AMERICANS
AND THEIR SCHOOLS

AMERICANS
AND THEIR
SCHOOLS

Erwin V. Johanningmeier
University of South Florida

WAVELAND
PRESS, INC.
Prospect Heights, Illinois

For information about this book, write or call:

Waveland Press, Inc.
P.O. Box 400
Prospect Heights, Illinois 60070
(312) 634-0081

In memory of
Erwin Frank Johanningmeier

Contents

Preface

While some Americans have viewed schools as important and integral to the cultural, social, and intellectual life of the nation, others have seen the schools' alleged failures and inadequacies as part of the crisis of today's society. Yet, schools have endured. As the nation was transformed from a predominately agrarian way of life to one lived for the most part in large metropolitan centers, schools grew in number and complexity.

In this text I have tried to show how Americans have thought about their schools and their relationship to the society as a whole. I have probably leaned more toward presenting the issues, problems, and ideals about which Americans have agreed than toward criticizing failures or emphasizing conflicts and differences. Wherever possible I have tried to examine issues in terms of the people who raised or discussed them because I believe history is ultimately for and about people. I have also tried to allow our ancestors to speak for themselves in a series of direct quotations.

Part I is an examination of the Colonial era during which many American values and characteristics began to take shape. At the period's beginning we were mostly Europeans; by its end we were a new people preparing to proclaim our independence from Europe. A discussion of three areas of early settlement—Massachusetts, Virginia, and Pennsylvania—gives the reader a fairly detailed appreciation of the diversity that was so quickly established on the new continent. In these three colonies we can see the origins of many characteristics that are especially American, such as the desire to establish homogeneous communities, the pursuit of wealth, and the belief that people can deliberately build a good society. We should note that the public schools were not a simple transplant of a European institution into an American setting but a seventeenth- and eighteenth-century invention of American society.

The duties, characteristics, and opinions about school teachers and the books from which they taught are examined in Part II. The new identity and national unity achieved by Americans immediately after the War of Independence was reflected in the books that were prepared for the schools. It was also reflected in the many educational plans of the new republic. During this period we begin to see differences between those who saw the school as an institution for individual needs and aspirations and others who began to conceive of the school as an institution to meet the needs of the nation. Whether the public school is to satisfy the needs of the individual or serve the interests of the nation is an issue that has yet to be clearly defined or easily resolved.

Part III shows America entering the nineteenth century with a full agenda. Almost immediately, the issues attendant on industrialism were apparent. While Americans argued about whether there should be public, tax-supported schools, they began to hear from those whose rights had been too frequently ignored. While women were presenting significant arguments about the relationship between school and society and contributing to the success of the new institution, many of their rights were still being denied. Finally, some attention is paid to the "new education," an attempt to improve and reform educational practices that had begun just one generation earlier. Chapters on American blacks and native Americans are included so we can see clearly that while Americans did successfully build a school system in the nineteenth century, they failed to build one that addressed the rights and needs of all Americans.

Part IV is devoted to the period during which nearly every facet of American life—economic, social, political, and intellectual—was transformed. Because of this transformation Americans had to learn to organize and manage their institutions in new ways. This era also marks the beginning of the growth of the American high school. From then onward, there would be many debates about whether the high school was to be an extension of the common school or a school to prepare a select few for higher education. The development of the new science of the mind, psychology, and its relationship to education is also examined. Frequently, this new science was used to defend and promote attempts at educational reform.

Part V includes a discussion of how schools were directly related to the defense needs of the nation during the post-World War II period, the role the media played in the education of Americans, and some recent developments and issues.

Throughout the text I have made every effort to render the pedogogy useful rather than cumbersome. Thus, no part of the text has been relegated to footnotes. Footnotes have been used to give authors their proper credit and to provide direction to those who may want to pursue a topic in greater detail. A "Guide to Educational Research" at the end of the book lists the standard collections of source materials for the history of education as well as basic reference works. Those who are assigned papers or wish to know more about the subject will find a beginning in these works.

The successful completion of any book requires the encouragement, good will, good humor, and patience of many. Some of these deserve special recognition. Some of my reviewers—James C. Carper of Tulane University and James R. Robarts of Florida State University—were generally constructive and helpful, if sometimes painfully frank. Henry C. Johnson, Jr. of Pennsylvania State University, another reviewer, has for years listened to my ideas, offered suggestions, and provided help too detailed to list here. At the University of South Florida many have helped; my former dean, Roger E. Wilk, offered encouragement of the kind all deans should give their faculties. During the early stages of the work Bruce Vaughan provided valuable assistance. Elizabeth Herman has checked references, made many trips to the library, developed an enviable rapport with the librarians, asked the right questions, and tended to many details with wit and dispatch. Alfredia Gambrell Brown not only assisted with the preparation of the manuscript but displayed a rare interest in its subject matter. Aileen Highsmith was always willing to retype a page at a moment's notice.

To two I owe a very special debt. From my daughter, Christina, I have learned that the interests and enthusiasms of my colleagues and I may not be the same as those of our children and students. Their world is different from ours. I hope I have provided for her and her generation an account that will enable us all to see our common heritage.

My other special debt is owed to Charles Weingartner, who read every version of the manuscript, quarreled, objected, insisted I read materials I would not otherwise have read, and shared the pain and joys of putting this book together.

E.V.J.

PART I

The Emergence of the Americans

The ideas, beliefs, values, and customs that gave American education its peculiar character started with the first settlements in the thirteen colonies. The first settlers at Jamestown (1607), Plymouth (1620), and Massachusetts Bay Colony (1630) crossed the Atlantic for a variety of reasons. Some came for religious freedom, some for political freedom, some for profit; some came or were sent because they had no place else to go. Many, but not all, were English. Others were Scots from the north of Ireland, Germans, Dutch, French, Swedes, Irish, Poles, Italians, Spaniards, and Africans.

By the 1700s—five generations after the first settlers had arrived—settlers were already acting and speaking as though they were a people, as though their home was the land they were inhabiting, not the lands across the Atlantic. By 1789 the settlers, their offspring, and their successors had managed to declare and win their independence from England, tested a confederation, and framed a Constitution that would govern how a new people and a new society managed its civil, religious, economic, and political affairs. To know something of them is to know something of our own difficulties and hopes.

In the following three chapters we shall examine the seventeenth-century settlements of Massachusetts, Virginia, and Pennsylvania. These three represent a variety of people and motives for settlement. We will examine not only the educational arrangements the settlers provided for themselves and their children, but also the issues and problems they met in settling a new land and creating a new society.

We will look at the relationship between religion, family, and education. By the middle of the eighteenth century, education was beginning to assume a new significance. In the view of Benjamin Franklin, for example, deliberately designed education was seen as the way to prepare youth for success in a new society. We will also see that education was generally more available in densely populated areas than in other areas. Why education prospers at times in the cities and not at other times is a question that must be posed.

New England: The First Community

New Knowledge and a New World

The settlers who came to the American wilderness had to adapt to a new environment and climate. Immediately, they had to make shelters, find food sources, and prepare defenses against possible attack. Before coming to America, they had already made a series of psychological and intellectual adjustments. In the preceding two centuries, the world of their parents had been challenged and frequently turned upside-down. A number of events, discoveries, and controversies had ushered in the arrival of what we now call the age of modernity. The discovery of the New World had expanded greatly the sphere of the European business world. As with any new economic development, there were opportunities for investment and employment, for getting rich quickly, and for bankruptcy.

While the Europeans' new world was expanding in the economic sense, it was contracting in another sense. The contraction may be said to have begun with the publication of Copernicus's *De Revolutionibus Orbium Celestium* in 1543. His argument that the sun—not the earth—was the center of the universe challenged traditional notions. The new theory was considered heresy at first, although Copernicus had only questioned the prevailing astronomical theory because its formulation seemed too sloppy to be the work of the Divine Artificer. Danish astronomer Tycho Brahe and his assistant Johann Kepler added refinements to the new view. Kepler argued that the orbits of the planets were not perfect circles but ellipses. Now we view the work of these scientists as brilliant astronomical and mathematical discoveries. In the early 1600s, it was viewed as an attack on the established teachings of the church, the teachings of Aristotle, and all that reasonable people knew was so.

In the following years, Galileo, Descartes, Bacon, and Newton were preeminent in formulating what we call the "scientific method." Although each made different contributions, as a group they symbolize the new age and the new method of seeking knowledge. Galileo demonstrated how knowledge about matter and motion could be acquired through the combined use of mathematics and observation. Descartes searched for certainties impossible to doubt and, in the process, found a way to combine geometry and algebra. That gave scientists a new tool, analytic geometry. Bacon effectively discredited deductive methods and showed how the human race could enter an entirely new world by asking not what the world meant, but by asking how it worked.

Newton developed a general theory of gravitation that viewed the earth and the heavens as bound together in one system. He thereby offered a theory of nature that was self-interpreting and self-justifying. Natural phenomena could now be understood and manipulated for human purposes. The Newtonian outlook held that humankind was fundamentally different from the remainder of nature. God had made the world and had placed in it beings with reason. Human beings could express how the world worked with scientific formulae, and, they themselves stood apart from it because they had rational thought and ethical sensibilities. This view of humanity was to stand until Charles Darwin revised and challenged all that and offered in its place a theory that made the human species a continuous part of nature.

New questions, new methods, and new inventions had undermined established world views, the teachings of the church, and reliance upon authority for the truth. The importance of observed facts, sense perception, experimentation, mathematics, and the efficacy of human reason became paramount. No matter where men and women looked—whether to see into a dewdrop or to observe the heavens—the newly invented microscope and telescope made it certain they would see farther and deeper than ever before.

Martin Luther and the Protestant Reformation

On Halloween night, 1517, Martin Luther nailed his ninety-five theses to the church door at Wittenberg, Germany. Luther may have meant only to reform the church and cleanse it of its corrupt practices; what he accomplished was the Protestant Reformation, a major revolution in the lives of the institutions of most Europeans. Within a generation, half of Europe became Protestant. Now the continent was dealing with new conceptions of the relationship of men and women both to their God and to their civil government.

The most revolutionary of Luther's ideas was his doctrine of the priesthood of all believers. As the eminent historian Vernon L. Parrington observed, "there was gunpowder packed away in Luther's doctrine of the priesthood of all believers, and the explosion that resulted made tremendous breaches in the walls of a seemingly impregnable feudalism."[1] The responsibility for an individual's salvation no longer rested with the church or the clergy, but with the individual. Traditional authorities and institutions had been shown to be vulnerable to the ideas and questions of individuals. Individuals would gradually be seen as having certain inalienable rights, independent of any earthly authority.

Protestant denominations developed quickly, creating new rituals, dogma, kinds of clergy, and forms of church governance. The new freedom was not complete. There were alliances between the new denominations and certain political rulers, for they could support one another. Eventually, there would be serious debate about separating church from state. For now, there was great interest in debating, examining, and establishing different forms of church governance: bishops in a hierarchy (episcopacy), elders and ministers (presbytery), or autonomous congregations (congregationalism).

The Reformation and Schooling

As individuals assumed the burden for their own salvation, they needed enough schooling to read and study the Scriptures for themselves. As editions of the Scriptures were prepared for readers in the vernacular languages, national identities and differences became more apparent and more important. To test the veracity of the vernacular editions, some needed to know Hebrew and Greek, or at least to trust those who did know those languages. Protestant leaders saw the idea of compulsory and state-supported education as necessary and mutually beneficial, and entered into cooperative relationships with civil governments.

Luther, for example, in his "Letters to the Mayors and Aldermen of All the Cities of Germany in Behalf of Christian Schools" (1524), stressed both the spiritual and civil importance of schooling. He argued that:

> ... even if there were no soul, and men did not need schools and the languages for the sake of Christianity and the Scriptures, still, for the establishment of the best schools everywhere, both for boys and girls, this consideration is of itself sufficient, namely, that society, for the maintenance of civil order and the proper regulation of the household, needs accomplished and well-trained men and women.[2]

Luther also told the mayors and aldermen that many parents were either too negligent, too ignorant, or too poor to be responsible for the necessary education of their children. The princes and lords, he complained, were capable, but too busy "with the weighty duties of cellar, kitchen and bedchamber" to tend to the education of the young. Consequently, education was the responsibility of the civil authorities. In the following generations and centuries, officers of government were to hear that argument again and again.

---

1. Vernon L. Parington, *Main Currents in American Thought: The Colonial Mind (1620-1800)* (New York: Harvest Books, 1954), p. 6.

2. Martin Luther, "Letter to the Mayors and Aldermen of All the Cities of Germany in Behalf of Christian Schools," reprinted in *Three Thousand Years of Educational Wisdom*, ed. Robert Ulich (Cambridge: Harvard University Press, rev. ed., 1963), p. 232.

The Reformation in England

Protestantism did not grow in popularity as quickly in England as it had on the continent. Although there was a Protestant party that had been heavily influenced by John Calvin and his followers of the Reformed Church, King Henry VIII in the early part of his reign stood firmly on the side of the Catholic Church, wrote a tract against Luther, and was even declared "Defender of the Faith" by the pope. The relationship between Henry VIII and Rome crumbled when the pope refused to annul the king's marriage to Catharine of Aragon. In 1534 Henry prompted Parliament to declare him the temporal head of the Church in England. His break with the papacy was basically personal and political; Henry assumed sovereignty over only temporal and jurisdictional matters. The dogma and ritual remained basically unchanged, and the episcopal system was maintained.

Under Henry's son, Edward VI, the Protestant faction made strong attempts to establish itself in England. A *Book of Common Prayer* and a series of Articles dealing with key religious issues were prepared, and every subject in the realm was expected to subscribe to them. But when Edward's sister, Mary Tudor, followed him to the throne, she immediately restored England to papal obedience and vigorously persecuted members of the Protestant party. Many Protestants fled to the continent, where they became even more committed to their views. Mary's reign was short, however, and her successor, Elizabeth, reestablished a non-papal national church to England. With the enactment of the Acts of Supremacy and Uniformity in 1559, the Anglican Church became the official church of England, and the crown became its temporal head.

Puritans and Separatists

Even after Elizabeth reestablished an independent English Church, many English citizens believed the church still had too many Roman, or papal, elements. These purifiers, who came to be known as Puritans, wanted to cleanse the church of those rituals, vestments, prayers, and celebrations—even Christmas—that could not be justified from their reading of the Bible. Chief among their purposes was the removal of the episcopal hierarchy. This rejection of the episcopal system was significant. While in an episcopacy, the pastor is sent to the people by the bishop, in non-episcopal systems the people call the pastor to them. Such a distinction has many implications when applied to questions of civil government.

As the Puritan movement grew, a division among its adherents became apparent. While all agreed that bishops were not sanctioned by the Scriptures, they did not agree upon a new form of church governance. Most wanted a presbyterian form patterned after Calvin: a hierarchy of governing bodies—presbytery, synod, and general assembly—consisting of ministers and ordained church elders. A minority of the Puritans, however, wished to abandon all ideas of a national church, whether ruled by bishop or national assembly. This minority believed that each church was a separate body organized on the basis of a covenant made between all those who confessed their faith and swore their allegiance to the covenant. Although these congregationalists wished to abandon the national church, they wanted a certain amount of support from the state. The state was to guarantee that nonmembers, those who could not make a confession of faith, would have no opportunity to spread heresies or form competing churches. Each congregation was to select its own pastor and church officers, and tend to the excommunication of its members when necessary.

An even smaller group of English protestants, different from either the presbyterian Puritans or the congregational Puritans, were those known as Separatists. The Separatists agreed with the agenda for purification. But rather than reform the governance of the church, they wished to separate themselves from it. They were mostly congregationalists who argued against any form of a national church. Their position was that a church could not be based on any geographical entity, whether it was as small as a parish or as large as a nation, but only on the will of the congregation. The Separatists quickly encountered difficulties because any act of separation from the Church of England was then tantamount to treason.

One of the separating churches was located at Scrooby in the west of England. In 1617 the Scrooby Separatists came to the attention of the authorities and were summoned to appear before the Court of High Commission. When they did not appear, they were fined and jailed. The group then decided that it would be necessary to leave England. Some made their way to Holland, first arriving in Amsterdam, a city then known for its toleration of religious differences and freedom of thought and speech. From Amsterdam they moved to Leyden, where they remained until 1620, when they decided to sail to America and establish a new community. They settled in Plymouth in 1620—ten years before the arrival of the Puritans—and came to be known as the Pilgrims.

The First Settlements

The Pilgrims' Voyage

The Pilgrims' voyage and their first years in the New World were difficult. They may not have known that their chances for surviving the voyage were only one in four, but they did know the dangers. In 1618, 180 of their fellow Separatists had set sail from Amsterdam to settle in Virginia, and only fifty had survived the crossing. The Pilgrims began their voyage in August of 1620 in the *Mayflower* and the smaller *Speedwell,* a ship they had purchased in Holland to serve as a consort and as a tender for fishing after their arrival. The smaller ship leaked so badly that it had to turn back after a few days at sea, and its passengers and provisions were transferred to the *Mayflower.* By then it was September, and the *Mayflower* encountered the predictable storms on the North Atlantic. During one storm, a beam cracked and some crew members wanted to turn back, but the captain directed that the beam be braced and the voyage continued.

Remarkably, all but one of the *Mayflower's* passengers survived the crossing. They had escaped the scurvy because their supply of onions and unpasteurized beer was sufficient for the voyage. However, it was not a comfortable trip. The

Pilgrims had to remain below deck, where they were allotted an average space of 17.5 square feet per person—an area about the size of a conventional single bed. They did not make landfall at their destination, Sandy Hook, but at Cape Cod, which was north of where their patent (the official land grant) from the Virginia Company entitled them to settle.

The Mayflower Compact, which has come to have great meaning for the democratic tradition, was the result of their landing at the wrong site. Because the patent was now invalid, and because some members of the group threatened disobedience, some formal agreement seemed necessary. On November 11, 1620 (Nov. 21 by our calendar), all forty-one free adult males aboard the ship signed the Compact and agreed to "covenant and combine ourselves together into a civil body politic . . . and by virtue hereof to enact, constitute, and frame such just laws, ordinances, acts, constitutions, and offices, from time to time, as shall be thought most meet and convenient for the general good of the Colony, unto which we promise all due submission and obedience."

On the same day, the Pilgrims dropped anchor in Provincetown Bay. For five weeks small landing parties explored the area, looking for a suitable site to settle. In early December the crew of the ship's shallop landed at Plymouth, where they found a cleared area and a supply of fresh water. A plague had struck the area in 1617 and killed its Indian inhabitants. The Pilgrims' first winter at Plymouth was disastrous. Half of the 102 *Mayflower* passengers were dead and buried in unmarked graves before summer arrived. The ship provided their only shelter; when weather permitted, they worked on shore, but much of their work was quickly undone by fire.

While the Pilgrims were not the first English people to visit Plymouth, they were its first permanent settlers. They were also the first permanent English settlers in North America to arrive with their wives and children. Obviously, the Pilgrims meant to stay. Not one of them was aboard the *Mayflower* when it sailed back to England in April 1621.

Plymouth Colony
Conditions improved for the Pilgrims during their first spring and summer in Plymouth. By the end of the summer, the Pilgrims had every reason to believe that their second winter would be better than their first. In November, however, the happy prospects for the coming winter were somewhat dampened when the *Fortune* arrived with thirty-six additional settlers who brought no provisions with them. The newcomers were welcome because more men and women were needed to perform the necessary labors, but to accommodate these thirty-six indigent settlers, the Pilgrims had to adopt an immediate policy of half-rations for everyone. The *Fortune* also brought good news. The *Mayflower* had returned safely to England, and the backers of the Pilgrims had obtained an appropriate patent for the Plymouth site. That meant that the Pilgrims' settlement was now legal.

Despite the Pilgrims' early handicaps and hardships, it appeared by the summer of 1622 that they would indeed survive. When the secretary of the Virginia Company paid the settlement a visit on his way home to England in 1622, he was impressed with everything he saw. A town had been built on the hillside with houses on either side of a wide street. The entire settlement had been enclosed with a palisade, and a fort was under construction on the hilltop.

Additional settlers arrived in 1623. Some were "particulars"—settlers whose passage had not been paid by the Virginia Company. Because the "particulars" had paid their own passage, they had no formal obligation to the Company and no reason to assume the economic obligations of the other settlers. Their presence challenged the well-integrated community. Before their arrival, the entire community shared political and economic motivations and, in some measure, religious beliefs (Separatists were outnumbered two to one on the *Mayflower* by non-Separatists). The "particulars" had to agree to obey the laws of the settlement, to pay taxes annually, and *not* to take part in the profitable trade with the Indians. The agreement with the "particulars" constituted a formal recognition of differing classes of citizenship. It also illustrates how little interest the early settlers had in extending freedom to others.

During the first years of the settlement, the Pilgrims operated under a communal system. They did not work for their own individual profit, but for the Company. Profits, harvests, or developed assets were divided equally. In 1623, Governor William Bradford was asked by the settlers to change the system so that each household head would work for himself and then pay taxes to the settlement. The taxes were necessary because the settlers still had to pay the Company in England. Bradford agreed to the change, and each family was assigned a plot of land, its size depending on the size of the family. Bradford wrote later that the new system was more effective than the original communal system. The individual economic system, he wrote, "made all hands very industrious, so much as much more corn was planted than otherwise whould have been."

Plymouth remained as a separate colony until 1692, when it was absorbed by Massachusetts Bay. Historically, it was in many ways the first instance of the new way of life that was shaped by the wilderness these English Separatists settled. The Massachusetts Bay Colony had a more favorable beginning, was larger and better equipped, and very quickly produced a vast and interesting literature. The Pilgrims did not give us any firsts in education or schooling, but they did leave their mark on the American character. We can attribute to them several basic beliefs: (1) individual economic incentive works better than communal arrangements; (2) a group of people can form a contract about how to govern themselves and make it work; (3) citizenship entails a sharing in the obligations and purposes of the community; and (4) commitment and determination can overcome hardships and handicaps. In their beliefs and practices was also the notion that matters of church and matters of state should be separate from each other. Their concept of freedom, however, had no egalitarian elements in it.

The Puritans have come to stand for a variety of paradoxical characteristics. Historians have found them fascinatingly complex. From the vantage point of the present, it would be a mistake to view the Puritans as primarily a religious sect. Today religion is often separated from other spheres of human activity, but such distinctions were, for the most part, foreign to the Puritans. They arrived in New England five generations before the Constitution formally separated church and state, public and private life. The settlers at Plymouth held to a belief that effectively separated church matters from matters of state, but they were small in number and were considered too radical by most of their contemporaries. Of course, it must be remembered that our view of the Puritans has been shaped by those who wrote, primarily the clergy; and their most passionate writings were composed in the eighteenth century as their communities began to move away from the old ways.

The Great Migration and Massachusetts Bay

The Great Migration of Puritans to New England began in 1629. When civil war came to England in 1642, some 20,000 English Puritans had already left for New England. During the same period, some 45,000 other English subjects settled in the West Indies or the southern colonies. This migration out of England was set in motion when Charles I came to the throne in 1625. To many of the English— Puritans and non-Puritans—Charles's policies appeared to be pro-Catholic and repressive. His Archbishop of Canterbury, William Laud, vigorously repressed dissent and enforced Anglican usages. By 1629 many Puritans thought they had good reason to carry on their way of life in New England rather than in England. There were enough prosperous English citizens who could risk investing in trading companies to send out settlers.

At Salem, a few men from an unsuccessful venture had settled under the leadership of Roger Conant. In 1628, the New England Company sent forty more men under the direction of John Endecott. Shortly thereafter the New England Company reorganized as the "Governor and Company of Massachusetts Bay" and sent out another expedition to Salem. The party included two clergymen, Francis Higginson and Samuel Skelton, recruited and sent by the Company. Higginson and Skelton had not conformed to Anglican rituals and usages, and Higginson was expecting to be brought before the High Commission to answer for his dissenting behavior.

Within six weeks of the expedition's arrival at Salem, a new church was established. The congregation, composed of most of the settlers, elected Higginson and Skelton to the posts of ministers and proceeded to ordain each of them with the traditional laying-on of hands. This ritual could have been construed as an act of separation, even an act of treason; the small group had put congregational theory into practice. They formed their own church, and elected and ordained their ministers without the bishops, the Prayer Book, and the ceremonies that Archbishop Laud had been trying to press upon them. The Great Migration of congregational Puritans had begun.

What these Puritans wanted was a minister who would preach an appropriate sermon rather than officiate at a fixed and unchanging ceremony. They wanted their ministers to put forth some practical and intellectual effort. For the Puritans the unadorned meeting-house was their school and the sermon was their lesson. In it they sought to know how the Scriptures applied to them in their present situation. They believed there to be a real and significant relationship between their lives, the world they lived in, current events, and the Scriptures. The minister was to speak on those relationships. The sermon was thus an indispensable part of their lives, more than merely a form of worship. For the Puritans, the pulpit was, as Lawrence Stone has observed, "the most important propaganda instrument of the day."[3]

The Massachusetts Bay Company was growing and was soon to experience another change. In the summer of 1629 it was suggested that the headquarters of the Company be moved to New England. Seven members of the Company agreed to emigrate to New England on the condition that they could take the charter with them, to prevent any attempts by the crown to change or revoke it. The plans for the charter revision were successful and the stockholders approved the changes. John Winthrop was elected governor of the revised Company in October 1629, and he immediately began to make preparations for the move to New England.

In the first six months of 1630 more than a thousand men, women, and children sailed in fifteen ships from England to Massachusetts. How the news of the expedition spread so quickly is not exactly known. There were no newspapers and there are no known broadsides. But the Puritan community was close-knit. Word about the expedition probably traveled through the traditional channels of communication wherever people regularly met: the smithy, the inn, the courts, and, of course, the church. Their motivations are clear: The king was unpopular; economic conditions were poor; and there was the strong desire to live a life based on religious beliefs, without interference from a government that held and was enforcing different persuasions. In a very short time hundreds of people sold their farms and most of their household goods, left the lands their families had occupied for generations, and prepared for the voyage to New England.

Like the Pilgrims, the Puritans had a difficult first year. Endecott and his men were expected to have raised sufficient crops to help feed the newcomers; but as it turned out, they had to rely on the stores of Winthrop's fleet. Fortunately, additional provisions arrived in time to avoid extreme hardship during the winter months. Enough news trickled back to England about conditions and the provisions that would be needed upon arrival to dispel the idea that the immigrants would be coming to a completely finished community. Nonetheless, successive waves of newcomers continued to expect more than they found in America. Perhaps many felt that almost anything would be better than what they had.

---

3. Lawrence Stone, *The Causes of the English Revolution, 1529–1642* (New York: Harper and Row, 1972), p. 66.

Education in the Bay Colony

Soon after their arrival, the Puritans turned their attention to education. The Boston Latin School traditionally is said to have been founded in 1635. Harvard College was begun the next year. The now-famous Massachusetts educational laws were passed by the General Court (the legislative body) in 1642 and 1647. These two laws reminded parents that they had an obligation to tend to their children. They warrant examination because successive generations of Americans have considered them so significant. According to some scholars, the notion of "free popular education" had its origins in early New England. Samuel Eliot Morison wrote:

> One trait in which New Englanders even excelled the old country was their emphasis on education. Free popular education has been the most lasting contribution of early New England to the United States, and possibly the most beneficial. . . . Compact villages made it possible to have and do, as well as talk about education. It is no accident that almost every educational leader and reformer in American history, from Benjamin Franklin through Horace Mann and John Dewey to John B. Conant, has been a New Englander of the Puritan stock.[4]

Morison's view is not unique. According to an early historian of education, the Massachusetts laws not only presented new educational ideas, but also laid the "foundation stones" of the American public school system.[5] Recent historians have not been as willing to accept this view; many features of New England Puritan education must be considered in determining the role of the Massachusetts laws in the history of American schools.

The Family and the School
Schools were neither new nor unimportant to the Puritans. In England—and in the thought of the Reformation—schooling was already growing in importance. According to Lawrence Stone, "Education at school replaced education in a noble household."[6] Yet the Puritans who came to Massachusetts did not abandon the family as an important educational institution.

The Puritans believed that each person had some particular talent—something he or she could do especially well. It was the responsibility of the family to ensure that the talent was properly cultivated. To ignore the talent was to cast aside God's gift and one's duty. Hence, the poor laws and the family laws typically spoke of the necessity of children learning a useful trade as well as reading and religion. One who was rightfully educated was literate, religious, and hard-working. The family that was fulfilling its responsibility usually arranged for an apprenticeship for its children. Male offspring typically engaged in a wide range of apprentice-

---

4. Samuel Eliot Morison, *The Oxford History of the American People*, vol. 1 (New York: New American Library, 1972), p. 113.

5. Ellwood P. Cubberley, *Public Education in the United States* (Boston: Houghton Mifflin, Co., 1919), p. 18.

6. Stone, *Causes of the English Revolution*, p. 74.

ships; female children were taught how to perform housewifely duties. The master to whom a child was sent was responsible for continuing the apprentice's education, as well as for teaching him or her the skills of a trade.

It may be most accurate to label the 1642 law a *family* law, rather than a school law. In the first lines of the law, the General Court stated that it took into consideration "the great neglect in many parents and masters in training up their children in learning, and labor, and other employments which may be profitable to the commonwealth." The law did not require the colonists to establish schools; its purpose was broader and more basic. It reminded all that it was the duty of parents to bring up their children so they would know how to read, how to understand and obey the laws of the country, and how to understand and live by the principles of their religion. It also required the officials of each town to make sure that the parents were doing their job properly. (Masters who supervised youth in apprenticeships were probably included because they served as substitute parents.)

It is evident that the leaders of the Bay Colony were ever watchful and concerned about the behavior of children and the relationships between parents and children. In 1646 the General Court declared that "any child above sixteen years old and of sufficient understanding who either hit or cursed his parents" could be put to death "unless it can be sufficiently testified that the parents have been very unchristianly negligent in the education of such children."[7] The Court allowed, however, that children had the right to defend themselves from "death and maiming" at the hands of their parents. In 1648, the Court revised the 1642 law to remind town officials that "the good education of children is of singular behoof and benefit to any commonwealth" and that many parents and masters were still "too indulgent and negligent of their duty."[8] This time the Court specified that the negligent parents and masters were to be fined twenty shillings for their failures.

The records of the Court indicate that the 1642 and the 1648 laws did not quite do the job. In 1654 the Court noted that "it appears by too much experience that diverse children and servants do behave themselves too disrespectfully, disobediently, and disorderly towards their parents, masters, and governors, to the disturbance of families and discouragement of such parents and governors." Convicted children were "to endure such corporal punishment by whipping."[9] "Ten stripes" was the maximum for one offense.

In the 1670s a new office, that of the tithingman, was established. He was to help the town selectmen and constables supervise how well families were fulfilling their duties and to report:

---

7. "Instructions for the Punishment of Incorrigible Children in Massachusetts (1646)," reprinted in, *Education in the United States*, ed. Sol Cohen (New York: Random House, 1974), p. 370.

8. "Massachusetts School Law of 1648," reprinted in Cohen, *Education in the United States*, pp. 394–95.

9. Reprinted in Robert H. Bremmer, et. al., eds., *Children and Youth in America* (Cambridge: Harvard University Press, 1970), vol. 1, p. 39.

...the names of all single persons that live from under family government, stubborn and disorderly children and servants, night walkers, tipplers, Sabbath breakers by night or by day, and such as absent themselves from the public worship of God on the Lord's days, or whatever else course or practice of any person or persons whatsoever tending to debauchery, irreligion, profaneness, and atheism amongst us, whether by omission of family government, nurture, and religious duties, or instruction of children and servants, or idle, profligate, uncivil or rude practices of any sort.[10]

Improper behavior was believed to be the result of family negligence or of the absence of a proper family atmosphere. In 1675, for instance, Captain James Johnson was the subject of a complaint in Suffolk Court, Massachusetts, and was accused of "disorderly carriages in his family, giving entertainment to persons at unreasonable hours of the night, and other misdemeanors." He was ordered "to break up housekeeping and to dispose of himself into some good orderly family within one fortnight."[11]

There is some temptation to infer from these laws that the Puritan family was breaking down shortly after its arrival in New England. It may be more accurate, however, to conclude that the family was adjusting to a new way of life. The amount of official attention the family received indicates that it was seen as vitally important. It also illustrates the Puritans' belief that each member of the community had an obligation to participate in the general education of the young. The family was so important that numerous laws were enacted to assist it in maintaining its strength as the chief educational institution. The New Englanders were trying to carry out their version of English ways. However, they could neither maintain them intact nor create exact reproductions.

Many settlers came from communities where their families had lived for generations. In America there were no familiar surroundings, no landmarks, monuments, cathedrals, or hallowed grounds. There was no network of friends and relatives. Familiar institutions had to be reestablished in a strange land—a land with a harsher climate and already inhabited by strangers whose responses and actions could not be predicted. The housing patterns of both the Puritans and the Pilgrims show that the newcomers built their dwellings in the customary pattern of the medieval manor village. There was a common village green with the meeting-house at one side. It served as a place of worship, as a place to do the town's business, and at times as the schoolhouse. Around the other sides of the green were the houses of the villagers. People lived close to each other and knew what their neighbors and their children were doing. Each day men went from the villages to the fields that had been assigned to them or to the woods for fuel or building supplies. Later social and educational commentators noted that in the industrialized cities a person's place of residence and place of work were separated, and because of that separation the school had to assume some of the family's responsibilities. For many early settlers home and work were also separated.

---

10. Reprinted in Bremmer, *Children and Youth in America*, vol. 1, p. 42.
11. Ibid., p. 50.

The "Old Deluder Satan" Act   The 1647 law, commonly known as the "Old Deluder Satan" Act, required that towns of fifty or more households appoint one of themselves to teach all children to read and write if the children were available for instruction. The wages of the teacher were to be paid either by the parents or master of the children, or by the inhabitants in general. The Act further required that once a town had grown to one hundred or more households, a grammar school be established to prepare youth for the university. The university was, of course, Harvard, the only college available to colonial youth unless they returned to England. Eligible towns that did not comply with the law were subject to a £5 fine.

The 1647 law may have been unprecedented, but it was not inconsistent with Puritan ways and beliefs. Puritans were Protestants, and so were committed to literacy so that people could read and study the Scriptures. They were also committed to some form of higher learning, especially the study of Latin, Greek, and Hebrew. Those languages were necessary for a deeper understanding of the Scriptures. The serious Protestant was not about to rely exclusively on the vulgar translation of the Bible. The first paragraph of the 1647 law dealt explicitly with the relationship between languages, Scripture, and Satan. It read:

> It being one chief project of that old deluder, Satan to keep men from the knowledge of the Scriptures, as in former times by keeping them in an unknown tongue, so in these latter times by persuading from the use of tongues, that so at least the true sense and meaning of the original might be clouded by false glosses of saint-seeming deceivers. . . .[12]

Martin Luther, early in the Protestant Reformation, had made remarkably similar points in his "Letters to the Mayors and Alderman." For Luther, languages were a gift from God that the devil could not take away, although he tried hard to limit their use.[13] Luther argued that it was "foolish to attempt to learn the Scriptures through the comments of the Fathers and the study of many books and glosses." Many of the church Fathers had presented "verbose expositions" that were wrong, wrong because their ignorance of language did not allow them to make the correct interpretations.

Luther was not content to have only "a pious life and orthodox teaching." It was also necessary to have proper exposition of the Scriptures. That, of course, required literacy. In like manner, the Puritans also sought more than piety and orthodoxy. They wanted the faithful to be literate and they wanted the clergy to fashion their sermons so that a dialogue could take place between the minister and the congregation. Reliance on the "oral tradition" was inadequate. Luther had warned emphatically that without learning the Germans would become "blockheads" and "brutes." The first paragraph of the 1647 Act also states that the Court

---

12. "Massachusetts School Law of 1647," reprinted in Cohen, *Education in the United States*, p. 394.

13. Luther, "Letter to the Mayors," reprinted in Ulich, *Three Thousand Years of Educational Wisdom*, p. 226.

did not want "learning . . . Buried in the grave of our fathers." At the end of the eighteenth century the famed *New England Primer* instructed its young readers that:

> He who ne'er learns his A. B. C.
> Forever will a blockhead be.

Compulsory Education and the Grammar School

A historian of the Massachusetts public school system interpreted the education laws of the 1640s in this way:

> It is important to note here that the idea underlying all this legislation was neither paternalistic nor socialistic. The child is to be educated, not to advance his personal interests, *but because the State will suffer if he is not educated.* The State does not provide schools to relieve the parent, nor because it can educate better than the parent can, but because it can thereby better enforce the obligation which it imposes.[14]

That schools are primarily for the benefit of the society and not necessarily for the benefit of the individual is a thesis with which some modern students of society would agree. A society's increased attention to its schools may be a signal that the society is undergoing some significant change.

By the standards of the day, the citizenry of the Bay Colony was very well educated. It is estimated that of the 20,000 settlers who had arrived by 1640, about 100 were graduates of either Cambridge or Oxford. That ratio of one college graduate in every 200 people was probably as large as existed in any seventeenth-century country. Moreover, English citizens had grown accustomed to having the state take an active part in education. During the reign of Henry VIII, specific texts were prepared for use in the schools—an "A B C" book, a primer consisting of prayers in English, and a Latin grammar. Henry's successors never doubted their right to control education throughout the realm.[15]

Compulsory Schooling

America's present-day public school systems are characteristically both *compulsory* and *free.* Schools are free in that no parent is billed directly for the schooling of his or her child. The entire community, directly or indirectly, pays the way of all students through taxes. The 1647 Massachusetts law permitted, but did not necessarily require, this system of financial support. The law simply stated that the teacher would be paid by the parents or by the community in general.

Many have interpreted the 1642 "family law," its revision in 1648, and the 1647 school law to mean that education was compulsory in the Bay Colony. In a

---

14. Cubberley, *Public Education in the United States,* p. 19.

15. James Murphy, "Religion, the State, and Education in England," *History of Education Quarterly* 8:1 (Spring 1968), p. 9.

sense, education was compulsory but formal schooling was not. The laws required only that schools be made available. Compulsory schooling as known in the contemporary United States did not come until the mid-nineteenth century. Massachusetts was the first state to pass a compulsory school law, but it was not enacted until 1852.

The Grammar School

Puritan schooling did not begin with elementary schools. In the early years of the seventeenth century, training in basic literacy, the Christian way of life, and citizenship was the responsibility *not* of the school but of the family. Training for stewardship—to be a guardian or officer of the town or the church—was the function of the secondary school. The first two educational endeavors in the Bay Colony were the establishment of the Boston Latin School (1635) and the founding of Harvard College (1636). The Latin School was a "grammar school," then the term given to secondary schools. At first grammar schools were seven-year schools; later they became four-year schools. The grammar school assumed that the students who enrolled already had learned to read and write either at home or in dame schools, which were conducted in the houses by women who taught youths to read and write, and sometimes to knit.

The curriculum of the Latin grammar school was not as narrow as the term "Latin school" may suggest. Although most masters probably devoted most of their time to language instruction, this emphasis on languages had originated in the revival of classical learning during the Renaissance. It was further strengthened by the Protestants' emphasis on literacy. John Milton, the greatest of the Puritan poets, who set his literary efforts aside to become Oliver Cromwell's Latin Secretary, offered a twofold aim of education when he made his proposal for an academy. The aim of education, he wrote in 1644, was "to repair the ruins of our first parents by regaining to know God aright, and out of that knowledge to love him, to imitate him, and to be like him." He believed "a complete and generous education" to be "that which fits a man to perform justly, skillfully, and magnanimously all the offices, both private and public, of peace and war."[16]

The American Puritans were not trying to retreat from the world, but to live a life based on the Scriptures. They were not much interested in theological explorations, but they were interested in applying the theology they accepted to their daily lives. The grammar school was not a school for religious education; that was the function of the home.[17] The grammar schools emphasized language because language was practical. The poet Milton had called language the "instrument conveying to us things useful to be known." The object of language

16. John Milton, "Of Education" in *Milton on Education,* ed. Oliver Morley Ainsworth (New Haven: Yale University Press, 1928), pp. 52, 55.

17. N. Ray Hiner, "The Cry of Sodom Inquired Into: Educational Analysis in Seventeenth-Century New England," *History of Education Quarterly,* 13:1 (Spring 1973), pp. 10–11.

was to get at "the solid things."[18] To study language simply to learn the language had no merit.

The grammar school and what, at its best, it stood for did not last very long. By the end of the seventeenth century, it was beginning to decline.[19] Some towns were reducing the support they gave to the required grammar schools, and others even closed their grammar schools. This decline can be viewed as a signal that a change was occurring in what the community wanted from its schools. Although towns were not observing the 1647 law, they were increasingly supporting the writing schools and the private vocational schools. There students could study writing and arithmetic, which they needed to become scriveners and bookkeepers. Those subjects had received little attention from the grammar school masters.

The rise of the writing schools and private vocational schools within two generations of the Great Migration indicates that the values of the community had undergone some change. The sons and daughters of the founders of the Bay Colony were sending their children to schools different from the ones of their own childhood. Another sign that the structure and institutions of the society were changing is the adoption of the famed Half-Way Covenant in 1662. It allowed the descendants of the "visible saints" (those who had publicly testified to their conversion to saving grace) a special status within the church even though they had not had the intense conversion experience themselves. With this Covenant, the Puritans could still maintain that the church consisted solely of the "elect" even though they had made the entrance requirements easier. In 1711 Cotton Mather wrote in his diary that the country was in need of "A Lively Discourse about the Benefit and Importance of Education."[20] The people, he claimed, were "perishing for want of it; they are sinking apace into Barbarism and Wickedness." From Mather's point of view the colony was declining; from our vantage point it appears that it was preparing for participation in the new mercantile system of commerce and industry. Eighteenth-century New England was to be very different from seventeenth-century New England.

Harvard and Yale

Harvard College was established on October 28, 1636, by a vote of the General Court of Massachusetts Bay. Its purpose (as we are told by *New England's First Fruits*) came from the Puritans' fear of leaving "an illiterate Ministery to the Churches, when our present Ministers shall lie in the Dust." It was patterned after Cambridge University's Emmanuel College, founded in 1584 by Sir Walter Mildmay, Chancellor of the Exchequer to Queen Elizabeth. It is reported that when the queen questioned Mildmay about his establishment of the Puritan foundation,

---

18. Milton, "Of Education," in Ainsworth, *Milton on Education*, p. 53.

19. Jon Teaford, "The Transformation of Massachusetts Education," *History of Education Quarterly* 10:3 (Fall 1970), p. 294.

20. Cotton Mather, *Diary of Cotton Mather: Volume II, 1709–1724* (New York: Frederick Ungar, 1957), p. 51.

Mildmay answered: "Far be it from me to countenance anything contrary to your establishment laws but [as he added] I have set an acorn which, when it becomes an oak, God alone knows what will be the fruit thereof."[21] Cambridge was to be the name of the town in which the New World version of Emmanuel College was established, because many of the Colony's leaders had been graduated from Cambridge University. The college received its present name from John Harvard, who held a Master of Arts from Emmanuel College. Upon his death in 1638, half of Harvard's estate and his entire library became the property of the newly founded college.

Although Harvard had no charter from the Court until 1650 and no charter ever from the crown, it began granting degrees in 1642. By granting degrees without specific permission of charter, Harvard was ignoring, if not violating, both English law and the traditional distinction between colleges and universities. Traditionally, colleges were self-governing institutions where students lived, studied, and received instruction. Universities conducted examinations, awarded degrees, and supervised professional courses—law, medicine, and theology. The only institutions authorized to grant degrees in the English realm were the two universities, Oxford and Cambridge. By assuming functions of both the college and the university, Harvard began the peculiar tradition of higher education in America, and perhaps fulfilled Mildmay's prediction about his "acorn."

Harvard's contribution to early New England was not confined to the education of its small student body. One of its early contributions was the almanac, an important tool of informal education that was nearly indispensable for those who spent their time in agricultural or navigational pursuits. The almanac contained information on weather, the phases of the moon, and the tides. Of forty-four almanacs produced prior to 1687, forty-one were prepared by graduates of Harvard.[22] In the almanac one could also learn about major intellectual and scientific issues. For example, in 1656 Thomas Shepard offered its readers an astronomical essay in accordance with the Ptolemaic cosmology; three years later, they were presented with an explication of the work of Copernicus.

The second college to be established in New England was Yale. The proposals for Yale grew out of the intimate life of the churches in the "religious colony" of Connecticut. The peculiar character of the New Haven colony had been made very clear in the 1630s by John Davenport, a founder and early pastor, who presented a learned exposition of it in his *Civil Government in a New Plantation Whose Design is Religion.* Yale's first trustees' meeting in 1701 began with an affirmation that the colonists—called the "now blessed fathers"—had come to America specifically to "plant" the Protestant religion, and that was the basic intention which, in their minds, made the founding of a school appropriate. Follow-

---

21. Quoted in "College American," *A Cyclopedia of Education,* ed. Paul Monroe (New York: Macmillan, 1911), vol. 3, p. 59.

22. Robert T. Sidwell, "Writers, Thinkers and Fox Hunters—Educational Theory in the Almanacs of Eighteenth-Century Colonial America," *History of Education Quarterly* 8:3 (Fall 1968), p. 276.

ing the advice of Judge Samuel Sewall, an urban site was chosen (at Saybrook) for Yale after the example of the great Dutch universities. In the original proposal for the new college, it was insisted that degrees not be granted and that diplomas or testimonials be awarded in order to avoid the appearance of pretension.

The chief immediate reason for the founding of Yale was probably the growing belief that Harvard no longer represented the purest religious ideals of Protestant New England. Increase Mather, who had recently been ousted as president of Harvard, offered the founders of Yale considerable advice. He suggested that they not bother with dormitories and that they avoid the expense of an elaborate commencement ceremony. In the early years, Mather's advice was followed. Students boarded with pious families recommended by the clergy. That practice was consistent with the Puritan emphasis on the family as the basis of Christian nurture; it was also a way to avoid English collegiate ways.

The role of religion was more important at Yale than at Harvard. The president's first duty was to lead prayers, conduct exercises in Scripture, Divinity, and Church History, and supervise the work and conduct of the tutors. He was also expected to preach publicly as often as possible. Yale's charter made it quite clear that the principal purpose of Yale was to train orthodox clergy. The founders were convinced that the task of "upholding and propagating" the Protestant religion required a "succession of learned and orthodox men." Harvard apparently had not been doing the job. It is estimated that only slightly over half its seventeenth-century graduates actually entered the ministry.

Like other New England institutions, however, Yale did not escape change. By 1717, after Yale had moved to New Haven, the religious intensity began to diminish. The needs of the citizenry were addressed and more emphasis was placed on traditional studies. Yale was successful, but it was not able to turn back the developments that had already overtaken less orthodox communities and institutions.[23]

---

23. In this section I have made extensive use of an unpublished paper, "Secularization in American Higher Education," by Henry C. Johnson, Jr.

The Virginia Colony: The Pursuit of Wealth 2

Jamestown: Gold and Adventure

In contrast to the respectable craftsworkers and professional men who served as leaders in the New England colonies, the dominant figure in the early Virginia Colony was Captain John Smith, an adventurer and soldier of fortune. Smith had fought the Turks in Europe, where he was taken prisoner and sold into slavery in Constantinople. He was only twenty-four when he escaped from slavery and found his way back to England in 1604.

There he found that a new wave of interest in establishing colonies in America was just beginning. Smith signed up with the London Company to sail for North America, and on December 19, 1606, he and others left Blackwall, London, for Virginia. The commander of the expedition was Captain Christopher Newport, a veteran of many raids on the Spanish West Indies.

The purpose of the planned settlement was to earn a profit for the London Company. The settlers had agreed to work for the Company for seven years in exchange for their passage, after which they were to be granted land and other considerations and allowed to carry on as they desired. During the first seven years, however, they were expected to engage in profitable trade with the Indians, harvest timber, raise crops, and above all else, find and send great quantities of gold back to London.

Unlike the later expeditions to New England, Newport's went by way of the longer, but less arduous, southern route. Late in April 1607, the fleet of three ships reached Chesapeake Bay. When the first landing party reached shore at Cape Henry, it was attacked by Indians, and several members of the party were seriously wounded. They then decided to cross the bay and sail up the nearest large river, hoping to find the Indians in the interior less hostile. On May 13, they found a place to settle, naming it Jamestown. A sealed box from the London Company was opened to reveal the names of the seven resident councilors who were to elect a president and advise him on the government of the settlement. John Smith's name was among the seven, but the others refused him his seat; some had already accused him of trying to undermine the venture and had therefore even suggested that he be hanged.

Jamestown seemed to be a good site. It was located on a navigable river with a channel deep enough to allow ships to anchor near the river bank. It was also nearly 60 miles from the ocean, so that any invading Spanish or French fleet could be sighted easily long before it actually arrived. There was an abundance of fish, game, and fowl in the area, as well as trees that could be cut for timber, clapboard, and masts and plenty of pines from which pitch and tar could be extracted.

On June 22, 1607, Captain Newport sailed back to England with the two largest ships loaded with clapboard and sassafras root. When Newport departed, the settlement seemed to be going well, but the pleasant May weather had prevented anyone from realizing that Jamestown was on a swamp. Within ten days of Newport's departure, nearly all the men were ill, overcome by a combination of hot weather, insects, bad water, and poor diet. By September, at least half the settlers had perished, most from disease, a few from Indian arrows (one was put to death for treason).

The winter of 1607–08 was especially harsh. When Newport returned to Jamestown in early January 1608, he found only 38 of the 105 men he had left behind. He brought fresh supplies and an additional 120 settlers. They were no better prepared for these conditions than the first contingent had been, and within a year most of them also died. A fire that burned the storehouse and most of their new dwellings added to their misery and disorganization.

In addition to their problems with hunger and disease, the Jamestown settlers constantly bickered among themselves. From the outset, the council and its president never seemed strong enough to order the colony's affairs properly. Moreover, the colony's relations with the Indians were unpredictable. After their first encounter, some Indians appeared and in a gesture of friendship gave them food, tobacco, and other gifts. Later, however, other Indians attacked the makeshift fort. Still later, others appeared and explained how the settlers could defend themselves from further surprise attacks.

Captain Smith was responsible for exploring the interior and negotiating with the Indians. While on an expedition in December 1607, he was attacked, captured, and taken to Powhatan, chief of the local Algonkians. With tricks with his compass and lies about the intentions of the settlers, Smith negotiated his release. During this expedition, Smith met Pocahontas, the daughter of Powhatan. Although the story that she offered her head in place of his may be only legend, she was very much drawn to him. In the ensuing years, she was to befriend the settlers and help them on many occasions. Smith and Powhatan did not develop a liking for each other, but each developed a healthy respect for the other's power that helped prevent open warfare between the Indians and the settlers.

Unlike the New England colonists, the first settlers of Virginia had no common cause strong enough to bind them together. Although the Charter of the London Company claimed the spread of the Christian religion to be among their purposes, religious motives seemed to make little difference in the daily lives of the settlers. They shared only a baseless belief that they would find great quantities of gold and become wealthy. The first contingent of settlers, in fact, included a perfumer, a jeweler, two gold refiners, and two goldsmiths. More important, the quest for gold was so strong that it distracted many settlers from tasks that would have increased their security and chances for survival.

The fortunes of the Virginia Colony began to improve somewhat in September 1608, when Smith became president. Soon all the councillors were gone, and he had a free hand in governing the colony. He had little patience with those who expected to find gold and insisted that each settler work at least six hours a day. He published lists of those who were working and those who were not. He promoted discipline by dividing the settlers into small groups, giving each a leader and a specific task to accomplish. Once a week he conducted military drills that were concluded with musket practice.

Shortly after Smith became president, Newport returned with new supplies, new settlers, and new instructions from the London Company. Newport was not to return to England until he had completed one or more of three assignments: to return with gold, to bring news of the discovery of a passage to the South Sea, or to find the survivors of the "lost colony" set up at Roanoke in the 1580s.

Although Smith wanted men who were used to hard work—carpenters, smiths, skilled farm workers—he was sent a lot of assorted gentlemen, artisans whose skills he did not need (including another gold refiner), and only twelve laborers. He did not even appreciate the Germans and the Poles who were sent because they were proficient in the making of tar, glass, and potash. He believed it was still too early for even rudimentary manufacturing enterprises. He strongly approved of the two women who came at this time, however; for he believed that families would contribute greatly to the development of a permanent colony.

Smith was not to see the development of a prosperous colony at Jamestown. In July and August 1609, a fleet of ships brought news that the Virginia Company of London had been reorganized and had changed the government of the colony. By October Smith was relieved of his command. Under his leadership, the colonists had lived better than in the first year and better than they would in the near future. While he was president, only 18 of the 200 people under his command died. When he left for England in October 1609, there were 300 colonists at Jamestown. Six months later 240 of them were dead.

In this first settlement in Virginia, there was little concern with family, church, or education. In retrospect, it seems surprising that the colony even survived. Thomas Jefferson Wertenbaker wrote:

> . . . the immigrant to Virginia [was] beset on all sides with deadly perils. If he escaped the plague, the yellow fever and the scurvy during his voyage across the Atlantic, he was more than apt to fall a victim to malaria or dysentery after

he reached his new home. Even if he survived all these dangers, he might perish miserably of hunger, or be butchered by the savage Indians. No wonder he cursed the country, calling it "a miserie, a ruine, a death, a hell."

It is remarkable that the enterprise, in the face of these stupendous difficulties, should ever have succeeded.[1]

Tobacco Brings Prosperity

King James I believed that, because of its moderate climate, Virginia would become a source of produce, which England had to import from the Mediterranean countries. But Virginia's eventual prosperity was based on a product for which James I could not give his personal approval—tobacco. The use of tobacco had spread throughout England after 1565 when John Hawkins returned with some fine Florida leaf. As neither the soil nor the climate of England was appropriate for its successful growth, England had to choose between tobacco from Spanish America or the harsh-tasting leaf grown by the Indians in Virginia.

In 1611, a Jamestown settler, John Rolfe, planted tobacco in Virginia, using seeds from Trinidad and the valley of the Orinoco River. Rolfe's tobacco was not as good as the Spanish-American tobacco but was much better than the Indians'. Samples sent to England in 1616 were declared satisfactory, and soon all the colonists were planting as much tobacco as possible. In 1615 they sent about one ton of tobacco to England. Within two years they sent ten tons. In 1620 they sent thirty tons. In 1639 they sent home seven hundred and fifty tons. The colonists had found a cash crop and were eager to plant as much as they could. At one time, the streets of Jamestown were even planted in tobacco. Tobacco had become the gold the first settlers had sought.

The tobacco fever led the colonists to become careless about their defenses against the Indians. When the new government assumed command after Smith's departure, a new site had been prepared for settlement at Henrico, about fifty miles upriver from Jamestown. Five blockhouses were erected along the river bank, and palisades and ditches were built so that the colonists would be secure from surprise attacks. But the desire to grow greater amounts of tobacco led the colonists outside their secure lands.

For a time, the influence of Pocahontas brought them security. The daughter of Powhatan had been captured and held by the colonists as a way of forcing the Indians to return stolen tools and imprisoned settlers. During her detainment in the colony, the colonists grew fond of her, while she learned English ways and became a Christian. In April 1614, John Rolfe and Pocahontas were married in the Jamestown church. The marriage created a peace between the Indians and the colonists, and allowed the settlers to make several favorable treaties with the Indians.

The marriage of Rolfe and Pocahontas was touted widely in England to convince the English that the race relations problem had been solved. To give the colony good publicity and promote further investment, Rolfe and Pocahontas

---

1. Thomas Jefferson Wertenbaker, *Virginia Under the Stuarts* (New York: Russell and Russell, 1959), p. 15.

visited England in 1616. Pocahontas was the chief attraction of English society for nearly a year, but contracted smallpox and died before she could return to Virginia.

The peace brought about by the marriage came to an abrupt end on Good Friday, 1622, with an attack planned by Chief Opechancanough, Powhatan's successor. A last-minute warning by some converted Indians saved Jamestown, but the outlying plantations fell to the Indians. In one day, the Indians killed nearly 350 people, slaughtered much of the livestock, and burned many of the buildings. The end of the peace forced the colonists back into their protected areas. Soon the old problems of disease and malnutrition were added to the renewed state of hostility between the Indians and the settlers.

By the 1620s, then, conditions were not greatly improved from what they had been in the first years at Jamestown. In 1619, Sir Edwin Sandys began to organize his plans to send women to the colony to serve as wives. Each prospective groom was to pay 120 pounds of tobacco for his wife. That was the beginning of a sizable migration to Virginia, but the colony claimed lives by the hundreds. It has been estimated that between 1616 and 1624, 5,000 people left England for Virginia. But in 1624 the total population was about 1,100, or only 200 more than it had been in 1619.

Children and the Law

In the early years of the Virginia Colony, children were so scarce and so valuable as a source of labor that attempts were made to recruit them. In 1619 the Virginia Company of London requested the officials of the City of London to send a hundred children, twelve years or older, to Virginia. It was argued that since London had a surplus of poor children for whom there was no work, sending them to Virginia would benefit all parties. The children would have work, Virginia would have much-needed laborers, and London would no longer have to care for those children. Boys were to be apprenticed until they were twenty-one, girls until they married or reached twenty-one. The Company promised the London officials that the children would then be placed on public lands, not as owners, but as tenants. They would become taxpayers.

The London officials agreed, but some children refused the opportunity presented to them. In 1620 Sir Edwin Sandys asked for, and was quickly granted, the authority to force the children to go to Virginia.

Not until 1646 was there a law in the Virginia Colony that directly concerned families or schooling. Earlier laws and directives from the colony's governors had ordered the settlers to attend church services, but these apparently were not systematically enforced and were designed mainly to encourage the settlers not to leave their work undone. Although the law in Massachusetts (1642) specified that it was the duty of parents to bring up their children so that they would know how to read, understand and obey the laws of the country, and understand and live by the principles of their religion, the Virginia Apprenticeship Law (1646) did not mention either reading or religion. Its emphasis was clearly the necessity of teaching the poor a useful trade. It cited English tradition (probably meaning the English Act for the Relief of the Poor, 1601) and began with a reference to Parliament which in its wisdom had established a number of statutes and laws in order to ensure that youth would be educated "in honest and profitable trades and manufactures." Such a law was necessary "to avoid sloath and idleness where-with such young children are easily corrupted" and to give relief to those parents "whose poverty" did not allow them to give their children the proper education. The law was also necessary for the good of Virginia. "God Almighty, among his many other blessings," read the law, "hath vouchsafed increase of children to this colony who now are multiplied to a considerable number, who if instructed in good and lawful trades *may much improve the honor and reputation of the country,* and noe lesse their owne good and their parents' comfort."[2]

Although both the Virginia law and the Massachusetts law made provision for binding out children as apprentices, the Virginia law was significantly different. It did not remind parents of their duties, although it explicitly recognized that parents were frequently unwilling to part with their children. Attributing parents' attachment to their children to either "fond indulgence or perverse obstinacy," it therefore ordered (in accordance with the "laudable custom in the kingdom in England") that "the commissioners of the severall countyes respectively do, at theire discretion, make choice of two children in each county of the age of eight or seven years at least, either male or female, which are to be sent up to James City between this June next to be employed in the public flax houses under such master and mistresse as shall there be appointed, in carding, knitting and spinning, etc."

The Problem of the Poor

While educational or apprenticeship provisions for the poor are sometimes viewed as philanthropic gestures, it is probably fair to conclude that the Virginia Colony was more interested in the honor and the economic welfare of Virginia than in the welfare of the children. Historically, the more favored classes and the churches had assumed responsibility for the poor. As the poor grew in number and threat-ened social tranquility, however, their problems became the problems of the collective society.

In a curious way, Virginia was both behind and ahead of its time. It was developing into a plantation society without any major cities. (Of the five major colonial cities, only Charleston, South Carolina, was in the South.) Virginia's plan-tation society and economy made it similar to fifteenth- and sixteenth-century England. Yet it was facing the problem of how to deal with the needs of special classes of children: the poor, the orphans, and illegitimate offspring. In that respect it was like seventeenth-century England. It could not rely on churches and privately

---

2. "Workhouse Law for Poor Children in Virginia," reprinted in *Education in the United States: A Documentary History,* ed. Sol Cohen (New York: Random House, 1974), Vol. 1, pp. 342–43. Emphasis added.

established foundations to tend to the poor, for it was still too new a society to have developed either in any significant number. It was, and would for a number of years continue to be, a frontier settlement—a colony without great population centers. Yet as soon as it became a colony with families, Virginia had to begin to attend to social problems. That it copied the 1601 English Act for the Relief of the Poor is not surprising. Most Virginians were English but, unlike the Pilgrims and the Puritans, they were not deliberately trying to live up to any special communal ideal. Rather, they were looking for wealth and trying to improve their stations in life within the framework of English society as they knew it. Their social heritage required that they look after those who could not tend to themselves. Others were expected to take care of themselves and their own.

Marcus W. Jernegan reported that colonial Virginia enacted seventeen laws in behalf of orphans. The first (1642) was intended to protect the estates of orphans from abuse by their guardians, but also stated that guardians were to ensure that their charges be taught the Christian religion and "the rudiments of learning." A 1705 law required that "the master of every such orphan shall be obliged to teach him to read and write." Subsequent acts in 1730, 1740, and 1748 indicate that making provisions for orphans and the handling (or mishandling) of their estates was a continuing problem. It was generally expected that orphans who had been left considerable estates would receive instruction in reading and writing, while those who had small or no estates would be bound out as apprentices. After 1751 poor and orphan girls as well as boys were supposed to be taught to read and write.[3]

The record books of two parishes that Jernegan examined show the proportions of poor, orphans, and illegitimate children as well as the kinds of apprenticeships to which they were bound. Such records also show the kinds of trades that were practiced and the kinds of artisans the colony needed. In the records of Fredericksville Parish, Louisa County, 1742–85, and Dettingen Parish, Prince William County, 1745–82, Jernegan found indentures for 120 boys and 43 girls. Poor children were the largest class; there were 64 so described. The others consisted of 62 orphans, 20 mulatto children, and 17 illegitimate children. The girls "were usually apprenticed as domestic servants with no particular trade mentioned." Sometimes it was specified that the girls be taught "to knit, spin, and sew." For boys, a variety of trades was listed. Shoemaking and carpentry headed the list. Others were blacksmith, cooper, weaver, bricklayer, saddle-maker, tailor, millwright, silversmith, and barber. Only 14 of the boys were assigned to become planters and farmers.[4]

Virginians followed the English tradition of making private provision for the "special classes." William Arthur Maddox wrote in his study of education in Virginia

---

3. Marcus W. Jernegan, "Compulsory Education in the Southern Colonies," The School Review 17:6 (June 1919), p. 408–11.

4. Marcus W. Jernegan, "Compulsory Education in the Southern Colonies: II, Virginia," School Review 18:2 (February 1920), pp. 137–38.

that "from the time of the bequest of Benjamin Syms, 1634, it was common practice among Virginians, as it was among pious English gentlemen everywhere, to remember the education of the poor in their wills."[5] Syms willed two hundred acres, eight cows, the milk from the cows, and the cows' calves for the establishment of a school in Elizabeth City. The Syms school opened in the late 1640s. In 1805 it was merged with the Eaton School, founded under the will of Thomas Eaton, also of Elizabeth City.

The first provisions made for children in Virginia were thus different from those made in Massachusetts. Virginians and other southerners were to continue their tradition of providing schools and orphanages through bequests throughout the eighteenth century. In Massachusetts, many communities abandoned their support of publicly supported schools; but when they did so, they turned frequently to private schools. In large measure the differences between the two colonies can be explained by the differences in both their patterns of settlement and their economies.

The Plantation Economy

The cultivation of tobacco as a cash crop required enormous expanses of land because tobacco soon depleted the soil of its minerals. The ambitious planter sought to secure as much land as possible for future crops. He used only a small portion (about 10 percent) of his land for tobacco, growing tobacco on the land for about four years, then using it for grain for a year or two, and finally giving it for a church or one of the field schools or simply abandoning it. While one plot of land was used for tobacco, others were being cleared for future crops.

The amount of tobacco a planter could grow was determined not only by the available land but also by the available labor. There were numerous complaints that workers made as much in a day in Virginia as they did in a week in England. The high wages and the prospect of acquiring one's own land prompted many English laborers to come to Virginia as indentured servants. The supply of labor began to change dramatically after 1619, when a Dutch ship arrived with twenty blacks who were sold as indentured servants.

For most blacks, indentured service developed into chattel slavery, and by 1650 there were about 300 black slaves in Virginia. The slave population then began to grow more rapidly. In the first decade of the 1700s more than 6,000 slaves were acquired by the Virginians. At that time slaves constituted about 20 percent of Virginia's population; by the time of the Revolution, they made up about half. The introduction of slavery into Virginia allowed the large plantations to grow even larger. At the same time, the number of small planters decreased dramatically. White servants and workers were soon discouraged from immigrating to Vir-

---

5. William Arthur Maddox, *The Free School Idea in Virginia Before the Civil War* (New York: Teachers College, Columbia University, 1918), p. 8.

ginia, for there were few positions for them. Virginia was to have its very prosperous and its very poor at the expense of the black slaves and the middle class.

Shipping facilities were crucial for the Virginia planters because the market for tobacco was in England. The tidewater area of Virginia could not have been better suited to the planters' needs. Chesapeake Bay is large and well protected and is fed by four large, navigable rivers: the James, the Potomac, the Rappahannock, and the York. Each of these rivers gives access to several other navigable rivers, creating an elaborate system of waterways that allowed nearly every plantation to have its own direct shipping connections with the West Indies, Bristol, and London. Planters had no need for a great commercial city or even for roadways.

Learning on the Plantation

Without nearby cities or even sizable towns, each plantation became a complete miniature community. Crops were planted and harvested. Lumber was cut from fields being cleared for future tobacco cultivation and made into packing crates, barrels, and furniture. People were born and buried. Out of necessity, the plantation owner became adept at a variety of trades, sometimes even practicing medicine. Perhaps the best example of the wide range of abilities and interests cultivated by a Virginia planter is Thomas Jefferson—a farmer, scientist, inventor, philosopher, and student and practitioner of politics. Jefferson, however, differed from other planters in that he was educated through both books and experience. Most Virginians, even the gentry, seemed to rely more on experience than on books.

In many respects, young people who lived on a plantation did not need access to formal schooling. The plantation was small enough for them to see all the agricultural, commercial, and manufacturing processes first hand. At the same time, the activities on a plantation were numerous and varied enough to enable the children to learn what they needed. What formal instruction they needed could often be secured in a nearby field school. However, as slavery grew, and the gap between the prosperous and the poor increased, another system developed. The children of the planters were provided with tutors, imported from Europe or from the North, with the result that access to schooling for others, especially the poor, was severely limited. Sometimes there was a field school for the poor, but it frequently opened only a day or two a week. It certainly was not comparable to the New England grammar school. It barely went beyond the basic skills and was often conducted by the Episcopal parish priest or the lay reader. Sometimes an indentured servant served as the master. The field schools were usually supported by the tuition paid by each student's parents, not by a tax on the entire community.

The life the Virginians were trying to live did not require the same commitment to literacy as that of the New Englanders. Those who became dominant in Virginia had been members of the English middle class who aspired to the life of the gentry, which was neither studious nor comtemplative. The role the Virginia man cast for himself was a practical one as manager of his plantation and public servant in his community. If called to serve on the vestry of the church or in the House of Burgesses, he did so.

Although much has been made of the libraries on the plantations, it is likely that the extensive collections of William Byrd II and Thomas Jefferson were not typical. Daniel Boorstin reports that "before 1700 a library in Virginia containing more than one hundred volumes was a rarity; even in the eighteenth century it was not unusual in inventories of the estates of leading Virginians to find but a dozen books."[6] Most books in the libraries were practical books, useful in conducting the numerous affairs of the plantation. The inventories of the libraries indicate that law books were deemed to be the most practical.

The College and the Church

Although the College of William and Mary was not founded until 1693, there had been earlier attempts to found a school or college in Virginia. A tablet in the arcade of the college's Christopher Wren building reads: "First College in the United States in its antecedents, which go back to the College proposed at Henrico. Second to Harvard University in actual operation." The Virginia Company, with the encouragement of King James I, did endorse a plan for a school at Henrico in 1619. The crown had even allocated 9,000 acres for a school, but the Indian massacre of 1622 put an end to those plans (and to the king's Privy Council, George Thorpe, who was to have started the school). The planned Henrico College was to have a branch for Indians, where the colonists could transform them into their own likeness.

In 1622, the year of the Indian attack, the Virginia Company endorsed a plan for the East India School, which was to be both a grammar school and a university. The plan for it was fashioned by the Reverend Patrick Copland, the chaplain aboard the East India Company ship *Royal James*. Having convinced the captain and his crew to contribute toward the establishment of good works in the Virginia Colony, Copland and the Company decided that a school was greatly needed. The Company agreed that a thousand acres and several workers should be designated for the school, but these plans, like later attempts in the 1660s, did not bring a college to Virginia.

The first Virginia college, William and Mary, was to be as different from Harvard and Yale as Virginia was different from New England. Harvard was founded to train ministers. Yale was founded because some believed Harvard had become too liberal. Throughout the 1600s and 1700s, in fact, the founding of colleges was frequently related to the specific sectarian interests of various groups. Frederick Rudolph writes, for example, that "Yale and Princeton contributed a new purpose to the life of the colonial college—the carrying on of sectarian

6. Daniel J. Boorstin, *The Americans: The Colonial Experience* (New York: Vintage Books, 1958), p. 303.

controversy, the pursuit of denominational survival in an environment of religious diversity."[7] Although the early purpose of the College of William and Mary was to educate a ministry as well as teach the young good manners and provide them with proper literary training, its relationship with Virginia's established Anglican religion seems comparatively weak.

Virginians thought religion important, but they did not fight about it. They maintained their relationship with the Church of England, managed to continue to be Episcopalians without bishops, and devised a way to have what amounted to a form of congregationalism without formally breaking from the episcopal system. In England, priests were appointed to their posts by the bishop. Once installed, the priest remained in the parish whether the parishioners were satisfied or not. The Virginians found a polite way to avoid such an eventuality. A priest could not be officially installed until he had been presented or nominated by the vestrymen to the Governor and the Council. The Virginians simply never took this step; rather, most parishes gave their priests one year's contract after another. The parishioners thus maintained the upper hand and created what was tantamount to a congregational system.

Virginia had no bishops throughout the colonial period, and the Church of Virginia was considered to be under the jurisdiction of the Bishop of London. The Virginians seemed not eager to have a bishop and the Bishop of London seemed to think it the better course of wisdom not to press the issue. Consequently, Virginia could not ordain its own priests, for there were no bishops to do so. The absence of bishops gave the Virginia Church a loose structure. It also required parish priests to be responsive to the will of the people.

In the 1680s Henry Compton, Bishop of London, began to send his personal representatives to the colonies. In 1689 Compton named the Reverend James Blair as his Commissary in Virginia. Although the Commissary represented the bishop and was the head of the Virginia Church, his powers were limited and not totally delineated. (He could not, for example, ordain priests for the colony.)

Blair had first been sent to Virginia by Compton in 1685 as a missionary. After becoming rector of a frontier parish at Varina in Henrico County, he married into an influential Jamestown family and developed social contacts that were to serve him in his later educational and political efforts (he was governor of Virginia, 1740–41).Soon after his appointment as Commissary, Blair called a meeting of the Virginia clergy at which he introduced the notion of founding a college in Virginia. Those present at the meeting endorsed the idea, and Blair took the idea to the Assembly. By 1693 he had made good use of his position and contacts in both Virginia and London and had secured from the crown a charter for the College of William and Mary. It named him the college's first president and Bishop Hampton its chancellor.

In the early years of the college, Blair's annual salary of £150 consumed most

---

7. Frederick Rudolph, *The American College and University* (New York: Vintage Books, 1965), p. 8.

of the available resources. Not until the 1720s did the college really begin to function as a college. Although it was founded by an Anglican and its faculty were required to be Anglicans, the college seems not to have been dominated by religious concerns. Nor did the presence of the college completely change the educational practices of prosperous Virginians, who continued to be educated by tutors and in the English schools. They did, however, develop the habit of spending a year at William and Mary either before or after their education in England. The time spent at William and Mary was useful in acquiring some knowledge of the politics of Virginia—the college was located in Williamsburg within sight of the Capitol—and in developing social contacts that would be useful in the political and commercial life of Virginia. This social function was, according to Phyllis Vine, one of the major functions performed by American colleges in the eighteenth century. By the middle of the eighteenth century, American colleges were serving a purpose that was more social than religious. For instance, Vine has found many instances in which young men married sisters of their classmates or the daughters of college officials.[8] She has concluded:

> By the middle of the eighteenth century, teachers and parents began to view the college as an institution which would abet weaknesses in the family's socialization of youth. As educators removed students from the immediate influence of parents, and provided opportunities for a broader range of personal and professional contacts, they established an institution that functioned to solidify an elite while training students to serve the public arena.[9]

---

8. Phyllis Vine, "The Social Function of Eighteenth-Century Higher Education," *History of Education Quarterly* 16:4 (Winter 1976), p. 415.

9. Ibid., pp. 416–17.

Pennsylvania: The Holy Experiment 3

The Quaker Aristocrat

The development of William Penn's proprietary colony, Pennsylvania, provides another example of the diversity of interests, motives, beliefs, and peoples in the North American colonies. William Penn was born in 1644 during the English Civil War, the son of a captain in the Parliamentary navy. After receiving high honors, gifts of property, and a promotion to admiral, the senior Penn fell from Oliver Cromwell's favor and retired to his lands. After Cromwell died in 1658, the senior Penn helped to restore the monarchy in England and was knighted by Charles II. In later years, William Penn, although he did not share his father's values and beliefs, would profit from his father's high station and friends at court, as well as the debts the crown owed his father.

To the puzzlement of his father, William Penn showed a keen interest in religious matters at an early age. During his second year at Oxford, he was expelled for making known his strong dislike for Anglicanism. He was sent to tour Europe with other young aristocrats, spent some time in France where he attended a Huguenot college, and was introduced at the Court of Louis XIV. When he returned to England, he gave the appearance of being a proper courtier. Penn began to read law at Lincoln's Inn in 1665 but soon left to escape the plague and went to Ireland to manage his father's lands. There he encountered the Irish Quakers, converted to their beliefs, and subsequently traveled about England preaching them. Periods in jail did not deter him. He stuck to his Quaker beliefs, wrote in defense of religious freedom, and married the stepdaughter of the Quaker leader Isaac Pennington.

The Religious Society of Friends

The Religious Society of Friends, nicknamed "Quakers," had been founded by George Fox in the 1650s. While Puritans set aside the authority of the church hierarchy in favor of the authority of the Scriptures, the Friends went a step further by insisting that the inner voice of Christ was in the heart of each person and that all people needed to know the truth and the way to live could be found in their own hearts. This idea developed into a set of beliefs that directed each person to do away with artificial social distinctions and titles, to refrain from oaths, and to refuse to support or engage in war. Unlike the Puritans, the Friends did not see themselves as a closed community, but wished to communicate their spiritual discoveries to others even when others did not want to listen.

During the first generation of Quakerism, many Friends were persecuted, not only for their beliefs but also for their insistence upon preaching where they had been asked not to preach. The Friends also refused to obey laws they considered unjust and were jailed and had their property confiscated. Like the Separatists before them, many felt English society to be corrupt and desired to purify it. By the 1670s some Quakers held that leaving English society would be an acceptable alternative to purifying it.

In the 1670s George Fox led a missionary expedition to the Americas, visiting the colonies. He and Penn later toured northern Europe together. During their travels, they learned that Quakers and members of other pietistic sects who feared they would not be long tolerated were willing and even eager to found a new colony. Perhaps it would be possible to live and practice their religious beliefs in safety in the lands across the Atlantic.

In June 1680, Penn petitioned Charles II for the land that now comprises Pennsylvania and in March 1681 was granted a proprietary charter. The land granted to Penn had belonged to the king's brother, the Duke of York, also a friend of the senior Penn. There seems to be no clear agreement about why Penn was granted the land, although many plausible explanations can be derived from his own and his father's activities.

The Holy Experiment

Penn managed the preparations, the settlement, and the government of the colony in accordance with his aristocratic station and tastes as well as his religious beliefs. Although he viewed the colony as a source of income for himself, he also saw it as an experiment where religious freedom could truly be tried. His advertisements for the colony were very much unlike the advertisements of other early colonizers. He did not promise gold chamber pots, immediate wealth, or an abundance of anything but hard work. He outlined what the journey would cost and what provisions would be needed, and warned prospective settlers of the difficulties that faced them. As in Virginia, each settler who brought an indentured servant was to receive a 50-acre grant. Two-hundred acre tracts could be had for a rent of a penny an acre. The price for a 5,000-acre estate was £100. With each estate the purchaser received a 10-acre city lot. Indentured servants were eligible for 50-acre tracts after they had completed their term of service.

The Pennsylvania Colony was not to be limited to either the Friends or the English. Advertisements were published in Dutch, French, and German. Penn promised the settlers considerable freedom, participation in the government, and free rents for the first five years. For those who were willing to live peacefully there was to be total religious freedom. There was no established church, although Quakers would be the dominant political force for at least two generations.

Penn's advertisements drew settlers from all the British Isles, Germany, Holland, and other American colonies. During the first year, 2,000 settlers arrived aboard twenty-three ships. By the end of 1685, almost 8,000 immigrants had come to Pennsylvania. A group of German Mennonites led by Francis Daniel Pastorius, whom Penn had met on his tour of northern Europe, founded Germantown. Besides the English Quakers and German Pietists, there were Scots-Irish Presbyterians, Dutch and Swedish Lutherans, and Catholics from England, France, Holland, and Germany. A corporation of Quakers, The Free Society of Traders began a general store, a whale-fishing industry, brick kilns, tanneries, glass works, and trade with the West Indies. In just four years, Penn's colony achieved in population what it had taken Virginia nearly three decades to accomplish. By 1690 Philadelphia was second only to Boston among colonial cities.

Conditions for new settlers were more favorable than in the other colonies. Several hundred Swedes and Finns, the remnants of the short-lived New Sweden colony, farmed near Philadelphia, ensuring a supply of food. Moreover, the settlers faced no problems with the Indians because of Penn's humane policies toward them. Pennsylvania had no difficulties with the Indians until the 1750s. By that time Philadelphia was secure, and the Indian attacks were confined to the frontier settlements.

When Penn arrived in his colony in October 1682, he had the city laid out according to the best thought of Renaissance planners. The result was the now-familiar grid pattern of parallel streets running at right angles. Some squares of the city were given to parks and others to building. Penn refused to name the streets after famous or prominent people; he chose instead to name them after the various trees in the area. In the future, many American cities would lay out their streets and name them just as they were in Philadelphia. Penn also directed that houses be built in the center of lots (to keep fires from spreading) and that each lot be planted with trees. Placing houses in the center of lots would help to prevent devastating fires. Penn's tree-lined streets were also copied throughout the country.

Although Penn himself was not to grow wealthy from his colony, Pennsylvania experienced remarkable economic growth. From the beginning, Philadelphia had the ingredients for a healthy economy. The surrounding farm lands were fertile, there was easy access to the Atlantic, and the first settlers included knowledgeable and established merchants and experienced craftsmen. Its economic diversity and the absence of either political or religious orthodoxy made it a much less homogeneous place than any of the other colonies. There could not have been a more hospitable place for a young man such as Benjamin Franklin to become the prototypical American.

The First "American"

Benjamin Franklin was not a native Philadelphian, but he had been one of its leading citizens for over fifty years when he was appointed in 1776 to the committee to help draft what became the Declaration of Independence. Although it was generally known and agreed that the young Virginian, Thomas Jefferson, would write the document, John Adams and Franklin gave not only geographic balance but considerable prestige to the undertaking. Franklin's experiments in electricity —the kite episode was but one of them—had brought him international fame as a scientist, as well as Master of Arts degrees from Harvard, Yale, and the College of William and Mary. His *Poor Richard's Almanack* (published from 1732 to 1757) also contributed to his reputation.

Franklin was born in Boston, and his parents had tried to bring him up in accordance with the traditional ways of New England. Their efforts in behalf of their tenth son were thoroughly consistent with the New England laws of the 1640s. His older brothers had been sent out to be apprentices in various trades at early ages, but his father intended to have Benjamin prepared for service in the church. Accordingly, he sent his son to the Boston grammar school when he was eight. Franklin excelled in the grammar school, according to his *Autobiography,* but his father removed him because the expense was too great. He was then sent to a writing school, where the master tried to teach him to write and do arithmetic. He left school at age ten, having learned to write. He would have to master arithmetic on his own at a later time.

After these two years of formal schooling, Franklin worked with his father, a soap boiler and tallow chandler. Franklin did not like that trade, however, and talked of going to sea, a prospect that did not please his father. To find an alternative for him, his father took him about the city to watch the various workers to determine whether some other trade might interest his son. To use an earlier Puritan idiom, Franklin's father was trying to determine what his son's "calling" was. Finally, when Franklin was twelve, his father apprenticed him to his brother who was a printer. Although he failed to complete his apprenticeship with his brother, he used what he learned to establish his own business in Philadelphia. Franklin had arrived in Philadelphia in 1727 at age seventeen with a Dutch dollar and about a shilling in copper in his pocket. He used the dollar to pay for his passage and began his career with the remaining copper. Thus began one of the most famous rags-to-riches stories in the history of America. At age twenty-four Franklin had his own shop and a newspaper, the *Pennsylvania Gazette.*

Arriving at Moral Perfection

While Franklin is indeed an exemplar of the rising American middle class, he is also an exemplar of a new morality—one that focused on what people did. Its origins were in Puritan New England. Franklin's family belonged to Cotton Mather's church in Boston, and Franklin claimed that Cotton Mather's *Essays to Do Good* had a lifelong influence on him. Franklin, however, would not adhere to the teaching of any particular denomination or any creed. He emphasized the behavior of people and found most religious dogma "unintelligible" or "doubtful."[1] The difficulty he had with dogma did not, however, take him away from morality. He simply wanted to transform "religious principles" into specific behaviors. As Franklin told it, he "conceived the bold and arduous project of arriving at moral perfection." Believing that a person could fashion himself or herself into a completely moral person, he devised a simple plan to do so, using an eighteenth-century version of behavior modification theory.

Franklin set out to achieve moral perfection with a simple apparatus—a pen and a few pieces of paper. First, he made a list of virtues (thirteen in all) and attached a precept to each. On another piece of paper he drew 91 squares: across the top of this page he entered the days of the week; down the left side of the paper he listed the virtues. He explained that he would attend to one virtue a week, striving to achieve no black marks for an entire week. He explained how the entire process worked in this way:

> I determined to give a week's strict attention to each of the virtues successively. Thus, in the first week, my great guard was to avoid even the least offence against *Temperance,* leaving the other virtues to their ordinary chance, only marking every evening the faults of the day. Thus, if in the first week I could keep my first line, marked T, clear of spots, I supposed the habit of that virtue so much strengthened, and its opposite weakened, that I might venture extending my attention to include the next, and for the following week keep both lines clear of spots. . . . I should have, I hoped, the encouraging pleasure of seeing on my pages the progress I made in virtue, by clearing successively my lines of their spots, till in the end, by a number of courses, I should be happy in viewing a clean book, after a thirteen weeks' daily examination.[2]

As Franklin worked his way down the list, managing to achieve rows of spotless squares, he had a built-in reinforcement schedule. Variations of Franklin's scheme have since been used countless times in schoolrooms.

Franklin explained that after he began his project he was surprised to learn that he had had so many faults. Still, he did have "the satisfaction of seeing them diminish." Ever the careful scientist, Franklin even designed improvements in his apparatus. As he used his little book over and over and rubbed out the spots, he eventually wore little holes in the pages. He then transferred the precepts and the

---

1. *Benjamin Franklin's Autobiography* (New York: Holt, Rinehart and Winston, 1953), p. 81.
2. Ibid. pp. 86–87.

tables "to the ivory leaves of a memorandum book." Those marks he "could easily wipe out with a wet sponge" and then start out with a clean slate.

Franklin had unquestionably worked a revolution in morality. Sin no longer soiled the soul; it soiled the page. Moral transgressions were not really sins; they were (as Franklin said when he described how he broke the indenture with his brother) "errata." Most important, people were now their own moral accountants. Gone was the notion that a God or an agent of God was keeping accounts. That was no longer necessary. Now people could balance their own moral accounts.

Franklin has not endured history without criticism. His life was so long and his activities so varied that it is not surprising that he met with successes and failures, praise and blame, friends and detractors. In education his record is a mixture of success and failure. He taught himself and did so very well. He saw his *Almanack* and the *Pennsylvania Gazette* as instruments for education. They were successful. He formed a subscription library and several self-improvement projects and they were long lasting. However, when he directed his efforts toward the establishment of an academy, the result was not quite what he had planned.

The Philadelphia Academy

Benjamin Franklin was the promoter, organizer, and designer of the Philadelphia Academy which opened in 1751. The school, however, took a course different from the one he had charted for it. He announced his plan for the Academy in 1749 when he published his *Proposals Relating to the Education of Youth in Pennsylvania.*

Franklin began *Proposals* with what amounted to an annotated bibliography. The annotations, however, told more about the authors than the works cited: "the famous Milton," "the great Mr. Locke," "the ingenious Mr. Hutcheson," "the learned Mr. Obadiah Walker," "the much admired Mons. Rollin," and "the learned and ingenious Dr. George Turnbull."[3] Perhaps Franklin cited these authors to show that he was sufficiently acquainted with educational matters to offer his own proposals, or perhaps he was trying to convince his readers of the soundness of his ideas with a splendid appeal to authority. It is also possible that he used them because they illustrated the points he wanted to emphasize. Indeed, most of the proposals are found not in the main body of the text but in the footnotes.

After introducing his authorities, Franklin appealed to the reader's civic and personal interests. The reader was reminded that "the good Education of Youth has been esteemed by wise Men in all Ages, as the surest Foundation of the Happiness both of private Families and of Common-wealths." Although that sentence appealed to traditional reasons for supporting education, Franklin admitted in a footnote that what he was proposing "may be found to differ a little from the Forms of Education in common Use."[4] He noted that Milton, Locke, Rollin,

---

3. Benjamin Franklin, "Proposals Relating to the Education of Youth in Pennsylvania," in *Educational Views of Benjamin Franklin,* ed. Thomas Woody (New York: McGraw-Hill, 1931), p. 150.
   4. Ibid., p. 151.

Turnbull, and others had recently observed that the old ways of education were wrong and that it was very difficult to change old ways. Pennsylvania, however, had a rare opportunity to proceed according to reason rather than custom because it scarcely had an educational tradition.

By the standards of his time Franklin's proposals were modern. He wanted to make the proposed academy an integral part of the city's life and to involve the city's citizens in the school's affairs. In recommending a location, urged "that a House be provided for the ACADEMY, if not in the Town, not many Miles from it: the Situation high and dry, and if it may be, not far from a River, having a Garden, Orchard, Meadow, and a Field or two."[5] (The sites of the Virginia field schools would not have been suitable.) The mention of a garden, orchard, meadow, and fields is reminiscent of what the Italian educator Vittorino de Feltre had called "the Pleasant House" and of Milton's call for "a spacious house and ground." On the other hand, while Franklin wanted a pastoral setting, he wanted it in or very near the city. He noted that if the school were in the city, a library would not be needed because students could use the town library. In a footnote he reminded the reader of "the English library begun and carried on by Subscription in Philadelphia," though he did not record that he had started it. There was also, he noted, an excellent collection that one of Philadelphia's leading citizens would make available to the students if the school were located in the city. He also observed that it would be easy for the citizens to watch over the behavior of the students.

Franklin did not urge parents to involve themselves in the school's affairs, but he did strongly urge the trustees to take an active part. He asked that the trustees frequently visit the students and wanted them to treat the students as though they were their own children. He even asked that they give preferential treatment to those who completed their studies. He wanted the trustees "to zealously unite, and make all the Interest that can be made to establish them, whether in Business, Offices, Marriages, or any other Thing for their Advantage, preferably to all other Persons whatsoever even of equal Merit."[6] Whether Franklin's request of the trustees was motivated by an attempt to relate schooling to the needs of a rising middle class or whether it was an attempt to find a substitute for what already existed in Europe is a matter for interpretation. In a footnote he pointed out that "something seems wanting in America to incite and stimulate Youth to Study." In Europe, he explained, there were more "Encouragements to Learning" (that is, more potential church and governmental posts) then in America.

The curriculum Franklin proposed for the Academy was not bound to tradition. The main subjects were not the classical languages; the central discipline was instead to be history. If history were "made a constant Part" of the students' reading, he said, it would naturally lead to other subjects: Geography, Chronology, Ancient Customs, and Morality. By "Morality" Franklin meant to convey something close to what we would now term "good citizenship." The study of proper history

---

5. Ibid., pp. 154–55.
6. Ibid., pp. 153–54.

would, he claimed, "fix in the Minds of Youth deep Impressions of the Beauty and Usefulness of Virtue of all Kinds." It would also show "the Necessity of a Public Religion, from its Usefulness to the Publick; the advantage of a Religious Character among private Persons; the Mischiefs of Superstition and the Excellency of the Christian Religion above all others ancient or modern."[7]

Franklin anticipated the arguments of many nineteenth-century proponents of public schooling in his argument that history would show the advantages humanity acquired from joining together in societies governed by law. Such arrangements protected people and their property, encouraged industrious behavior, and generally made life more comfortable than it would otherwise be. Franklin's appeal to Christianity without specification of any sect and his appeal to what might be called domestic tranquility were to be repeated in nearly every generation.

In his discussions of education as well as in his many other endeavors, Franklin linked morality to what was socially useful. Like his ancestors in Massachusetts, he was more concerned with living a good life than with any theological or sectarian niceties. Vernon L. Parrington described Franklin as a man "less concerned with the golden pavements of the City of God than that the cobblestones on Chestnut Street in Philadelphia should be well and evenly laid."[8]

Breaking with Classical Tradition

Franklin's clearest break with tradition in educational matters was the emphasis, or lack of emphasis, on languages. Classical languages were reduced to electives, although he did suggest that students would want to learn Latin, Greek, and other languages after they discovered that the people whose feats they were reading about could be further explored in all their rich detail only by reading their works in the original. Recommendations for the study of languages, however, were directly related to the profession toward which the student aspired. Accordingly, those who wanted to enter the ministry were advised to study French as well as Latin and Greek. Future merchants were advised that modern languages— French, German, and Spanish—would be useful. No student was to "be compell'd to learn Latin, Greek, or the modern foreign Languages."

In this matter, Franklin had gone beyond what was customary, even beyond the authors he cited. Milton had emphasized "that language is but the instrument conveying to us things useful to be known" and stated that those who knew languages but did not know the "solid things" in them were no better educated than "any yeoman or tradesman competently wise in his mother dialect only."[9] However, Milton's insistence that languages be useful was not a rejection of them. They were still an integral part of his curriculum.

---

7. Ibid., p. 170.

8. Vernon Louis Parrington, *Main Currents In American Thought I: The Colonial Mind (1620–1800)* (New York: Harvest Books, 1954), p. 180.

9. John Milton, "Of Education" in *Milton on Education,* ed. Oliver Morley Ainsworth (New Haven: Yale University Press, 1928), p. 53.

William Penn also had argued for a new approach to language instruction, though not for dropping the study: "We press their Memory too soon, and puzzle, strain and load them with Words and Rules: to know *Grammer* and *Rhetorick,* and a strange Tongue or two, that it is ten to one may never be useful to them."[10] Penn observed that youth had a natural interest in nature and in mechanical things and wondered why those interests were so often ignored. It was, he wrote, "A Pity therefore that Books have not been composed for *Youth,* by some curious and careful *Naturalists,* and also *Mechanicks,* in the *Latin* Tongue, to be used in Schools, that they might learn Things with Words: Things *obvious* and *familiar* to them, and which would make the Tongue easier to be attained by them."

Franklin's views on the classical languages were, however, to be echoed in successive generations. In 1762, Parson James Maury, who had been Thomas Jefferson's teacher, advised another teacher that Latin and Greek were necessary for those who were to enter one of three professions: the ministry, medicine, or law. Maury was not certain that Latin and Greek were necessary and "proper for all our Youth."[11] But Maury and Franklin did not represent the majority of those who were then making recommendations about what should be taught. In time, others would endorse positions similar to theirs, yet, Latin and Greek, especially Latin, remained an important part of the school curriculum for many generations. How useful Latin is was still being debated in the 1920s and later.

Any doubt that Franklin was trying to break with educational tradition was eliminated in 1751 when he sketched out his "Idea of the English School" for the Academy's trustees. There he outlined what each of the six classes was to study. The first class was to learn the rules of English grammar and orthography (spelling). The second class was to attend to "Reading with Attention, and with proper Modulations of the Voice according to the Sentiments and Subject." For the third, Franklin recommended the study of "the Elements of Rhetoric" so students could learn "Speaking properly and gracefully." They were also to begin the study of history in the third class. It becomes clear that Franklin was proposing a program to equip students to know the English language in all forms: reading, speaking, letter writing, and composition. Good writing was to be second only to good speaking. (Good handwriting, it must be remembered, was as important in an eighteenth-century commercial city as typing and shorthand would be at a later date.) The texts prescribed for the sixth class were either those of contemporary English authors or translations of the classics—Homer, Vergil, and Horace. After the sixth and final class, the students would be prepared for "any Business, Calling or Profession except such wherein Languages are required."[12]

Although Franklin was the first president of the board of trustees of the

---

10. William Penn, "Fruits of Solitude," in *American Issues, Volume I: The Social Record,* ed. Willard Thorp, Merle Curti, and Carlos Baker, rev. ed. (New York: J. B. Lippincott Co., 1955), p. 26.

11. Quoted in David B. Tyack, *Turning Points in American Educational History* (Waltham, Mass.: Blaisdell Publishing Co., 1967), p. 35.

12. Benjamin Franklin, "Idea of the English School" in Woody, *Educational Views of Benjamin Franklin,* p. 129

Academy, he was unable to persuade the other trustees to adopt his views. When the Academy opened, it professed no specific religious mission, although most trustees were Anglicans. As the trustees organized the school, they showed that they were more closely wedded to tradition than Franklin was. The school's advertisements said that Greek, Latin, French, and German would be taught. A Latin master was not only hired but also made rector of the school, and his salary was twice that set for the English master. The English master was expected to teach a class of forty while the Latin master was to teach a class of twenty. The trustees appropriated £100 for supplies and books for the Latin course. There was no appropriation for the English course. In fact, no English master was hired until the second year.

In 1775 the Academy was reorganized and granted a new charter, becoming the College, Academy, and Charitable School of Philadelphia. The philosophical and classical courses were located in the college division of the new school under the direction of William Smith, the school's first provost. Smith, who had earlier written plans for educational reform and had tried to become the first president of Kings College (Columbia University), organized a curriculum that included both traditional and modern subjects. Students were required to study the classics, Scripture, and the modern authors, including Bacon, Locke, and Newton.

After the Declaration of Independence was signed, the College of Philadelphia became the University of Pennsylvania. Unlike the first institutions of higher education in New England, the University of Pennsylvania had no explicit religious mission. The Friends did not need advanced schools for their clergy and did not express any interest in founding a school for the higher learning until 1827 when the Friends Central College was opened. Franklin can be given credit for working to establish what became the first college in Pennsylvania, for trying to reform education in Philadelphia—and for demonstrating that it is easier to plan educational reforms than to institute them.

Pennsylvania School Laws

In the first Frame of Government that Penn fashioned in 1682 for his new colony, it was specified "That the Governor and Provincial Council shall erect and order all public schools, and encourage and reward the authors of useful sciences and laudable inventions in the said province."[13] Penn also wanted a committee of the Provincial Council to supervise the "manners, education, and arts" to prevent "all wicked and scandalous living" and ensure that the young be brought up "in virtue and useful knowledge and arts." In March 1683, the Assembly met and passed a law somewhat like those of Massachusetts and Virginia. It required all parents and guardians of orphans to attend to the instruction of their charges so that all

---

13. Qyoted in Robert E. Potter, *The Stream of American Education* (New York: American Book Co., 1967), p. 56.

"may be able to read the Scriptures and to write by the time they attain to twelve years of age."[14] It also directed that children be taught a "useful trade or skill." This law was not, however, the usual "poor law." In good Quaker fashion, it was explained that everyone needed instruction in a "useful trade" so "that the poor may work to live, and the rich if they become poor may not want." This law did not endure, for William and Mary exercised their right to veto it, as specified in Penn's charter. Another early law that was not observed called for the publication of all the colony's laws so they would be available as a text for the schools.

After the enactment of the 1683 law, the Pennsylvania Council called upon Enoch Flower, who had been a schoolmaster in England for twenty years, to open a school in Philadelphia. The school was supported not by taxes but by "rates" that were to be paid by those who attended. Those who wanted to learn how to read English had to pay four shillings a quarter. The rate for reading and writing was six shillings. For two shillings more, one could also be taught to cast accounts. For £10 a year, one could have instruction in all the branches as well as room, board, and laundry service.

When Penn returned in 1699 for his second visit to his colony, he brought a new Frame of Government. It included no educational laws, and the rest of the eighteenth century, education was left to the people without any direction from the government. There seemed to be no inclination to impose any specific form of schooling on the people. Whether such an imposition would have been successful is doubtful. In many ways, Pennsylvania was a colony of colonies. As the various groups with their distinctive religious persuasions arrived, they set out to live their lives in accordance with those beliefs. That included the nurture of their children. For government officials to attempt to direct educational matters would have been tantamount to attempting to direct the family customs and religious practices of those many groups. It would probably have met with considerable suspicion, if not actual resistance. Although most people would have agreed that proper education was necessary for proper civil order, they probably would not have agreed to accept state-directed education.

Friends' Schools

The absence of state laws on educational practices can not be construed to mean that there were no educational opportunities and interests in Pennsylvania. In Philadelphia the Friends founded and supported elementary schools that were open to all boys and girls whose parents could pay tuition. For those who could not pay the tuition, scholarships were provided by affluent Friends. For girls, the private schools were more plentiful and better equipped than in many other colonies. Young women in Philadelphia were taught more than the domestic sciences. Eventually, students from other nearby colonies—New Jersey, Delaware, and Maryland—were sent to Philadelphia for their schooling.

---

14. Reprinted in Sol Cohen, ed., *Education in the United States: A Documentary History* (New York: Random House, 1974), p. 359.

Although the Friends were not especially interested in secondary education as a way of educating a ministry, they were not antagonistic toward secondary education. Like other "nonconforming" groups, they were opposed to traditional forms of schooling that gave students a polish but not an education. As early as 1689, the Quakers appointed George Keith as a master of a newly founded grammar school. It was open to all children regardless of their family's religious persuasions, and scholarships were available for the children of the poor.

Schools of Other Sects

Outside Philadelphia, schools were founded by other religious sects. The Reverend William Tennent, a Scots-Irish Presbyterian, opened a school at Nashiminy in 1726 to train clergy. Tennent's school was one of several opened by the Presbyterians during the years of the Great Awakening. The graduates of what came to be known as Tennent's "log college" were responsible for opening several academies where the quality of instruction was exceptional. They included an academy at Nottingham on the Maryland-Pennsylvania border, Samuel Blair's academy at Faggs Manor, and Robert Smith's at Pequea. After Tennent's departure from the "log college" in 1742, several of his students organized the Presbyterian College of New Jersey, which was to become Princeton University. The Great Awakening prompted a movement for educational reform and expansion in some subjects. Many of the revivalists once again emphasized the basic Protestant notion that because all people were capable of conversion to God's way, all needed to know how to read. Their attacks on the abundance of abstractions in religion served to support those who wanted schooling that would be useful.[15]

Francis Pastorius, who had led German Pietists to settle Germantown, taught his people classics after a two-year service in the Penn Charter School. Finally, in 1770 Christopher Dock of the Mennonites published his *Schulordnung,* the first pedagogical work to be published in North America. Dock became known for his use of humane methods in the classroom. He set aside the birch rod in favor of exhortations and admonishments. Even today, Dock's writings are useful to teachers. They show how a classroom can be organized to promote learning even when children arrive at different times of the day and when there is no great supply of ready-made materials.

As in Massachusetts, religious beliefs were an essential part of the lives of the first settlers in Pennsylvania. There was a greater variety of beliefs, however, and they were expressed in many different ways. In Pennsylvania toleration of wide diversity among people and their beliefs was generally the rule. In an address sent to the governor of Barbados in 1671, George Fox reminded the Friends that it was the duty of the master of every household to look after all who were members of that household and all who belonged to it, including "Negroes, Tawnies and Indians."

---

15. Douglas Sloan, ed., *The Great Awakening and American Education* (New York: Teachers College Press, 1973), pp. 36–41.

The spirit of those directions found its way to Pennsylvania. Action was taken to build schools for black and mulatto children. Serious attempts were made to treat the Indians fairly. And there was the Quaker reformer John Woolman, who from the 1740's till his death in 1772, journeyed from settlement to settlement, preaching that the exploitation of black people was wrong. Woolman reminded his fellow Friends that the whole system of slavery was built on an "Unrighteous Foundation."

PART I

The Emergence of the Americans

By the time the Declaration of Independence was signed in 1776, there were two and a half million people in the colonies and there were five major colonial cities: Charleston, Philadelphia, New York, Providence, and Boston. City dwellers had to confront problems of fire, fuel for the winter months, sanitation, clean water, overcrowded and inadequate streets, and crime. They found ways to meet these problems and to tend to other needs as well. Streets were paved, sidewalks were laid in some places, and some streets were even lit (usually with whale oil). Printers and booksellers had customers. Those who could not afford to attend the grammar schools or the academies could frequently find a private night school where they might learn skills appropriate for the developing commercial cities.

In the seventeenth century, colonies were fairly isolated from one another. Communication and trade were commonly easier to effect with England than with the other colonies. However, as the colonies, the cities, and their commercial activity grew, so did communication among them. As trade and communication increased, the similarities among the colonies became more important than the differences.

Some sense of the growing unity among the colonists can be seen in John Dickinson's *Letters from a Farmer in Pennsylvania,* written in 1767 and 1768. The language Dickinson used and the audience his letters found are as significant as the arguments they present about the rights of Parliament in relation to the colonies. The letters were printed in three different newspapers, and within two years at least ten editions were distributed in pamphlet form. When Dickinson began his letters with the salutation, "My Beloved Countrymen," he was addressing not only Pennsylvanians, but all the colonists. Writing in Philadelphia, he wrote of his hope "for the happiness of British America." In the third letter he wrote of Great Britain *and* of America. His language showed that a distinction between America and England had already been made in the minds of many.

The case of John Dickinson perhaps symbolizes the main development in the last part of the eighteenth century in America. Dickinson was not arguing for a new society or a new form of government. He was arguing that England's right to interfere with how Americans were living was severely limited. From that perspective the Revolution can be viewed not so much as an attempt to create a new society and a new government as an attempt to protect a way of life that had developed during the previous century and a half. There was no widespread attempt to enlist the schools in creating a new social order—it had already been developed. After the Revolution, however, a number of citizens saw that a new way of life had been won and tried to fashion systems of schooling to ensure its success.

Although by the Northwest Ordinance of 1785, the new nation provided grants of land for the support of education, it made no other significant attempts to exercise control or give direction to the process of educating the citizenry. The Constitution did not mention education, leaving the matter entirely to the states. Many leaders of the Revolutionary generation and the early Republic presented plans for an education that would relate the process of schooling to the political ideals of the new nation. As will be seen in Part II, these plans were rejected. Some attempts, however, were made to make existing schools and existing educational practices distinctively American.

PART II

The Early Republic

The last half of the eighteenth century, the Age of the Enlightenment, was an era that saw two major revolutions, the American and the French. It was an age during which people were breaking away from traditional ways and beliefs and were trying to build new social, intellectual, and political orders. In his distinguished work, *The Enlightenment,* Peter Gay emphasized that "there were many philosophies in the eighteenth century, but there was only one Enlightenment." In two sentences, Gay presented what is perhaps the best and most concise description of the Englightenment:

> A loose, informal, wholly unorganized coalition of cultural critics, religious skeptics, and political reformers from Edinburgh to Naples, Paris to Berlin, Boston to Philadelphia, the philosophes made up a clamorous chorus, and there were some discordant voices among them, but what is striking is their general harmony, not their occasional discord. The men of the Enlightenment united on a vastly ambitious program of secularism, humanity, cosmopolitanism, and freedom, above all, freedom in its many forms—freedom from arbitrary power, freedom of speech, freedom of trade, freedom to realize one's talents, freedom of aesthetic response, freedom in a word, of moral man to make his own way in the world.[1]

The subtitle of Gay's work, "The Rise of Modern Paganism," not only reminds us of the philosophes' rejection of Christianity but also brings to mind what may be an incorrect impression of what the Enlightenment was in America. Certainly there was more to it than a handful of articulate French writers, with a few allies from England and its American colonies, doing triumphant battle against political corruption and religious superstition.

---

1. Peter Gay, *The Enlightenment: The Rise of Modern Paganism* (New York: Alfred A. Knopf, 1966), p. 1.

A student of the Enlightenment in America, Henry F. May, has shown that while there may have been a rise of "modern paganism," Christianity certainly endured in America, though it was modified and perhaps weakened by its conflicts and compromises with Enlightenment doctrines. For years many Americans were not to worry about the separation of church and state. May has also shown that American society and American institutions were not the immediate consequence of the Americans' declaring themselves free from England.[2] Rather, these were the results of a variety of people with a variety of beliefs working together to achieve stability. Once Americans had achieved their formal independence, they tried to maintain order by working out compromises: striking delicate balances between science and religion, passion and reason, democracy and aristocracy, freedom and order. After the Revolution, Americans showed a remarkable ability to articulate what they had done and what they were doing, and to lay plans for maintaining what they hoped to accomplish in the future. They saw the dangers to their new social and political order and tried to devise ways to overcome them.

Perhaps the Americans who participated in the Enlightenment had an advantage over their European counterparts. What Americans abolished was housed, at least symbolically, not in their midst but in England. The American Revolution was more a severance than a revolution. Once the break was made, American social and political theorists could tend to finding ways to preserve what they had developed. The literature they produced shows that many were aware and even somewhat fearful of the problems created by the successful War of Independence. Two major problems that concerned many were how to maintain order and how to maintain unity among the people. For many, order and unity were even more important than freedom and equality. Some decided that schools should be deliberately designed as the instrument for preservation of the Republic.

In this second part of the text, we shall examine some of the plans that were offered for educating the new citizen. As background, we shall survey the characteristics of seventeenth- and eighteenth-century schoolteachers and schoolbooks, and how some of the materials assumed an American form after the Revolution. We shall also review some of the educational proposals made at the end of the eighteenth century. Although they are proposals that Americans did not accept, they are nonetheless important. They show that many American political theorists paid attention to the process of schooling, that many believed there to be a strong relationship between the kinds of schools a nation had and the strength of that nation. That these plans were not accepted tells us that from their very beginnings, Americans have been reluctant to accept the advice of educational theoreticians and reluctant to surrender the control of their children's education to a distant government.

---

2. Henry F. May, *The Enlightenment in America* (New York: Oxford University Press, 1976).

Schoolkeeping and Schoolbooks in the Colonies 4

The Colonial Schoolmaster

Many of the teachers in the grammar schools of the colonial period were well prepared for their tasks. Some were not. Nearly all were men, for women did not yet have access to those schools that would have prepared them to teach Latin and a little Greek, as these secondary schools required. Some spent but a few years teaching. Often they were graduates who had prepared for the ministry and were awaiting a call to a church. Some taught because they had nothing else to do. Others made teaching a life's work and often spent many years in the same community.

Perhaps the most widely acclaimed of the colonial schoolmasters was Ezekiel Cheever, who set the pattern by which Latin would be taught for over a century. Cheever, a native of London educated at Emmanuel College, arrived in Boston in 1637, when he was twenty-three. He soon left Boston to help John Davenport and Theophilus Eaton establish the new colony at New Haven. There he found a wife, became the town's schoolmaster, and assisted in other community affairs. On occasion he substituted for the minister in the pulpit. Cheever remained in New Haven for twelve years and might have stayed even longer had he not encountered difficulties with the church. His next post was at Ipswich where he taught for eleven years, earning a reputation that made him and the school there well known throughout New England. Students came from the neighboring towns to be schooled in their Latin by Cheever. He then taught in Charleston, Massachusetts for nine years and in 1670, at age fifty-six, was asked to teach in Boston. In 1687 Cheever wrote to Sir Edmund Andros, the royal governor, to ask that he be allowed to retain his post and pay. He told the Governor that God had been merciful to him and that he still had his "abilities in mind," "health of body," "vivacity of spirit," and still found "delight" in his work. It was, he explained, the only work for which he was "fit" and "capable."[1] The governor granted his petition, and Cheever taught in Boston until he died at age ninety-four.

Those who did decide to make a life's work of teaching had the chance of finding a secure position, although there were no tenure laws. Many, like Cheever, taught until their deaths, for there were no retirement plans. Richard Norcross, for example, accepted a position in Watertown, Mass., in 1651 and in 1700, at age seventy-nine, was still teaching there. (He did, however, occasionally take a year off). John Lovell served as the master of the Boston Latin School for forty-two years. After teaching in other places, John Tileston began his career at the North Writing School in 1762 and remained until 1818 when, at eighty-five, "feeling the infirmities of age increasing with the decay of strength natural to so long and laborious a life, he found it necessary to resign and retire from active service."[2] His retirement ended a 70-year career as a schoolmaster.

Recruitment of Teachers

The town's selectmen were usually charged with finding a schoolmaster, but frequently, there were just not enough good teachers to be found. Harvard produced some teachers, but it was a limited and transient supply. Most Harvard graduates preferred other forms of public service, medicine, or the ministry. Many of those who eventually became clergymen spent some time as teachers. However, only about three percent of Harvard's graduates actually made a career of teaching.

Many towns nevertheless exercised considerable care in the selection of their teachers. Candidates for posts who were not ordained ministers could expect to be examined carefully. Usually the selectmen and the clergy of the town would look into the nature and quality of the candidate's religious beliefs. If the candidate could pass that screening, he would be appointed to the post if the townspeople voted favorably at the town meeting.

Towns sometimes had to enlist the local physician, the town clerk, the church deacon, or any available person who could read to serve as a schoolmaster. According to Walter Herbert Small, the first teacher in Braintree (Mass.) was a Mr. Thompson, who is also believed to have been the town's first doctor. When "urgent cases" arose, "he was obliged to close his school to attend to his professional duties." In Medfield, Mass., the town's first doctor, Return Johnson, was appointed schoolmaster for a month's trial period in 1684. At the end of the month, it was decided that he could tend to both duties, and he was given a year's appointment. He was allowed to close the school for two weeks in the spring to look after his practice, provided he made up the time at the end of the school term. He was also required to make up other time lost to medical emergencies. At the end of the year

---

1. Reproduced in Edgar W. Knight and Clifton L. Hall, eds., *Readings in American Educational History* (New York: Appleton-Century-Crofts, 1951), p. 20.
2. Walter Herbert Small, *Early New England Schools* (Boston: Ginn and Co., 1914), p. 102.

Johnson and the town agreed that he could not handle both jobs. He gave up teaching.[3]

Community Service

A schoolmaster in colonial America might be expected also to carry messages for the court, be a summons server, conduct the church choir, ring the bell to announce the start of public worship, dig graves, and serve as a substitute minister. For example, when John Hoffman agreed with the Congregation of the Reformed Church at Lancaster (Pennsylvania) to serve as a schoolmaster in 1747, he also "promised in the presence of the congregation to serve as chorister, and as long as we have no paster, to read sermons on Sunday."[4] Johannes van Eckkelen's contract, written in 1682, with the townspeople of Flatbush (New York) contained one section outlining his "school service" and one section outlining his "church service." The portion of the contract devoted to "church service" also specified what payment Van Eckkelen could expect to receive for some of his services. Part of the contract read as follows:

> He shall give the funeral invitations, dig the grave, and toll the bell, for which service he shall receive for a person of fifteen years and upwards, twelve guilders, and for one under that age, eight guilders. If he should be required to give invitations beyond the limits of the town, and if he should be required to cross the river, and go to New York, he shall receive four guilders.[5]

Some teachers were part-time surveyors; some drew up legal papers; and others served as recording secretaries for the selectmen.

Teacher Requirements

In 1706 the Society for the Propagation of the Gospel in Foreign Parts (S.P.G.) advised its missionaries that upon their arrival in the New World they were not to "board in, or frequent Publick-houses, or lodge in Families of evil Fame." They were to "abstain from Gaming" and "converse not familiarly with lewd or prophane Persons, otherwise than to order to reprove, admonish, and reclaim them." Their public behavior was to be "circumspect and unblameable" and they were to "take special Care to give no offence to the Civil Government, by intermeddling in Affairs not relating to their own Calling and Function."[6] In 1711 the Society also set forth requirements for its schoolmasters. No person was to be accepted as a teacher until complete information about age, marital status, temper, education, political preferences, and religion were ascertained.[7] Before and after the Revolution, many Americans consistently tried to adhere to the standards embodied in the

---

3. Ibid., p. 98.
4. Reproduced in Knight and Hall, *Readings in American Educational History*, p. 30.
5. Ibid., p. 19.
6. Ibid., pp. 22–23.
7. Ibid., p. 28.

Society's regulations, showing their concern with prospective teachers' religious orthodoxy and political loyalties.

The Statutes of South Carolina show that to teach in the school at Charleston, one had to "be of the religion of the Church of England, and conform to the same," as well as be able to teach Latin and Greek and instruct children in the "principles of the Christian religion, as professed in the Church of England."[8] In 1747, however, a Presbyterian teacher, Mackenzie, was hired after he "promised in every thing to conform exactly to the Rites of the Establish'd Church."[9] A contract between the congregation at New Providence (Pennsylvania) and a schoolmaster shows that "special regard" was to be paid "to the purity of his doctrine and his life." The master was to ensure that the children did not use "profane language either in or out of school" and see that the children behaved "not like the Indians."[10] In 1760, Thomas Boone, the governor of New Jersey, issued a proclamation that reminded the populace that only "Persons of good Character" were to be employed as teachers and instructed the magistrates "to inform themselves sufficiently of the Character of the School-Masters."[11]

During the Revolution, some of the former colonies required loyalty oaths of teachers. An act passed in 1777 in New Jersey shows not only the political rhetoric of the era but also the belief that children could be ruined for life in their early years at school. It began:

> AND WHEREAS it is of the last Moment to a free and independent State, that the rising Generation should be early instructed in the Principles of publick Virtue, and duly impressed with the amiable Ideas of Liberty and Patriotism, and at the same Time inspired with the keenest Abhorrence of despotick and arbitrary Power: AND WHEREAS publick Teachers and Instructors may be greatly instrumental in tincturing the youthful Mind with such Impressions, either in Favour of a just and equal Administration, or of a slavish Submission to lawless Rule, as in their riper Years are not easily obliterated, and are, for that Reason, important Objects of legislative Attention. . . .[12]

Because the youthful mind could be so easily influenced, non-Quaker teachers had to swear to an oath of loyalty (Friends were allowed simply to affirm their loyalty). In 1776 Massachusetts disallowed payment to any teacher who had not signed a declaration of allegiance. Requirements that teachers swear to their political loyalty did not end with the War of Independence. Thomas Jefferson urged after the Revolution that teachers be required to "give assurance of fidelity to the commonwealth." (During the Civil War and during the two world wars, teachers would also be asked to take loyalty oaths.)

As the colonies and their schools grew in size and number, good teachers grew scarcer. Many proposals for schools included plans for training teachers—

---

8. Ibid., p. 29.
9. Ibid.
10. Ibid., p. 30.
11. Ibid., p. 36.
12. Ibid., p. 37.

not specific programs to prepare teachers for their duties, but recommendations that students who could not continue their schooling could become teachers. Teaching was something less than a first-rate activity. When the Common Council of Philadelphia voted to make a donation to Benjamin Franklin's Academy, it did so on the grounds that the Academy would produce teachers who might be better than those who were currently available. The Minutes that show the members' concerns and prejudices read as follows:

> That a number of the poorer Sort will be hereby qualified to act as Schoolmasters in the Country, to teach Children Reading, Writing, Arithmetic, and the Grammar of their Mother Tongue, and being of good morals and known character, may be recommended from the Academy to the Country Schools for that purpose; The Country suffering at present very much for want of good Schoolmasters, and obliged to employ in their Schools, vicious imported Servants, or concealed Papists, who by their bad Examples and Instructions often deprave the Morals or corrupt the Principles of the Children under their Care.[13]

Whether "poorer" was meant to describe the size of the student's purse or the student's scholarly prowess is not completely clear. It is not unreasonable to assume that it was meant to refer to the student's scholarship. Poorer students frequently were seen as fit teachers. When Jefferson recommended that ten of the twenty "public foundationers" who completed his proposed grammar school be sent on to the College of William and Mary, he also suggested that the ten who were not selected for advanced study could become grammar school teachers. A plan that Samuel Knox offered to the American Philosophical Society in 1797 suggested that some provisions be made for those whose parents were too poor to pay for their schooling and that such students could, upon completion of their studies, become teachers.

Not all teachers were the most reputable of citizens, and some found themselves cast in the role of runaways. A contract was a contract and an indenture was an indenture; some holders of the "paper" advertised in attempts to regain the services due them. For example, in 1751 Samuel Jaques and James Marshall advertised in the *Pennsylvania Gazette* for the return of Edward Kite who was "a cooper by trade, but has lately taught school." A reward of £4 was offered. In 1756 Richard Arrell offered twenty shillings reward for "a schoolmaster, named Samuel Willis, of little stature, thin face, and pale complexion" who had left Depford township in West-Jersey without permission.[14]

Although many towns found themselves in want of good teachers, the esteem in which the teacher was held was not great and the pay was even less. Noah Webster, for example, complained that parents sent their children to teachers with whom the "parents themselves will not associate." According to Denison Olmsted,

---

13. Ibid., p. 31.
14. Reproduced in Ellwood P. Cubberley, ed., *Readings in Public Education in the United States* (Boston: Houghton Mifflin, 1934), pp. 70–71.

the situation was not greatly improved in the first years of the nineteenth century. In a speech delivered at Yale in 1816 he charged that "the great defect" in education was "the ignorance and incompetency of schoolmasters." He claimed that the teachers' "geography scarcely transcends the mountains that bound their horizon" and that their "science is the multiplication table." All the teachers knew of history, language, and literature, claimed Olmsted, could be found "in the American Preceptor and Webster's spellinq book."[15] In 1824 James G. Carter, an educational reformer from Massachusetts, warned that no good use of appropriations for education could be made until something was done about the preparation of teachers. They needed to know what they were to teach and how to communicate it to the students. As Carter expressed it, *"Instructors and pupils do not understand each other. They do not speak the same language."*[16]

Hornbooks and Primers

The hornbook was the book from which colonial children at home or in the dame school learned their alphabet, numerals, and possibly the Lord's Prayer. It was typically made of a paddle-shaped slab of wood on which was pasted a paper showing the alphabet, the nine numerals, and if space allowed, the Lord's Prayer or some religious admonitions. The name refers to a transparent sheet of horn that served to protect the paper from the wet and dirty fingers of children, but hornbooks had no horn at all. These were usually made of wood or metal, with the letters and numerals carved or pressed on them. Much like the hornbook was the "battledore." It too depicted the alphabet, numerals, and sometimes the Lord's Prayer. It was usually made of stiff paper or cardboard that had been varnished. In time the battledore became simply a piece of stiff paper or cardboard that could be folded and fastened.

The English Primer
The first primers were not books especially designed for children, but prayer books or devotional manuals designed for use by the laity who knew no Latin and whose literacy was limited. Primers made their appearance in England before the Reformation. After the Reformation, the various sects produced their own unauthorized primers. After Henry VIII severed his relationship with the pope, he too issued a primer. It was described as "A prymer in Englyshe with certeyne prayers and goodly meditations, very necessary for all people that understonde not the Latyne tongue." In 1534, Henry issued a revised primer called the "Goodly in Englysshe." It was "newly corrected and printed, with certeyne godly Meditations and Prayers

15. Quoted in Small, *Early New England Schools*, p. 93.

16. James G. Carter, *Essays upon Popular Education Containing a Particular Examination of the Schools of Massachusetts, and an Outline of an Institution for the Education of Teachers* (Boston: Bowles and Dearborn, 1826), p. 45.

... very necessarie and profitable for all them that ryghte assuredly understande not ye Latine and Greke tongues."[17] In 1545 Henry issued still another primer.

To each of his primers Henry attached a preliminary book much like those that the Roman Catholic Church had been attaching to its primers since the fifteenth century. Henry called this attachment "The A B C." Besides the alphabet, it included the Lord's Prayer, the Hail Mary, the Creed, the Ten Commandments, and "various Graces for before and after 'dyner' and for 'fysshe dayes'."

As the Reformation continued and as various sects produced their own successful primers, Henry grew concerned that they were fostering "contentions and vain disputations" rather than edifying the people. He attempted to establish order in the realm by insisting that only authorized primers be used to teach children and serve as prayer books for those who knew no Latin. But sects and religious differences continued to multiply.

Although Henry's primers were intended for children, they never became schoolbooks in the contemporary sense of the word. The primer itself was in fact the forerunner of *The Book of Common Prayer.* Henry's primers appeared as deluxe editions, expensive and handsomely bound. The price and the limited subject matter of the primer made it impractical as a schoolbook. Furthermore, as the primer and the ABC were works authorized by the crown, only authorized printers were allowed to print and to sell them. With this effective monopoly on the books, licensed printers had no reason to produce inexpensive editions.

Early efforts to produce combination schoolbooks and catechisms occurred outside England. In 1591 in Edinburgh, a catechism with an A B C attached appeared under the sponsorship of Jeremias Bastingius. A similar book, Bishop Bedell's *Catechism,* appeared in Dublin in 1631. In 1646 the Church of Scotland issued a primer with an A B C. But in England, attempts at such publications were few, for the authorities strongly discouraged them. In 1666, for example, Benjamin Keach published *The Child's Instructor, or a New and Easy Primer,* but the crown did not approve of his leanings toward anabaptism and sentenced him to the pillory.

The New-England Primer

The *New-England Primer* was produced in Boston in 1690 by Benjamin Harris, who earlier had run afoul of the authorities in England for printing his "Protestant Petition" (1681). The *Primer* appears to have been a reissue or a revision of the *Protestant Tutor,* which Harris is believed to have printed in England before coming to Massachusetts. Both the *Tutor* and the *Primer* contained the alphabet, a syllabary, the Lord's Prayer, the Ten Commandments, the names of the books of the Bible, and numerals. The *Primer* was remarkably successful, and other materials were added from time to time by the various printers who produced it during the next century and a half of its use.

---

17. Paul Leicester Ford, ed., *The New-England Primer* (New York: Teachers College Press, 1962), p. 5.

The frontispiece of the *Primer* depicted the burning of the Reverend John Rogers at the stake in the presence of his wife and nine children. There was also an account of the execution that very closely paralleled the story in Foxe's *Book of Martyrs*. By modern standards such a picture and account may seem gruesome and inappropriate for children. However, such a reminder of the persecutions suffered by early Protestants was certainly consistent with the interests, concerns, and practices of the New England community. Moreover, for many New England Puritans, executions of wrongdoers were public and religious events. They lasted for hours and were attended by nearly the entire community; people would travel from outlying areas to attend and to take the opportunity to hear a good sermon. Sometimes, even the condemned participated by offering a sermon.

Perhaps the most memorable part of the *New-England Primer* was its illustrated rhyming alphabet. The 1727 edition has a picture and a rhyme for each of the twenty-four letters (*I* and *J* were considered interchangeable, as were *V* and *U*). The rhymes themselves reveal the changing beliefs and preferences of the citizens of the New World. Early editions were not so greatly influenced by scriptural considerations as some later editions were. In an early edition, children were taught the letter *E* with the rhyme: "An Eagle's Flight / Is out of Sight." A later edition replaced the Eagle with "Elijah hid / By Raven's fed." Rhymes that were not scriptural still were meant to be instructive. One edition warns readers: "The idle Fool / Is whipt at School." The rhymes for *K* and for *Q* reflected changes on the English throne. "King Charles the Good / No man of Blood" had to be changed when William and Mary took the throne. When Queen Anne followed William and Mary, another change was necessary: "K. William's Dead and left the throne / To Ann our Queen of great Renown." In time a rhyme suitable for any male occupant of the throne was fashioned: "Our King the good / No man of Blood." As the colonists began to question the rights of the throne, however, the rhymes instructed that "Kings should be good / Not men of Blood." After the Revolution the young were taught that "The British King / Lost States thirteen" or that "Queens and Kings / Are Gaudy things."

The *Primer's* syllabary consisted of letters, syllables, and words. Somehow children were to begin to become proficient in language through learning "ab, eb, ib, ob . . . ha, he, hi, ho . . . ti, to, tu." After mastering more than a hundred such syllables, the neophyte readers were to proceed to lists of words of one syllable, then to two-syllable words, and on through the list of six-syllable words. (A printer pressed for space might omit the larger words, thereby reducing the requirements for the pupil.) After completing the syllabary and the rhyming alphabet, the student was introduced to "An Alphabet of Lessons for Youth." It consisted of a lesson drawn from Scripture appropriate for each letter of the alphabet. For example, for the letter *Z* students learned: "Zeal hath consumed me, because thy enemies have forgotten the words of God.

During the eighteenth century when many were fearful of the loss of religious orthodoxy, the *Primer* included one of two catechisms: John Cotton's "Spiritual Milk for Boston Babes in either England, drawn from the Breasts of Both Testaments for their Souls' Nourishment" or the catechism of the Westminster Assembly. Those who read the Westminster catechism learned that "Baptism is not to be administered to any that are out of the visible Church, till they profess their Faith in Christ, and Obedience to Him, but the Infants of such as are Members of the visible Church are to be Baptised." Among the other 106 answers to be learned was "Adoption is an Act of God's Free Grace, whereby we are received into the Number, and have Right to all the Priviledges of the Sons of God." Those who were taught from editions with Cotton's catechism may have had an easier time of it, for it had forty-three fewer questions, and the answers were shorter than those in the Westminster catechism. Whatever edition the students used, their task was to memorize the answers. At specified times of the year they were expected to recite them before the congregation at the meeting-house.

The *New-England Primer* underwent innumerable editions and variations. It is estimated that during 150 years, six to eight million copies were sold. At times printers attempted to give it a new title. It appeared as *A Primer for the Colony of Connecticut* and as *The New York Primer*. After the Revolution it became *The American Primer* and *The Columbian Primer*. There was even an edition with a brief federal catechism that asked who had betrayed the country and who had saved the country. (The answers: George Washington and Benedict Arnold).

Early Arithmetic Books

Placing "'rithmetic" last in the "three R's" reflects the lesser amount of attention given to arithmetic in the schools of the seventeenth and eighteenth centuries. In the seventeenth century, students frequently made their own arithmetic books by recording the teacher's remarks in their copybooks. In the eighteenth century, Thomas Dilworth, author of a well-known and widely used spelling book, provided an arithmetic that was highly regarded in the colonies. Originally published in England in 1743, Dilworth's *Assistant* was used in Boston during the Revolution; there is evidence that it was in use as late as 1796. Described as "a compendium of Arithmetic, both Practical and Theoretical," Dilworth's text treated five major topics: (1) "Arithmetic in whole Numbers," (2) "Vulgar Fractions," (3) "Decimals," (4) "A large Collection of Questions with their Answers, serving to exercise the foregoing Rules, together with a few others, both pleasant and diverting," and (5) "Duodecimals, commonly called Cross Multiplication."[18]

Colyer Meriwether reported that among the "pleasant and diverting questions" in Dilworth's text was a version of the logic problem about the farmer who needs to cross the river with his corn, a fox, and a goose. It was presented in this way:

> A farmer with a fox, a goose and a peck of corn has to cross a river in a boat so small that he can take only one of these three burdens with him at a time. How can he so handle matters that nothing will be destroyed, because

---

18. George Emery Littlefield, *Early Schools and School-Books of New England* (New York: Russell and Russell, 1965), pp. 173–175.

he cannot leave the fox and the goose together nor can he leave the goose and the corn.[19]

Dilworth also attached to his book "An Essay on the Education of Youth," in which he urged parents to send their daughters as well as their sons to school. Observing that girls could not write, spell, or cipher, he urged that they be sent to school "as early as boys."

In 1729, the first arithmetic text published in the colonies was brought out by Isaac Greenwood, Hollisian Professor of Mathematics and Natural and Experimental Philosophy at Harvard. Like many others of the period, it was filled with rules and examples and lacked material that would encourage mathematical reasoning. By providing blank space for the student to practice after each set of examples however, Greenwood may have offered one of the earliest workbooks.

The first arithmetic to appear after the Revolution was Nicholas Pike's *New and Complete System of Arithmetic* (1788), which claimed to be "Composed for the Use of the Citizens of the United States." Among the endorsements Pike received for his text was that of George Washington, who wrote Pike that the work would bring honor to the United States. Washington even suggested that mathematics might be more important than Pike himself thought and expressed the belief that training in mathematics would lead to clear thinking.

> The science of figures, to a certain degree, is not only indispensably requisite in every walk of civilised life, but the investigation of mathematical truths accustoms the mind to method and correctness in reasoning, and is an employment peculiarly worthy of rational beings.[20]

Washington's endorsement may have helped the sales of Pike's arithmetic, which was soon adopted in the Boston schools and was used for more than fifty years. In subsequent generations many teachers would echo Washington by telling their pupils that mathematics was not only practical but also useful in organizing one's rational abilities.

At least one of Pike's problems demonstrated that knowledge of arithmetic could be useful in the marketplace.

> An ignorant fop wanting to purchase an elegant house, a facetious gentleman told him he had one which he would sell him on these moderate terms, viz. that he should give him a penny for the first door, 2 *d.* for the second, 4*d.* for the third, and so on, doubling at every door, which were 36 in all: It is a bargain, cried the simpleton, and here is a guinea to bind it; Pray, what would the house have cost him?[21]

The doubling pennies totaled £286, 331, 153, 1*s*. 3*d*.

In 1796, ten years after Congress decided that the "federal money" should be divided according to the decimal plan, Erastus Root published *An Introduction*

---

19. Colyer Meriwether, *Our Colonial Curriculum, 1607–1776* (Washington, D.C.: Capital Publishing Co., 1907), p. 166.

20. Reproduced in Littlefield, *Early Schools and School-Books*, p. 181.

21. Reproduced in Clifton Johnson, *Old-Time Schools and School-Books* (New York: Dover Publications, Inc., 1963), p. 305.

to Arithmetic. It paid special attention to the new monetary system and to its political significance. Root's comments about the decimal system demonstrate that not even arithmetic is free of political considerations:

> Let us, I beg of you, Fellow-Citizens, no longer meanly follow the British intricate mode of reckoning.—Let them have their own way—and us, ours.— Their mode is suited to the genius of the government—for it seems to be the policy of tyrants, to keep their accounts in as intricate, and perplexing a method as possible; that the smaller number of subjects may be able to estimate their enormous impositions and exactions. But Republican money ought to be simple and adapted to the meanest capacity.[22]

Nonetheless, fifteen years after Root offered his text and plea, there were still texts that presented problems in terms of pounds, shillings, and pence. Some offered students practice in measures that had gone out of date in the 1500s.

Geography

In the colonial and even the early post-colonial schools, geography was not commonly taught as a specific school subject. Under the heading of "reading" students learned geography, history, manners, civics, and perhaps even some natural history and astronomy. Several geographies and some histories were available in the eighteenth century for reading in the schools. The English theologian and hymn writer, Isaac Watts, published a handbook of astronomy and geography in 1725: *The Knowledge of the Heavens and the Earth made easy; or the First Principles of Astronomy and Geography explained by the Use of Globes and Maps.* In 1754 Daniel Fenning introduced *A New and Easy Guide to the Use of the Globe; and the Rudiments of Geography.* By 1770 there was a third edition of Fenning's work that included six maps, two of which were of North America. In 1740 John Holmes offered *The History of England* "adapted to the Capacities and Memories of Youth at School."

After 1800 the reading of geography grew more popular, largely because of Jedidiah Morse, a Yale graduate whose text earned him the title of "the first American geographer." His *Geography Made Easy,* printed in 1784, and its many revisions and abridgments were used in the schools for nearly half a century. Those who read his text learned about more than mountains and rivers. They learned that the quadruped animals made their way to America by land passages that must have connected the Old World and the New before they were "sunk by violent earthquakes." They learned that squirrels frequently travelled in great numbers and had a unique way to cross rivers. According to Morse, the squirrels set a suitable piece of wood upon the water, placed themselves upon it, and raised their tails to form sails.

Morse's descriptions of places and of people would not have won him a job as a writer of travel brochures. He wrote that his fellow citizens in Connecticut, while "generally industrious" and "hospitable to strangers," were also "intemper-

---

22. Ibid., p. 306.

ately fond of lawsuits and little petty arbitrations." "The ladies," he wrote, were "modest, handsome, and agreeable," though "fond of imitating new and extravagant fashions."[23] New York City, he reported, suffered "a want of good water" which was "a great inconvenience to the citizens."[24] Along the coast in Carolina, the summer and autumn brought the people "intermittent fevers, which often prove fatal." They developed "a pale yellow cast" and experienced "bilious symtoms." The people of Maryland, Virginia, and North Carolina were reported to be "excessively fond of the diversion of horse racing." In those states, Morse lamented, "every poor peasant has an horse or two and all the family in ruins."[25]

Morse's descriptions of the climate of New York, New Jersey, Pennsylvania, Delaware, and the territory northwest of the Ohio River included several graphic comparisons with places he had never visited:

> The changes of weather are great, and frequently sudden. On the whole, it appears that the climate is a compound of most of the climates of the world. It has the moisture of Ireland in spring; the heat of Africa in summer; the temperature of Italy in July; the sky of Egypt in autumn; the snow and cold of Norway in winter; the tempests (in a certain degree) of the West Indies, in every season; and the variable winds and weather of Great Britain in every month in the year.[26]

Morse also offered descriptions of the people and their ways in places even more remote than Europe. He wrote that Laplanders court their prospective spouses by providing the father with brandy, and reported with authority that the Chinese had a language that contained only 330 words, all of one syllable. Abridged editions of Morse's geographies were not always as detailed and colorful as the original edition. They did, however, continue to characterize peoples of non-European countries as less than civilized.

Noah Webster's Speller

Noah Webster first presented his speller in 1783 under the awkward title, *A Grammatical Institute of the English Language*. Later it was called the *American Spelling Book* and the *Elementary Spelling Book*. The covers of early editions were made of thin pieces of oak covered in light blue paper, while later editions were covered in bright blue paper, giving Webster's book its nickname of "the old blue-back." It was successful from the very beginning and eventually sold over twenty-four million copies, providing Webster with sufficient income to support himself, his family, and his other literary endeavors. After its introduction, spelling became a popular, recognizable, and important school subject. The spelling bee, not unknown in eighteenth-century America, grew in popularity in the nineteenth century.

Webster believed that Americans could use language to build national unity

23. Ibid., p. 328.
24. Ibid., p. 329.
25. Ibid., pp. 330–331.
26. Ibid., pp. 328–329.

and a national culture. In 1789, just six years after the appearance of his speller, Webster argued that "as an independent nation, our honor requires us to have a system of our own, in language as well as in government."[27] England could not serve as our model in language because the "taste" of the English writers was "already corrupted" and, even if the language were not in a state of decline in England, England was simply too far away from America to serve as a useful model. Webster, however, was content to use English as the "common root or stock" from which the national language would be developed. He predicted that America would grow and become powerful and that traces of all other languages would eventually disappear. All Americans would use and pronounce the language in the same way. "Provincial accents" had to be eliminated, for they were the seeds of potential discord.

Webster insisted that "nothing but the establishment of schools and some uniformity in the use of books, can annihilate differences in speaking and preserve the purity of the American tongue." He had already provided the Americans with a speller and was to work on a dictionary. He proposed to establish some order and consistency in spelling practices in a period when it was not uncommon for even the educated to spell the same word several different ways in the same work or even on the same page. Pronunciations were to be determined by the spelling of the words, not dictated by a special or select social group. Webster wanted to democratize language by freeing it from class distinctions.

Webster's "old blue-back" was remarkably similar to the *New-England Primer* in its format and even its content. It did not contain a rhyming and illustrated alphabet, but it did have a syllabary. The 1831 edition began with a section on the "analysis of sounds" in which the reader immediately learned that "language, in its more limited sense, is the expression of ideas by articulate sounds." It went on to discuss vowels, consonants, diphthongs, accents, cadence, and a pronunciation key. Then followed the alphabet and lists of syllables and words. Webster did not provide accounts of early Protestant martyrs or selections from Cotton's *Spiritual Milk,* but former readers of the *Primer* could easily find selections to which they could give their approval.

> He that speaks loud in school will not learn his own book well, nor let the rest learn theirs; but those that make no noise will soon be wise, and gain much love and good will.
> Shun the boy that tells lies, or speaks bad words; for he would soon bring thee to shame.[28]

Webster also included scriptural passages that all Christian sects were to find agreeable. At the end of the 1831 edition there was "A Moral Catechism" that gave instruction on humility, mercy, purity of heart, anger, revenge, justice, generosity, charity, avarice, cheerfulness, and other vices and virtues.

---

27. Noah Webster, *Dissertations on the English Language: With Notes, Historial and Critical* (Boston: Isaiah Thomas and Co., 1839), p. 20.

28. Henry Steele Commager, ed., *Noah Webster's American Spelling Book* (New York: Teachers College Press, 1962), pp. 61–63. Unless otherwise noted all quotations from Webster's *Speller* are from the 1831 edition.

Readers of Webster also were told that dogs growl, cocks crow, and oxen low. There were passages about the seasons of the year and what months belong to what seasons. And there was much advice. Readers were told to "prefer solid sense to vain wit" and to "let no jest intrude to violate good manners." There was even advice for those who were seeking a partner in marriage. Young men were instructed:

> Obey the ordinance of God, and become a useful member of society. But be not in haste to marry, and let thy choice be directed by wisdom.
>
> Is a woman devoted to dress and amusement? Is she delighted with her own praise, or an admirer of her own beauty? Is she given to much talking and loud laughter? If her feet abide not at home, and her eyes rove with boldness on the faces of men—turn thy feet from her, and suffer not thy heart to be ensnared by thy fancy.

For young women Webster had similar advice:

> Be cautious in listening to the addresses of men. Art thou pleased with smiles and flattering words? Remember that man often smiles and flatters most, when he would betray thee.
>
> Listen to no soft persuasion, till a long acquaintance and a steady, respectful conduct, have given thee proof of the pure attachment and honorable views of thy lover. Is thy suitor addicted to low vices? Is he profane? Is he a gambler? A tippler? A spendthrift? A haunter of taverns? Has he lived in idleness and pleasure? Has he acquired a contempt for thy sex in vile company? And above all, is he a scoffer at religion? Banish such a man from thy presence; his heart is false, and his hand would lead thee to wretchedness and ruin.

Those who had already found a wife were told to treat her "with tenderness and respect." Likewise, wives were told to respect their husbands and to "oppose him not unreasonably." By yielding their "will to his" they would "be blest with peace and concord." Webster also had instructions for parents, brothers, sisters, and daughters.

A 1798 edition of the *Spelling Book* included a "Federal Catechism." It told of the disadvantages of despotic governments, aristocracies, and democracies. Webster described the defects of democracy in this way:

> In a democracy, where the people all meet for the purpose of making laws, there are commonly tumults and disorders. A small city may sometimes be governed in this manner; but if the citizens are numerous, their assemblies make a crowd or mob, where debates cannot be carried on with coolness and candor, nor can arguments be heard: Therefore a pure democracy is generally a very bad government. It is often the most tyrannical government on earth; for a multitude is often rash, and will not hear reason.

Better than democracy, according to the "Federal Catechism," was a "representative republic," the form of government in which the people elected their "deputies to make laws for them." Representative governments were more orderly and responsive to the needs of all citizens:

> . . .But the great security of such a government is, that the men who make

laws, are to be governed by them; so that they are not apt to do wrong willfully. When men make laws for themselves, as well as for their neighbors, they are led by their own interest to make *good* laws.[29]

There were few subjects that did not receive some attention in the speller. There were many fables, each with a clear lesson. There were lessons on measurement, tables of state populations and of the chief rivers in Europe, Asia, and Africa. There were names of lakes, oceans, bays, gulfs, and mountains. There should be little wonder that Webster's speller was so successful. It was more than a speller. In modern terms, it was a curriculum guide for the elementary grades.

---

29. Noah Webster, "A Federal Catechism," reprinted in *Education in the United States: A Documentary History*, ed. Sol Cohen (New York: Random House, 1974), p. 770.

Educational Plans for the New Republic

5

The Effects of Revolution

In his *History of the American Revolution,* written soon after the war (1789), David Ramsay attempted to assess "the influence of the Revolution on the minds and morals of the citizens." He observed that "the literary, political, and military talents of the citizens of the United States have been improved by the revolution, but their moral character is inferior to what it formerly was." Revolution, Ramsay feared, could breed constant turmoil. The forces let loose in 1776 could be used to promote future disturbances. He feared that the ability Americans had developed to overthrow a government could be used continuously by "factious demagogues." He warned that "a long time, and much prudence, will be necessary to reproduce a spirit of union and that reverence for government, without which society is a rope of sand." [1]

Many who contemplated the meaning of the Revolution wanted to ensure that what had been fought for would endure. One way to make sure that the new citizens of the new nation would choose the correct way was to build a system of education that would teach them the correct ways. Many believed that human beings were malleable, and the thinking of the Enlightenment convinced many that deliberate and effective education was possible. Several grand educational plans were proposed to transform the young into good American citizens. They reveal that many people were more concerned with maintaining their vision of the good society than with looking after individual interests and welfare.

---

1. David Ramsay, *The History of the American Revolution* (1789; New York: Russell and Russell, 1968), vol. II, pp. 323–324.

Thomas Jefferson and the Meritocracy

Thomas Jefferson devised plans only for education in Virginia, but his stature and role in the founding of the new republic have given them the status of national plans. His plans were neither classical nor vocational; they were political. For Jefferson, education was an instrument whereby liberty and equality could be understood, secured, and protected.

When Jefferson wrote in the Declaration of Independence that "all men are created equal," he set down a principle that still shapes debate about political and educational matters. As a philosophical and ethical doctrine his notion of equality maintains that all people are equal in that all have been endowed with "certain inalienable rights." No person, no group, no government can ever have the right to deprive any individual of his or her rights. No person can even grant another person freedom because no person's freedom is ever rightfully another's to give. It is, however, the right and the duty of every individual to protect liberty, for without liberty there can be no equality.

If Jefferson's notion of equality had been a psychological concept, then he would have been arguing that all people have the same interests, inclinations, drives, motives, abilities, skills, needs, and capabilities in the same amounts. There is no evidence that Jefferson believed in that kind of psychological equality; nor did he seem to want to promote it. He clearly believed, however, that individuals were capable of learning, that they had a right and a duty to learn in order to protect their freedom, and that experience and accomplishment were more important than inherited status and privilege. In this, education was fundamental and essential. It was fundamental in that whatever people became was a consequence of their education. Moreover, they acquired those skills needed to experiment, innovate, and thereby promote the goddess of the eighteenth century—change. Education was essential because without it people had no way to protect their liberty or to achieve whatever might be possible to achieve.

In his "Bill for the More General Diffusion of Knowlege" (1779), Jefferson, then governor of Virginia, presented what he believed was the relationship of freedom and education. Although some forms of government were better designed than others to protect the individual's freedom, all, Jefferson maintained, had the potential to become tyrannical. The best way to prevent the rise of tyranny and the loss of freedom was, he wrote, "to illuminate, as far as practicable, the minds of the people at large." Through learning history, people would "be enabled to know ambition under all its shapes," and thus be empowered to defeat the forces that were opposed to liberty.[2]

In the Jeffersonian view of the world, good laws and good administration of the laws promoted both the happiness and the freedom of the people. The good-

---

2. Thomas Jefferson, "A Bill for the More General Diffusion of Knowledge," reprinted in *Crusade Against Ignorance: Thomas Jefferson on Education*, ed. Gordon C. Lee (New York: Teachers College Press, Columbia University, 1961), p.83.

ness of the laws was directly related to the qualities and capabilities of those who wrote and administered them. Jefferson wanted those who had been blessed by nature with superior abilities to be especially prepared to look after the affairs of state. He believed that it was

> ... expedient for promoting the public happiness that those persons, whom nature hath endowed with genius and virtue, should be rendered by liberal education worthy to recieve, and able to guard the sacred deposit of the rights and liberties of their fellow citizens, and that they should be called to that charge without regard to wealth, birth or other accidental circumstances. . . .[3]

For Jefferson, the Creator and nature were separable. The Creator had endowed all people with certain rights, and because all had been so endowed all were equal to each other. However, nature had not endowed all with the same capabilities. Because nature did not necessarily bestow more "genius and virtue" upon the offspring of the wealthy than upon the poor, it was necessary to devise special means to identify and prepare all who might benefit from a liberal education. It was unfortunate and wasteful that poverty kept many from properly educating their children, for those poor but capable children could, if educated, "become useful instruments for the public." To ensure that the best would govern rather than the worst, Jefferson proposed that capable students "should be sought for and educated at the common expense of all." The alternative was to leave the happiness and freedom of the people in the hands of the "weak and wicked."

Had Jefferson's bill been enacted by the Virginia legislature, the Virginia landscape would have been covered with schools. He wanted each county to be divided into sections that he called "hundreds." Once the counties were so divided, the electors in each county were to meet and decide where to build schools. For every ten schools there was to be a supervisor who made periodic visits and certified that the instruction was being conducted properly. Jefferson also urged that the state be divided into larger districts of three to five counties each, in which county officials were to determine a central location for a grammar school. Like most eighteenth-century social planners, Jefferson specified details: that each site have a supply of fresh water and be near " to plentiful supplies of provision and fuel," that the school be built of "brick or stone," that rooms be provided for the master and usher, that there be a hall for dining and "ten or twelve lodging rooms for scholars."

The plan for "hundred" schools and grammar schools supported through taxation was designed to add to the natural aristocracy the best possible talent regardless of its social origin. As Jefferson stated the case in his *Notes on the State of Virginia* (1781), it was a system that would ensure that "the best geniuses will be raked from the rubbish annually, and be instructed, at the public expense."[4]

This selection process was to begin in the early years of the "hundred" schools, which would be open to all free boys and girls for three years without

---

3. Ibid., p. 84.
4. Jefferson, "Notes on the State of Virginia," reprinted in Lee, *Crusade Against Ignorance,* p. 94.

charge for tuition. Those who wished to remain longer could do so "at their private expense." Those who wanted to go on to the grammar school could also do so at their own expense. However, some boys (not girls) who showed outstanding ability but whose parents were too poor to pay for their schooling were to continue in school at the public's expense. Each supervisor of a "hundred" school was to select annually "someone of the best and most promising genius and disposition" to attend the district grammar school.

Overseers of the district grammar schools in turn were to examine students annually and eliminate one third of the "public foundationers" who had completed one year there. Of the "public foundationers" who had completed two years, all but one were to lose their scholarships. The one judged to have "the best genius and disposition" was to be "at liberty to continue there four years longer on the public foundation." In his *Notes*, Jefferson explained that each year twenty "public foundationers" would complete the grammar school. Ten were to be selected for further schooling at the College of William and Mary at the public's expense. The other ten, he suggested, could become teachers.

Jefferson also specified what the students should study. The "hundred" schools were to teach reading, writing, and arithmetic. Reading was to be taught from history books so that students would learn the history of Greece, Rome, England, and America as they learned to read. He urged against "putting the Bible and Testament into the hands of the children at an age when their judgments are not sufficiently matured for religious inquiries." Rather, history and the "first elements of morality" were to be emphasized. In the early years the schools would lay the foundation for good public order by showing children that happiness was not dependent upon "the condition of life in which chance has placed them" but was the outcome of "a good conscience, good health, occupation, and freedom in all just pursuits."[5] History was to be emphasized because it would teach students that they had a right to determine the course of their society as well as give them the knowledge to make them wary of government. If people did not have the schooling to participate in their government, it would degenerate in the hands of the few. Thus, Jefferson argued to amend the Virginia Constitution to allow taxation for public schools.

Teachers and Curriculum

Jefferson's recommendations for the grammar school curriculum were traditional. Unlike Franklin, he did not question the value of the classical languages, but included "Latin and Greek languages, English grammar, geography, and the higher part of numerical arithmetic, to wit, vulgar and decimal fractions, and the extraction of the square and cube roots." In the *Notes,* Jefferson observed that although European schools were beginning to eliminate instruction in Latin and Greek, he thought this "would be very ill-judged." In the age range of the boys in grammar

---

5. Ibid., pp. 96–97.

school (eight to fifteen years), the mind, like the body, was not suited "for laborious and close operations." The memory, however, was "most susceptible and tenacious of impressions." There was no better time to teach the boys languages.

Like many educational planners and philosophers before him, Jefferson was concerned about the influence teachers could have on their students, particularly in terms of political views. As was mentioned in Chapter 4, he wanted teachers to take loyalty oaths and "give assurance of fidelity to the commonwealth."[6] He apparently feared that the impressionable grammar school students would be wrongly impressed with anti-republican doctrines. Once the youths were ready to leave the grammar school and begin the collegiate course, however, Jefferson was prepared to allow them to study whatever subjects interested them.

Jefferson wanted these students to study in Virginia rather than in Europe, however. While in Paris in 1785, he wrote a letter outlining the disadvantages of a European education. Except to study medicine, there was no reason for American youth to go to Europe for their college years; a European education would teach them the wrong values and allegiances. Among those disadvantages that a student could expect to encounter, Jefferson listed the following:

> If he goes to England, he learns drinking, horse racing and boxing. These are the peculiarities of English education. The following circumstances are common to education in that and the other countries of Europe. He acquires a fondness for European luxury and dissipation and a contempt for the simplicity of his own country; he is fascinated with the privileges of the European aristocrats, and sees, with abhorrence, the lovely equality which the poor enjoy with the rich, in his own country; he contracts a partiality for aristocracy or monarchy; he forms foreign friendships which will never be useful to him, and loses the seasons of life for forming, in his own country, those friendships which, of all others are the most faithful and permanent; . . .he returns to his own country, a foreigner, unacquainted with the practices of domestic economy, necessary to preserve him from ruin. . . .[7]

Jefferson also noted that one would not become proficient in speaking and writing one's native language if he did not practice those skills in his own country between ages fifteen and twenty.

The Virginia legislature, however, did not enact Jefferson's 1789 proposal. When in 1817 he presented another bill for a system of public education, the legislature once again demurred. Most of Jefferson's educational plans remained but plans. In the last years of his life, he managed to get the University of Virginia underway and in 1825, a year before his death, finally saw its first class of forty students begin their studies. The University of Virginia used many of Jefferson's ideas. There were no uniform entrance requirements and no prescribed courses. Lectures were offered in eight areas: ancient languages, modern languages, math-

---

6. Jefferson, "Bill for the More General Diffusion of Knowledge," reprinted in Lee, *Crusade Against Ignorance*, p. 90.

7. Thomas Jefferson to John Banister, Jr. in Lee, *Crusade Against Ignorance*, pp. 107–108.

ematics, natural philosophy, natural history, anatomy and medicine, moral philosophy, and law. Students were expected to concentrate their efforts in some of the areas, but the selection was theirs.

Apparently neither the rich nor the poor saw enough benefit in Jefferson's other educational proposals to lobby for their adoption. In the eighteenth century, there was no reason for the poor to see education as a way to improve their social and economic standing. Moreover, as only ten students a year would have been sent to William and Mary, the opportunity did not benefit an entire class of people. Opportunities to acquire land or to start a business would probably have been more appealing. Virginians who were already established and prosperous were not especially eager either to increase their taxes or to expand the role of government.

Perhaps Jefferson himself gave the best explanation of the proposal's failure in Virginia as well as in many other legislatures. In 1802, when Jefferson was President of the United States, his friend Joel Barlow proposed a national institution to support scientific research and to serve as an agency to supply the nation's schools with textbooks. Jefferson cautiously submitted the plan to Congress. In 1806, explaining to Barlow that the plan had failed, he wrote:

> There is a snail-paced gait for the advance of new ideas on the general mind, under which we must aquiesce. A 40-years' experience of popular assemblies has taught me, that you must give them time for every step you take. If too hard pushed, they baulk, and the machine retrogrades. . . .People generally have more feeling for canals and roads than education.[8]

In future years, and into the twentieth century, legislatures were to continue to reject Jeffersonian schemes for education.

National Plans for the "General Welfare"

On May 1, 1795, the American Philosophical Society for Promoting Useful Knowledge (a society originating in the educational efforts of Benjamin Franklin) offered a $100 prize for the best essay "on a system of liberal education and literary instruction, adapted to the genius of the government and best calculated to promote the general welfare of the United States: comprehending also a plan for instruction and conducting public schools in this country on principles of the most extensive utility."[9] The offer was consistent with the society's history and wide-ranging interests, which included topics such as agriculture, chemistry, natural history, how to secure firewood at reasonable cost, moral science, and

---

8. Thomas Jefferson to Joel Barlow, quoted in Henry F. May, *The Enlightenment in America* (New York: Oxford University Press, 1976), p. 312.

9. Minutes of the American Philosophical Society, March 6, 1795, quoted in Merle M. Odgers, "Education and the American Philosophical Society," *Proceedings of the American Philosophical Society,* 87:I (July 1943), p. 13.

politics. On December 15, 1797, the Society decided that the prize should be divided between two contestants: the Reverend Samuel Knox and Samuel Harrison Smith.

Samuel Harrison Smith's Plan

Samuel Harrison Smith, a graduate of the University of Pennsylvania and a Philadelphia journalist, was only twenty-five when he won half the APS prize, but the essay he submitted was well suited for the Society. He demonstrated his familiarity with classical and modern authors: Lucretius, Quintilian, Bacon, Montesquieu, Rousseau, and Locke. Siding with the adherents of the Enlightenment, he argued that Education was the key to social progress and the improvement of humanity.

Smith assumed that a system of national education was both desirable and necessary. He accepted the notion that "under a republic, duly constructed, man feels as strong a bias to improvement as under a despotism he feels an impulse to ignorance and depression." In a republic, the ways to happiness were available to all, but happiness could not be achieved unless people had ways to improve their minds and interact with others who had taken the opportunity to improve theirs. People needed to live in a land where there was a "general diffusion of knowledge" and where there was opportunity to develop the "capacity to think and speak correctly."[10]

Smith agreed with those who believed the state had the right to insist that all children be educated by the public. This was certainly not a new idea; Aristotle wrote that "we ought not to think that any of the citizens of the state belongs to himself, but that all belong to the state." For Aristotle those systems of education that allowed parents to teach their children whatever and however they saw fit were contrary to the best interests of the state. Later, Quintilian argued that public education was better than private or tutorial education. Students were exposed to more incentives in a public educational scheme than in a private, or tutorial, setting. Smith believed that the effects of compulsory education were so obviously beneficial that the state could expect "a general acquiescence" from the people should it exercise this duty.[11] Smith cited a French statesman who had participated in the writing of the Napoleonic civil code, Jean Jacques Regis de Cambacères, who had declared: "It is proper to remind parents that their children belong to the state and that in their education they ought to conform to the rules which it prescribes."[12] It was, according to Smith, "the duty of a nation to superintend and even to coerce the education of children."

Smith evidently believed that the state had a greater interest in the education of boys than in that of girls. He did not want to risk a recommendation on a subject

---

10. Samuel Harrison Smith, "Remarks on Education: Illustrating the Close Connection Between Virtue and Wisdom. To Which is Annexed a System of Liberal Education. . . ." reprinted in *Essays on Education in the Early Republic*, ed. Frederick Rudolph (Cambridge: Harvard University Press, 1965), pp. 188–189.

11. Ibid., p. 190.

12. Ibid.

where there was an "existing diversity of opinion," and was willing to remark only that "it is sufficient, perhaps, for the present that the improvement of women is marked by a rapid progress and that a prospect opens equal to their most ambitious desires."[13] (Smith himself, however, was not willing to aid these desires.)

Smith wanted all boys between the ages of five and eighteen to attend primary schools, each of which would enroll fifty boys and be divided into two divisions. In the first division, boys between the ages of five and ten were to be instructed in reading, writing, and arithmetic and be required to memorize and deliver selections that inculcated "moral duties," described "natural phenomena," or displayed "correct fancy." In the second division, the boys were to pursue the studies of the first division into their more complex parts and begin work in general history, "the history of our own country," geography, and the laws of nature with practical illustrations from agriculture and mechanics.

Smith's essay also proposed colleges and a national university. Each college was to have 200 students and to accept scholarship students from each of the primary schools in its district. The preceptor of each primary school was to select one boy each year whose "industry and talents" made him worthy of education at "public expense." College students were to continue the studies of the upper division of the primary school as well as begin the study of "polite literature." Those with ability could add new subjects: modern languages, music, drawing, dancing, and fencing. Smith suggested that permission to persue these additional subjects could be the "reward of diligence and talents." The faculty of the colleges were to select annually one out of every ten students for promotion to the national university, where the "highest branches of science and literature" would be taught.

Samuel Knox's Plan

Samuel Knox, who shared the Society's prize with Samuel Smith, was a native of Ireland who had recently immigrated to the United States. When his prize-winning essay was published in 1799, he was headmaster of the Frederick Academy in Maryland. Although he had been pastor of a Presbyterian church in Bladensburgh, Maryland, Knox wrote in his essay: "It is a happy circumstance peculiarly favorable to an uniform plan of public education that this country hath excluded ecclesiastical from civil policy and emancipated the human mind from the tyranny of church authority and church establishments." He went on to suggest that each religious denomination could open its own school for the study of theology and the preparation of clergy. Those who wanted to prepare for the ministry would do better in such specialized schools. According to Knox, the "licentious habits" and "domestic indulgences" of nondenominational public schools would be "little suited to the pious examples and virtuous dignity of the sacred function."[14]

---

13. Ibid., p. 217.
14. Samuel Knox, "An Essay on the Best System of Liberal Education, Adapted to the Genius of the Government of the United States. Comprehending also, an Uniform General Plan for Instituting and Conducting Public Schools, in This Country, on Principles of the Most Extensive Utility" reprinted in Rudolph, *Essays on Education,* pp. 315–316.

Knox's recommendations for education in the new republic were more Jeffersonian than Smith's. Knox, who was proficient in Latin and Greek, urged that youth study those languages. Like Jefferson, he believed that the study of language was "most proper as a preparation for scientific improvement" and also would promote a better understanding and use of one's own language. He suggested that "the mere comparing or contrasting of two languages together must afford considerable improvement to the mind."[15]

Like Smith, Knox thought that public (what he termed "academical") education was preferable to private, or tutorial, education. He acknowledged the standard arguments against public education and then gave the outweighing advantages: in public schools, students benefited from the principle of emulation. Desires to earn praise, to excel, and to compete could be met under the supervision of a competent teacher. Incompetent teachers were more likely to be discovered in schools with many students than in a private tutorial setting.

Admitting that public education typically required schools to be placed in "populous towns" where "opportunities are thereby given for corruption by scenes of vice and examples of debauchery," Knox voiced the subtle but enduring American prejudice against city life and the belief that rural life was somehow more virtuous. He acknowledged also that in a public school there were students of all sorts, or what he termed "complexions." The public school, however, did give "youth an opportunity to form such friendships and connections as often in a literary and interested view contribute eminently to their future prosperity and happiness."[16] The final and most important argument for public education, in Knox's estimation, was that it provided a way "for distinguishing literary genius and merit and consequently pointing out to public view such talents as are best fitted to fill the various stations and offices which the different exigencies of the state and the many departments of society require."[17] Like Jefferson, he believed schooling could be used to promote a meritocracy; the school was to be the place that prepared youth for civil service jobs.

As Knox moved from general observations about the worth and nature of education to his educational recommendations for the new republic, he reminded his readers of the size and of the diversity of the United States. It was populated with people from various places with different customs and manners; their morals and literary attainments were uneven, varying from one place to another. The tremendous diversity of the nation could, he believed, be harmonized with a "uniform system of national education."

Knox then advised that the content of education should be selected in a liberal manner, guided by a twofold aim: "the improvement of the mind and the attainment of those arts on which the welfare, prosperity, and happiness of society depend."[18] A curriculum that emphasized only practical subjects might be understandable in

---

15. Ibid., pp.301–393.
16. Ibid., p.306.
17. Ibid., p.308.
18. Ibid., p.312.

a nation without wealth, but the United States had sufficient wealth to support instruction in all the appropriate subjects. Besides, instruction in only the practical or "lucrative" subjects would lead to the destruction of the people's character and taste and ultimately to the destruction of the nation. For Knox, appropriate educational fare would include "a classical knowledge of the English, French, Latin, and Greek languages, Greek and Roman Antiquities, ancient and modern geography, universal grammar, *belles-lettres,* rhetoric and composition, chronology and history, the principles of ethics, law, and government, the various branches of the mathematics and the sciences founded on them, astronomy, natural and experimental philosophy in all their various departments" as well as "drawing, painting, fencing, and music." This curriculum was for all students, whether they planned to enter business, the government, or the professions.

Knox wanted students to begin their schooling in local primary schools, which would be in a "proper house" situated on a few acres of land and large enough to accommodate thirty to thirty-five students. Unlike Smith, he did not want compulsory attendance for all students at the public's expense. He did urge, however, that each school enroll "at least three promising boys, whose parents could not afford to educate them." These "public foundationers" were to become teachers when they finished their schooling. At age twelve the boys were to leave the local schools and move on to the county schools where they would reside with 200 or 250 other boys until age fifteen. Each country school was to offer five scholarships for worthy and needy students. Between the ages of fifteen and eighteen the boys were to attend college, continuing the studies begun in the country schools until they earned a Bachelor of Arts degree. From the colleges the young men could then go on to the national university, where they could earn a Master of Arts degree, a medical degree, or a law degree. Some scholarships were to be available for the colleges and the national university. The entire system was to be uniform from one place to the next. To ensure such uniformity, Knox proposed that there would be common textbooks, licensed printers in each state, and federal supervisors.

Other Approaches to National Education

The prize-winning essays written by Smith and Knox were published and so have been available for study and inspection by several generations of Americans. Some of the other essays, however, have survived in the files of the American Philosophical Society. Frederick Rudolph identified five others who wrote and published essays on education between 1786 and 1799.[19] All shared a belief that

---

19. The other five authors whom Rudolph has identified and whose works he has made available are: Robert Coram, Simeon Doggett, Amable-Louis-Rose de Lafitte du Corteil, Benjamin Rush, and Noah Webster. In Allen Oscar Hansen, *Liberalism and American Education in the Eighteenth Century* (New York: The Macmillan Co., 1926) are discussions of eighteenth-century educational theorists, including several of the group above: Benjamin Rush, Robert Coram, James Sullivan, Nathaniel Chipman, Samuel Knox, Samuel Harrison Smith, Amable-Louis-Rose de Lafitte du Corteil, Pierre Samuel Du Pont de Nemour's and Noah Webster.

people could shape their world for their own betterment and that Americans had the ability to transcend regional peculiarities and to consider the needs of the entire nation. Two of these essayists were Benjamin Rush and Noah Webster, better known today for other accomplishments. Both these writers gave attention to education for women as well as for men.

Benjamin Rush

Benjamin Rush was one of the busiest men in Philadelphia, as well as the country's most prominent physician. Like his fellow Philadelphian Benjamin Franklin, he seemed always to be either studying to improve himself or proposing a plan to remedy some social problem. A signer of the Declaration of Independence, Rush served as military surgeon during the Revolution and provided his friend Tom Paine with the title for his pamphlet "Common Sense." Throughout his career, Rush devoted himself to the improvement of the practice of medicine, agriculture, the mechanical arts, the treatment of criminals and the mentally ill, government, and education. His educational efforts reflected his belief that the human condition can be improved through the continued advancement of learning, his very strong commitment to the new republic, and his unswaying commitment to Christianity.

When Rush offered his "Thoughts upon the Mode of Education Proper in a Republic" in 1786, he had no doubts about what was necessary. Traditional methods of schooling had to be examined carefully and adapted to the new form of government brought about by independence. Schools would have to create unity out of the extant diversity. The citizens of Pennsylvania and of all other states had come from not one but many places in Europe. Schools, if properly conducted, could "render the mass of the people more homogenous and thereby fit them for uniform and peaceable government."[20] Schools were to convert men into "republican machines," teaching the student that nothing except his duty to God was more important than the republic, and that he did not belong to himself, but was public property. Above all, Rush's model student was to be transformed into the perfect citizen, setting aside amusement for work. The good citizen was to love all humanity but have a special regard and affection for his fellow citizen.

Unlike Knox, Rush was not willing to set aside the study of religion or place it in special schools. For Rush there could be no separation of church and state. He admitted that his views on the role of religion in education were contrary to "those paradoxical opinions with which modern times abound." He argued that while the modern view maintained that students should have no instruction in religious matters until they had reached full use of their rational powers, children were allowed to learn other subjects and develop other tastes and inclinations at an early age. Moreover, in Rush's estimation, the teachings of Christianity were thoroughly supportive of his view of the good republican citizen. "A Christian," he

---

20. Benjamin Rush, "Thoughts upon the Mode of Education Proper in a Republic," reprinted in Rudolph, *Essays on Education*, p. 10.

believed, "cannot fail of being useful to the republic, for his religion teacheth him, that no man 'liveth to himself'." The teachings of the Old Testament constituted the "best refutation that can be given to the divine right of kings," while the teachings of the Gospel inculcated "those degrees of humility, self-denial, and brotherly kindness, which are directly opposed to the pride of monarchy and the pageantry of a court."[21]

Rush understood that patriotism had an emotional as well as an intellectual base. As students formed their strongest prejudices and friendships during their first twenty-one years, it was imperative to plan carefully how they would be educated. Their sleep, their diet, and their associations with each other had to be supervised. Rush even questioned the wisdom of what Knox called "public" or "academical" education. To put all students under one roof away from their families would make them scholars but would not necessarily make them good Christians and good republicans. Young people had to be separated from each other when not at study so the family would have an opportunity to play its part in the educative process.

Although Rush did not advocate the abolition of schools he wanted to control their size and location. The size of the student body, he believed, was directly related to the development of the students' character and habits. In his "Plan for the Establishment of Public Schools" (1786), he advocated that four colleges be established in Pennsylvania rather than one because "there is a certain size of colleges, as there is of towns and armies, that is most favorable to morals and good government." England, he related, had only two major institutions of higher learning—Oxford and Cambridge—and they had become "seats of dissipation." Scotland had a greater number of schools, with smaller student bodies, and they were known for "the order, diligence, and decent behavior of their students."[22]

Like many others of his era, Rush wanted a system of education that would include elementary schools in every township of one hundred families, academies in each of the counties, colleges, and a university. All members of the community were to be taxed for the schools, even "the estates of orphans, bachelors, and persons who have no children." To those who objected that there were already too many taxes to pay, he answered that taxes for schools would lead ultimately to a reduction of taxes: schooling would increase the knowledge and therefore the productivity of manufactures and agriculture as well as lead to a significant reduction in crime. An educated people would constitute an efficient, safe, and moral community where all would benefit. According to Rush, the following catalogue of benefits could be derived from a system of universal schooling:

> The bachelor will in time save his tax for this purpose by being able to sleep with fewer bolts and locks on his doors, the estates of orphans will in time be benefited by being protected from the ravages of unprincipled and idle boys,

---

21. Ibid., p.11.
22. Benjamin Rush, "Plan for the Establishment of Public Schools," reprinted in Rudolph, *Essays on Education,* pp. 4–5.

and the children of the wealthy parents will be less tempted, by bad company, to extravagance. Fewer pillories and whipping posts and smaller jails, with their usual expenses and taxes, will be necessary when our youth are properly educated than at present. I believe it could be proved that the expenses of confining, trying, and executing criminals amount every year, in most of the counties, to more money than would be sufficient to maintain all the schools that would be necessary.[23]

Rush would not be the last to argue that an investment in schools would serve as a deterrent to crime or that schools were less expensive than jails.

Rush on the Education of Women

Rush's support for the education of women was also based on the good of the republic. He believed, in fact, that education of men could never be effective until women agreed with the nation's laws and were inculcated with a strong sense of their republican duties. Rush explained that "the opinions and conduct of men are often regulated by the women in the most arduous enterprises of life, and their approbation is frequently the principal reward of the hero's dangers and the patriot's toils."[24] Moreover, since a child's first impressions came from women, women should be as committed to the republic as men.

When Rush addressed the students and friends of the Young Ladies Academy in Philadelphia, he instructed them that those who questioned or opposed the education of women were possessed of "little minds" and were no better than those who opposed "the general diffusion of knowledge among the citizens of our republic." If the women of the nation were properly schooled, they would have not only the power to exert a strong and positive influence over the making and the administration of the country's laws, but also the opportunity to improve the manners and the character of the people. He told the women that they should show men that "the female temper can only be governed by reason" and confessed that he had "sometimes been led to ascribe the invention of ridiculous and expensive fashions in female dress entirely to the gentlemen in order to divert the ladies from improving their minds and thereby to secure a more arbitrary and unlimited authority over them."[25] Above all, women were to be instructed in the principles of Christianity, for "the female breast," wrote Rush, "is the natural soil of Christianity."[26]

Noah Webster

Several years after the publication of his speller, Noah Webster gave his views on what education in general was appropriate for the new republic in his *American*

23. Ibid., pp. 6–7.

24. Rush, "Thoughts upon the Mode of Education Proper in a Republic," reprinted in Rudolph, *Essays on Education,* p. 22.

25. Benjamin Rush, "Thoughts upon Female Education, Accommodated to the Present State of Society, Manners, and Government in the United States of America," reprinted in Rudolph, *Essays on Education,* p. 39.

26. Ibid., p. 32.

Magazine (1787–88). He believed that in Europe education had no significant influence on national character and that in all nations there was "an inseparable connection" between morals and education. America, as a new country, had the opportunity to fashion a system of education that would "implant in the minds of the youth the principles of virtue and of liberty and inspire them with an inviolable attachment to their own country."[27]

While Webster shared the belief that people were capable of improving themselves and their society through deliberate educational efforts, he also did not advocate a completely secular form of education. He agreed with Rush that religion was a proper subject for the schools but did not agree that the Bible should be used extensively. Rush thought the only possible objection to the Bible was "its division into chapters and verses and its improper punctuation which render it a more difficult book to read *well* than many others."[28] Webster, however, argued that if the Bible were used frequently, it would lose its power to make an impression. He explained that while in some nations the common people were not allowed to read the Bible at any time, in the United States, it was too often "as common as a newspaper" and read with no more respect. Although it was advisable to use selected passages to teach "a system of religion and morality," the Bible should not be used in place of other books.

In his discussions of the location of schools, Webster argued that villages were better settings because "large cities are always scenes of dissipation and amusement, which have a tendency to corrupt the hearts of youth and divert their minds from their literary pursuits."[29] Like Rush, he wanted students to be closely supervised and separated from each other when not studying. He advocated a practice—one he may have learned as a student at Yale—of having the students "live in decent families" while attending school rather than in dormitories. He also questioned the wisdom of keeping all students together in one class. As all were not preparing themselves for the same careers, it was not reasonable that all study the same subjects. Superior students, he urged, should be allowed to move to the higher classes as a "reward for their superior industry."

Teachers, Webster advised, should have absolute authority. "Strict discipline" was essential; it was "the best foundation of good order in political society." Answering those who claimed that teachers with unlimited authority might abuse the children, Webster retorted that the public would simply have to secure the services of good teachers. The "displeasure" of a good teacher whom students respected would be all the force needed in the classroom.

The quality of teachers, according to Webster, was generally less than it should be:

---

27. Noah Webster, "On the Education of Youth in America," reprinted in Rudolph, *Essays on Education,* p. 45.

28. Rush, "Thoughts upon the Mode of Education Proper in a Republic," reprinted in Rudolph, *Essays on Education,* p. 12.

29. Webster, "On the Education of Youth," reprinted in Rudolph, *Essays on Education, p. 52.*

Will it be denied that many of the instructors of youth, whose examples and precepts should form their minds for good men and useful citizens, are often found to sleep away in school the fumes of a debauch and to stun the ears of their pupils with frequent blasphemy? It is idle to suppress such truths; nay more, it is wicked. The practice of employing low and vicious characters to direct the studies of youth is in a high degree criminal; it is destructive of the order and peace of society; it is treason against morals and of course against government; it ought to be arraigned before the tribunal of reason and condemned by all intelligent beings. The practice is so exceedingly absurd that it is surprising it could ever have prevailed among rational people. Parents wish their children to be *well-bred,* yet place them under the care of *clowns.* [30]

Webster pointed out that teachers were frequently so low in the eyes of the community that parents refused to associate with them; and still they sent their children to school and expected them to behave properly. Good teachers, he felt, were so essential that he was nearly willing to "adore that great man who shall change our practice and opinions and make it respectable for the first and best men to superintend the education of youth." [31]

Webster on the Education of Women

Like Rush, Webster believed that women could exert considerable influence over men. The desire of men for the "company and conversation" of women of good character had saved many men, he claimed, from lives of ruin. Women had a moral stamina superior to that of men; though delicate, they were "generally the last to be corrupted." In America the education of women was particularly important because American women typically did not consider themselves "above the care of educating their own children." They had to be educated so they would tend to their children properly.

Female education, like that of males, was to be suited to the government of the United States and the character of American society. Women were to be taught to have good manners, how to maintain respectability in their families, how to be agreeable in society, and to be useful. To be "useful" women had to know their own language; French was sometimes "convenient" but usually a "luxury." "Young ladies," Webster declared, "should be taught to speak and write their own language with purity and elegance, an article in which they are often deficient." [32] For reading matter he recommended history, *The Spectator,* and poetry. "A taste for poetry and fine writing should be cultivated," he explained, "for we expect the most delicate sentiments from the pens of that sex which is possessed of the finest feelings." Novels were not recommended, for one could read a hundred of them "without acquiring a new idea." Novels were "the toys of youth, the rattle boxes of sixteen," and therefore unsuitable for women. [33]

---

30. Ibid., pp. 60–61.
31. Ibid., p. 64.
32. Ibid., p. 70.
33. Ibid., p. 71.

For Webster, a major reason for educating women was to enable them to bring up their children properly, to "enable them to implant in the tender mind such sentiments of virtue, propriety, and dignity as are suited to the freedom of our governments."[34] Because children were apt to learn what they saw and heard in the home, their upbringing had to be supervised very carefully so improper or distasteful traits would not appear in their adult behavior. The nursery was to be kept free from all that was vulgar, obscene, or illiberal.

Education and Nationalism

The practice of sending youth, especially young men, to Europe for their schooling, or of bringing teachers from Europe, ceased to be acceptable when the political relationships with England were severed. Education abroad was "to be discountenanced, if not prohibited." Like Jefferson, Webster believed that the character and attachments formed during youth were lasting and determined the quality of persons as well as their patriotism. American youth had to be educated in America, for young people took on the manners and developed an allegiance for the country in which they were educated.

The objection to sending American youth abroad for their education, was a sentiment that was widely shared in the early years of the republic. In 1785, for example, the Georgia legislature enacted a law that effectively disenfranchised those who went to Europe for their education. Any youth under age sixteen who spent three or more years in a school in Europe was upon his return to be treated as an alien and "not be eligible to a Seat in the Legislature or Executive authority or to hold any office civil or military in the State for that term and so in proportion for any greater number of years as he . . . shall be absent. . . ."[35] Such students were not, however, to be deprived of their other constitutional rights.

When George Washington wrote to Robert Brooke in 1795 about his advocacy of a national university, he wrote, "It is with indescribable regret that I have seen the youth of the United States migrating to foreign countries, in order to acquire the higher branches of erudition, and to obtain a knowledge of the sciences. . . . A serious danger is encountered by sending abroad among other political systems those who have not well learned the value of their own."[36] In 1795 the Virginia House of Delegates passed a resolution in favor of establishing a national university because "the migration of American youth to foreign countries, for the

---

34. Ibid., p. 68.

35. "Declaration by the Georgia Legislature that Youths Who Study in Europe Shall be Aliens" 1785), in *Education in the United States: A Documentary History*, ed. Sol Cohen (New York: Random House, 1974), p. 800.

36. "George Washington Favors a National University," in Cohen, *Education in the United States*,). 806.

completion of their education, exposes them to the danger of imbibing political prejudices disadvantageous to their own republican forms of government. . . ."[37] Benjamin Rush, who is generally regarded as having first proposed the idea of a national university, wanted to make graduation from it a condition for holding public office.

The first six Presidents of the new United States supported the idea of a national university, but Congress rejected the idea whenever it was proposed—as too costly, unnecessary, impractical, or a boon for the rich.[38] The idea also failed to receive widespread public support. When John Quincy Adams proposed a national university and observatory, newspapers made light of his idea by writing of his "lighthouses of the skies." Adams's argument that educational facilities in England, France, and Russia were better than those in the United States did not inspire the Congress to act on his plan. After that, no President mentioned the idea of a national university until Grant did so in 1875. The notion appeared again in the administrations of Hayes, McKinley, and Wilson. When the idea was presented during McKinley's administration, Andrew Carnegie showed some interest in supporting it, but concluded that it might jeopardize the positions of the already existing colleges. He then established the Carnegie Institution in 1901 to aid higher education, effectively supporting diversity rather than uniformity in American college education.

37. "Resolution of the Virginia House of Delegates on a National University" (1795), in Cohen, *Education in the United States*, p. 806.

38. Albert Castel, "The Founding Fathers and the Vision of a National University," *History of Education Quarterly"* 4:4 (December 1964), pp. 280–302.

PART II

The Early Republic

After the Revolution was won, many Americans deliberately tried to assure the success of the new republic. They sought to establish institutions: language, literature, values, and schools that would be uniquely and distinctively American. David Tyack has described the mood as "an all-out effort to Americanize through the schools, the press, the pulpit, the work of the artist, the courtroom, the political assembly—by all the means of shaping character and intellect."[1] In some ways they were successful. Recognizing that their loose Confederation was not working, they wrote and adopted a Constitution and before it was too late added a Bill of Rights. They had learned the lessons of the Enlightenment very well. Believing that education could indeed do everything, they developed plans designed to create the perfect and free American, an American who would not question the new social-political order. Some, like Rush, even used the mechanistic language of the Enlightenment and asked for the production of "republican machines."

The leaders of the new nation did not, however, convince the new citizens that the federal government should tend to their education. Rather, the people decided either that they did not need to partake of a general diffusion of knowledge or that their educational needs could be better satisfied through local efforts. The advocates of national systems of education nevertheless provided the arguments and articulated the beliefs that were to be believed and used, frequently successfully, by later generations: that people were educable; that people could improve themselves and their society through deliberate educational efforts; that the investment of resources in schooling would return itself in the form of reduced crime and reduced poverty; and that the strength, security, and reputation of the nation depended on its educational strength. The advocates of grand educational systems were not united on whether religion should be part of the schools, but the Christian tradition was part of the American tradition and so remained in the schools. In fact, when Americans began to expand educational opportunities for their children in the 1830s and 1840s, they frequently turned to the *Readers* of the Reverend William Holmes McGuffey, which supported patriotism and nonsectarian Christianity.

The textbooks used in the schools may represent the values and beliefs of Americans better than the eloquent statements and plans of the nation's articulate leaders. To be sure, they frequently celebrated the founding of the new nation and extolled the virtues of the new experiment in government. The texts, however, do not indicate that people set aside their old values. To their

---

1. David Tyack, "Forming the National Character: Paradox in the Educational Thought of the Revolutionary Generation," *Harvard Educational Review* 36:1 (Winter 1966), p. 32.

long-standing commitments they added a new one, patriotism. Their basic values did not undergo any sudden and revolutionary change. The texts showed a strong attachment to religion.

During the war, organized religion did suffer. Some congregations were divided by the war, some churches were disbanded, and some church buildings were destroyed. Inflation and other economic difficulties of the postwar years made it difficult for many to support their churches as they had in earlier times. Many members of the clergy feared that religious indifference and deism would overtake the country. But in the 1790s a second religious revival began. Between 1790 and 1830, churches were reorganized and new sects were formed; the Baptists and Methodists grew and became the two most powerful religious sects in America. In 1831 the French observer of American ways, Alexis de Tocqueville, noted that "there is no country in the world in which the Christian religion retains a greater hold over the souls of men than in America."[2]

In the 1820s and 1830s Americans finished reorganizing their religious affairs. The idea of separation of church and state was beginning to take form, and many learned that they could be faithful to their beliefs and conduct social and political debate outside their churches. Those concerned with the development of a national and uniquely American literature found hope in the work of James Fenimore Cooper. Americans also attended to developing a new culture by tending to their history. However, contrary to the grand designs of many leaders and social theoreticians, they concentrated on the writing of state and local histories. In the first third of the nineteenth century, numerous regional historical societies were formed.

After the Americans had got their church, their literature, and their histories in order, those who did not move across the Allegheny Mountains to settle the new wilderness turned their attention to what we now call social problems. They began to consider seriously the need for public schools as we now know them. Those considerations and developments will be examined in Part Three.

---

2. Alexis de Tocqueville, *Democracy in America*, ed. Phillips Bradely (New York: Vintage Books, 1958), vol. I, pp. 303–304.

PART III

A New Institution in a New Era: Successes and Failures of the Common School

The election of Andrew Jackson to the presidency in 1828 is often cited as the event that dramatically signified a new era in American history, one usually seen as the era of the common man and of social reform. Such periods of social reform are usually interesting because they are times of sharp differences of opinion. They are times of contest, when people are not only trying to change important parts of their social, economic, and political lives, but are also trying to adjust to changes that have already occurred. Invariably, there are those who approve of new ways and there are those who prefer more familiar ways. In the early 1800s, the new nation faced a number of developments and choices that would ultimately shape how people would live, work, do business with each other, and govern themselves. As the new nation grew, ways had to be devised to reconcile the rhetoric of the Revolutionary Period with the social and political facts of life. The contest was between democratic and aristocratic conceptions of government. In formal political terms, the issues were those that usually divided the Federalists and the Republicans. The election of Jefferson to the presidency may have taken the office from those who were inclined toward some form of aristocracy. It did not, however, give clear meaning to the terms *liberty* and *equality*, just as it did not solve the problems of the common man.

Problems attendant to industrialism appeared as early as 1791, when the first textile mill in America was set up in Rhode Island by Samuel Slater. Soon those who valued and wanted to maintain an agrarian society had to contend with those who wanted to build a commercial and capitalistic society. Industry and commerce promoted the rapid growth of cities, but cities were feared as the breeding places of social and human problems.

The nation and its cities grew quickly after the Revolution. Between 1790 and 1830 the nation's population increased by over 300 percent, from 3.9 million to 12.8 million. By the time of the Civil War it had more than doubled again, to 31.4 million. At the beginning of the nineteenth century only about five percent of the nation's people lived in cities with populations of 8,000 or more. The five largest cities in the United States in 1800 were, by modern standards, not very large. New York, however, was the fastest growing, and by 1820 was the largest city in the country. By 1830 it had nearly 200,000 people.

As urban populations grew, the fears of the agrarianists were frequently realized. Polluted water, streets strewn with garbage and overrun with pigs, nightly fires, crime, and poverty became standard features of life in the cities. By 1840 New York had slums that many thought were even worse than those of London. As the cities grew, their problems—and the problems of the poor who lived in them—became increasingly apparent. Densely populated areas in which people were segregated by social and/or economic position transformed individual misfortunes into social problems and responsibilities.

In the 1820s it was difficult not to have an opinion about such issues as the need for schools, the conditions of the prisons and asylums, temperance, slavery, the role and rights of women, and the rights of workers to organize and make their needs known. In the 1830s the number of immigrants increased, presenting Americans with a new problem—how to extend freedom to newcomers and still maintain the existing order and tradition.

All these issues have reappeared in successive generations. The sweeping changes brought by industrialization, however, changed the world for many people in the early 1800s. In Chapter 6, the early attitudes and responses to industrialism will be examined, as well as some of the early attempts to provide education for the poor. In Chapter 7 we will examine how some outstanding women responded to the educational issues of their day, as well as consider attitudes toward the education of women—white and black—an issue that was eloquently raised at the end of the eighteenth century. In Chapters 8 and 9, the movement leading to the establishment of free public education will be discussed. A generation after the leaders advocated a national system of public education, Americans decided to begin to build such systems. Instead of one national system, however, they built many systems, community by community, state by state.

By the 1876 centennial, the nation had expanded and prospered, built new institutions, gained some international respect, proved that its republican form of government was durable, and survived a bloody and costly civil war. Many things that had been new and threatening at the beginning of the century were now largely familiar and comfortable. There were, however, new issues to confront that had been previously set aside or ignored. As the frontier moved westward, the white settlers had to come to terms with what they often called the "Indian question." After the Civil War it was no longer possible to assume that the Indians could be continuously pushed farther west. As Samuel Chapman Armstrong observed in 1883, "our frontier line is pushing westward, at the rate of twenty miles a year; has already wrapped itself around and is pressing hard upon the reservations."[1] According to Armstrong, the only solutions to the "Indian question" were "extermination" or "civilization." The settlers set out to convert the Indians to their ways. In Chapter 10 we look at the kinds of education they chose to try to accomplish this.

Slavery and its legacy were paramount among the old issues. At the Civil War's end, the nation, North and South, had to tend to the need for education of the newly-freed black people. By the end of the nineteenth century, Americans had worked out another compromise in the history of the relationships between blacks and whites. In the South, legislators enacted "Jim Crow" laws, based on the notion that "separate but equal" schooling was just, legal, and viable. On May 17, 1954, the Supreme Court declared (in the "Brown decision") that "separate but equal" schooling was an unconstitutional concept. Consequently, segregation of the races was unconstitutional. In principle, children could no longer be assigned to schools simply because they were of one color or another. In actuality, such practices continued, and de facto segregation persists, but it continues to be challenged. Subsequent to the Brown decision, several federal district courts ordered the deliberate desegregation of public schools. The United States was entering a new social and a new educational era.

Chapter 11 discusses how important blacks saw the education of black Americans, focusing on the works and views of Frederick Douglass as well as those of Booker T. Washington and one of his critics, W. E. B. DuBois.

At the end of the Civil War the idea of the common school was already a generation old. Many of the original crusaders had departed. Among the more prominent of the new educators were Edward A. Sheldon, Col. Francis Wayland Parker, and William Torrey Harris. They worked to consolidate the gains of their predecessors, to raise this new occupation of education to professional status, and to show what a school system could do for the nation and its people.

In those areas of the nation where schools had been established there was still some debate about whether the public school was a good idea. However, the major questions were about the school's pedagogy: how might classroom practices be rendered more interesting for students and more humane? As Sheldon, Parker, and others sought to answer the question, they developed "new education." In the early years of the twentieth century the

---

1. Samuel Chapman Armstrong, *The Indian Question* (Hampton, Virginia: Normal School Steam Press, Print, 1883), pp. 20–21.

"new education" was justified with theories from the "new psychology" and became progressive education. In Chapter 12 a sample of the educational reforms of the second half of the nineteenth century will be examined.

In the chapters that comprise this section we can see that while schools were being improved for some Americans, others barely had a chance at what those Americans were taking for granted. Few of the mainstream reforms took into account the meager educational opportunities that were provided for black Americans and American Indians. As the efforts and programs of Booker T. Washington are examined, it is easy to ask whether he might have been hailed as one of the founders of progressive education had he not been black. Certainly, he saw clearly the relationship between schooling and the lives people led; that he had to make compromises should tell us something about a nation that all but neglected some of its people while it tried to reform its schools for others.

Industrialism and Early Responses

6

The Debate over Industrialism

One of the earliest and most articulate advocates of industrialism in the United States was Alexander Hamilton. In his report on manufactures in 1791, he saw three major advantages in the factory system of production and the division of labor. First, the worker's "constant and undivided application to a single object" led, he believed, to "greater skill and dexterity." As the task was simplified, the worker's skill increased. Second, time was gained, for there was no time lost as the worker moved from performing one task to the next. Third, he thought division of labor would stimulate the worker's imagination: "A man occupied on a single object will have it more in his power, and will be more naturally led to exert his imagination, in devising methods to facilitate and abridge labor, than if he were perplexed by a variety of independent and dissimilar operations."[1]

When Alexis de Tocqueville toured America in the 1830s and observed the growth of factories, he saw consequences that Hamilton had not considered. While Tocqueville agreed that the division of labor might lead to greater efficiency, he also asked how it might affect the worker. His conclusions were very different from Hamilton's:

> When a workman is unceasingly and exclusively engaged in the fabrication of one thing, he ultimately does his work with singular dexterity; but at the same time he loses the general faculty of applying his mind to the direction of the work. He every day becomes more adroit and less industrious; so that it may be said of him, that in proportion as the workman improves the man

---

1. Alexander Hamilton, "Report on Manufactures," in *The Reports of Alexander Hamilton*, ed. Jacob E. Cooke (New York: Harper Torchbook, 1964), pp. 128–129.

is degraded. What can be expected of a man who has spent twenty years of his life in making heads for pins? and to what can that mighty human intelligence, which has so often stirred the world, be applied in him, except that it be to investigate the best method of making pins' heads?[2]

Tocqueville also observed the beginnings of a new aristocracy in the United States. Unlike traditional aristocracies, it was not defined by territory and would not be bound by human relationships. In traditional aristocracies there was an obligatory relationship between rich and poor: the poor were expected to defend the rich and the rich were expected to protect the poor. They lived in the same place, knew each other, and were bound to each other by habit and duty. In the new aristocracy, the expectations rich and poor had of each other were limited to wages and labor. Outside the factory, they did not know each other. The new aristocracy did not govern or protect people; it only used them.

The new aristocracy was but a collection of individuals connected by economic interests. According to Tocqueville, they had "no feelings, or purposes in common, no mutual traditions or mutual hopes." Although he warned that the new aristocracy could become the mechanism whereby "permanent inequality of conditions" could "again penetrate into the world," he concluded that the aristocracy he described was one of the world's "least dangerous," though also "one of the harshest which ever existed. . . ."[3]

Tocqueville's analysis of the effects of industrialism was not unlike Karl Marx's (published ten years later) in that he foresaw the possibility of a working class growing ever larger and a class of owners growing ever smaller. Other analyses, however, described the human consequences in harsher terms, foresaw the possibility of social upheavals, and offered some form of socialism as a solution. One such analysis was that published in the 1840s by Parke Godwin, an advocate of Fourierism.

The Communal Societies

The social critic Parke Godwin argued that the philosophies of the American and the French revolutions could be realized only in a society organized in the communal pattern set down by Fourier. He believed that although the modern democratic revolutions had accomplished much, equality was still more an abstraction than an actuality. While privileged classes no longer had constitutional protection and status, he maintained that people were still governed by classes.[4] For Godwin, the problem lay in the country's lack of social and economic organization, not in its laws.

Godwin warned that the *laissez-faire* economic system, uncontrolled, was "anarchical." It lowered the workers' wages; promoted "an endless warfare between human arms, and machinery and capital"; created uncontrollable economic

---

2. Alexis de Tocqueville, *Democracy in America*, in *American Issues: The Social Record*, ed. Willard Thorp, Merle Curti, and Carlos Baker (New York: Lippincott, rev. ed., 1955), vol. 1, p. 406.

3. Ibid., p. 408.

4. Parke Godwin, *Democracy, Constructive and Pacific* (New York: J. Winchester, 1844), p. 10.

recessions and depressions; and was reducing the "middling and lower classes to a precarious and miserable existence."[5] "Human beings," said Godwin, "are not mere commodities, whose price auguments and diminishes with the supply in the market." Society owed its membership "a guaranty of life and work." Each person had a right to labor, for it was "the most sacred of all rights," and people also had a right to expect an opportunity to develop their moral and intellectual faculties, for God had "placed them on earth to advance."[6]

According to Godwin, neither political discussion nor political action could change the relationships between rich and poor: "Politics has never been thorough enough to touch the root of our social distress."[7] He wanted a reorganization of society in which each town would combine all its capital resources and issue shares to all according to their contributions. Members were to have access to the common funds even if they had not been able to contribute to the "fixed property" of the township. At the end of each year, the profits were to be divided among all members—men, women, children—according to how much they had worked and how difficult their work had been. Godwin suggested also that people might leave their individual dwellings and move into "a large building, or rather, in a row of buildings." Such structures could be arranged so that each family would have its privacy and still be able to have the economies of shared fires, light, cooking, and common cellars.

There were many attempts at communities in which sharing and cooperation were to take the place of competition and rigid status systems, although some such communities lasted longer than others. The community formed by Robert Dale Owen at New Harmony, Ind. was probably the most successful and long-lived of the attempts. Another well-known social experiment was the Transcendentalist community at Brook Farm, which attracted such members as Nathaniel Hawthorne and Charles A. Dana. Most Americans, however, did not choose such alternative communities. Many learned to adjust to the new system and even to defend it.

Godwin and others showed that American society was altering people's lives. Even Alexander Hamilton saw and admitted that factories changed the lives of people, although he viewed them as giving people a chance to make extra money. He noted that "in general, women and children are rendered more useful, and the latter more early useful by manufacturing establishments." In England, slightly over half those employed in the cotton mills were women and children, and many of the children, he reported, were "of a tender age."[8]

---

5. Ibid., p. 21.
6. Ibid., pp. 20–21.
7. Ibid., pp. 20, 25.
8. Alexander Hamilton, "Report on Manufactures," pp. 130–131.

Mills and Millworkers

When Francis Cabot Lowell visited England in 1810–12 and saw the squalor of the factory towns, he decided that his textile mills at Lowell, Mass., would be different. In some respects they were different. They were set in the country and care was taken to provide a suitable environment for the young women who came to work in them. Some efforts—classes, lectures—were made to give the workers leisure and education. Between 1842 and 1847, the women workers of the Lowell mills were allowed to publish the *Lowell Offering,* the first magazine published solely by women. One 1844 issue contained an article, "Factory Labor," in which there is a conversation between Miss S and Miss B about the advantages and disadvantages of working in the mills. Miss B, however, does not accept any of Miss S's objections to work and life in the factory. Miss S charges that the girls must work so many hours, but Miss B's answer that there is "abundant proof that unremitted toil is not always derogatory to improvement." According to Miss B,

> A factory girl's work is neither hard or complicated; she can go on with perfect regularity in her duties, while her mind may be actively employed on any other subject. There can be no better place for reflection, when there must be toil, than the factory.[9]

Miss B also reports that the "factory girls" made very good use of newspapers, periodicals, and the "well-worn" libraries. They also had opportunities to attend evening schools, churches, and "sabbath schools" where they could find improvement for both "mind and heart."

Davy Crockett on the Mills

Proponents of the factory system also found support from Davy Crockett who visited Lowell on a political tour in 1834, two years before his death at the Alamo. Crockett related that he wanted to visit the mills because he "wanted to see how it was that these northerners could buy [southern] cotton, and carry it home, manufacture it, bring it back, and sell it for half nothing." When he arrived at the mills, the workers were on their way to dinner, "pouring out of the houses like bees out of a gum." As they passed, Crockett observed them and found them "all well dressed, lively, and genteel in their appearance." They looked so fine that it seemed "they were coming from a quilting frolic."[10] During his visit to the factory, he found none of the girls "tired of her employment, or oppressed with work; all talked well and looked healthy."

> I could not help reflecting on the difference of conditions between these females, thus employed, and those of other populous countries, where the female character is degraded to abject slavery. Here were thousands, useful to others, and enjoying all the blessings of freedom with the prospect before

9. "Factory Labor," from *The Lowell Offering,* in Thorp, Curti, and Baker, *American Issues,* vol. 1, p. 411.

10. David Crockett, *An Account of Col. Crockett's Tour to the North and Down East* (Philadelphia: E. L. Carey and A. Hart, 1835), p. 91.

them of future comfort and respectability: and however we, who only hear of them, may call their houses workshops and prisons, I assure my neighbours there is every enjoyment of life realized by these persons, and there can be but few who are not happy.[11]

Lowell was, by Crockett's account, a perfect setting. It was built upon what had been a sheep pasture. What had been a small village became a prosperous town of 14,000, which had nine meeting-houses and free schools that served 1,200 students daily.

Herman Melville on the Mills

But all accounts of mill life were not so favorable. In the spring of 1855 Herman Melville published an attack on what the machine did to those who had to attend it. He described his visit to a paper mill that was located in a valley he named "Devil's Dungeon." What Melville saw was "rows of blank-looking counters" where there were "rows of blank-looking girls, with blank, white folders in their blank hands, all blankly folding blank paper." In the paper mill, the workers and the machines seemed to have taken each other's place: "The girls did not so much seem accessory wheels to the general machinery as mere cogs to the wheels."[12] In other parts of the factory, Melville found places where the workers were exposed to cutting machinery and a place where "the air swam with the fine, poisonous particles, which from all sides darted, subtilely, as motes in sunbeams, into the lungs."

At the end of his tour, the narrator of Melville's story asks his guide: "Why is it, sir, that in most factories, female operatives, of whatever age, are indiscriminately called girls, never women?" His guide fashions a quick and instructive reply:

> Oh! as to that—why, I suppose, the fact of their being generally unmarried —that's the reason, I should think. But it never struck me before. For our factory here, we will not have married women; they are apt to be off-and-on too much. We want none but steady workers: twelve hours to the day, day after day, through the three hundred and sixty-five days, excepting Sundays, Thanksgiving, and Fast-days. That's our rule. And so, having no married women, what females we have are rightly enough called girls.[13]

Schools for the New Society

Factory work changed the education of Americans by changing their homes. As men, women, and children spent more time away from home, their range of associations with others was wider and frequently different from what they would have found at home. Moreover, to change what people do for most of the day, how

---

11. Ibid., p. 92.

12. Herman Melville, "The Paradise of Bachelors and the Tartarus of Maids," in *Harper's New Monthly Magazine*, April, 1855, p. 675.

13. Ibid., p. 678.

they do it, and where they do it is to provide a new set of experiences by which they judge and interpret their world.

As Americans considered the establishment of public school systems, some argued that the school was a better place for children than factories. Some argued that all would be better workers and better citizens if they were schooled before entering the factories. Others claimed that the school would have to do what the family used to do. Some, like Catharine Beecher, suggested that men should take jobs in mills so that women could take jobs as teachers in the public schools.

Even before the War of 1812 the need for some schooling for the very poor was apparent to many. In New York, the Society to Promote Manumission was organized in 1785 to help alleviate the effects of slavery, protect the legal rights of blacks, and provide educational opportunity for poor black children. In 1787 the Society opened a school for blacks that received occasional aid from the city and the state. The Association of Women Friends for the Relief of the Poor opened a free school for the children of the poor in 1801. Such societies were philanthropic endeavors. "Free school" meant charity school. The parents of those who attended could not afford other alternatives.

The Monitorial System

In 1805 DeWitt Clinton, then mayor of New York, organized the New York Free School Society, to provide for the poor who were not receiving help from any of the religious societies in the city. Its first school, opened in 1806, was a monitorial school. This system was an import from England developed by two men who had been working independently of each other, Andrew Bell and Joseph Lancaster.

Andrew Bell was an Anglican clergyman who had stopped at Madras on his way to a new post in Calcutta, but was convinced to stay there as military chaplain and superintendent of the Military Male Orphan Asylum. Because the school had insufficient materials and too few teachers, Bell adopted practices from the local schools. In place of paper and pencils, for instance, he used sand tables for students to practice their writing. When the teachers of the Asylum objected, refused to use his methods, and eventually quit, he appointed some of the boys to supervise others and to serve as assistant teachers. In 1798, he published *An Experiment in Education, made at the Male Asylum at Madras, suggesting a System by which a School or Family may teach itself under the Superintendence of the Master or Parent*. Later, in 1807, he published *A Sketch of a National Institution for Training up the Children of the Poor in Moral and Religious Principles, and in Habits of Useful Industry*. By 1807 the Archbishop of Canterbury had become acquainted with Bell's system and aided its introduction into many schools in England. It offered a way to educate the poor, make them Christians, and make them productive, all with a minimum of expense.

In 1811, Bell charged another teacher, Joseph Lancaster, with stealing his ideas, thus giving both systems publicity. Lancaster was a Quaker who had opened his own school in the late 1700s. It was soon so successful and popular that he had more pupils than he could handle. Having no funds to hire teachers, he too re-invented the system of having the more accomplished pupils teach the less accomplished ones. Lancaster also found ways to compensate for the lack of books and other school supplies. In place of a book for each student he used large reading charts; in place of paper or copybooks he used slates that could be wiped clean and used repeatedly. Lancaster published an account of his system in 1803. Like other books of that era, its title tried to tell the entire story: *Improvements in Education as it respects the Industrious Classes of the Community, containing a Short Account of its Present State, Hints towards its Improvement, and a Detail of some Practical Experiments conducive to that End.*

At the end of his book, Lancaster related that he had recently seen Bell's work, found it useful, and wished he had known it earlier. Bell's charge of "piracy," as well as the religious differences between the two, served to publicize the monitorial methods in the press and the pulpit. The influence of the two was in fact divided. Bell's program was followed in Ireland and Canada, while Lancaster's work spread to Europe and to the United States.

Lancaster's system was precisely what organizers of charity schools needed: a way to school many with a minimum of expense for teachers and equipment, and with little knowledge of schoolkeeping. Lancaster offered detailed instructions. He advised his readers that it was important to keep children busy at all times; one way was to give each a special assignment. Accordingly, there were monitors for all sorts of functions: in charge of tuition, in charge of keeping order, in charge of cleanliness.

Lancaster also gave detailed descriptions of disciplinary methods. He explained that on occasion "boys are put in a sack, or in a basket, suspended to the roof of the school, in the sight of all the pupils, who frequently smile at the *birds in the cage.*"[14] The "cage" was infrequently used, for the mere mention of it usually produced the desired behavior from the pupils. There were a variety of other methods that could be used to maintain order, too. To encourage cleanliness among the pupils an elaborate form of punishment was devised:

> When a boy comes to school with dirty face or hands, and it seems to be more the effect of habit than of accident, a girl is appointed to wash his face in the sight of the whole school. This usually creates much diversion, especially when (as previously directed) she gives his cheeks a few *gentle strokes of correction* with her hand.[15]

For some offenses pupils had labels attached to them that told of their transgressions. For additional emphasis "a tin or paper crown" was placed upon the offender's head, and then the guilty one was led about by two classmates who

---

14. Joseph Lancaster, *Improvements in Education, as it Respects the Industrious Classes of the Community* (London, 1805) in *Education in the United States: A Documentary History*, ed. Sol Cohen (New York: Random House, 1974), vol. 2, p. 883.

15. Ibid., pp. 883–884.

announced his or her arrival and proclaimed the faults. Lancaster advised that such methods turned "the *public spirit* of the whole school against the culprit."

Both Bell and Lancaster, probably not deliberately, were following the methods of the factories. Proponents of the factory system in the early 1800s emphasized the efficiency achieved through carefully planned division of labor. Monitorial schools were similarly efficient in making the maximum use of people and materials. For example, Lancaster described a method "whereby one Book will Serve instead of Six Hundred Books."

> It will be remembered, that the usual mode of teaching requires every boy to have a book: yet, each boy can only read or spell one lesson at a time, in that book. Now, all the other parts of the book are in wear, and liable to be *thumbed* to pieces; and, whilst the boy is learning a lesson in one part of the book, the other parts are at that time useless. Whereas, if a spelling book contains twenty or thirty different lessons in that book, it would be equivalent to thirty books for its utility. To effect this, it is desirable that the whole of the book should be printed three times larger than the common size type, which would make it equal in size and cost to three common spelling books. . . . Its different parts should then be pasted on pasteboard, and suspended by a string, to a nail in the wall. . . .[16]

Advocates of Lancaster's monitorial system saw the possibility of classes of 300, 500, even 1,000 pupils. In 1818 DeWitt Clinton, then governor of New York, recommended the system to the state legislature in these words:

> Having participated in the first establishment of the Lancasterian system in this country, having carefully observed its progress, and witnessed its benefits, I can confidently recommend it as an invaluable improvement which by a wonderful combination of *economy in expense and rapidity of instruction* has created a new era in education; and I am desirous that all our common schools should be supplied with teachers of this description. As this system operates with the same efficacy in education that *labor-saving machinery* does in the useful arts, it will be readily perceived that it is peculiarly adapted to this country.[17]

Like most innovations in schooling, the Lancasterian method found many adherents, received generous praise, met with criticism, and finally fell into disuse. In 1828 the Boston School Committee received a report on its merits. The authors of the report were impressed by the great savings of time and money they found in the New York schools they had visited. They noted that only three schools and three teachers were needed to school more than 1,500 boys. In Boston there were at least seven schools and fifteen teachers for that many students. The ratio for girls' schools was not as large, but there was still a noticeable difference. In New York there was one woman teacher for 400 girls; in Boston there was one for every 56 pupils.

---

16. Ibid., p. 881.

17. *Messages from the [New York] Governors,* volume 2 in Edward A. Fitzpatrick, *The Educational Views and Influence of DeWitt Clinton* (New York: Teachers College, Columbia University, 1911), pp. 48–49.

Communities that did not have or thought they did not have sufficient capability to school all children saw in the method a way to school the poor. An editorial in an 1814 issue of the *Raleigh [N.C.] Register* endorsed the plans of the local Academy to adopt the system because "the children of all such parents in the city and neighborhood as are unable to pay their tuition, may be taught without additional expense."[18] When the system started in 1815, an editorial in the *Register* again noted that those whose parents were too poor to pay could attend without charge. Parents needed only to apply to a school trustee and receive an introduction to the school's treasurer. By this process, no one but the trustee and the treasurer would know which students had paid and which were "taught gratis."[19] The system removed the stigma of being a charity case, which frequently kept many out of school.

Advocates of Lancaster's system promised more than economical and efficient instruction in reading, writing, and arithmetic. And those who adopted it expected more. An advertisement in the *Western Carolinian* explained that Lancasterian schools were designed to "lessen the load of human misery; and to better the religious, moral, and social condition of society by teaching those who attend not only to read and write, etc. but what is infinitely of more moment, the fear of the Lord, veneration for his holy word—for the ordinances of the Lord's house, and a due observance of the Lord's day."[20] An advertisement for a Lancasterian manual that appeared in 1817 in Philadelphia emphasized not only the system's economy but also "its morality and the peculiar and happy fitness of all its details to the capacities and feelings of children."[21]

DeWitt Clinton, who continued as president of the New York Free School Society after he became governor, constantly argued for a concept of education that included more than the "three R's." In an 1809 address, he claimed that the Lancasterian system comprehended "knowledge of Holy Scriptures" as well as the three R's. Among the monitorial system's "peculiar improvements" over other educational systems were the opportunity it gave students to be active in the schoolroom and its attempt to foster "order and emulation."[22] Clinton also praised the system's method of enforcing discipline through "shame rather than by infliction of pain."

The Free School Society not only introduced the Lancasterian system in its schools, but advocated the spread of the system to other communities. It was soon

---

18. *Raleigh [North Carolina] Register,* April 1, 1814, in *Readings in Public Education in the United States,* ed. E. P. Cubberley (Boston: Houghton Mifflin, 1934), p. 140.

19. *Raleigh [North Carolina] Register,* March 17, 1815, in Cubberley, *Readings in Public Education,* p. 141.

20. *Western Carolinian,* November 8, 1822, in Cubberly, *Readings in Public Education,* pp. 139-140.

21. *Aurora General Advertiser,* August 21, 1817, in Cubberley, *Readings in Public Education,* p. 137.

22. DeWitt Clinton, "Address on the Opening of a New School Building" (December 11, 1809), in William Oland Bourne, *History of the Public School Society of the City of New York* (New York: Wm. Wood, 1870), p. 18.

extended to the city's female schools and to the schools of the Orphan Asylum and the Economical School. The tenth report of the Society (1815) records that Lancasterian schools had been organized in several communities: Philadelphia, Baltimore, Georgetown, Albany, Hartford, New Brunswick (N.J.), Flushing, and Burlington and Mount Holly (N.J.).

Although Clinton strongly endorsed the inexpensive monitorial system, he also tried for years to convince the state to support education. In his 1826 message to the legislature about education (a message that is Jeffersonian in both style and substance) he declared:

> The first duty of government and the surest evidence of good government is the encouragement of education. A general diffusion of knowledge is the precursor and protector of republican institutions, and in it we must confide as the conservative power of the state that will watch over our liberties and guard them against fraud, intrigue, corruption and violence.[23]

Earlier Clinton had declared that the "best bulwark" of free institutions was education. It promoted "the culture of the heart and the head." It included "piety and morality." Later, Clinton reminded the legislature that "the mind duly enlightened and the heart properly cultivated can never submit to dominion of anarchy and despotism." Like others before him, he was trying to ensure the success of republican government with education, concluding that "upon education we must therefore rely for the purity, the preservation and the perpetuation of republican government."[24]

The Demise of the Monitorial System

Although Clinton and others tried to spread the monitorial system and constantly extolled its virtues, it met with difficulties and criticisms. Its fatal weakness turned out to be its original strength, the monitors. A report of a committee in Philadelphia in 1826 noted that the Lancasterian schools would have to find better monitors if the system were to work effectively. Students were too much alike to be effective monitors: "the tender age, intimate association, sameness of pursuits and pastimes, and perfect equality *out of doors,* all unite to deprive these childish tutors of that influence and authority *in school* which is requisite for the maintenance of discipline, and a proper attention to the routine of instruction."[25]

The Philadelphia committee was echoing objections that had been raised earlier in Detroit. A writer for the *Detroit Gazette* described the Lancasterian system as "specious" and "pernicious," and posed a number of questions to show what the difficulties were:

> But what . . . can be hoped for from a system where the juvenile monitor is alone responsible for the good behavior and moral as well as scientific

23. *Messages from the [New York] Governors.* volume 3 in Fitzpatrick, *Educational Views and Influence of DeWitt Clinton,* p. 49.

24. Ibid., pp. 48–49.

25. "Annual Report of the Controllers of the Public Schools of the First District of the State of Pennsylvania, 1826" in Cubberley, *Readings in Public Education.* p. 142.

advancement of his little school-fellows, who are also his pupils and playfellows? Can advice, reproof, or instruction, come with proper effect from those who practice all the wild extravagancies which they affect to condemn in others? It can surely be little else than 'hide my faults and I'll hide yours,' amongst these ephemeral teachers.[26]

For the Detroit writer, the solution was a return to the "good old system." For the Philadelphia committee, the answer was a better monitor. They recommended that older pupils, those who were at least age fifteen, be persuaded to become monitors. The committee recommended that these students be offered three-year appointments, given an opportunity to enroll in the high school while serving as monitors, and be furnished "with a suit of clothes or a moderate sum of money per annum." Older monitors would, the committee advised, "hold a standing detached from and superior to the mass of the pupils." That social distance would give the older monitors "a superior degree of authority" over the smaller and younger pupils.

The Philadelphia committee's solution was tantamount to the first step in the dissolution of the system. The monitors were to become a kind of assistant teacher, moving closer to the teacher in status. In earlier times they might have been called "ushers." Later they would be called "teacher aides." A few other modifications—dividing the large class into smaller classes with a monitor for each group, assigning spaces for each group—would produce the beginnings of an elementary school similar to those of today.

The student-monitors' inability to maintain discipline was not the only shortcoming of the Lancasterian system. As long as the monitors were drawn from the class, severe limitations were placed on what could be taught to students, how it could be taught, and how quickly students could progress in their work. Frequently, the monitor was only able to determine whether students made exact copies of what was on the reading chart or their own slate. Variations became errors.

Where the monitorial system did work as designed, close interaction between teacher and student was severely limited, if not completely eliminated. But from colonial times on, Americans had expected teachers to attend personally to their charges. In nearly every period of Western civilization, in fact, teachers have been expected to be models for students to imitate. The monitorial system was not designed to meet such expectations.

Infant Schools

Another form of schooling that Americans imported from England during the early 1800s was the infant school, the invention of Robert Owen. Owen was a self-educated, reform-minded mill owner in New Lanark, Scotland, and is generally

---

26. *Detroit Gazette*, November 23, 1821 and February 15, 1822, in Cohen, *Education in the United States*, p. 989.

considered the founder of English socialism. Aware of the problems created by the factory system, he fashioned plans to create a classless society. (Owen later began the utopian community at New Harmony, Ind.) In 1809 he began a school for boys and girls between the ages of six and twelve. In 1816 he opened a school for those under six, the first infant school. He began with a class of about a hundred workers' children. In charge of his school was one male teacher assisted by a seventeen-year-old female teacher.

Owen's school came to the attention of Samuel Wilderspin, a schoolmaster, who borrowed and modified its plan. The purpose of Owen's school was not to teach traditional school subjects, but to look after the development of the young children and their characters. Accordingly, children were taught to be neat and clean, to respect each other, and to develop a sense of order through dancing and military drills. Wilderspin turned Owen's plan inside out. He sought to teach the "infants" the rudiments of reading and arithmetic, bits of geography, history, natural science, and how to memorize parts of the Bible.

While Americans knew about both Owen and Wilderspin, they generally copied Wilderspin's schools, which appeared to be an easy way to teach children at least the rudiments of literacy before they began to work. Most infant school societies were formed as charitable undertakings, although in 1818 Boston appropriated funds to start infant schools as part of its school system. Between 1827 and 1828 three infant school societies were founded in Philadelphia. In 1828 the New York Free School Society assumed responsibility for one that had been opened a year earlier. In 1853, when the New York Board of Education assumed responsibility for the schools of the New York Free School Society, there were more than fifty infant schools under the Society's direction.

A report of the New York Free School Society suggests that the infant school filled the same needs as modern day care centers. Children were "allowed to come early in the morning, and to remain till near dark, bring their dinners with them, or to attend during the usual school hours only." The Society viewed the infant school as a place where children of the poor could spend the day in comfort and receive some "instruction" and some "amusement." It was an alternative to having the children spend their days "wandering the streets" where they would be "exposed to the contamination of vice."[27]

Like most innovations, the infant school aroused controversy. In 1829 William Russell addressed the Boston Infant School Society about the European infant schools that he had seen while traveling. Russell found that "intellectual instruction" was limited to "a few simple but useful and interesting elements." Children were taught a little arithmetic, some reading and spelling, and even more about natural objects and familiar household items. The noteworthy feature of the infant school, said Russell, was "the excellence of its moral instruction."[28]

---

27. Bourne, *History of the Public School Society of the City of New York*, p. 660.
28. William Russell, "An Address on Infant Schools" (Boston, 1829), in Cubberley, *Readings in Public Education*, p. 143.

Many proponents of the infant school viewed children not as passive agents who were to have moral precepts impressed upon them, but as active participants in the school community. According to Russell, the primary method of the school was "the personal influence of the teacher," who sought to maintain a "cheerful" setting for the children and then relied upon their natural tendency to imitate. Although the infant school appeared to pay only "incidental" attention to the development of the intellect, the result was to "inspire it with a healthy and natural vigour." Children were "advanced as a living whole."[29]

A few years later, however, the Boston Infant School Society reported that the enthusiasm for the infant school was waning. Many infant schools, it said, had been "misemployed" and "in some instances perverted." Infant schools were not to be machines for filling small intellects with "the words and thoughts of others" and for converting little children into "prodigies in mere intellect."[30] They were mainly to provide the care that some parents could not give their children.

Infant schools had been introduced when many were already pressing for the establishment of tax-supported public schools, and these advocates wanted more emphasis on "intellect" than the infant school was designed to provide. It is doubtful whether the charitable societies that supported many infant schools could have provided enough of them to meet the growing demand for schools.

The Sunday School

Another form of schooling imported from England was the Sunday School. Robert Raikes, a Gloucester printer, is usually considered its founder. In 1780, wishing to do something for the poor children in his community, Raikes hired four women to teach them to read and to recite their catechism. He chose Sunday because it was the only day the children were not otherwise occupied. Raikes printed a description of his charitable work in a pamphlet, and others followed his example. In 1785 the Society for Promoting Sunday Schools throughout the British Dominion was formed to promote the new form of schooling. In 1786 a Sunday School was opened in Hanover County, Va. The next year, a Sunday School for blacks was opened in Charleston, S.C. In 1791 the Society of Friends founded a First-Day School in Philadelphia. After the War of 1812, many Sunday Schools appeared along the eastern seaboard. By 1824 there were enough local Sunday School societies to make possible the formation of a national society, the American Sunday School Union.

The first Sunday Schools typically were nondenominational in their instruction. By the 1820s, however, especially in the densely populated areas where other forms of schooling were becoming available, most Sunday Schools were conduct-

---

29. Ibid., pp. 143–144.
    30. *Report of the Boston Infant School Society* (1833). in Cubberley, *Readings in Public Education*. p. 145.

ed by churches and were assuming their present denominational form. As Americans moved westward, the Sunday School frequently followed close behind. In many places, the Sunday School was the only school, and few people objected to their children's learning to read from the Bible. In 1831 the American Sunday School Union held a meeting in Washington, D.C., to consider providing Sunday Schools for the Mississippi Valley. A report of the meeting in the *American Annals of Education* indicates that the Union's purpose was to promote "Bible education." Those who attended the meeting—including several congressmen—seemed to agree that "Bible education" was a good way to promote "national improvement and happiness" among the people.[31] The Sunday School movement did aid the development of the common schools, and many people who were active in the Sunday School movement were also active in the movement to establish publicly supported weekday schools.[32]

Sunday schools, infant schools, monitorial schools, and other charitable efforts did not satisfy either the needs or the aspirations of Americans. They wanted more. In retrospect it can be seen that Americans were indeed rejecting what they viewed as the two-track European school systems. They were not willing to accept a clear division between rich and poor. They did not want charity schools for the poor and private schools for the wealthy. The lives of Americans were being transformed by the growth of the country, the growth of industrialism, the development of urban centers, the westward movement of the frontier, and the arrival of many immigrants. As people's life conditions changed, they called for changes also in their institutions, arguing that new social roles and rights be sanctioned. Proponents of tax-supported schools campaigned for their cause at the same time workers' organizations made their desires known. Before the Civil War, nearly all American institutions became the objects of reform.

31. In Edgar W. Knight and Clifton B. Hall, eds., *Readings in American Educational History* (New York·.Appleton-Century-Crofts, 1951), p. 151.

32. William Bean Kennedy, *The Shaping of Protestant Education* (New York: Association Press, 1966), p. 25.

Women's Call for Educational Reform 7

The Colonial Background

Historically, there has been a two-track system of education, one for men and another for women. Formal schooling, until recently, has not always been part of the women's track. At times, the two tracks have been comparable; at others, they have been very different. The repeated use of the term "co-education" is evidence that when the two tracks have been combined, many still assume the existence of both.

The situation in the seventeenth-century American colonies reflected the colonists' backgrounds. As in Europe at the time, female children did not enjoy the same access to schools as did males. The first schools in New England were grammar schools, which were preparatory schools for the college, where young men would be trained for the ministry or service to the state, careers that were not open to women. Girls did attend the same schools and even the writing schools in New England. There they learned to count and how to read the *Primer.* By the late 1700s, girls were sometimes allowed to attend early-morning sessions at the town schools before the arrival of the boys. New York and Pennsylvania may have paid more attention to the schooling of girls in the first years of settlement than New England did, but girls still were not thought to need much more than rudimentary literacy. The domestic skills they needed, many believed, could be learned easily enough at home.

As the colonies grew and prospered in the eighteenth century, educational entrepreneurs opened private schools to teach subjects not available in the grammar schools to the children of affluent families. After about 1750, young women could receive private instruction in academic subjects as well as in music, dance, and needlework. By the end of the 1700s, some of the educational theorists of the early republic, such as Rush and Webster, began to address themselves to the question of the education of women.

Typically they endorsed a two-track system, with the sole aim of helping women become better wives and mothers. Most who did work in behalf of increasing educational opportunity for women clearly saw that the issue had ramifications for the values of the whole society. The ideas of democracy and individual rights put forth in the American and French revolutions encouraged the English writer Mary Wollstonecraft to challenge the patriarchal organization of school and society and the segregation of the sexes in schools.

Mary Wollstonecraft

Mary Wollstonecraft was an active participant in that international eighteenth-century group that writer Peter Gay described as "a loose, wholly unorganized coalition of cultural critics, religious skeptics, and political reformers." Her circle of friends and acquaintances included the Americans Tom Paine, Joel Barlow, and Gilbert Imlay. Her first political work, *A Vindication of the Rights of Men* (1790), was a rebuttal of Edmund Burke's attack on the French Revolution (*Reflections on the Revolution in France*). Soon she realized, however, that the new political theories were not designed to change the situation of women. The plan for a national system of education that Tallyrand submitted to the National Assembly in September, 1791, was a plan for the education of boys; it excluded girls. The "rights of man" were for men, not for mankind. She then turned her efforts to *A Vindication of the Rights of Women,* raising arguments that still have currency.

Wollstonecraft refused to accept that the sole purpose of women was to serve and satisfy men. She argued that mind, not gender, was the defining characteristic of humanity. As long as society continued to deprive women of their civil, political, and economic rights, it was squandering half its assets and depriving women of their right to be free moral agents. She likened the relationship between the two sexes to that of master and slave, and pointed out that it was degrading for both.

Educational Reform and Beyond

To remedy the untenable and unjust relationship between the sexes, Wollstonecraft proposed a new system of education. By twentieth-century standards it was not a radical proposal: she wanted national day schools where boys and girls between the ages of 5 and 9 would be schooled together. The schools were to be supported by the government, not by parents. Higher standards could be enforced in governmentally-supported schools; if the schools were supported by the parents, the schoolmaster would only have to satisfy them. Too often parents were too ignorant to demand what was necessary for their children.

In the elementary schools all children were to be treated alike, dressed alike, and expected to comply with the discipline set down by the school. Those who did not want to comply were to leave. The school was to be on "a large piece of ground" so there would be sufficient room for the children's necessary physical activity. Seatwork for more than an hour at a time was inappropriate. Children were to learn botany, mechanics, astronomy, reading, writing, arithmetic, natural history, and science, but learning these subjects was not to "encroach on gymnastic plays in the open air." The academic subjects should not be "dryly laid down" but "introduced as a kind of show."[1] Through "conversations in the Socratic form," children were to learn religion, history, and politics.

After elementary school, students were to be separated according to ability and aims. Those who were "intended for domestic employments or mechanical trades" would go to appropriate places for their vocational training in the afternoons. In the mornings, they were all to continue their education together. Students with exceptional abilities or with sufficient funds, whether they were male or female, were to continue their study of history and politics and begin the study of "their dead and living languages and the elements of science."[2]

Wollstonecraft wanted to put an end to "gallantry and coquetry." In their place she wanted "friendship and love." She asserted that if her plan were adopted "the constitution of boys would not be ruined by the early debaucheries, which now make men so selfish" and the girls would not be "rendered weak and vain, by indolence, and frivolous pursuits." Recognizing that many parents would object to her notions, she said that all there was to fear was that "some early attachment might take place" among some boys and girls.[3]

In the *Vindication of the Rights of Women,* Wollstonecraft was arguing for more than educational reform. She wanted a society in which intellectual and professional accomplishments, values, and political and civil rights would have no relationship to sex. Women would have the opportunity to enter the professions, politics, and business, and their rights and responsibilities would not be determined by their marital status.

Although Mary Wollstonecraft's *Vindication* was read in the United States, her arguments and the cause of rights and education for women did not become a popular issue immediately. Nor did any American women become active reformers at that time. Popularization of the arguments for the rights of women was still a generation away.

Frances Wright

Frances Wright was born in Scotland three years after the appearance of Wollstonecraft's *Vindication.* Having inherited a considerable fortune of her own, she

---

1. Mary Wollstonecraft, *A Vindication of the Rights of Women* in Edgar W. Knight and Clifton B. Hall (eds.), *Readings in American Educational History* (New York: Appleton-Century Crofts, Inc. 1951), p. 704.

2. *Ibid.,* pp. 704–705.

3. *Ibid.,* p. 705.

was able to travel as she wished. Wright became acquainted with the philosophical radicals Jeremy Bentham and James Mill, and with many other prominent English, American, and European liberal political thinkers. After her first trip to America, she published her *Views of Society and Manners in America* (1821), depicting the new nation as a society with political and social ideas and institutions shaped by reason. Her second tour of the United States, with the Marquis de Lafayette, brought meetings with Jefferson, Madison, John Quincy Adams, and Andrew Jackson, and interested her in the problem of slavery and in experiments in communal living. She decided that many slaveowners wanted to disassemble the slave system but did not know how to go about it.

Her own experimental community, in Nashoba, Tennessee, was designed to prepare slaves for freedom and eventual colonization abroad, but it failed in 1830. She became interested in Robert Owen's colony at New Harmony, Ind., and bought an interest in Owen's journal. Under the name of the *Free Enquirer,* she used it and the lecture platform to spread her ideas of wide-ranging social reform. For a woman to give lectures in public was considered both radical and scandalous. What she had to say was even more scandalous to many. She attacked the work of religious groups, objected to the missionary societies and the growth of religious revivals, and to the attempts of the churches to influence American politics. She waged a campaign against debtor's prisons and capital punishment. She took up the cause of the workingman, claiming that his labors were the source of wealth and that he did not receive his fair share of that wealth. She argued for the emancipation of women, insisting that they needed equal educational opportunities so that they could be truly equal to men. At the foundation of all her reform ideas was the need for radical changes in education.

"Children of a Common Family"

Wright noted "the noble example of New-England" in establishing common schools. She added, however, that the common school was not the answer to America's needs; its purpose was limited to teaching reading and writing, some arithmetic and a bit of science. Even if its purpose were expanded to include "all the branches of intellectual knowledge," it would still not be equal to the task at hand. Building schools, she said, was like building churches: "When you have them, you need some measure to ensure their being occupied." Her observations of social conditions in American cities led her to conclude that it would be difficult to fill additional schools. The typical family needed "the united efforts of all its members" in order to earn enough money for food, clothing, and shelter. Children could not enroll in the common school and still have time to learn "the trade necessary to their future subsistence."[4]

To solve social problems and to build a strong and unified nation Wright urged a program of euthenics, a program that would completely control every detail of

---

4. Frances Wright, *Course of Popular Lectures* (London: James Watson), p. 113.

the environment of all children. She suggested that people direct their state legislatures to replace all schools and all institutions that looked after children with "establishments for the general reception of all children."

In these nurseries of a free nation, no inequality must be allowed to enter. Fed at a common board; clothed in a common garb, uniting neatness with simplicity and convenience; raised in the exercise of common duties, in the acquirement of the same knowledge and practice of the same industry, varied only according to individual taste and capabilities; in the exercise of the same virtues, in the enjoyment of the same pleasures; in the study of the same nature; in pursuit of the same object—their own and each other's happiness—say! Would not such a race, when arrived at manhood and womanhood, work out the reform of society—perfect the free institutions of America.[5]

All students live in a national institution as "children of a common family" and learning to be "citizens of a common country." Parents were to be allowed to visit the children at "suitable hours," but they were not to "interfere with or interrupt the rules of the institution."[6]

Two kinds of taxes were to support the residential schools. The first was to be a tax on parents of children aged 2 to 12. In levying the parental tax, proper attention was to be paid "to the varying strength of the two sexes, and to the undue depreciation which now rests on female labour."[7] Parents were to be allowed to pay their tax in money, produce, goods, or labor. Wright believed that the parental tax would also cause young people to consider their "fitness" before assuming the responsibilities of parenthood. The second tax was a progressive property tax. The rich would thereby contribute to the relief of the poor and help to strengthen the country by producing "an enlightened and united generation."

Wright's reform measures offered a good society in which all would be truly equal. The price was total state control over the education of all children. This idea was unacceptable. Wright did present a problem that could not be set aside. Industrialism had taken hold in America; she helped convince Americans that there was a relationship between education and the social problems presented by industrialism. It became apparent that neither individuals nor charitable organizations could handle all the needs of the growing, changing society, and more people agreed that the state had an obligation to provide education for all children. Some agreed that the state had a right to insist that all children be sent to school. Wright's plan for full state responsibility, however, was simply too radical for Americans. Although she offered it as a way to achieve true equality for all classes and both sexes, it would have changed the basic structure of the American family. Americans have never been willing to surrender formally—to the state or the schools—their right and responsibility to raise and nurture their own children.

---

5. *Ibid.*, p. 116
6. *Ibid.*, p. 114.
7. *Ibid.*, p. 115.

Emma Hart Willard

By the early 1800s, more American women had begun to speak out for social changes and reforms. Many saw education as crucial to change. Emma Hart Willard was one of the most successful and influential proponents of education for women in the early nineteenth century. She was also an effective worker for the improvement of the common schools and for better salaries for teachers. Born in 1787, Willard attended the local district school and the Berlin (Conn.) Academy, and at 16, began to teach in the village school. While teaching, she continued her own education at private schools in Hartford. In 1807 she took charge of the Female Academy at Middlebury, Vt.; she married in 1809 and her husband's nephew, a student at Middlebury college, lived with the Willards. From him she learned about the courses that women were never offered, borrowed his books, and embarked on a course of study of her own. She began with geometry and then went on to study Paley's *Moral Philosophy* and Locke's *Essay Concerning Moral Understanding*. In 1814 she opened a school for girls, teaching them geometry and philosophy instead of sewing, dancing, music, and decorative arts. Her students' success convinced her that young women could study mathematics and philosophy without injury to their health, charm, or womanhood.

Willard's successful experiment inspired her to look for a way to provide improved educational opportunity for women. In 1818 she submitted a "Plan for Improving Female Education" to New York's governor, DeWitt Clinton, asking for funds for the founding of schools for women. Her plan was not to give women the same education as men, but to provide an opportunity for higher education appropriate to them. She also tried to show how the state would benefit from properly educated women. Clinton liked the plan, but the legislature voted it down.

Willard had moved her school to Waterford, New York, and secured a charter from the state legislature, but no financial help. The refusals embittered her toward politicians, but they did not dissuade her from her purpose. In 1821 she moved her school to Troy, New York, where she had been offered land and buildings. As principal of the school, 1821–28, she built a program that did indeed provide higher education for women. She established a self-perpetuating board of trustees for the school to ensure its continuation, and supported it with royalties from the several texts she wrote.

Willard's success was due to her own pedagogical abilities and her remarkable ability to combine traditional and newer concepts of education. Many people believed it unnecessary and perhaps even frivolous to send women to a secondary school. Willard, however, argued that she was not trying to give women a man's education, but to enable them to be better mothers and to know the theory of housewifery rather than mere practice.

The curriculum at the Troy Seminary was not, however, an elaboration of the household arts. At a time when women were not supposed to be exposed to the human body and its workings, Willard introduced the study of physiology. Some visitors to her school left classrooms rather than watch a lesson in which a student drew the circulatory system on the chalkboard. Bowing to contemporary sensibilities, Willard pasted heavy paper over the pages of the text that depicted the human body so that the girls' modesty might be preserved. Students at Troy also studied history, geography, mathematics, and chemistry, and had opportunities to work in a chemistry laboratory. Willard believed mathematics increased the mind's intellectual power and she was certainly one of the first, if not the first, to teach higher mathematics to female students. At both Waterford and Troy, she studied topics in mathematics herself, taught the class until one of its members could take it over, and then introduced a new mathematical topic.

Training Women as Teachers

The higher education for women at the Troy Female Seminary may not have been equivalent to the courses in men's colleges, but it came close. Willard saw her school also as a school for the training of teachers, and it gave better training than many other schools of the era. She saw in the growth of the common school an opportunity for her graduates, and, like many others, felt that women were better equipped by nature than men to be teachers. She also noted that the public would not have to pay women as much as men. She wrote:

> That nature designed our sex for the care of children, she has made manifest, by mental as well as physical indications. She has given us, in a greater degree than men, the gentle arts of insinuation, to soften their minds, and fit them to receive impressions; a greater quickness of invention to vary modes of teaching to different dispositions; and more patience to make repeated efforts. There are many females of ability, to whom the business of instructing children is highly acceptable; and who would devote all their faculties to their occupation. . . . If then women were properly fitted by instruction, they would be likely to teach children better than the other sex; they could afford to do it cheaper; and those men who would otherwise be engaged in this employment, might be at liberty to add to the wealth of the nation, by any of those thousand occupations, from which women are necessarily debarred.[8]

Proposing to educate women so they could be hired to teach for less money than was paid to men was not an uncommon suggestion. For Willard's purposes, it was shrewd. Women, especially married women, had few or no rights, and teaching would give them some income and independence. Her plan also made good economic and demographic sense. Northeastern states were losing their men to the frontier. Willard's proposal would release the men from the schoolhouse and allow them to work at other jobs. While attempts were being made to improve and expand the schools, opponents of educational expansion argued that it was too costly. With lower-paid women teachers, more students could be schooled for the same expenditure.

The view that women were intellectually and physically inferior, though moral-

8. Emma Hart Willard, *An Address to the Public; Particularly to the Members of the Legislature of New York, Proposing a Plan for Improving Female Education* in Sol Cohen (ed.), *Education in the United States: A Documentary History* (New York: Random House, 1974), Vol. III, p. 1580.

ly and aesthetically superior, did not give way completely, but it was adjusted enough to allow women to become schoolteachers. As the years passed, women were hired in larger numbers. In 1843 Horace Mann reported that, in a five-year period ending in 1842, there was an increase of 691 women teachers in the Massachusetts schools compared with an increase of only 131 males. (The women were paid nearly $13 a month; the men were paid a little over $32.)[9]

When Catharine Esther Beecher wrote *The Evils Suffered by American Women and American Children* in 1846, she suggested that the roles of many men and many women could easily be reversed. Men could take the places of the women in the factories and the women could take the places of the men in the schools. She asked: "Now without expressing any opinion to the influence, on health and morals, of taking women away from domestic habits and pursuits, to labor with men in ships and mills, I simply ask if it would not be *better* to put the thousands of men who are keeping school for young children into the mills, and employ the women to train the children?" Beecher observed that schools fared better when they were under the direction of women. She reported that "in Massachusetts, where education is the highest, five out of seven of the teachers are women; while in Kentucky, where education is so much lower, five out of six of the teachers are men."[10] At mid-century Sara Josepha Hale, the editor of *Godey's Lady's Book,* told her readers that women could afford to take jobs as teachers for half, and sometimes even less than half, what men had to be paid. By the end of the nineteenth century most teachers were women; in fact, they outnumbered men by nearly two to one. The 1896–97 *Report of the United States Commissioner of Education* showed that there were 271,947 women teachers in the nation's public schools and only 131,386 men teachers.

Although Willard's proposals were to a degree compatible with the prejudices and misconceptions of her day, she was nonetheless trying to change how society treated and molded women. She complained that society had not set down a systematic set of principles for how women were educated, but left it to "chance and confusion." Even the rich, who could afford to educate their daughters properly, allowed them to play while their sons were prepared for a useful future. Willard asked: "When the youth of the two sexes has been spent so differently, is it strange, or is nature in fault, if more mature age has brought such a difference of character that our sex have been considered by the other as the pampered wayward babies of society, who must have some rattle put into our hands to keep us from doing mischief to ourself or others?"[11] Patterns of differential treatment also existed among less affluent families. Sons were allowed to attend school

---

9. Robert E. Potter, *The Stream of American Education* (New York: American Book Co., 1967), p. 238.

10. Catharine Esther Beecher, *The Evils Suffered by American Women and American Culture: The Causes and the Remedy* in Robert H. Bremner, *et. al.* (eds.) *Children and Youth in America: A Documentary History* (Cambridge, Mass.: Harvard University Press, 1970), Vol. I, p. 482.

11. Emma Willard, *A Plan for Improving Female Education* (1819), in Bremner (ed.), *Children and Youth in America,* Vol. I, p. 511.

while daughters remained behind to help at home or worked to contribute to their brothers' education. The educated young men too frequently looked down upon their sisters as "rustic innocents" or drudges. That, wrote Willard, was not as "pernicious" as what happened to the girls from the rich families but it was "pathetically unjust."[12]

Willard's account of how women sacrificed to support the education of men was not an unusual story. One woman who had worked in the Lowell mills since age ten recalled:

> The most prevailing incentive to labor was to secure the means of education for some *male* member of the family. To make a *gentleman* of a brother or a son, to give him a college education, was the dominant thought in the minds of a great many of the better class of mill-girls. I have known more than one to give every cent of her wages, month after month, to her brother, that he might get the education necessary to enter some profession.[13]

Some men who were educated at the expense of women "sometimes acquired just enough learning to make them look down upon the social position in which their women friends and relatives were forced to remain." Frequently, the woman's only reward was "to be the *mother* or *sister* of somebody."[14]

Willard's Achievements
By the 1870s—some fifty years later after the school opened—more than 13,000 students had enrolled in the Troy Academy. Graduates were presented with signed certificates that testified to their ability to teach. Many took Willard's advice and their certificates and found jobs as teachers in the South and on the frontier. When Willard left the principalship in 1838, she continued to work for the expansion and improvement of education for women. In 1837 she formed an alumnae organization and in 1839 presented her "Letter to the Willard Association for the Mutual Improvement of Female Teachers" in which she argued for better salaries for women teachers. In the 1840s she worked for improved common schools, joining Henry Barnard in Connecticut, visiting schools, and giving model lessons in mathematics and geography.

At the time of her death in 1870, her work had earned her a national and international reputation.

Mary Lyon and the First Women's College
Mary Lyon's early life followed much the same pattern as Emma Willard's, a pattern typical of women of their economic position and background. Born in Buckland, Mass., in 1797, she attended rural district schools and began teaching while still in her teens. While teaching, she continued her own education, attending

---

12. *Ibid.*

13. Harriet H. Robinson in the *Fourteenth Annual Report of the Massachusetts Bureau of Statistics of Labor* (1883) in Miriam Schneir (ed.), *Feminism: The Essential Historical Writings* (New York: Random House, 1972), p. 54.

14. *Ibid.*

both the Sanderson Academy and the Amherst Academy. At 24, an age when most people thought that schooling should be over, she went to the seminary at Byfield, Mass., where the director, Rev. Joseph Emenson, had a reputation for advocating women's education. There she developed an enthusiasm for Christian social service. After she left Byfield, Lyon returned to the pattern of studying and teaching at the same time.

The Adams Academy in New Hampshire, where Lyon taught in the summer, was conducted by Zilpah Grant (later Banister) who had been one of the teachers at Byfield. When she opened a school for girls at Ipswich in 1828, Lyon agreed to teach there during the summer months. In 1830 she was made vice-principal of Grant's school. Grant was unable to secure an endowment to ensure the continuation of her school at Ipswich, and so Mary Lyon decided to establish a school of her own. She envisioned a school of collegiate grade that would be good enough to attract the daughters of the wealthy *and* economical enough to allow those of moderate means to enroll. Determined to secure sufficient funds and pledges to insure the permanence of the school, she quickly raised a thousand dollars, a fourth of which came from her former students, many of whom had become teachers. The balance was solicited from the women in and about Ipswich. Initially, she believed that the local ministers and businessmen who had agreed to serve as the school's trustees would raise the $27,000 needed to construct the school's first building, but the sluggish economy that was to bring about the economic "panic" of 1837 hindered fund-raising. So from 1834 to 1837 Lyon toured the countryside seeking donations for her school. It was certainly not customary for a woman of that era to solicit funds door-to-door. At the same time, however, the Grimké sisters were traveling about Massachusetts seeking support for the abolition movement and women's rights. Mary Lyon raised the needed $27,000, and in 1836 secured a charter for Mount Holyoke College. The next year the new college accepted its first students.

To ensure that young women of moderate means could afford to attend Mount Holyoke, Lyon kept the school's operating costs as low as possible. Each student had to share in household duties, but they were not taught. Teaching housework was not, for Lyon, the function of a college. Holyoke's three-year curriculum was patterned after that of Amherst College. To emphasize that the school was of collegiate grade, she did not include a preparatory department; she also insisted on entrance examinations.

Although the press ridiculed Mount Holyoke in its early years, sometimes referring to it as a "Protestant nunnery," the school was successful. It was the first college for women to open with property, buildings, a library, a laboratory, and equipment that had been specifically pledged and designated for women's education. The curriculum included English, Latin, mathematics, philosophy, and science, and was soon expanded to include music and modern languages. The regular faculty of Mount Holyoke were women, but members of the faculties at nearby Amherst College and Williams College frequently came to lecture.

The *Catalogue* for the 1837–38 school year instructed that the beginning student was required to have "an acquaintance with general principles of English Grammar, a good knowledge of Modern Geography, History of the United States, Watts on the Mind, Colburn's First Lessons, and the *whole* of Adam's New Arithmetic, or what would be equivalent in Written Arithmetic."[15] The 1848–49 *Catalogue* emphasized that no student would be allowed to enter the Junior Class (the first class) "without passing a good examination on all the *preparatory studies,* whatever may be their attainments in other branches." At this time the entrance requirements were spelled out in greater detail than they were earlier. For some it was possible to enter without having met requirements in Latin and Ancient Geography; these students were to spend two years in the Junior Class "to make up the deficiency."

Lyon's enthusiasm for Christian social service became an evangelical commitment that she tried to share with her students. Mount Holyoke was sometimes thought of as a seminary for the preparation of missionaries. She instituted a yearly Pentecost, when those who believed that they had properly embraced the Christian faith were to convince others to do likewise. She also delivered daily sermons, a not unusual practice by the standards of the day. Before her death in 1849, she grew increasingly concerned with the spread of Christianity. She canvassed her faculty, her students, and the community for funds to aid missionaries and frequently brought missionaries to campus to talk to the students.

Although Lyon's concern with the spread of Christianity colored the perception many had of Mount Holyoke in its early years, her school was the first true college for women in the United States. (The Georgia Female College at Macon was also chartered in 1836, but it did not open until 1839.) By insisting on strict entrance requirements, a rigorous curriculum, a three-year course (rather than the usual two), and a board of trustees, she built the college to endure. Mount Holyoke students did not receive merely a smattering of many subjects, and the school's academic prestige grew.

Making higher education available to women, however, did not offer a solution for women who were not academically oriented or not able to afford such an education. These women were the concern of other kinds of reform ideas.

Catharine Beecher

Catharine Esther Beecher was the eldest of the numerous talented children of the revivalist clergyman Lyman Beecher. Although she was given the usual education for young women of her background—drawing, music, painting—the intellectual atmosphere of the family also allowed her to learn Latin, philosophy, and mathematics on her own. When her fiance, a Yale mathematics professor, was lost in a shipwreck, she took it as a sign of a change of direction in her life and thereafter

---

15. In Beth Bradford Gilchrist, *The Life of Mary Lyon* (Boston: Houghton Mifflin Co., 1910), p. 437.

worked to improve the lot of young women. Although she did not seek to change women's role, she worked to convince society that the role was an important one and deserved a higher status than it had. She also felt that women needed better opportunities to prepare themselves properly for their roles.

In 1824 she opened a private girls' school in Hartford, Connecticut. Like Emma Willard in Troy, Beecher offered young women a chance to study something more than the mere basics of schooling. In her school, students learned to write from Catharine Beecher herself and her sister Harriet (later the author of *Uncle Tom's Cabin*). The school gained a reputation for its sound curriculum and good teaching. When Lyman Beecher was invited to Cincinnati to assume the presidency of the Lane Theological Seminary in 1832, however, she gave up her interest in the school to accompany him. In Cincinnati she organized another school, the Western Female Institute, along the lines of the school in Hartford, but poor health and the financial crisis of 1837 caused her to give it up.

Beecher continued her work in other ways. In some ways, she was more like a revivalist preacher than a teacher, carrying her message from place to place, publishing books and articles, and lending her efforts to a number of causes and organizations. In Boston she aided in the organization of the Ladies' Society for Promoting Education in the West. After she moved to Cincinnati (then thought of as the West) she continued to urge the young women of the East to take teaching posts in the West and the South. She helped to open schools for women in Burlington, Iowa, Quincy, Ill., and Milwaukee, Wisc.

Although she worked to promote increased educational opportunity and higher status for women, Catharine Beecher did not challenge the traditional roles assigned to women. She repeatedly emphasized that women were particularly suited to be teachers, nurses, and mothers. Those were important roles, she said, and tried to show how they could be performed with dignity, efficiency, joy, intelligence, and success.

The titles of some of her books illustrate her concerns: *An Essay on Slavery and Abolitionism with Reference to the Duty of American Females* (1837); *A Treatise on Domestic Economy for the Use of Ladies at Home and at School* (1841); *Miss Beecher's Domestic Receipt Book* (1846); *The Evils Suffered by American Women and American Children: The Causes and the Remedy* (1846); and *Woman Suffrage and Woman's Profession* (1871).

Beecher discovered that most women suffered from what seemed to her too many ills—invalidism, spasms, backache, neurasthenia—and that many feared marriage because they feared the pain of childbirth, nursing, and the rearing of children. She planned a program of physical education. She had introduced a calisthenics program in her Hartford school in the 1820s; later she published *Physiology and Calisthenics for Schools and Families* (1856). Writing in *Harper's New Monthly Magazine,* she instructed her readers that they should heed the lessons of an earlier era, when "our early mothers worked and trained their daughters to work, and thus became healthy, energetic, and cheerful." Young women of her day, especially those from well-to-do families, did not use their muscles in domestic work or in any other form of labor. The lack of proper exercise and excessive study and reading were leading to "the decay of the female constitution and the ruined health of both women and girls."[16] To improve women's physical well-being, Beecher explained in great detail how houses should be built and organized so they could do their work properly and enjoy good health.

Lyman Beecher had maintained that a strong, cohesive family was essential to the stability of society, and Catharine Beecher adopted her father's views, using them to restore dignity to the traditional role of women. Nothing was more important than family management, and as women were the center of the family, it was essential that they receive the proper education for that role.

Beecher's emphasis on the importance of the home and the family was a different approach to giving women a position of higher status. She did not question the subordinate position women held in the social structure. She agreed that social hierarchies were necessary for stability, order, and the maintenance of a stable democracy.

From her subordinate position in the home, however, the properly educated woman (Beecher thought) would save the Republic from corruption and vice. As mothers, women would train their young and use their superior moral qualities to produce good and honorable citizens. For those women who did not marry there was a suitable alternative—teaching. As teachers, women could also exert their influence to mold youth. Woman was the "residing genius" who was to govern society from either the home or the schoolhouse.

The positions Beecher articulated in the 1830s and 1840s were gaining popularity in many parts of the nation. Her claim about the importance of the first impressions mothers made on children was consistent with the growing concern for the development of the child's nature. Her argument that mothers and teachers were especially important in the process of teaching habits of obedience and self-control to the young complemented the position of those who argued that schools were necessary to develop an orderly society. In fact she maintained that the school was nearly as important as the home, and could in some cases counteract the influence of a bad home. School was more than a place where children were sent "simply to learn from books." Their teachers and classmates influenced the formation of "their habits, opinions, and character."[17] Beecher was in effect asking that the school share the power and responsibility that had traditionally been reserved to the family and the church. As this view grew popular, schools were looked upon more favorably, although they were also increasingly held responsible for a number of social problems.

For Beecher the school was to serve as a restraining influence on America's unprecedented social experiment—democracy. Because American government was not "despotic," force could not be used to restrain the people. The only

---

16. In Barbara M. Cross (ed.), *The Educated Woman in America* (New York: Teachers College Press, 1965), p. 95.

17. *Ibid.*, p. 68.

alternative was to rely upon *"virtuous* intelligence,"[18] and the surest way to promote such intelligence was through schools that based their programs on a foundation of moral and religious instruction. As virtue and intelligence had their origins in women, the very existence of the nation depended upon its women, as mothers or teachers. To make her case for women's education, Beecher combined two powerful motives: self-interest and patriotism.

Like many of her contemporaries, Beecher saw that the social changes of her era were not leaving women untouched. There were others, however, who saw those same changes and asked for even more than Beecher did. Emma Willard and Mary Lyon wanted educational opportunities for women that would be comparable to those men enjoyed. Some wanted equal access to jobs as well as education. Margaret Fuller, for example, wrote in 1855 that she asked men "to remove arbitrary barriers" and proclaimed: "let women be sea captains if they will."[19] Others argued for Constitutional equality, but for the most part all that was achieved was not much more than Benjamin Rush had urged a generation earlier.

The Debate Over Women's Role

Discussion about the education of women continued throughout the nineteenth century. There were advocates and there were opponents. Stephen Simpson, for example, a candidate for Congress on the Working Men's Party ticket in the 1830s, addressed himself to the topic in his campaign literature. Simpson wanted no part of "the new fangled projects of the celebrated reformers" who were trying "to reduce the mother of our race to a destructive equality with man."[20] Both nature and reason, he believed, clearly showed that men and women had very different roles to perform in society. "As the MOTHER of the human race," advised Simpson, "quiet seclusion, and domestic tranquility with much suffering is her lot."[21] Those who thought the sexes were equal were suffering from a "fatal delusion." No good, he warned, could come from equal education for the sexes. Rather, such a scheme was likely to unsettle the economy, disturb nature's harmony, "diminish the happiness of mankind," and "prostrate the barriers of chastity and virtue."[22]

Even after the Civil War there was still opposition to allowing women the same educational opportunities as men. There was less opposition in the West than in the Northeast. While Oberlin College, Antioch College, and the Universities of

---

18. *Ibid.,* p. 71.

19. Sarah Margaret Fuller, *Woman in the Nineteenth Century* in Willard Thorp, Merle Curti, and Carols Baker (eds.), *American Issues: The Social Record,* rev. ed. (New York: J. B. Lippincott, 1955), pp. 463–464.

20. Stephen Simpson, *The Working Man's Manual* (1831) in Rena Vassar (ed.), *Social History of American Education* (Chicago: Rand McNally and Co., 1965), p. 188.

21. *Ibid.,* pp. 187–188.

22. *Ibid.,* p. 190.

Michigan and Wisconsin were allowing women to pursue the same course of study as men, educators in the East were still explaining why this should not occur. In 1874, for example, a Harvard professor, Edward Clarke, published his views on the subject in *Sex in Education or a Fair Chance for Girls.* He concluded that the strain of education would surely weaken women and result in either consumption or mental breakdowns. Besides, he argued, abstract learning had nothing to do with the essential roles of women.

Education for Black Women

Opportunities for formal schooling for most blacks, male or female, in the nineteenth century were limited, chancy, and frequently nonexistent. (See Chapter 11.) Ironically, this situation to an extent prevented the development of the two-track system common in white education of the era. Though education for black children was inadequate, what there was was shared by girls and boys both before and after the Civil War.[23] Another difference between black and white attitudes toward education for women lay in the expectations that these women had for their future. Black women, in general, were brought up with the idea that they would have to work at a job or a career.

Nonetheless, black women who sought an education faced an extra barrier of race discrimination. Those educators who fought for education for blacks tended to leave women out of their arguments.

Whether a black woman was educated or not, she certainly did not have the same rights and opportunities as either white women or black men. Sojourner Truth made that point very clearly in 1867 at the first annual meeting of the American Equal Rights Association. She told her audience that she came from a field different from most of theirs—"the country of the slave"—and warned that "if colored men get their rights, and not colored women get theirs, there will be a bad time about it." No matter what black women did, they were not rewarded as well as men. In fact, her own experiences taught her that both black and white women did not receive their due:

> I used to work in the field and bind grain, keeping up with the cradler; but men never doing no more, got twice as much pay. So with the German women. They work in the field and do as much work, but do not get the pay. We do as much, we eat as much, we want as much.[24]

Sojourner Truth warned men that when women got their rights and a little money, they would be free. That women were not paid as men were, and that they had to go to men for money, constituted a form of slavery that she wanted to end. She observed that it would be difficult for men to surrender their hold on women,

---

23. Gerda Lerner, *Black Women in White America* pp. 75–76.

24. Sojourner Truth, "When Woman Gets Her Rights Man Will Be Right" in Philip S. Foner (ed.), *The Voice of Black America* (New York: Simon and Schuster, 1972), p. 346.

but that once the dependency of women on men was broken, all would benefit: "When woman gets her rights man will be right."[25]

But by the end of the nineteenth century, black women like many white women, were still set apart from men's activities. In a section of Booker T. Washington's *Working with the Hands,* his wife Margaret Murray Washington described the insignificance of the role women were given at the first Negro Conference for farmers, held at Tuskegee in 1892:

> Sitting in that first meeting of the Negro farmers and hearing the resolutions which stood as the platform of the conference, I felt that history was repeating itself. In the days of Lucretia Mott, and the early struggles of Susan B. Anthony, women had no rights that were worth mentioning, and, notwithstanding the fact that there were many women present at this first conference, they had little actual place in it.[26]

Margaret Washington devised a way to help the women in the Tuskegee area. She noted that many women came to the village each Saturday, and so she decided to conduct a brief conference for them then. On her first attempt, six women came, and she presented her idea to them. Ten years later, she reported that the conferences were held for two hours each week and were attended by more than 300 women. The topics they discussed included: "Morals among young girls; The kinds of amusements for young girls; A mother's example; A mother's duty to her home; Dresses for women and children; Poultry raising for women; The part a woman should take in securing a home; Fruit canning, etc."[27]

As the popularity of the conferences grew, many women who could not leave their children at home began to bring them along. Soon there was a parallel session for the children, where they were "taught simple lessons, and, at the same time, received short practical talks on behavior at home, on the streets and elsewhere."[28] A small library was assembled for them, and they were allowed to borrow the books to read at home.

Soon Margaret Washington developed an extension program to complement the work of the conference. Visits were made to homes to "see that the lessons are put into practice." Pictures were given to women for their walls so that "the cracks might be closed against the wind and rain, and that the children of the home might have something besides the dark and cheerless logs to look at."[29] For those who could not attend the conferences, the talks were printed in little books to which were added "recipes which any woman may need in her country home, especially when there is sickness in the family.[30] Leaflets were sent out so that teachers and other women would know how to organize "home-union meetings for mothers."

25. *Ibid.*
26. Booker T. Washington, *Working with the Hands* (New York: Negro Universities Press, 1960), pp. 119–120.
27. *Ibid.,* p. 123.
28. *Ibid.,* p. 122.
29. *Ibid.,* p. 123.
30. *Ibid.,* p. 124.

Women were to be encouraged to discuss their plans openly so they could learn from each other. Teachers were cautioned "not to be dictatorial while visiting." There were leaflets to teach women how to prepare their homes for meetings. Topics for discussion at the home meetings centered mainly on child-raising, running a home, family problems, home-buying, and education in the home. They were home- and family-oriented, but as Margaret Washington wrote, "Eighty percent of our women have their homes in the country or on the plantations, they live in the oldtime log cabins, but they have hearts, they have aspirations for the future."[31]

Vocational Education

Booker T. Washington's approach to education for blacks emphasized practical, vocational training at the expense of academic education. In the late 1890s, he "became impressed with the idea that there was a wider range of industrial work for our girls." The only reasons for a lack of suitable jobs for women were "traditional prejudice" and "lack of skill."[32] During slavery, he explained, many believed that white women should not do housework and their education should consist of art, music, and literature. When the slaves were freed, many black women believed they should be similarly educated. Washington fought that notion and eventually convinced the women who attended Tuskegee that training in the household arts was of paramount importance. There were, however, other jobs for women.

Washington's observations at the agricultural college for women at Swanley, England, his observation about the differences in the economies and the climates of the North and the South, and his desire to find better jobs for black women led him to establish a program of agricultural training for women. In England, he observed women who spent their mornings in the laboratories and the classrooms and their afternoons "at work in the field with the hoe or rake, planting vegetable seeds, pruning fruit trees or learning to raise poultry and bees and how to care for the dairy." If such work, he reasoned, was "necessary for a people who have back of them the centuries of English wealth and culture, it is tenfold more needful for a people who are in the condition of my race at the South."[33]

Washington enlisted the aid of his wife in the program at Tuskegee. At first many women resisted, and those who tried the program were embarrassed to be seen working in the fields. However, by winning the confidence of the "social leaders of a certain group," Margaret Washington was able to get the work underway. Eventually, there was a complete course that offered instruction and practice in dairying, poultry raising, horticulture, floriculture and landscape gardening, market gardening, and livestock.

Washington saw many advantages to outdoor work for women. There was no

---

31. *Ibid.*
32. *Ibid.*, p. 107.
33. *Ibid.*, p. 109.

doubt that "life out in the sweet, pure, bracing air is better from both a physical and a moral point of view than long days spent in the close atmosphere of a factory or store." The program he designed also had "the advantage of a superior mental and moral growth."

Higher Education

Attempts to provide higher education for black women lagged behind those for white women. Like white women, however, black women found their first career opportunities in teaching, though, of course, they could teach only in black schools. One of the first colleges to offer college work for black women was Spelman College in Atlanta. Though it was founded by two women from Boston, Sophia B. Packard and Harriet Giles, Spelman did not adhere to the argument that women should study what men studied. Spelman sought to prepare black women to be teachers and church workers. Mary Jane Patterson, probably the first black woman to be awarded an A. B. degree (Oberlin, 1862) went on to teach in the Institute for Colored Youth in Philadelphia, a school that produced a number of black women teachers. Patterson later became principal of the Preparatory High School for Negroes in Washington, D.C.

Those black women who did manage to acquire an education often were criticized and found themselves alienated from their friends and families. For example, Mary Church Terrell, who was among the first to earn a bachelor's degree, had to contend with the displeasure of her father. She related that:

> It was held by most people that women were unfitted to do their work in the home if they studied Latin, Greek, and higher mathematics. Many of my friends tried to dissuade me from studying for an A. B. degree. After I had finished college my father did not want me to get a job teaching. He felt that he was able to support me. He disinherited me, refused to write to me for a year because I went to Wilberforce to teach. Further, I was ridiculed and told that no man would want to marry a woman who studied higher mathematics.[34]

Educated black women were also viewed as influences for "moral good" and as uplifting helpmates for men. At the 1898 Hampton Negro Conference, S. B. Stevens, a black woman, related that there were two kinds of education, ornamental and utilitarian. "Ornamental" education was what Southern white women pursued before the Civil War. "Utilitarian" education was what the black women needed so they could "help cheerfully to bear the burdens of life instead of fretting because their homes . . . are not handsomely furnished out of a meagre salary."[35] In 1908 the Dean of Howard University, Kelly Miller, argued that black men should study the liberal arts and that black women should study the domestic sciences. Writing in *Alexander's Magazine* in 1906, Thomas Nelson Baker argued that the need for black women to be educated was greater than the need for black men

---

34. Quoted in Jeanne L. Noble, *The Negro Woman's College Education* (New York: Teachers College Press, 1956), p. 23.

35. *Ibid.*, p. 157.

to be educated. His reason was simple: "Mothers of men should be superior in order to rear superior men."[36] Over a hundred years after the American Revolution, it was still held that black women were not to be educated for themselves but for their race and for men.

---

36. *Ibid.*

The Move Toward Public Education

8

New Advocates and New Purposes

The statesmen of the early republic had argued that the new nation needed a uniform system of schools to ensure its permanence and stability. Yet there was nothing approaching a uniform system. There were public schools and private schools, though in some places the distinction between the two was blurred. The Constitutional principle of separation of church and state frequently meant little in schools. Tradition, not newly articulated principles, determined how schools were organized and conducted, and in many places the need for schools was acknowledged but unmet; at times, it was met through charitable societies. In the 1820s a campaign began, especially in the Northeast, to improve and extend public schooling. By the end of the Civil War, the idea of the common school was widely accepted.

No one person, group, or reason can be given credit for the founding of this new institution. Its development was the consequence of many interests seeking to solve many problems and to realize many purposes. Many women who objected to the meager educational opportunities provided for them not only helped to articulate the arguments in support of increased educational opportunity, but also assumed the responsibility of staffing the schools. Working men through their organizations helped to spread the notion that all citizens had a right to education. Politicians supported universal schooling for various reasons: to teach people their responsibilities to the state and the established order, to teach immigrants the American way and promote social unity.

This variety of people advocated the development of the common school in a variety of ways. Some groups organized and sent memorials and resolutions to state legislatures. Some used the quickly growing magazines and newspapers to advocate or learn about the benefits and dangers of public education. The Lyceum was another source of information and arguments in behalf of public education. In the 1820s, '30s, and '40s, people debated the idea of providing education for all at the public's expense. Their purposes were not always as clear and high-sounding as those of the statesmen of the early republic. Their efforts were, however, more effective.

Workers' Organizations

As cities grew in number and in size, workers began to organize to protect and state their common interests. In 1794 Philadelphia shoemakers met and organized themselves into the Federal Society of Journeymen Cordwainers in Philadelphia. In 1799 the Cordwainers called a strike to express their displeasure at the wage cuts their masters had announced. Within a generation there were many more such organizations as well as more strikes. By the mid-1830s there were more than fifty groups each in Philadelphia and New York, more than twenty in Boston, and a few less than that in Baltimore. The effectiveness of the societies and the strength of their support for free schools can be questioned, but their very existence and growth are significant.

These working men's societies were not entirely comparable to contemporary unions. Members were artisans and craftsmen, not factory workers. In their early years, factories, especially mills, employed mostly women and children, who were, regarded as temporary factory workers. The banding together of the artisans to protect and express their interests is evidence that their traditional ways of working and their independence were being threatened by the changing social conditions. In the first half of the nineteenth century, however, it was frequently difficult for the workers to effect their desires through collective action, for most courts held that strikes were illegal, a conspiracy against free trade. That view did not begin to change until Chief Justice Shaw of the Massachusetts Supreme Court ruled in 1842 that workers had the right to organize.

The working men's organizations advocated political action and even organized political parties. A working men's political party was organized in Philadelphia in 1828. Soon similar parties were organized in New York and Massachusetts. In their political platforms, the workers took positions on a wide range of social issues, including education. The platform published by the Boston Working Men's Party in 1830 contained fifteen planks. Two dealt directly with education: The fifth plank reminded legislators that they could ensure "the continuance of our national independence" by establishing "a liberal system of education" that would be "attainable by all." The sixth plank called for the diffusion of that knowledge that directly related to "mechanical employments" and to the "politics of our common country." The other planks dealt with a variety of issues. Some objected to the recent "multiplication of statutes," and emphasized that people had the right "to understand every law made for their government, without paying enormous fees for having them expounded by attorneys."[1] Other planks objected to those who would disturb the social order by pairing political doctrines with religion. There was even a plank calling for a reform in the state's militia. By taking stands on such a wide variety of issues, the workers' organizations and parties may have weakened their chances to improve their own working conditions, although they contributed significantly to the discussion of many social issues that reformers were raising. On the other hand, the workers themselves did not enjoy any widespread sympathy from other reformers. Those who spoke in their behalf frequently took positions that were too radical for most politicians and newspaper editors.

The workers' organizations frequently selected education as *the* solution to the social problems they had identified. To the old arguments in favor of education they added the claim that education was a natural right of all men (women were frequently excluded from their proposals) regardless of the social and economic station that one had been assigned by birth. As early as 1799 the Mechanics and Manufacturers Association of Providence (Rhode Island) expressed the view that education was "the common right of every child to enjoy."[2]

The Halloween, 1829, issue of the *Working Man's Advocate* told of the reasons for forming an Association for the Protection of Industry and for the Promotion of National Education. (By "industry" the association did not mean a system of factories but the workers' own labor. The workers' industry was unprotected and inadequately rewarded. Moreover, workers and their children did not have access to a system of education "befitting a republic." There was, the Association maintained, no system of education

> ... which secures the equal maintenance, protection, and instruction of youth
> —of the children of the poor as of the rich; none which is at once free from
> sectarian and clerical influences, and from aristocratical distinctions; none
> which is calculated to induce in the rising generation those habits of industry,
> those principles of sound morality, those feelings of brotherly love, together
> with those solid intellectual acquirements, which are necessary to secure to
> all the fair exercise of those equal political rights set forth in the institutions
> of the land.[3]

Like many reformers who were to follow, they believed that presentation of the facts would quickly lead to social changes. They were wrong.

The Association strongly questioned whether either religion or the rich, two traditional sources of support for education, could serve the needs of workers. "State religion and monied ascendancy," it stated, "have done much harm to the people in every age and in every nation." The Association wanted a sharp separation between church and state, between what was private and what was public.

---

1. *Boston Courier*, August 28, 1830, in *Education in the United States: A Documentary History*, ed. Sol Cohen (New York: Random House, 1974), p. 1059.

2. Ibid., p. 1051.

3. *Working Man's Advocate* (New York City), Oct. 31, 1829, in *Social History of American Education*, ed. Rena Vassar (Chicago: Rand McNally, 1965), p. 165.

It suggested that those who were religious could be so in the "closet when the door is shut, but not in public."[4]

In effect, the workers were arguing that what they had traditionally received as "charity" from the rich and from organized religion was rightfully theirs. Education was a right, not a gift. Government had the responsibility to take an active role in the social affairs of all its citizens. The report of a workers' meeting in Philipsburgh, Pa., on September 26, 1829, shows that some in the workers' movement wanted schools to promote social equality as well as teach the traditional "three R's." Acknowledging that there were "natural inequalities among men," the workers agreed, however, that it was "the duty of a wise government to soften and modify" those inequalities "as much as possible."[5] Under no circumstance was it proper for government to contribute to increasing those natural inequalities. Yet, said the workers, it appeared that government was doing so. While Congress levied tariffs that made goods more costly for workers but protected the interests of the manufacturers, "thousands of dollars of the public money [had] been appropriated for building colleges and academies for the rich."[6]

In earlier times, the report continued, workers could avoid the pauper stigma and still secure some education for their children through the apprentice system. After the Revolution, however, the apprentice system had, the workers reported, "greatly diminished." Workers' choices were severely restricted: they could accept the stigma of charity or pauper schools or they could argue that their children had a right to education.

The workers' contention that the state had the obligation to provide education for all children was in fact a proposal for the construction of a new institution, the common school. In the typical state constitution, the only provisions for state-supported schooling were those made for the dependent classes, the poor, the abandoned, and orphans. To send one's child to such a pauper school was to admit to a form of dependence that simply was inappropriate for free citizens of a republic.

In 1830 the *Working Man's Advocate* published another report emphasizing that "there are great numbers, even of the poorest parents, who hold a dependence on the public bounty to be incompatible with the rights and liberties of an American citizen, and whose deep and cherished consciousness of *independence* determines them rather to starve the intellect of their offspring, than submit to become the objects of public charity."[7] "Each human being" the report went on, "has an equal right to a full development of all his powers, moral, physical, and intellectual."[8] Stephen Simpson, the first candidate for Congress from the Working Men's Party of Philadelphia, objected bluntly to "the odious system of charity

---

4. Ibid., p. 166.
5. Ibid., p. 168.
6. *Ibid.*
7. *Working Man's Advocate*, March 6, 1830, in Vassar, *Social History*, p. 172.
8. Ibid., p. 175.

school." Even the idea of a charity school could not help but impress "a consciousness of degradation."[9] In *The Working Man's Manual* that he published as part of his unsuccessful campaign for Congress in 1831, Simpson argued:

> ... we created the necessity of universal education, by adopting a form of government, whose existence and purity depended on the exercise of reason, and the preservation of public virtue. Where every man is an *elector,* and bound to judge and to choose those who may make laws, and administer the government;—everyone ought to receive an education, commensurate to his duties, as such; and where individual opulence does not furnish the means, the public are bound to impart the blessing in the fullest measure, and to the widest extent, at the common cost of society: not however, as a bounty, or a *charity,* but as a *right;* that as *all* contribute their share of labour to the expense and support of government, so *all* are equally entitled to the great benefits of popular instruction.[10]

Just as the Constitution was an instrument designed to protect liberty without regard to any citizen's economic status, Simpson went on, education also was necessary for all people. To have "a *popular government* devoid of *popular education*" was, he claimed, tantamount to having a "civilized society destitute of a *system of industry.*"[11]

For Simpson there seemed to be no social problem and no fault of character that education could not remedy. He told his readers:

> I hold it to be an indisputable maxim, that knowledge not only prevents crime, but increases industry—that it adds to the excellence of the human character in all its bearings—that it snatches men from low and grovelling vices, and gives them a fresh impulse to the acquisition of perfection of every kind. How seldom do we behold a *tavern* frequented by men of good education, and cultivated intellect? How seldom do we find men of educated minds, slaves to the beastly vice of intemperance?—Give education to the people, and you give them the spur to every virtue; the rein to every vice.[12]

In time, both supporters of public schooling and professional educators would similarly promise the public that better schools would rid society of its ills and ensure that children would grow up to be honorable, productive, and orderly citizens. (As a corollary, once schools were established, they were frequently held responsible for the ills of society and wayward youth.)

The American Lyceum

Long before the introduction of television into American society, there were many who would sit and listen while some one spoke at them. In the early days of the Massachusetts Bay Colony, the Puritans demanded that their clergy provide them

9. Stephen Simpson, *The Working Man's Manual* (1831), in Vassar, *Social History,* p. 182.
10. Ibid., p. 183.
11. Ibid., pp. 183–184.
12. Ibid., p. 185.

with good sermons. The sermon was a social occasion, a time for the community to meet together; sermons were given at commencement exercises and even at hangings. When church attendance began to decline, revivals were instituted, and many came out to hear what the new-style clergymen had to say and observe how they said it. Two hundred years after the founding of the first New England colonies, Americans were still eager to hear a good talk. Daniel Boorstin has recorded that "all over the country—less in the Old South, but in ever-growing numbers in the Southwest and West—audiences sought men of eloquence, of presence, and of reputation, who could hold their attention."[13] In Boston during the 1830s and 1840s, "the craze for lecturers reached phenomenal proportions."[14] During the winter of 1837–38, for instance, Bostonians had their choice of twenty-six different courses of lectures, each with no less than eight sessions. Theodore Parker, the noted pastor of Boston's Twenty-Eighth Congregational Society and a popular orator of the mid-nineteenth century, observed that "the business of lecturing is an original American contrivance for educating the people." In the American lecture, said Parker, "are combined the best things of the Church, and of the College, with some of the fun of the theatre."[15]

The American Lyceum, founded by Josiah Holbrook, became both a system of education and a movement for the development and improvement of public schools. It was a vehicle for secular sermons. Holbrook, an 1810 graduate of Yale, had first tried to organize an experimental school on his father's farm, combining farm work and manual training with the traditional school subjects. He also attended the science lectures of Benjamin Sillman at Yale, and then took to the lecture circuit to deliver lectures on scientific subjects. In 1826 Holbrook wrote his plan for the Lyceum (he then called it a Society for Mutual Education) and published it in William Russell's newly founded *American Journal of Education.*

The plan set forth two major objectives for the societies. The first was to provide "an economical and practical education" for youth and "to diffuse rational and useful information through the community generally." The second was to show how science and other branches of education could be applied "to the domestic and useful arts, and to all the common purposes of life."[16] Holbrook suggested that each participant in a society pay a small yearly fee of one dollar so that books and other equipment could be purchased. He especially urged societies to buy cabinets for displaying minerals and apparatus for demonstrating scientific principles. Holbrook foresaw the possibility of a national organization of societies devoted to mutual education. The system was to have the form of a pyramid, with the local societies at the base and a General Board at the top, embracing all the societies in the United States.

---

13. Daniel Boorstin, *The Americans: The National Experience,* (New York: Vintage Books, 1965), p. 315.

14. Carl Bode, *The American Lyceum* (New York: Oxford University Press, 1956), p. 49.

15. Quoted in David Mead, *Yankee Eloquence in the Middle West,* (East Lansing: Michigan State University Press, 1951), pp. 145–146.

16. Bode, *The American Lyceum,* p. 12.

In 1826, the same year he made his proposal, Holbrook organized the first Lyceum—Lyceum No. 1 at Millbury, Mass. The following year the Worcester, (Mass.) County Lyceum Association was founded, and three years later there was a state lyceum association in Massachusetts. By 1831 nearly a thousand towns had lyceums, and more than fifty counties. In less than ten years more than 3,000 lyceums had been organized.

In the early promotional literature Holbrook prepared on the lyceum, public schools received some attention, but they were clearly not the primary focus. An 1826 leaflet was entitled: *American Lyceum of Science and the Arts, Composed of Associations for Mutual Instruction and Designed for the General Diffusion of Useful and Practical Knowledge.* Of the six advantages it described for those who organized a lyceum, one was that lyceums could contribute to the improvement of the common schools. The lyceum idea, however, began to move toward a closer identification with the common school movement. In the December 1828 issue of the *American Journal,* readers were told that besides encouraging the opening of libraries and stimulating geological and agricultural surveys, the lyceum would benefit infant schools, the common or district schools, and the academies. The title of an 1829 edition of Holbrook's leaflet shows that the lyceum was adopting the common school as one of its major concerns: *American Lyceum, or Society for the Improvement of Schools and Diffusion of Useful Knowledge.*

In this leaflet Holbrook explained that the lyceums had discovered a growing interest in the common schools. He discussed the growing number of teachers and the importance of improving their abilities. Holbrook indicated that the local lyceums had been helping the schools by offering their facilities "for the improvement of their teachers" and by making lyceum courses available to the oldest common school students. The lyceum courses were "of a higher character" than those that could be provided by the common school, where there was frequently a "promiscuous assemblage of children."[17]

On May 4, 1831, Holbrook's hope for a national lyceum was realized. The first national meeting, attended by representatives from seven states, was held in New York City. The constitution of the newly founded American Lyceum Association gave considerable attention to the common schools. Among its purposes were (1) fostering of legislation supportive of common schools; (2) upgrading teachers' qualifications; (3) building better relationships between the common schools and the colleges and universities; (4) finding better teaching methods and improved ways of securing school discipline; (5) adding natural science to the schools' courses of study; (6) supplying books and other educational apparatus to the schools; and (7) promoting an interest in the education of women.

At each of the nine national meetings held subsequently by the ALA, considerable attention was given to the common school and its problems. At the first meeting, delegates discussed the introduction of the natural sciences into the

17. Ibid., p. 25.

common school, the teaching of the Bible in the schools, teachers' qualifications, and the need for teacher training institutions. At the second national meeting, the president, John Griscom, delivered an address on problems of school discipline. The suitability of the monitorial system for the common school was discussed by Walter Rogers Johnson. At later meetings, delegates gave their attention to manual training, teacher training, teacher methods, the education of women, stammering, and the education of the deaf. Science education and the use of the Bible in the schools were discussed at several meetings.

At the ninth (and last) annual meeting of the ALA, Charles Brooks asked the delegates to sponsor a special meeting to consider an ambitious program for promoting the development of the common schools. Brooks offered six major points for consideration: (1) the collection of educational statistics; (2) a report on the status of the common schools in the various parts of the country; (3) an examination of European practices that might be appropriate for adoption in the United States; (4) an investigation of normal schools to determine whether they were of any use; (5) an inquiry to determine where the best information could be secured on available school supplies as well as models of schoolhouses; and (6) a petition to the United States Congress to direct that the next Census determine how many people sixteen years of age had not received any public school instruction.

The meeting was held in Philadelphia in November 1839. Delegates agreed to urge the several state legislatures to create state boards of education, with the secretary of each state board serving as the superintendent of schools. This recommendation, eventually adopted by many states, moved responsibility and control of education from the district or town level to the state level. Most reformers then believed that state control of public education and uniformity of school practices were in the best interests of the public.

At their 1840 meeting in Washington, D.C., the delegates tried to draw national attention to the common school movement and secure the interest of the United States Congress. Committees were established to ask Congress that the proceeds from the sale of public lands be used for education and that a portion of the legacy of British philanthropist James Smithson be used for education. Congress, however, did not appropriate any funds for public education. In fact, it gave no indication that it had even heard the plea of those who were calling themselves the National Convention of the Friends of Education.

Carl Bode, the historian of the lyceum, has concluded that the lyceum's "paramount" contribution to the common school movement was the creation of a favorable atmosphere for public schools. It became a forum where the idea of the common school, its needs, and its advantages were discussed. Even those who did not attend could read newspaper reports of the discussions. Local lyceums conducted surveys of educational conditions and the needs of children in their communities. They sent memorials to the county officials and to their state legislatures. Some provided a platform for those who wished to introduce new educational methods and materials. At times the lyceum served as an institute for the training of teachers.[18]

The Print Explosion

Between 1825 and 1850 there was what one media historian has called "the great magazine explosion."[19] Estimates are that in 1825 there were less than a hundred periodicals and by 1850, nearly 600. If the many periodicals that were started and then quickly and quietly died are included in the count, it is likely that there were between 4,000 and 5,000 periodicals published in that period. The *New York Mirror* observed in 1828 that periodicals were springing up "as fast as mushrooms." The "magazine explosion" was in part the result of the growth of cities and of technological improvements such as the rotary press. The common school movement and the magazines complemented each other. Increased literacy created a potentially larger market for the magazines, while magazines served as a forum where the cause of the common school could be expressed, challenged, and advocated.

Nearly every issue of the day was catalogued and discussed in the periodical press. There were many attempts at specialized magazines for special interests. For example, in 1834 Lewis Gaylord Clark began the *Knickerbocker,* which subsequently published the work of such authors as Washington Irving, James Fenimore Cooper, William Cullen Bryant, Nathaniel Hawthorne, Henry Wadsworth Longfellow, and John Greenleaf Whittier. The census of 1850 reported that half of the nearly 200 religious publications in the country were magazines. There were magazines devoted to agriculture, science, women's interests, horse racing, and even crime (the *National Police Gazette*). Those who did not have access to a school or lyceum could pick up a magazine for instruction or amusement.

Sarah Josepha Hale and *Godey's Lady's Book*

In 1827 the Reverend John L. Blake, an Episcopalian priest, invited Sarah Josepha Hale to come to Boston to edit a new magazine for women. She was to become one of the most successful and most influential magazine editors of the time. Hale understood the world in which she lived and worked, and in the first issue of the *Ladies Magazine* (1828), she advised the husbands and the fathers of her prospective readers that the magazine would provide a wholesome diversion for women while the men were away from home tending to their business affairs.

In her editorials Hale continued to instruct her readers in the women's point of view. Through the magazine, she taught women about the realities of the world in which they lived. She promoted better education for women, encouraged women to become teachers, and advocated women's rights. She gave her editori-

---

18. Ibid., pp. 113–119.
19. John Tebbel, *The Media in America* (New York: Mentor Books, 1976), p. 163.

al support to the work of Catharine Beecher, Emma Willard, Mary Lyon, and others who were working in behalf of women. As editor, Hale often reminded her readers of numerous instances of the oppression of women and instructed them that they must work out their survival in a world that was controlled by a sex that did not always look kindly toward them.

In an era when many magazines lasted for only a few issues, Hale's *Ladies Magazine* survived for nine years. Then Louis Godey its chief competitor, merged it with his own magazine. Hale became the editor of the new *Godey's Lady's Book,* and continued to instruct her readers. By 1850 *Godey's* had a monthly circulation of 40,000; in 1860 its circulation was 150,000. (*Harper's* had 110,000). Continuing as editor, Hale was introducing to many readers ideas about the roles of women in school and society that they had never met during their youth.

The Educators' Magazines

The first educational journals in the United States were published by Albert Pickett, who in 1811 introduced the *Juvenile Monitor or Educational Magazine.* Although the *Monitor* survived less than a year, Pickett and his son John tried again in 1818 with publication of the *Academician.* The Picketts also wrote several textbooks, owned a school in New York City, and were officers of the Incorporated Society of New York Teachers. Though it too lasted only a year, the *Academician* presented extensive discussions of English language and grammar, arithmetic and geography, the conditions of education, teachers' qualifications, and the educational practices and philosophy of the Swiss educator Pestalozzi. They initiated a "mathematical department" in the magazine, a feature that was adopted by most of the educational journals founded in the next fifty years.[20]

After 1826 many new educational journals began to appear. Many disappeared quickly; some endured. In January 1826, William Russell began publication in Boston of the *American Journal of Education.* Russell gave a generous amount of space to the lyceum movement, and for a while the magazine was known as the *American Journal of Education and American Lyceum.* In November 1826, J. L. Parkhurst began the *Teachers' Guide and Parents' Assistant* in Portland, Maine. It was merged with Russell's journal in March 1828. During its short life, the *Teachers' Guide* offered material on infant schools, Pestalozzi's educational methods, and quotations on education from several prominent authors. In 1830 Russell's *Journal* was merged with the newly founded *American Annals of Education and Instruction and Journal of Literary Institutions,* which lasted until 1839. Only two of the nearly thirty educational periodicals started by 1840 continued publication into the 1840s: Horace Mann's *Common School Journal* (1839–1852) and the *District School Journal for the State of New York* (1840–1851).

According to Sheldon Davis's study of the early educational press, nine educational journals were attempted between 1811 and 1830, all of them in either the

---

20. Sheldon Emmor Davis, *Educational Periodicals in the Nineteenth Century* (U.S. Department of Interior, Bureau of Education, Bulletin No. 28, 1919), p. 11.

Northeast or the East.[21] The first western journal was issued in Cincinnati in 1831. During its one-year life, the *Western Academician and Journal of Education and Science* discussed Pestalozzi (who was fast becoming a prominent figure in nearly all the educational literature), Victor Cousin's and Calvin Stowe's reports on the Prussian educational system, female education, and the Lancasterian system.

As the brief lives of most of the early educational journals suggest, their circulations were severely limited. Paid subscriptions were usually considerably fewer than the circulation, for early postal laws allowed publishers to exchange their magazines through the mail without charge. However, most educational periodicals failed to achieve any significant circulation outside the area in which they were published. When large circulations were achieved, it was typically the results of free distributions. For example, J. Orville Taylor, editor of the *Common School Assistant* in Albany, New York was able to distribute nearly 40,000 copies monthly of his magazine with the help of a "number of philanthropic gentlemen."[22] Those free samples seem not to have helped very much, for the *Assistant* expired in April 1840, early in its fifth year. The low circulation figures and the comments of several editors indicate that teachers did not read the journals. Frequently, the journals were especially prepared for members of school committees, but there were also complaints that they did not read the educational literature either. Readers were mainly the advocates of public education, school officials, prominent citizens who were sympathetic to an expanded school system, the clergy who were traditionally associated with educational endeavors, and those few teachers charged with some supervisory and administrative duties.

As the various states began to take action to improve and expand their public school systems, they established educational journals to promulgate their rules and regulations to the local school officers. Newly formed teacher associations also sponsored journals as a way to communicate information and advice about their tasks. Collectively, the various educational journals helped serve the cause of the common school in several ways. They publicized the various efforts to improve and extend the common schools; supplied information about teaching methods, new textbooks, educational apparatus, and school equipment; and offered advice on how to teach the various school subjects and maintain order in the classroom. Through their reports and discussions of the work of European educators, they helped to introduce new educational ideas to the United States.

One of the later and more successful of the educational journals was Henry Barnard's *American Journal of Education* (1855–1881). When he began it, he envisioned it as a national journal that would serve to lessen sectional differences in the country and provide a wide range of information. Barnard collected and reproduced materials on the history of education in the United States and Europe; materials on non-school agencies of education such as museums, the lyceum and libraries; accounts of new educational practices; biographies of important educa-

---

21. Ibid., pp. 92–94.
22. Ibid., p. 93.

tors; and materials on the school laws and school systems of the various states. Throughout the second half of the nineteenth century, Barnard's *American Journal* was *the* handbook for a nation that was building many school systems.

The Campaign for the Common School

Besides convincing many people that all children had a right to an education and that the state had a duty to provide that education, the common school crusaders of the early nineteenth century transformed that idea into a workable institution. Collectively, they demonstrated the injustices and inequities that resulted from allowing local districts to decide whether and to what extent they would support education. They instituted instead uniform state-wide systems of public education. The crusaders also attended to the specific features necessary for a workable system. They introduced graded schools, built teacher-training institutions, devised methods for the supervision of instruction, and centralized the administration and supervision of schools. They tended to the construction and furnishings of schoolhouses. They produced, secured, and distributed educational materials. Most important, they attempted to replace blind and sometimes erratic adherence to traditional school routines with a new, unified system patterned after what they had found in Europe, especially Germany.

The Northeast
The first attempts to enlist state government in an active role in public education occurred in the Northeast. By 1784 New York had organized the Board of Regents of the University of the State of New York to look after secondary and higher education, and in 1795 it established a system for financing its schools. Like most early educational legislation, however, it was not always honored and by 1800 it had in effect expired. In the early 1800s DeWitt Clinton and his associates successfully generated interest in the problems and advantages of the public schools, and in 1813 New York became the first state to appoint a state superintendent of schools. In Massachusetts, James G. Carter and Horace Mann have traditionally

been given credit for the establishment of the common school. The movement also had other able spokesmen, most notably Daniel Webster and Edward Everett. Henry Barnard worked in two states, Connecticut and Rhode Island, and developed a reputation that led to his appointment in 1867 as the first United States Commissioner of Education.

In Pennsylvania, Governor George Wolf and Thaddeus Stevens, a former schoolteacher who was beginning his political career in the legislature, worked to enact the Public School Law (1834), which would allow local districts to tax themselves to support public schools that would serve all children, not just the children of the poor. As local school districts opted to exercise the taxing authority this law granted them, considerable opposition came from prosperous farmers and from religious groups who had their own private schools. They viewed the law as a license to tax them once more than necessary. Both houses of the Pennsylvania legislature quickly responded to the pressure and began to take action to repeal the 1834 law. Replying to those who asserted that it was unfair to tax citizens to support schools they or their children would never use, Stevens pointed out that there were many governmental agencies that citizens paid for and never planned to use. He reminded his colleagues that:

> The industrious, thrifty, rich farmer pays a heavy county tax to support criminal courts, build jails, and pay sheriffs and jail keepers, and yet probably he never has, and never will have, any personal use of either. He never gets the worth of his money by being tried for a crime before the court, by being allowed the privilege of the jail on conviction, or receiving an equivalent from the sheriff or his hangman officers![1]

Stevens did convince the legislators to change their minds and even to enact his own bill, which strengthened the 1834 law. Although Stevens made his plea from sketchy notes, after the session he prepared a complete draft of his remarks. The speech was widely distributed inside and outside Pennsylvania and it became part of the common school campaigners' repertory. To many it must have seemed a powerful weapon. In 1834 Pennsylvania had about 800 free public schools; three years later it had more than 3,400.

Michigan, Illinois, and Indiana

Isaac Crary and John Pierce were among the early workers for schools in Michigan. Crary and Pierce joined forces to convince the first Michigan constitutional convention that the state should have one state system of public education rather than a collection of local systems. In 1836 Michigan created the post of Superintendent of Public Instruction, a title inspired by Crary's and Pierce's recent reading of Cousin's account of the Prussian school system. Not surprisingly, Pierce became Michigan's first superintendent.

---

1. "General Education—Remarks of Mr. Stevens," *Hazard's Register of Pennsylvania*, vol. 15 in *Education in the United States: A Documentary History*, ed. Sol Cohen (New York: Random House, 1974), p. 1066.

The advocates of the common school in Illinois were not so successful as those in some other states. The Illinois constitution (1818) ignored the issue of public schools, but in 1825 the legislature passed a measure introduced by Joseph Duncan. It is generally believed that the bill Duncan introduced was written by the governor, Edward Coles, who had been discussing education in an exchange of letters with Thomas Jefferson. The preamble of the bill echoed Jefferson's 1779 *Bill for the More General Diffusion of Knowledge,* as it proclaimed that "it is generally true that the people will be happiest whose laws are best administered" and that good administration depended on an enlightened citizenry. It also declared that expediency dictated "that those persons whom nature hath endowed with genius and virtue, should be rendered by liberal education worthy to receive . . . the sacred deposit of the rights and liberties of their fellow citizens."[2] However, the Duncan-Coles Bill was only slightly more successful than Jefferson's had been in Virginia. The 1826–27 Illinois Assembly emasculated it by adding that "no person shall hereafter be taxed for the support of any free school in his state unless by his own free will and consent, first had and obtained in writing."[3]

In 1852, Illinois Governor Matteson convinced the legislature to separate the position of Superintendent of Public Instruction from that of Secretary of State. He appointed Ninian W. Edwards as his first chief state school officer. Edwards, the son of the Illinois Territory's first governor, knew the state well. In 1855 the Illinois Assembly passed most of what he had recommended in the 1855 Public School Law. In the thirty-year interval between the two school laws, the interest in free public schools was kept alive by newspapers and the periodical press, especially John S. Wright's *Union Agriculturalist and West Prairie Farmer.*

In Indiana, the new state constitution adopted in 1851 provided for a state-supported system of education. The article dealing with education was in many aspects the result of several years of agitation by Caleb Mills, who since 1846 had given annual messages to the Indiana lawmakers. Mills had come to Indiana to be the principal of a new Presbyterian School at Crawfordsville, which eventually became Wabash College. From the college, Mills began to take an interest in the educational situation in Wabash County and in the state as a whole. In his first message to the legislature he used familiar themes. Education could, he wrote, "benefit every part of the State, improve every class in the community, give permanence to our civil and religious institutions, increase the social and literary capital of our citizens, and add materially to the real and substantial happiness of everyone."[4] Like most other advocates of the common school Mills believed that the common school could offer something to everyone, offend no one, and give stability and order to the society.

---

2. W. G. Walker, "The Development of the Free Public High School in Illinois During the Nineteenth Century," *History of Education Quarterly* 4:4 (December 1964), p. 267. Also see John D. Pulliam, "Changing Attitudes Toward Free Public Schools in Illinois, 1825–1860," *History of Education Quarterly* 7:2 (Summer 1967), pp. 191–192.

3. Pulliam, "Changing Attitudes," p. 193.

4. Caleb Mills, "Addresses to the Legislature of Indiana," in Ellwood P. Cubberley, *Readings in Public Education in the United States* (Boston: Houghton Mifflin, 1934), p. 172.

Leaders of the Common School Crusade

James G. Carter

From a boyhood education in winter schools, James G. Carter went on to Groton and Harvard. He supported himself by teaching in the district schools and singing schools and by lecturing on Masonry. After graduation from Harvard, he taught in Cohasset and then developed an impressive following at a private school in Lancaster, preparing many students for Harvard and tutoring those already in the college.

In 1821 Carter began a series of letters to the *Boston Transcript* criticizing the poor support and condition of the Massachusetts schools. These appeared in 1824 with the title: *Letters . . . on the Free Schools of New England: With Remarks Upon the Principles of Instruction.* In his letters Carter touched on nearly every aspect of education. He gave a detailed account of early educational legislation in Massachusetts, thus helping to establish the tradition of citing the Massachusetts laws of the 1640s as the beginning of public education in the United States. He decried the decline and neglect of the free schools, told how matters might be improved, warned of the consequences of bad teachers and bad texts, and urged that a science of education be developed.

Carter appealed to the history of Massachusetts to win his readers to his views, but he was not calling for a restoration of earlier school practices such as having the town's selectmen and the minister examine the character and qualifications of a prospective teacher.

In his later letters, Carter discussed the typical ways in which arithmetic was being taught. He complained that students learned mechanical rules but seldom acquired any "knowledge of the principles of the rule."[5] At the end of the last letter, he reflected on the role of tradition in education. "Reverence for antiquity" was, he conceded, "a salutary check upon rash innovation," but it was also "a troublesome barrier against wholesome improvement."[6] While the other sciences had made considerable progress, he said, education continued to base its practices on principles that were at least two thousand years old.

Carter continued his crusade after the publication of the *Letters.* During the winter of 1824–25 he published a series of essays in the *Boston Patriot* under the pseudonym "Franklin." In 1826 they were assembled and published in one small volume, *Essays on Popular Education and an Outline of an Institution for the Education of Teachers.* In the first essays Carter discussed education in its widest possible sense, trying to show his readers that what does or does not happen to children in their early years can influence their entire lives. He tried to show how the private academies were destroying the free schools and how that trend was inconsistent with the traditions established by the first settlers. He warned that the common schools were not growing as fast as the population and that their con-

---

5. James G. Carter, *Letters on the Free Schools of New England* (Boston: Cummings, Hillard and Co., 1824), p. 115.

6. Ibid., p. 121.

tinued neglect would eventually destroy them. Soon many would have to accept good instruction as a "charity" rather than a "birthright."[7]

In his discussion of the education of teachers, Carter posed questions that still await a satisfactory answer. He observed that little or no attention had been paid to the distinction between what the teachers knew and how well they could communicate what they knew.

> When we are looking for a teacher, we inquire how much he *knows,* not how much he can *communicate;* as if the latter qualification were of no consequence to us. Now it seems to me, that parents and children, to say the least, are as much interested in the latter qualification of their instructor as in the former.[8]

The frequent inability of teachers and students to communicate effectively with one another was a problem that Carter believed had to be addressed in programs specifically designed for teachers. He was particularly concerned about the qualifications of the women who typically taught in the summer primary schools. "They are a class of teachers," he proclaimed, "unknown in our laws regulating the schools unless it be by some latitude of construction."[9] Any young women who wanted to keep school and who could find a district to employ her could do so, and teaching posts were easy to find because the pay was so low that others were unwilling to compete for the jobs. The difficulty, according to Carter, was that no distinction was being made between *keeping* school and *teaching* school.

Carter recommended a special school for the training of teachers, realizing that such a school could not be categorized as a school of science or of literature. It would be related to these traditional categories, yet be unlike them. Carter described it in this way:

> The institution from its peculiar purpose must necessarily be both literary and scientific in its character. And although, with its design constantly in view, we could not reasonably expect it to add, directly, much to the stock of what is now called literature, or to enlarge much the boundaries of what is now called science; yet, from the very nature of the subject to which it would be devoted, and upon which it would be employed, it must in its progress create a kind of literature of its own, and open a new science somewhat peculiar to itself—the science of communicating knowledge from one mind to another while at a different stage of maturity.[10]

At the same time, Carter himself was the co-publisher of the *United States Literary Gazette* (begun in 1826), a literary review specializing in American themes and writing. He later published textbooks on geography.

---

7. James G. Carter, *Essays Upon Popular Education Containing a Particular Examination of the Schools of Massachusetts, and an Outline of and Institution for the Education of Teachers* (Boston: Bowles and Dearborn, 1826), p. 41.

8. Ibid., p. 45.

9. Ibid., p. 36.

10. Ibid., p. 47.

Carter next set out to secure political action in support of his proposals. In 1827 he asked the Massachusetts legislature to appropriate funds for a state normal school for the training of teachers. The bill failed by one vote in the state senate. In 1830, Carter was elected to the legislature, and by 1837 he was chairman of the House Committee on Education, which drafted the bill creating a state board of education. After the bill passed the senate, many expected Governor Everett to reward Carter's efforts by appointing him the first secretary of the board. Although he was appointed to the newly created board, the rotation system made his term only a year. According to one account, Carter's failure to win the appointment as secretary was due to the political liabilities he had collected, especially among the clergy, while trying to promote school reform.[11] Governor Everett also passed over two other likely candidates, the Reverend Charles Brooks and George B. Emerson. Instead, he named Horace Mann, who up to that time had not been associated with the common school movement.

Horace Mann

Although Horace Mann had had very limited experience with education, he was the president of the Massachusetts state senate and had been active in a number of other reform movements. He was largely responsible for the establishment of the first hospital for the mentally ill in Massachusetts (and in the United States), was an untiring worker in the temperance movement, and had worked to improve conditions for paupers and debtors. Mann's appointment was thoroughly consistent with the views of Governor Everett, for both men were politicians who did not reject reform but consistently worked for it within the system. They sought not so much to transform society but to reform it where it had somehow gone awry.

As secretary of the state board of education, Mann sought to persuade people that their interests and public schooling were complementary. He promised no immediate social reforms but did suggest that the schools would prevent social problems in the future. Mann's platform for schools was broad but basically conservative. He taught that the schools could promote social unity by teaching the common principles of republicanism and of Christianity. There was, he believed, a core of principles to which nearly all Americans subscribed. He also sought to prevent schools from being captured by special interests and urged that they avoid controversial issues.

By the time Mann resigned in 1848, he was regarded as an educational expert throughout the nation. His accomplishments were the results of his own ability and work. The legislature provided no staff and gave him no executive authority. The Act that created the position simply stated that the Secretary was to "collect information of the actual condition and efficiency of Common Schools, and other means of popular education; and to diffuse as widely as possible . . . information

---

11. Jonathan C. Messerli, "James G. Carter's Liabilities as a Common School Reformer," *History of Education Quarterly* 5:1 (March 1965), pp. 14–25.

of the most approved and successful methods of arranging the studies, and conducting the education of the young.[12]

Whenever there was a meeting to discuss education in Massachusetts, Mann seemed to be there. For the first five years of his tenure in office, the state sponsored an annual convention for the "friends of education." Mann attended and delivered an address to each gathering. The state directed the counties to hold educational conventions; Mann attended these, too, and delivered an appropriate lecture. Those speeches, the *Common School Journal* that he edited for ten years, and the twelve *Annual Reports* he wrote for the Board constitute an impressive body of literature on the problems and issues in the nineteenth-century education.

Mann quickly learned about the schools in Massachusetts and made good use of what he learned. When he spoke to members of school committees, teachers, and other citizens, he could discuss actual conditions because he had visited many of the state's schools. In the first address he prepared for delivery to the county common school convention (1837), he discussed, with some humor, the conditions of the schoolhouses he had recently visited.

He told one story about visiting a schoolhouse "which the scientific would probably call the sixth order of architecture." It was a "summer-house for winter residence," a place where the ink froze in the pens while still in the students hands. In the center of the schoolhouse, near the stove, the temperature was typically 90 degrees. At the perimeter of the room, it was frequently near 30 degrees. The teacher allowed the center of the room to exceed ninety degrees only when the perimeter fell below thirty degrees. As Mann saw the room, it was not without pedagogical promise, for, he said, "It was an excellent place for the teacher to illustrate one of the facts in geography; for five steps would have carried him through the five zones." As for the students, Mann related that some "suffered the Arctic cold of Captains Ross and Perry" and some endured "the torrid heat of the Landers," but none was awarded "the honors of a discoverer."

At another school Mann observed a roof that made him wonder whether it had been "designed to explain the Deluge." He asked the school's mistress whether "she and her little ones were not sometime drowned out." The teacher replied that she and the students were in no danger because "the floor leaked as badly as the roof, and drained off the water."[13] After his amusing accounts, Mann lectured his audience about the other common defects in the schools that were not as obvious but more dangerous. He explained that each child needed to inhale one gallon of fresh air each minute. Schools without proper ventilation deprived children of the air they needed and caused them to inhale that second part of the air, the part meant not for people but for plants. He asked his audience why the public had tended to ventilation in jails but not in schools.

---

12. Horace Mann, *Lectures on Education* (Boston: Idle and Dutton, 1855), p. vii.
13. Ibid., p. 24.

Women in Teaching. In his first county lecture, Mann remarked that he regarded "it as one of the clearest ordinances of nature, that woman is the appointed guide and guardian of children of a tender age."[14] In his second county lecture, he returned to this topic. Mann believed that women were better suited than men to teach the young. Women could discern the status of a child's mind, follow its workings, determine whether it had strayed, and bring it back to the proper course more readily than could men. Increasing the proportion of woman among the teaching force—he estimated that there then about two women for every three men—would improve instruction as well as make good use of talent that had been allowed to lie "dormant for want of some genial sphere of exercise."[15]

Mann evidently knew that some women were asking for increased status and opportunity in the social arena, but he offered neither strong support nor strong objections. While noting that "Christianity and other conspiring causes" had been working for "the elevating of the character, the condition and the social rank of the female sex," he reminded the women in the audience that "new privileges" brought "new duties." The duty Mann assigned them was the teaching of those of a "tender age."

> Is there not an obvious, constitutional difference of temperament between the sexes, indicative of a prearranged fitness and adaptation, and making known to us as by a heaven-imparted sign, that woman by her livelier sensibility and her quicker sympathies, is the forechosen guide and guardian of children of a tender age?[16]

However, to Mann, the difference that made women most fit to teach the younger children also weighed against their being placed in charge of the older ones. After the world had hardened the mind of the young, it was time to subject it "to the firmer grasp, to the more forcible subduing power of masculine hands."[17]

The advantage of this distinction, for Mann, was that men could continue to teach the upper grades without any threat of their status being diminished by the entrance of women. Women who wanted to teach would constitute a ready supply of teachers for the schools Mann was seeking to expand and improve.

Throughout his tenure as secretary, Mann sought to show how his proposals for schools were consistent with his constituents' beliefs and aspirations. When he spoke of equality and the power of education, he assured his audience that the schools would not and could not turn out students "like so many half-dollars struck at the government mint."[18] Even when he spoke of the necessity of educating both boys and girls, he adhered to traditional conceptions. A son, he suggested, should be prepared to "superintend some part of the complicated social machinery of

---

14. Ibid., p. 26.
15. Ibid., p. 73.
16. Ibid.
17. Ibid., p. 74.
18. Ibid., p. 80.

life." A daughter was to be prepared "to answer the claims of humanity whether those claims require the labor of the head or the labor of the hand." He did suggest also that a daughter should be "so trained that she can bear, with dignity and self-sustaining ability, those revolutions in Fortune's wheel which sometimes bring the kitchen up and turn the parlor down."[19]

Mann's Reports. In his twelve *Annual Reports* as secretary of the state board, Mann touched on nearly every facet of public education. He reported on the need for good schoolhouses, the character and composition of the local school committees, public apathy as the chief enemy of good schools, the need for trained and qualified teachers, the best ways to teach reading and spelling, the need for libraries, the problems of school discipline, the need for school consolidation, the need to prohibit religious differences from disrupting the development of the schools, the need for instruction in health and hygiene, and many other topics. In particular, the *Fifth Report* (1841) was widely circulated outside Massachusetts, and the *Seventh* (1843) precipitated a great deal of controversy.

Most of the 1841 *Report* was devoted to showing the propertied classes and manufacturer that paying for public schools served their interests. Mann was certainly not opposed to the accumulation of wealth; nor did he want to redistribute it. The acquisitive instinct, he had said, was "the parent of industry and frugality," which were "blood-relations to the whole family of the virtues."[20] To the businessmen and manufacturers, Mann explained that support of schools would not diminish the nation's wealth but would contribute to its growth. Properly schooled people would behave in ways that would complement the strength and vitality of the nation's economy. Mann's position won him the support of important interests in Massachusetts and earned him recognition outside the state. His friend Francis Dwight, editor of the *District School Journal* for the state of New York, devoted an entire issue of his journal to Mann's *Fifth Report.* With the assistance of some "friends of education," Dwight even provided German translations for "thousands of immigrants who are equally with ourselves interested in the only means of preserving the institutions of our common country."[21]

On May 1, 1843, Mann was married to Mary Tyler Peabody. During their five-month wedding tour, Mann visited schools throughout Great Britain and northern Europe. The major portion of his *Seventh Report* dealt with school practices in Europe. Like others before him, Mann was impressed with the Prussian schools. Several schoolmasters took umbrage at his *Report,* for they believed Mann was attacking them. In the next two years Mann and the Boston teachers exchanged a series of lengthy attacks and replies. In the course of the controversy Mann secured a good amount of publicity for the schools and their difficulties, and the public seemed to endorse his views. In his final reply in 1845, Mann established

---

19. Ibid., p. 92.
20. Ibid., p. 89.
21. In Jonathan Messerli, *Horace Mann* (New York: Knopf, 1972), p. 372.

that the controversy had brought his *Seventh Report* to the attention of at least 100,000 readers. It also served to publicize the pedagogical reforms Mann had been advocating for several years. Two of them still have currency: whether to begin the teaching of reading with words or letters; and whether corporal punishment should be abolished.

1848 was an eventful year in the history of the western world. In Europe, it was a year of revolution and social upheaval. Karl Marx published the *Communist Manifesto* and the revolutions convinced many that the social order would indeed be rent by a series of class conflicts. For a full generation many Americans and observers of the new nation had examined the social and economic order of the United States. Some warned that a harsh class system was being fashioned, and some, as we have seen, like Frances Wright and Parke Godwin had proposed solutions.

In 1848 Mann wrote his *Twelfth Report.* In it he wrote about the European and the American systems of social classes. Dissociating America from Europe, he wrote that in the United States, education had the power "to obliterate factitious distinctions in society." The common school was to be "the balance-wheel of the social machinery."[22] It would prevent revolution and even the necessity of redistributing wealth by teaching all people in all classes how to create new wealth. The common school was the bulwark of American society and its institutions.

Mann's Achievements. In 1848 Mann resigned from the board of education to take John Quincy Adams's place in Congress. His twelve years in office had brought about an impressive list of improvements in the Massachusetts schools. Annual expenditures for the common schools had doubled and many new schools had been built. The salaries of male teachers increased by 62 percent, those of the women teachers by 51 percent. There were many more women teachers than at the beginning of the period. Three schools for the training of teachers had been opened. The average length of the school year increased by a month. The frequency and quality of school supervision was improved. Teaching methods and discipline methods were reformed according to new educational theories. New textbooks were provided and school libraries were enlarged or built. New high schools were opened, and the private secondary schools were no longer more important than the public ones. Children were attending school in greater numbers than ever before.

Mann was clearly an effective worker for the common schools of Massachusetts, and influential in other parts of the nation. Yet it may be a mistake to attribute all the improvement to Mann's efforts alone. Before Mann, James G. Carter and other members of the American Institute of Instruction worked for better schools. Also, the increasing wealth of the state helped make the improvements possible. These other factors suggest that the creation of the common

---

22. Horace Mann, *Twelfth Annual Report,* in *The Republic and the School: Horace Mann on the Education of Free Men,* ed. Lawrence A. Cremin (New York: Teachers College Press, 1957), p. 87.

school was the result of people responding individually as well as collectively to the changes in their lives.

Henry Barnard

Henry Barnard's career paralleled Mann's in many respects. Each had planned to make the law his career, but was drawn into a new professional field, education. While Horace Mann was closing his law office and preparing to assume his new post, Barnard was being elected to the Connecticut legislature. Like Mann, Barnard was a Whig and was fearful of the social disorder he associated with the Jacksonians. As a legislator, Barnard worked for many of the humanitarian causes of the day: public libraries; reorganization of the county jails; help for the blind, the deaf, the mentally ill, and the poor. In 1838 he presented to the Connecticut House of Representatives a bill that urged the creation of a Board of Commissioners of Common Schools and the office of Secretary of the Board. His bill passed both houses without a dissenting vote, giving Connecticut an act much like that in Massachusetts. Barnard was appointed to the board and named another educational reformer to serve as secretary, the Reverend Thomas H. Gallaudet. Gallaudet declined, and the other members elected Barnard to fill the position.

The Connecticut law required the Secretary to inspect and report on the condition of the schools, to prepare reports and recommendations to the legislature, to address the county educational conventions, to edit an educational journal for the state, and do whatever else was necessary to improve the schools. At the end of his first year in office Barnard submitted his required *Report*. It showed that he had secured and managed a great deal of information. He presented statistical information for more than 1,200 schools. He had addressed county educational conventions, delivered addresses to other public meetings, visited 200 schools and nearly two-thirds of the state's teachers, and seen to the publication and distribution of 60,000 copies of the *Connecticut Common School Journal.*

Like many other school reformers of his day, Barnard was well acquainted with the Prussian school system. An entire issue of the first volume of the *Connecticut Common School Journal* was given to an examination and discussion of that system. Barnard pointed out that in Connecticut, society was "new and unfixed," and its people enjoyed social, commercial, and political freedoms unknown to Prussians. Yet it was clear that Barnard found the Prussian system "admirable" because it was carefully designed to satisfy the requirements of Prussian society. The message was clear: Connecticut should and could have a comparable system. However, an essential feature of the Prussian system was compulsion. That was not possible in Connecticut. Even if the state built a school system and then attempted to compel people to comply with its requirements, public opinion would wreck it. What puzzled Barnard was the willingness of the public to accept compulsion in other aspects of their lives. He noted that:

> . . . the right of the State to enforce parents to educate their children, would be denied and resented. And yet they will submit to perform military duty or pay their fine—to serve as jurors or incur the penalty—to sell their lands and

their homestead to make room for the railroad or canal, or else yield to an arbitrary apprizal—all this and much more they will do, because the Law enjoins it as a public duty. But to educate children, by which society may be shielded from their vice, and poverty, and crimes, and be made happy by the correct exercise of the duties of the elector, juror, citizens, is regarded as a duty entirely parental, and which the Law cannot make compulsory.[23]

Not until the 1850s did states begin to pass compulsory school attendance laws, and those early laws were not systematically enforced. Some allowed exemptions, and most laws failed to define adequately either truancy or attendance. In 1842 Connecticut demonstrated that it certainly did not want any compulsory school laws—perhaps no school laws at all. The Whigs lost the governor's office and the legislature to the Democrats, who repealed the 1838 School Law. Friends of education were dismayed, and Barnard was out of office.

Barnard then set out on a fifteen-month tour of the United States to collect materials for a planned history of education. While on tour, he lectured to eleven state legislatures and to others who wanted to learn about the benefits of the common school. Before he could begin writing his history, he was invited to Rhode Island to discuss the common school problem there. Soon Barnard was visiting schools in Rhode Island and talking to teachers, citizens, and public officials. After eighteen months of fact-finding, he wrote a bill that became Rhode Island's school law in 1845. Barnard became the new Commissioner of Public Schools in Rhode Island.

In 1849, he resigned his post in Rhode Island because of failing health. He went on to a series of educational positions and a number of illnesses, but lived until 1900. (He was eighty-nine years old at his death.)

Through the 1850s, Barnard served as principal of the Connecticut State Normal School and State Superintendent of Common Schools; chancellor of the University of Wisconsin and agent of the newly created Normal School Regents in that state. In 1867 the Congress established the Department of Education, and President Andrew Johnson appointed Barnard the first U.S. Commissioner of Education. Now he was to collect and diffuse educational information for the nation.

Barnard lacked the necessary administrative ability, however, and encountered difficulties with Congress and a disappointed rival for his office. In 1869 the Department of Education was made a bureau in the Department of the Interior; President Grant appointed John Eaton as commissioner. Barnard returned to Connecticut to work on his history (which was never finished) and on the *American Journal of Education,* which he had begun in 1855. Most of his time and energy, and a great deal of his own money, went to the magazine.

As an administrator and a politician, Barnard was not so successful as Mann. He made an impressive contribution to the literature of education, however, helping to give definition to a new social institution and a new profession. In the

---

23. In Daniel Colhoun, ed., *The Educating of Americans: A Documentary History* (Boston: Houghton Mifflin, 1969), p. 196.

American Journal and his other writings, he provided the materials from which others were to write many histories of education in the United States and Europe. He also contributed to the daily routines of school teaching in school administration by making information available to teachers, superintendents, and school committee members.

School Architecture. Barnard's *School Architecture,* published in 1848, was a handbook for those faced with building a school system. An examination of Barnard's book shows just what the Americans in the first half of the nineteenth century needed to know and do to build a school system: how school buildings should be built, heated, and ventilated; where they should be located on the lot; how they should be maintained, how they should be furnished; and what kinds of materials would be needed for the teaching that was to occur within them.

Barnard also directed his readers' attention to the people who were to work in the schools. He advised that the room be arranged so that the teacher could see the entire school "at a glance," address the entire school from one position, be able to approach any one student without interfering with any other, and conduct recitations with some of the class without disturbing those who were doing seatwork. Barnard also provided specific directions on how to arrange the schoolroom: The teacher's desk was to be at the front of the room on a platform and students' seats properly arranged in aisles. No matter where the recitation area was, it was important that the teachers know the advantages of each area. The rear of the room was a good position from which to detect misconduct; the front was a good place from which to prevent misconduct. If the teacher did move about the room, Barnard cautioned, "the mischievous scholars will shape their devices for concealment accordingly." From the front of the room, "the eye of the teacher, that great instrument of moral discipline," could be employed effectively.[24]

The most important piece of schoolroom apparatus, according to Barnard, was the blackboard. He advised that each school have several. Recitation rooms, he suggested, should be lined with blackboards. Where there was but one, he instructed, "it should be movable . . . suspended on hooks, or rings, inserted in the upper edge, or what is better on a movable frame, like the painter's easel."[25] For those who were teaching in schools without blackboards, Barnard even provided a recipe for making one by coating a board with a mixture of lampblack, flour of emery, and spirit varnish.

Barnard also told teachers what to put on the blackboard: "the elements of the written characters classified in the order of their simplicity, and guide-marks to enable a child to determine with ease the height, width, and inclination of every letter" and "the musical scale."[26]

---

24. Jean and Robert McClintock, eds., *Henry Barnard's School Architecture* (New York: Teachers College Press, 1970), p. 74.

25. Ibid., p. 75.

26. Ibid., p. 245.

Throughout *School Architecture,* Barnard gave ample descriptions and directions on how to acquire and use school furniture and school apparatus. He provided pictures, names of supplies, and prices. He told how the apparatus was to be used and why. He could have titled his work "How to Keep School."

Calvin Stowe and Education in the West

The Ohio Territory was the first of the western lands to be settled after the Revolution, and in 1803 Ohio became the seventeenth state. Cincinnati, located on the northern bend of the Ohio River, had already became the largest city. The river brought goods and settlers from the East, and Cincinnati soon acquired its share of urban characteristics. Like many western cities, it attempted to pattern itself after Philadelphia, laying out its streets in the familiar checkerboard pattern. It even had its own version of Benjamin Franklin, Dr. Daniel Drake, sometimes known as the "Franklin of the West." Drake promoted the founding of the local lyceum, a circulating library, a Lancasterian school, a museum, and a number of debating societies. He also campaigned for public health measures and ran a drugstore in which he introduced soda water to Cincinnati.[27]

The advocates of education and the common school in Ohio were concentrated in Cincinnati. By 1829 the town had a system of forty-seven private neighborhood schools that enrolled more than 1,600 children.[28] Those schools could not provide schooling for all children, especially the poor, and in the 1820s Cincinnati began to lobby for a statewide system of common schools. The rest of the state was not yet ready to consider such action, but in 1829 the town did secure an amendment to its charter enabling it to operate its own system of common schools.

A number of those who had worked for improved educational facilities in the Northeast had moved West. Albert Pickett, who had run a school in New York City and published two educational journals, was among those who had moved to Cincinnati. In 1828 Pickett and Alexander Kinmont founded the Western Academic Institute, later the Western Literary Institute and College of Professional Teachers. The Institute held annual meetings, published its proceedings, and worked to promote interest in the development of a system of common schools. Among the members and participants were Lyman Beecher, Thomas S. Grimké, Henry Barnard, Walter S. Johnson, William Holmes McGuffey, Emma Willard, Catharine E. Beecher, Almira Lincoln Phelps, Lydia H. Sigourney, Samuel Lewis (Ohio's first superintendent of schools), and Calvin Stowe.

Calvin Stowe, a graduate of Bowdoin College and Andover Theological Seminary, had been persuaded by Lyman Beecher to leave his professorship of Greek at Dartmouth College and move to Cincinnati to assume the chair of Biblical Literature at Lane Theological Seminary in 1833. (Beecher, a prominent New

---

27. Richard C. Wade, *The Urban Frontier: The Rise of Western Cities, 1790–1830* (Cambridge: Harvard University Press, 1959), p. 114.

28. Ibid., p. 244.

England clergyman, was president of the new seminary. He was also the father of many gifted children, notably Catharine, Harriet, and Henry Ward.)

Although he was a student of the classical languages, Stowe did not advocate the restoration of the traditional grammar school where students were drilled in the rudiments of Greek, Latin, and Hebrew. Rather, he saw the common school as an institution that would simultaneously ensure the preservation of the existing American culture and promote the country's economic development. In an address delivered to the fifth annual meeting of the Western Institute, Stowe told his audience that "the wave of immigration has begun to roll from the old world to the new, and no human power can stop it." It was essential, he said, that the immigrants be Americanized and lose their European characteristics.

> It is altogether essential to our national strength and peace, if not even to our national existence, that the foreigners who settle on our soil, should cease to be Europeans and become Americans; and as our national language is English, and as our literature, our manners, and our institutions are of English origin, and the whole foundation of our society English, it is necessary that they become branches of the parent stock; improve its fruits, and add to its beauty and its vigor. . . .[29]

Stowe argued that the best way to secure the proper "harmony of national feeling and character" was to bring all children together in the common schools. Public schools had to be the best schools so that they could attract the rich as well as the poor, native Americans as well as immigrants. The school would promote the "commingling of different ingredients" and produce a strong and even improved national character.

Daniel Drake shared Stowe's concerns and proposals. Drake likened the school to the crucible, the schoolmaster to the alchemist, and the children of immigrants to "crude and discordant materials" out of which the schoolmaster-alchemist would produce "fine gold."[30] For two generations, Stowe's and Drake's views were to be restated many times.

In 1836, a few months after he and Harriet Beecher were married, Stowe planned a trip to Europe to purchase books for the library of the seminary. Before Stowe's departure, the Western Literary Institute persuaded the Ohio legislature to commission him to inspect the schools of Europe and prepare a report. In 1837 Stowe presented the famous *Report on Elementary Education in Europe,* in which he compared educational practices in Ohio with those of Prussia and Württemberg. The Ohio legislature printed 10,000 copies of the report and distributed it to the school districts of the state. Subsequently, other states—Pennsylvania, Massachusetts, Michigan, North Carolina, and Virginia—did likewise. Although other Americans had traveled to Europe and appraised European schools, Stowe's *Report* was the first to receive general and widespread attention. He was im-

---

29. "Transactions of the Fifth Annual Meeting of the Western Literary Institute and College of Professional Teachers" (Cincinnati, 1836), in *Turning Points in American Educational History,* ed. David B. Tyack (Waltham, Mass.: Blaisdell Publishing Co., 1967), p. 149.

30. Ibid., p. 150.

pressed with the frugality and efficiency the Prussian schools engendered in their students. Those were qualities that could benefit America because, according to Stowe, "the productions of our country for some years past have by no means kept pace with the increase of our consumption, and many an American family during the last season has felt a hard pressure, where they never expected to feel one."[31]

Stowe told the Ohio legislature that the state could have a system of schools as good and as effective as those of Prussia. Ohio only needed the will, for the will of the people was even more powerful than that of any foreign monarch. The state, however, did not act to make its schools truly free to all until 1853. Yet Stowe's *Report* (1837), the translation from the French of Victor Cousin's report on the Prussian schools (1834) and Horace Mann's *Seventh Report* (1843), provided the advocates of the common school with arguments, plans, procedures, and a standard by which they could measure their own progress.

---

31. In Sol Cohen, ed., *Education in the United States: A Documentary History* (New York: Random House, 1974), p. 929.

Education for the Native American   10

That American Indians were not granted citizenship in the United States until 1924 tells much of the story about the education of the native Americans. Successive waves of white settlers saw the Indians either as enemies who had to be defeated or as savages who had to be "civilized" and so made harmless to the society the white settlers were building. Rarely was the Indian seen either as one who could participate equally in the white society or as one whose native language and culture were rich and valuable. Efforts at providing education for the American Indian were usually separate from those the white settlers made in providing for their own children. At best, Indians were to be transformed into English Christians or Christian Americans and taught how to conform to the ways and demands of the white settlers. Paul Horgan's observations of the "irrelevant" education of the Pueblos in the Southwest in the 1930s describes what typically was done to American Indians in the name of education:

> Indian children are placed in Government Indian schools, where they learn orthodox school subjects, and military drill, and football. When they are old enough to graduate as young men and women, they are turned out, equipped by rote to compete in modern life, but wholly unequipped by temperament, heritage, and desire. One of two courses confronts them: They may either take some menial job in the white man's scheme, a job for which their formal education has provided nothing, or they may return to the pueblo, where the values of a formal education are laughable![1]

Rarely were attempts made to determine what the Indians' values and aspirations were so that a suitable system of education could be established. Rather, the attempts were to restructure the lives and ways of the Indians so that they could be controlled.

---

1. Paul Horgan, "The Three Southwestern Peoples," in *Living Ideas in America,* ed. Henry Steele Commager (New York: Harper and Row, 1964), pp. 42–43.

New England: "Christianizing the Natives"

As the Indians and the New England settlers interacted, each showed the other new and different ways. Those exchanges constituted a mutual education and offered each group an alternative way of life. The white settlers, however, were not content to learn from the exchanges with the Indians. Believing that their own ways and beliefs were superior, they set out to teach them the "Christian way of life."

The first attempts at either schooling or converting the Indians were severely limited by the barriers of language. Two clergymen, Thomas Mayhew and John Eliot, began to use Indian interpreters and to study the Algonkian language. Through the efforts of Mayhew, Eliot, and others, Parliament in 1649 created the Society for the Propagation of the Gospel. The Society paid missionaries and teachers to work among the Indians; bought tools, building supplies, and clothing for the Indians; financed the building of an Indian College at Harvard that never really served Indians; and paid for the printing of several books in Algonkian. Among the translated books were a grammar, a primer, a catechism, Richard Baxter's *A Call to the Unconverted,* and Eliot's translation of the Bible, published in 1661–63.[2]

Believing that the Indians' conversion had to include a complete transformation of their civilization, Eliot by 1651 had convinced several leaders to assist in establishing what came to be known as a "praying town." He secured 2,000 acres on the Charles River. Streets were laid out, lots for houses and plots for farming assigned, and a meeting-house with a room for Eliot built. With funds provided by the Society for the Propagation of the Gospel in New England, thirteen other such "praying towns" were organized in the next fourteen years. By 1675 there were about 2,500 converted Indians (about a fifth of the Indian population in the area) and most of them lived in New England praying towns.[3]

The Indian Charity School

Like many clergymen of his era, Eleazar Wheelock of Connecticut taught as well as preached. Among the pupils he took into his home in 1743 was Samson Occom of the Mohican tribe. Wheelock soon decided to establish an Indian missionary school. In 1754 a Connecticut farmer, Joshua Moor, donated two acres and a house in Lebanon, Connecticut. By 1762, when Wheelock wrote "Of the Original Design, Rise, Progress and Present State of the Indian Charity School in Lebanon, Connecticut," he had nearly twenty Indians in his school.

In his description of the Indian Charity School, Wheelock offered several reasons for educating the Indians. He reminded his readers that it was a God-given

---

2. Lawrence A. Cremin, *American Education: The Colonial Experience 1607–1783* (New York: Harper and Row, 1970), p. 160.

3. Ibid.

duty to look after the physical and spiritual well-being of the Indians. They had neglected this duty, and so God was punishing them by "permitting the savages to be such a sore scourge to our land, and make such depredations on our frontiers. . . ."[4] Furthermore, the colony's charter was secured from the crown with a claim that "Christianizing the natives" was one of the motives for establishing the colony. Conversion also would make the Indians loyal to the English crown. Finally, in a familiar argument, Wheelock claimed that conversion and schooling would be the cheapest possible form of defense against the Indians.

Because the Indians moved about "fishing, fowling, and hunting," Wheelock decided to train Indian boys to work as missionaries among their own in concert with the English missionaries. His work also included instructing Indian girls "in whatever should be necessary to render them fit, to perform the female part, as housewives, school-mistresses, tayloresses, &C." No matter where the Indians were, there would be teachers and missionaries who could "recommend to the savages a more rational and decent manner of living.[5] Thus Wheelock advised that it usually was pointless to have the missionaries establish schools for the Indians, for their temperament and lifestyle made schools ineffective. If schools were established, Wheelock thought it was necessary that children be "taken quite away from their parents, and the pernicious influences of Indian examples."[6]

Wheelock advised that at such schools there should be skilled farmers and tradesmen to instruct the boys and "mistresses to instruct the girls in such manufacturers as are proper for them" when they are not in the classroom. The Indian boys, as well as English boys who were willing to devote their lives to the missionary service, were to learn the languages of the Indians (Wheelock termed them "pagan languages"). Although the studies were especially designed for missionary work, students were also to learn Latin and Greek. Each day of school began and ended with prayer. The senior students read passages from Scripture and then followed drill in *Assembly's Catechism.*

Wheelock's first Indian student, Samson Occom, became a successful missionary, and in 1766 joined the Reverend Nathaniel Whitaker on a journey to England to secure an endowment for the Indian school. They secured subscriptions totaling nearly £10,000, and the Earl of Dartmouth was named president of the board of trustees. In 1770 Wheelock's school was moved to what is now Hanover, New Hampshire. To the Indian school was added a college, and Dartmouth College was founded. It remained separate from the Indian school, however. Dartmouth was not for the American Indian.

---

4. "Wheelock's Narrative (1762)" in *Old South Leaflets* 1:22 (Boston: Directors of the Old South Work, Old South Meeting House), p. 2.

5. Ibid., p. 3.

6. Ibid., p. 8.

"Habits of Civilization"

When the U.S. Office of Indian Affairs was established in 1819, government funds for schools for Indians became available. Before then, any education provided for the Indians came from either missionaries or religious organizations. The government, however, adopted the policies of the religious organizations and enlisted their aid in providing instruction. The object of education was still to "civilize" the Indians.

On the recommendation of President James Monroe in 1818, Congress appropriated $10,000 to introduce "the habits and arts of civilization" to the Indians who lived close to the nation's frontier settlements. Curiously, the program was administered by the Secretary of War. The War Department invited missionaries and other charitable organizations to apply for funds to enable them to teach the boys the "mechanic arts" as well as the "three Rs" and agriculture, and to teach the girls to spin, weave, and sew.[7] The department also emphasized that those who worked in the schools for Indians were expected "not only to set a good example of sobriety, industry, and honesty, but as far as practicable, to impress on the minds of the Indians, the friendly and benevolent views of the government toward them."[8]

In a report to John C. Calhoun, Secretary of War, on the condition of schools in the Choctaw mission run by the American Board of Commissioners for Foreign Missions, the Reverend Cyrus Kingsbury recorded that the Lancasterian methods were used in the boys' school. When not in the classroom, the boys worked at planting, hoeing, and clearing the land—some worked in the blacksmith's shop— and the girls did domestic work.

By 1824 many believed that success in educating and "civilizing" the American Indians was very near. The Committee on Indian Affairs of the House of Representatives reported that the funds spent for Indian education had been "very judicious." Schools for Indian children and houses for the teachers had been built. Children were being instructed in practical matters as well as traditional school subjects, and they were even having a positive influence "in inducing their parents to become less fond of an erratic life."[9]

The "Indian Question"

The committee's belief that its program would soon transform the lives of Indians in "geometrical proportion" turned out to be overly sanguine. Even after the defeat

---

7. *The works of John C. Calhoun*, vol. V., reproduced in Robert H. Bremmer, et. al. (eds.) *Children and Youth in America: A Documentary History*, ed. Robert H. Bremmer et al. (Cambridge: Harvard University Press, 1970), vol. I, p. 548.

8. John C. Calhoun, "Regulations for the Civilization of the Indians," reproduced in Bremmer, *Children and Youth in America*, vol. I, p. 549.

9. Reproduced in Bremmer, *Children and Youth in America*, vol. I, p. 551.

of General George Armstrong Custer in 1876, Americans still clung to a concept of the Indians that was not significantly different from that of the first settlers. In a pamphlet entitled "The Indian Question" (1883), Samuel Chapman Armstrong, who had founded Hampton Institute for black freedmen, wrote that even in "civilized" tribes the Indians seemed "to a large extent . . . fixed in a half civilized, half pagan state. . . ."[10] By modern standards, Armstrong was insensitive to the Indians' needs and their right to maintain their own way of life. For his own time, he was sympathetic, although his sympathy was mainly directed to those Indians who were willing to adopt the ways of the white society. He wanted to educate the Indians for a proper role in white society just as he had worked to help black Americans fill their specified roles.

Armstrong strongly criticized how Americans were dealing with the Indian question. Although he found the reservations "necessary expedients," he described them as "merely places for herding Indians" that "may become growing evils." The mistaken notion that the Indians should be treated as a "separate people" had led to the disruption of the lives of too many Indians in the eastern United States, where "thrifty farms and fruitful orchards" were needlessly exchanged "for a Western wilderness, where thousands have died from exposure."[11]

Armstrong recognized that the white settlers' transformation of the American continent had largely destroyed the Indian way of life. His claim that "the destruction of the buffalo has been more trying to the Indian than was the sudden emancipation of the Negro" was insightful as well as debatable. The destruction of the buffalo did in fact destroy the basic elements of many Indians' way of life. He observed that the "human machine, after running for centuries, does not readily reverse itself."[12] His answer to "the Indian question," however, was brutally simple: he suggested that the best way to civilize the Indians was to all but destroy them and regulate their vital provisions. After defeat and surrender, Armstrong advised, the white society should appeal to the Indians' stomachs to convert them to the proper ways.

Hampton and Carlisle

In November 1878, Armstrong accepted fifty Indian students from the Indian Bureau into Hampton Institute. The following year, the federal government established a training school for Indians at Carlisle, Pennsylvania, along the lines of Hampton Institute. In 1883 Armstrong reported that there were 90 Indian students enrolled at Hampton and more than 300 at the Carlisle school. The progress of the Indians in these schools was so satisfactory, he explained, that he recommended their education be expanded. He cautioned that "the aims and methods

---

10. Samuel Chapman Armstrong, *The Indian Question* (Hampton, Va.: Normal School Steam Press, 1883), p. 4.

11. Ibid.

12. Ibid., p. 5.

of most white schools render them unfit for Indians."[13] Rather, he wanted to place the Indian students in the schools already established for black Americans, "the Negro institutions at Nashville, Tenn., at Talladega, Ala., and elsewhere." At Hampton, Armstrong reported, the black students and the Indian students worked well together. The two races "were mutually helpful" to each other; and, "a race that had been led," he claimed, "is leading another."[14]

The educational program that was provided for the Indians at Hampton and at Carlisle was "practical," designed to "fit them to take care of themselves." The students' days were divided equally between study and labor. More attention was given to mechanical skills than to agriculture because tradesmen earned better wages. Students made shoes, tinware, harnesses, and other products. They were successfully taught to learn from books, and to be neat and industrious.

When Armstrong opened Hampton Institute after the Civil War, he operated on the principle that blacks should be taught to support and teach themselves. He tried to convince others that the same principle could be used to solve the Indian question. He noted that the free school system for blacks in the South was "vitalized" by a number of central institutions that chose and trained youth of the race as teachers. Certainly, Eastern charity could help establish a system of schools in which the best Indian boys and girls could be trained to teach their peers in the classroom, as well as in the community through good example. Like many others in the nineteenth century, Armstrong believed that women had a particular role to play in society, and that teaching was an especially appropriate job for them. In the Fall of 1881 he took twenty-five Indian boys and five Indian girls back to their Dakota homes. The boys were easily placed in areas where they could practice the trades they had learned at Hampton; for the girls it was a different matter. They could sew and do housework, but they had no trades, and there were no "suitable situations" for them. The girls were returned to their mothers and grandmothers, who "would sell them to the brave who would pay the most ponies for them." Armstrong did not recommend that the girls be taught trades, but rather said that they should be teachers. He compared the girls' career in teaching to that of black women in the South; it was one way for the girls to "be more than drudges." And, like many others before him, he claimed that it was upon the Indian girls that "the hope of the race rested."

Once they returned home, Indian students did not always find it easy to live as school had taught them. In the winter of 1883, Armstrong received word about some of his former Hampton students from the Reverend Thomas L. Riggs, a missionary to the Sioux Indians in Dakota. For example, Riggs wrote that of the five Indian boys at the Cheyenne River Agency who had been to Hampton, every

---

13. Ibid., p. 15.
14. Ibid., p. 16.

one had, during the summer, "put on the blanket and leggins."[15] Riggs went on to counsel Armstrong that he should not be overly discouraged by the apparent failures, for it was not reasonable to expect "to lift up a savage people by giving to a few boys and girls a three years' course of study alone."[16] He also observed that many of the government agents did not know how to judge the Hampton students. An Indian agent at Lower Brule, Dakota, complained in 1882:

> As a matter of fact, the boys returned to this agency with a three years' training at Hampton have thus far proved a failure. At the start they promised well, but they have all returned to their old way, having learned just sufficient of the vices of the whites to make them worse than at the beginning. I am exceedingly mortified to make this admission, but if the truth be not told the evil will go on, and both time and money be expended, and little or no good result from the expenditures.[17]

Armstrong's reaction to the criticisms of the Hampton students was to call for better agents and a more efficient and responsive government: "The difficulty is not with the Indian who is today most improvable and ready to do his part, but in the well-meant but complicated hydra-headed administration of his affairs at Washington. . . ."[18]

Sarah Winnemucca

Princess Sarah Winnemucca was educated for her career as a mediator between Indians and whites by her grandfather, Captain Truckee, chief of the Piutes. Her success as an educator was brought to the attention of the white society in 1886 when Elizabeth Peabody communicated it to the editor of the *Christian Union,* Lyman Abbot. Abbot then reproduced a letter from Winnemucca that he had earlier sent to the school trustees of Inyo.

> Hearing that you are about to start a school to educate your children, I want to say a word about it. You all know me; many of you are my aunts or cousins. We are of one race,—your blood is my blood,—so I speak to you for your good. I can speak five tongues,—three Indian tongues, English, and Spanish. I can read and write, and am a school teacher. Now, I do not say this to boast, but simply to show you what can be done. When I was a little girl, there were no Indian schools; I learned under great difficulty. Your children can learn much more than I know, and much easier; and it is your duty to see that they go to school. There is no excuse for ignorance. Schools are being built here and there, and you can have as many as you need; all they ask you to do is send your children. You are not asked to give money or horses,—only to send your children to school. The teacher will do the rest. He or she will fit your little

---

15. Letter from the Reverend Thomas L. Riggs to Samuel Chapman Armstrong, January 2, 1883, in Armstrong, *The Indian Question,* p. 24.

16. Ibid., p. 27.

17. Quoted in Armstrong, *The Indian Question,* p. 31.

18. Armstrong, *The Indian Question,* p. 33.

ones for the battle of life, so that they can attend to their own affairs instead of having to call in a white man. A few years ago you owned this great country; today the white man owns it all, and you own nothing. Do you know what did it? Education. You see the miles and miles of railroad, the locomotive, the Mint in Carson, where they make money. Education has done it all.[19]

The *Daily Alta California,* which had also published Winnemucca's letter, urged that she be placed in charge of an Indian school. The paper reported that "she is very active for her people and loses no opportunity to urge them to send their children to school."

However, she was able to start her own school for the children of her brother, Chief Natchez, and other Indian children in the area with a grant of land from California Senator Leland Stanford. Help also came from Elizabeth Peabody and others who wanted to ensure Winnemucca's independence of the government agencies. Like Armstrong and others, Peabody was not sure that the government agencies helped the Indians. She wrote that they, in fact, prevented "civilization by insulting and repressing that creative self-respect and conscious freedom to act, from which alone any vital human improvement can spring."[20]   Yet, there was no question that Elizabeth Peabody was endorsing a person and an approach that would bring the Indians to the ways of the white society. She wrote that she wanted to ensure that Winnemucca would have an opportunity to help Indians begin a "self-supporting, self-directed life on the ground of their inherited domestic moralities which . . . are very pure."

When Winnemucca began her school in a brush arbor, the student's first lessons were "gospel hymns and songs of labor that she interpreted in Piute."[21] She taught them to spell English, and as soon as they could handle some of the language, she began instruction in reading, writing, and ciphering. She also taught drawing and sewing. A small group of local citizens visited to observe the progress of the children reported that the children were able "to name all the visible objects, repeat the days of the week and months of the year, and calculate to thousands." The children also took turns going to the blackboard where each printed his or her name. Even more impressive (to the visitors) was the students' knowledge of religion and gospel hymns.

Peabody wrote that the chief "drawback" for Winnemucca's students was that they could not stay the summer at the school, but had to join their parents on the hunt for winter provisions. The parents of the schoolchildren were said to be saddened by their inability to pay for their children's board during the summer, "and they compared [Winnemucca's] school, where the children were so happy in learning, to the Reservation schools, where they were *whipped* and taught

---

19. Quoted in Elizabeth P. Peabody, *Sarah Winnemucca's Practical Solution of the Indian Problem: A Letter to Dr. Lyman Abbot of the "Christian Union"* (Cambridge, Massachusetts: John Wilson and Son, 1886), pp. 5–6.

20. Ibid., p. 8.

21. Ibid.

nothing, but on which the Government wasted millions of dollars every year."[22]

Peabody also received reports from a teacher whom she identified only as "a lady who has been for twenty years engaged practically in public and private education West and East." The "lady visitor" observed that "every lesson was read in English and in Piute" and that when Winnemucca read the Bible to the students she read in both languages.[23] Peabody came to think that "the education was superior instead of inferior to the average white education in our primary schools, being based upon the method of the "New Education," in which doing leads thinking, and gives definite meaning to every word used."[24] She compared the education the children received at Winnemucca's school with that introduced in the Quincy schools by Col. Francis Parker. The "lady visitor" also found the writings and drawings to be decidedly superior" to those done by children in other schools with which she was familiar. The children not only did well in the traditional studies but participated in the maintenance of the school. When they were not at schoolwork, they tended to other chores. The visitor saw the boys digging a cellar and the girls "assisting Sarah about the cooking and cleaning."

Elizabeth Peabody raised some funds for Winnemucca's school and convinced others to make contributions. While there were some in the West who applauded and supported Winnemucca's efforts, others tried to undermine them and also to destroy the progress her brother Natchez was making in agriculture. Successful, independent Indians were threatening to many whites who were making less than honest livelihoods by working as Indian agents. Winnemucca and her brother were demonstrating that perhaps reservations were not necessary, that Indians could live and learn on their own. It was to be a long time before white society would be able to accept such a notion.

The Government's View of Indian Women's Education

The aim of education for American Indians consistently was to convert them to the ways of the white society. (See Chapter 10.) The attitude of the government schools toward Indian women was a reflection of society's view of all women. It persisted, however, after reforms had begun in the larger society. For example, in 1911, the United States Office of Indian Affairs circulated an outline of studies entitled "Some Things That Girls Should Know How to Do." Its contents are reminiscent of the counsel that Catharine Beecher gave to middle-class women a generation earlier. The booklet began with the presumption that Indian girls "will not go out to work but will return home after finishing the day or reservation

---

22. Ibid., p. 14.
23. Ibid., p. 17.
24. Ibid., p. 18.

boarding school course."[37] They were to be taught how to be good homemakers according to the norms of white society.

The outline told what articles the Indian girls should be taught to make and actually make while in school, the domestic processes they needed to learn, and presented lists of equipment that would be needed for a suitable kitchen. Outlines of lessons were given for such topics as "Equipment of Kitchen and Preparation of Food," Care and Equipment of Bedrooms," "Laundering," and "Care of Camp Animals."

Among other articles, Indian girls were to be taught how to make a sewing bag, an iron holder, a mattress cover, shirts, and handkerchiefs. They were also to learn to make bread, candy, and pickles; how to sew, mend, and darn; and do dry cleaning and embroidering. They were to learn that the cost of a one-quart enamel stewpan was forty cents, and that quart glass fruit jars went for $1.40 a dozen. They were taught that rugs and curtains for a sitting room could be "home made" and that an organ for that room would cost $35.

The Office of Indian Affairs instructed its teachers to teach Indian girls "the desirability of a large house." They were "not [to] be satisfied with one room."[38] Teachers were encouraged to conduct field trips to country stores and to use the boxes in which supplies were shipped to show how simple furnishings could be made for the home. Privately run schools took much the same viewpoint. Samuel C. Armstrong of Hampton Institute pointed out the futility of education for young Indian women: "They had no trades, and though they could make their own garments, and do housework, there were not suitable situations for them, and they returned to their mothers and grandmothers, who would sell them to the brave who would pay the most ponies for them." Armstrong, however, did not recommend that the Indian girls be taught the trades taught to the boys. The only alternative for the girls was teaching: "Teaching is the career of Indian girls, as it has been the one way for colored girls of the South to be more than drudges: it is their only field for a womanly ambition.[39] But, just as other educators had spoken of black women and white women, he claimed that it was upon the Indian women that "the hope of the race rested."

The efforts of the nineteenth-century reformers did not bring women equal opportunities for education, but they succeeded in breaking down some formidable barriers. The reformers won acknowledgment from many people of the fact that women were capable of learning and understanding abstract studies and that they deserved opportunities for higher education and for jobs other than those of mother, nurse, and teacher. A few pioneers, both black and white, managed to enter the professions and become doctors and lawyers. Full acceptance, econom-

37. U.S. Office of Indian Affairs, *Some Things That Girls Should Know How to Do and Hence Should Learn How to Do When in School* (Washington, D.C.: Government Printing Office, 1911) p. 5.

38. *Ibid.*, p. 9.

39. S. C. Armstrong, *The Indian Question* (Hampton, Va.: Normal School Steam Press, 1883) p. 17.

ic equality, and true equality in education for jobs and professions, however, were still a long way from being achieved. Women still had neither the economic power nor the political power to win equality in education.

A Tradition of Failure

Neither private efforts nor governmental programs succeeded in transforming the Indian to meet the specifications set down by the white society. In 1916 the Bureau of Indian Affairs produced a new course of study for the Indian schools that was supposed to improve significantly the Indians' opportunities and education. The government's schools were designed to teach Indian boys gardening, dairying, poultry-raising, plant production, farm carpentry, and other related subjects. Girls were to be taught cooking, poultry-raising, sewing, nursing, and other related subjects.

After World War I, the Bureau of Indian Affairs began trying to close as many Indian schools as possible, reduce the enrollment in Indian schools, and close boarding schools where possible. Attempts were being made to identify and remove ineligible students from the Indian schools, identify those who could afford to send their children to public school, and to make arrangements for the federal government to pay local school districts to accept Indian students. The commissioner, Cato Sells, explained:

> . . . the public school of the State is the place for the children of those Indians who have been released from guardianship. The combined capacity of Government schools is not sufficient for all, and the real Indian should be given preference as to educational opportunity.[25]

The Bureau of Indian Affairs never managed to close all of its Indian schools. Nor was the white society completely successful in converting the Indians to its language and ways. As late as 1970, the Bureau of Indian Affairs was still conducting more than 75 boarding schools and nearly 150 day schools for Indians. Nearly 300 Indian languages are still used today, and most students entering the Bureau's schools do so as non-English speaking students.

Not only the effectiveness of the Bureau's schools has been a subject of continuing debate and controversy. More recently, the entire purpose and objectives of such schools have been questioned as many native Americans have once again articulated their right to maintain their heritage and culture.

---

25. *Report of the Commissioner of Indian Affairs* (Washington: Government Printing Office, 1919), p. 22.

The Education of Black Americans 11

The Black Immigrants

There is no way to tell precisely how many black people were brought to the Americas from Africa; estimates vary from 15 million to 60 million. Nor is there any authoritative record to indicate when the first black person arrived in America. An estimated 900,000 blacks were brought to South America to work as slaves during the 1500s. The first blacks to come to North America were with Menendez in 1565, when St. Augustine, Florida, was founded by the Spanish. Traditionally, the first blacks in America were those who arrived at Jamestown in 1619 on a Dutch ship. They were sold as indentured servants.

For blacks in the colonies, the system of indentured service soon became a system of chattel slavery. At the beginning of the eighteenth century there were about 28,000 slaves in the colonies (19 percent in the North and 81 percent in the South), and by 1750 there were 236,000 (13 percent in the North and 87 percent in the South). On the eve of the Revolution the total population of the colonies was 2.6 million, of which half a million, or nearly 20 percent, were black slaves. In 1790, blacks comprised 19 percent of the population of the United States. Of the 697,000 blacks then in the country, only 59,000 were free.

White European immigrants to the Americas usually came with others who shared the same language, culture, and traditions, and had similar religious and political beliefs. If their purposes were not identical, they were usually compatible. But in addition to being brought forcibly to a strange land against their will, the black immigrants frequently were strangers to each other. Africa is not, and was not, a homogeneous continent. In any given slave ship, there were likely to be people from many places with different traditions, cultures, and languages. When they arrived, they worked for a master whose language they did not know. Frequently, their peers also spoke a language they did not know. Effective communication was extremely difficult, if not impossible.

To survive in the new land, blacks had to abandon all they knew and learn the ways of a radically different social system. The dominant white society tried to exercise careful control over what elements of the social system blacks learned, and how well they learned them. At times blacks were allowed to organize themselves into families, but most of the time they were not. When black families did exist, their existence was totally dependent on the desires of the owners. At times blacks were taught to read or allowed to learn to read. At other times, legislation specifically prohibited their education.

Education and Slavery

Most blacks in slavery were deprived of the opportunity to attend school, public or private. Some did have educational opportunities, both formal and informal. Early in the eighteenth century the Society for the Propagation of the Gospel in Foreign Parts instructed its missionaries and teachers to teach the fundamentals of Christianity to blacks as well as whites and Indians. Some slaves were taught to read and write so that they could carry out the duties their owners wanted to assign to them. Some were taught to read and write either with their owner's children or, on occasion, by the children. Those who were selected to work in the houses commonly had educational opportunities that field workers did not have. Some learned to identify with the values of their owners and became the teachers of the white children, often instructing them in matters of dress, deportment, and other social skills and values. Some were taught trades that were necessary to the maintenance of the plantation; some were taught trades so they could be hired out, even though that practice was usually illegal.

At the beginning of the nineteenth century, education for slaves was in what may be called a "permissive" phase.[1] They were being taught many skills and even given some formal instruction. By the 1820s and 1830s, however, as the institution of slavery was being challenged, the "permissive" phase began to end. Some thought that legislating against teaching blacks would help sever the communication between the free and those in slavery. Others believed that blacks who could not read would remain ignorant of antislavery arguments. Making education illegal, however, only made it more appealing and valuable.

Even after it was generally against the law to educate black slaves, many people continued to do so. Sarah and Angelina Grimké, the daughters of a justice of the South Carolina Supreme Court, deliberately violated the law against teaching slaves. Sarah Grimke described the scene: "The light was put out, the keyhole secured, and flat on our stomachs before the fire, with spelling books in our hands, we defied the laws of South Carolina."[2]

---

1. Henry Allen Bullock, *A History of Negro Education in the South* (Cambridge: Harvard University Press, 1967), p. 7.

2. Ibid., p. 10.

In various ways many blacks, free and slave, found ways to learn to read and write. In some northern cities, blacks were able to secure their right to public-supported education.[3] In slave states, many used or created whatever opportunities they could.

Religion and Oratory

Blacks demonstrated a remarkable ability to use the institutions of their oppressor to their own advantage. From the time of the earliest settlers, Americans have liked to gather together to listen to a sermon or a lecture. In the early 1800s, besides the Lyceum, Americans went out to hear other lectures. There were lectures on prison reform, temperance, the common school, and other subjects. The abolition societies—by 1827 there were more than a hundred—also offered lectures. In the years before the Civil War, Southerners, according to some observers, developed a passion for oratory.[4] Like the people around them, blacks learned to gather together to listen to a sermon or a lecture. They also learned the art of oratory.

Activity on behalf of abolition was not the exclusive province of white Americans. A black abolitionist movement was begun early in the nineteenth century, and before 1830 there were some fifty black abolitionist societies. The beginning of the movement can be attributed, at least partially, to the founding of the American Colonization Society in 1816. The Colonization Society's well-meant purpose was to return free blacks to Africa. Many free blacks objected immediately. In 1817 James Forten and Richard Allen, who had earlier founded the Bethel (African Methodist Episcopal) Church in Philadelphia, called a meeting of blacks in Philadelphia to protest the plan to move blacks from what was now their native land. Three thousand free blacks attended. In the same year there was a similar convention in Richmond, Va., and more meetings were held subsequently. In September 1830, representatives from seven states met at the Bethel Church to organize aid for a group of blacks who wished to leave Cincinnati and its racial strife and move to Canada. That meeting was the first of what became the Convention Movement. There were six such national conventions in the 1830s and three more in the 1840s. There were also many such meetings at the state level. One issue discussed at these conventions was whether it was appropriate to support emigration as a solution to their problems. Though there was never complete agreement (and some blacks did go to Africa), the majority resisted the idea of emigration or colonization. Many believed that leaving the United States would be tantamount to betrayal of the blacks still in slavery. Moreover, to emigrate was to leave one's native land. Blacks had been in the United States as long or longer than most white Americans.

While slavery made it impossible to establish and maintain many institutions,

---

3. C. G. Woodson, *The Education of the Negro Prior to 1861* (Washington, D.C.: Associated Publishers, Inc., 1919), 2nd ed., pp. 307–335.

4 Waldo W. Braden, ed., *Oratory in the Old South. 1828–1860* (Baton Rouge: Louisiana State University Press, 1970), p. 3.

one, the church, became important. Most of the religious beliefs and rituals of the African peoples had been suppressed just as the other elements of their heritage were ripped away and discarded. In place of their own religious beliefs, blacks were taught many varieties of Christianity. At first, slave owners did not allow their slaves to be instructed in Christianity because of the Christian tradition that Christians could not be held in bondage. However, that tradition was legislated away, and the Bishop of London, for instance, emphasized that Christian slaves would be more compliant and docile. But as the abolition movement grew, and as Southerners grew increasingly fearful of northern missionaries who were spreading doctrines that challenged the legitimacy of slavery, proponents of slavery set out to teach black slaves their own version of Christianity. At midcentury many were considering the advantages and disadvantages of segregated churches and integrated churches. Their reasoning is interesting. For instance, Reverend C. C. Jones advised that *"in the slave States it is not advisable to separate the blacks from the whites."* According to Jones:

> This mingling of the two classes in churches creates a greater bond of union between them, and kinder feelings; tends to increase subordination; and promotes in a higher degree the improvement of the Negros, in piety and morality. The *reverse* is, in the general, true of *independent church organizations of the Negros,* in the slave States.[5]

Despite such reasoning and the efforts of some Southerners, blacks did find ways to have their own churches or religious meetings. These were commonly illegal, yet many plantation owners allowed them. Frederick Law Olmsted observed in the 1850s that church services were the major, if not the only, source of relief for their participants.[6] The church provided an occasion for genuine emotional and aesthetic expression, and was often the only semblance of community available to many blacks. Most of the communicants, and frequently the minister, were illiterate. Consequently, they relied on the spoken word. Through oratory, articulate black speakers could exercise their talents and their ability to persuade and to lead. Oratory appeals to the emotions *and* the intellect, and its structure often depends on differences or conflicts between the real and the ideal. For blacks in slavery, it was not difficult to imagine a world better than the reality in which they lived, and Biblical promises were a ready source for the ideal.

The importance of the church and ministers in the slave society was as great, if not greater than, their importance in the free society. Robert L. Allen has noted that the black conventions of the 1830s and 1840s drew their leadership primarily from the ministry. According to Allen, the ministry became the "natural training ground for black leaders not only for the churches but for all other spheres of

---

5. Quoted in Daniel J. Boorstin, *The Americans: The National Experience* (New York: Vintage Books, 1965), p. 197.

6. Ibid., p. 197.

social life," because it was "the only profession easily accessible to blacks."[7] For over a century the church produced eloquent spokesmen for the rights of American blacks. Richard Allen (founder of the Philadelphia Bethel Church) and Henry Highland Garnett were ministers who played important roles in the Convention Movement. The church and its ministers also served as models for other black leaders. Allen has noted that both David Walker, author of the *Appeal* (1829), and Frederick Douglass "were strongly influenced by the teachings of the church and the oratorical style of black preachers."[8] In *Black Religion* (1964), Joseph R. Washington, Jr. , reported that "the social role of Negro churches is one of great importance."[9] Washington's description of the community's expectations for the black Baptist ministers is reminiscent of the early New England Puritans:

> . . . the Baptist minister [is] the news medium of the community. He is expected to gather local news and circulate it through his sermons on Sunday. In fact, almost all ministers in southern Negro communities are looked to as the disseminators of information, and the pipeline of the community leads directly to them.[10]

Washington also noted that it was not at all unusual that the meetings held during the Montgomery, Ala., bus boycott "were held in church buildings, and were presided over by ministers."[11] Leaders in the earlier fight for abolition also were found among those who spoke and wrote movingly and effectively. The same tradition of leadership produced several of the most prominent civil rights leaders, notably Dr. Martin Luther King, Jr., a major figure in the civil rights movement.

Frederick Douglass

In 1838, at the age of 21, Frederick Douglass, a self-educated slave, fled from his Maryland owner to New Bedford, Mass. At an antislavery meeting in 1841, he met William Lloyd Garrison, an ardent abolitionist and editor of the *Liberator*. Impressed by Douglass's extemporaneous speech, Garrison encouraged him to continue speaking for abolition. In 1845 Douglass successfully toured England speaking against slavery. Some of his English friends arranged to buy his freedom, and he returned to the United States a free man. In 1847 he began publication of his own newspaper, *The North Star*. In 1851 he disagreed with Garrison's contention that the solution to slavery was for the North to secede from the Union and that the Constitution was a proslavery document. More conservative, Douglass believed that Congress had the responsibility to abolish slavery, and that the

7. Robert L. Allen, *Reluctant Reformers: Racism and Social Reform Movements in the United States* (New York: Anchor Books, 1975), p. 18.

8. Ibid.

9. Joseph R. Washington, Jr., *Black Religion: The Negro and Christianity in the United States* (Boston: Beacon Press, 1964), p. 2.

10. Ibid.

11. Ibid., pp. 2–3.

North's secession would abandon the slaves in the South. He chose not to abandon his people, to work within the existing political framework, and to encourage blacks to help themselves and each other.

In 1848 Douglass asked, in his newspaper, "What Are the Colored People Doing for Themselves?" His approach was that blacks were not doing enough either for themselves or for each other. They had to prove themselves worthy of freedom, for what was not worth working for was not worth having. He argued that unless black people undertook to effect their own "regeneration and improvement," they would have to continue in their "present miserable and degraded condition for ages."[12] Douglass soundly rejected those who reasoned that "our fathers got along pretty well through the world without learning and without meddling with abolitionism, and we can do the same." He told his audience that they should be seeking more than "heaven when they die."

Douglass argued that the black cause could be greatly improved if "three pulpits" would work toward that end: the Bethel Church in Philadelphia, and the Zion Church and St. Phillip's Church in New York. He believed these three churches were sufficiently powerful to effect "a revolution in the condition of the colored people" in just three years. The Bethel Church in Philadelphia was the center of a large network of churches, with "small Bethels" all about the city as well as in other parts of the country. Douglass described the contribution the "large Bethel" could play:

> The Bethel pulpit in Philadelphia may be said to give tone to the entire denomination—"as goes large Bethel, so go the small Bethels throughout the Union." Here is concentrated the talent of the church, and here is the central and ruling power.—Now, if that pulpit would but speak the right word—the word for progress—the word for mental culture—encourage reading, and would occasionally take up contributions to aid those who are laboring for their elevation, as the white churches do to aid the colonization society to send us out of the country—there is no telling the good that would result from such labors.[13]

Douglass urged his audience to be self-reliant and to rely on education as a solution to their problems. He rejected the notion that a small number of prominent blacks would solve the problems of all black people.

Douglass admitted that society had placed many barriers on the blacks' road to progress. "Though born on American soil," he reminded his audience, blacks had "fewer privileges than aliens."[14] Yet there were some signs that blacks were gaining access to education. He argued that blacks had to avail themselves of the opportunities that existed even at the expense of a "few fine garments" and "a coarser and scantier diet."

---

12. Frederick Douglass, "What Are the Colored People Doing for Themselves?" in *The North Star* (July 14, 1848), in *Negro Social and Political Thought, 1850–1920,* ed. Howard Brotz (New York: Basic Books, 1966), p. 205.

13. Ibid., p. 206.

14. Ibid.

Through his speeches, his writings, and the *North Star*, Douglass's views reached many people. Booker T. Washington described how what he heard about Douglass affected his own desire for schooling:

> Even before I had learned to read books or newspapers, I remember hearing my mother and other coloured people in our part of the country speak about Frederick Douglass's wonderful life and achievements. I heard so much about Douglass when I was a boy that one of the reasons why I wanted to go to school and learn to read was that I might read for myself what he had written and said.[15]

Booker T. Washington

Like Frederick Douglass, Booker T. Washington was born a slave. However, unlike Douglass, he did not have to flee from slavery to gain his freedom. Born in 1856, he was freed in 1865 by President Lincoln's Emancipation Proclamation. Unlike many born into slavery, Washington was not separated from his mother. In *Up From Slavery,* he told how his mother had prayed for freedom for her children and how she moved the family from Franklin County, Virginia, to Malden, West Virginia (a free state). There she obtained a copy of Noah Webster's "old blue-back" for him, and Washington learned the alphabet. As a boy, Washington worked at a nearby salt furnace and sometimes attended a local elementary school that had been established for the newly freed. Sometimes he got his lessons in the evening from the teacher after finishing a day's work. At other times he worked at the salt furnace for five hours in the early morning, then went to school, and returned to work at the end of the school day. In 1872 Washington returned to Virginia to seek admission to the Hampton Normal and Industrial Institute.

Hampton Institute had been founded in 1868 by Samuel Chapman Armstrong, the son of missionaries in Hawaii. Armstrong had led an all-black regiment in the Civil War and then been appointed as an agent of the Freedmen's Bureau. While in charge of a camp for blacks at Hampton, Armstrong decided to help blacks help themselves by setting up school similar to one he had seen in Hawaii, the Hilo Manuel Labor School. The Hilo School was a boarding school for boys. To pay their tuition the boys were required to work at a trade, tend gardens, or perform other necessary chores. In 1867 Armstrong submitted his idea for a school for blacks that would tend to "mental culture and manual training" to the American Missionary Board. The Board agreed to purchase the mansion and land where the camp was located, and Armstrong opened his school. It would later accept Indians as well as blacks.

Washington was admitted to Hampton and took a job as janitor to help pay his tuition. He graduated after three years and returned to Malden to teach at the

---

15. Booker T. Washington, *My Larger Education* (1911), (Miami, Fla.: Mnemosyne Publishing Co., 1969), pp. 103–104.

elementary school he had earlier attended. At Hampton, Washington absorbed much of Armstrong's attitude: that manual labor was necessary to teach students there was dignity in labor, and that manual training also helped to build character and develop economic independence. Washington also learned "a great deal more about Frederick Douglass" at Hampton and followed Douglass' career with "great interest." Washington was to spend the remainder of his life as an educator building on what he learned from Douglass and Armstrong.

After teaching for several years, Washington enrolled in the Wayland Academy in Washington, D.C. There he found further reason to stick by the lessons Armstrong taught him. He found his classmates at Wayland to be superior to the students at Hampton in several ways. They were better dressed, had more money, and were in many cases more able than the Hampton students. But the Wayland students were also inferior to the Hampton students in several ways; they were more concerned with maintaining the proper appearance than with developing independence and self-reliance. They were, to Washington's chagrin, not willing to assume posts as teachers in the remote rural communities in order to help those who were less fortunate than they were.

Tuskegee

In 1879 Washington delivered the annual post-graduate address at Hampton Institute, and he was then invited to become the first black faculty member. He taught night classes for students who spent their days working in the school's laundry or at the sawmill. When Armstrong accepted a group of Indian students from a Western reservation, Washington took charge of them. He also served as Armstrong's secretary. When Armstrong was asked to send someone to Tuskegee, Alabama, to begin a normal school for blacks, Washington was an obvious choice. In May 1881, Washington set out for Tuskegee, where he expected to find a school. He found nothing, for the legislature had not planned to spend any money for the new school until October. Washington decided that the school should be opened on Independence Day. He rented a building, collected some old books, gave speeches at all the local churches, and recruited students. On July 4, 1881, he opened the school with forty students.

Washington set out to model Tuskegee after Hampton Institute. But while Armstrong had begun with a building and land, Washington began with nothing. He had to secure land, buildings, and money as he began the school. He had to be supervisor of instruction and fund-raiser. He also had to contend with rapidly growing enrollment. Four months after he opened the school, its enrollment had more than doubled. He borrowed money to purchase a farm, hired three teachers, traveled to the North to raise funds, and put the students to work. At Hampton, students worked because Armstrong believed it was necessary to build character. At Tuskegee, the students worked to build both their character and their school. Students and faculty members made the bricks, built the buildings, and raised crops to feed themselves and raise cash.

By 1884 Tuskegee was a going enterprise, and Washington was able to express very clearly its purpose and philosophy. In an address delivered before the NEA in Madison, Wisconsin, he told how Tuskegee was helping the people in the nearby areas. Within a twenty-mile radius of the school there were 25,000 blacks. Many lived in remote areas far from even a railroad track. Many had no access to any school. What schoolhouses there were were badly equipped and rundown. Many of the teachers could do little more than write their names. The people in Tuskegee's service area needed "teachers with not only trained heads and hearts, but with trained hands." Tuskegee's purpose was "not to send into these places teachers who will stand off and tell the people what to do, or what ought to be done, but to send those who can take hold and show the people *how* to do."[16] The teacher trained at Tuskegee was not a "proud fop" who sported "a beaver hat, kid gloves, and walking cane," but a well-trained worker.

Industrial Education

The heart of Washington's program at Tuskegee was industrial training. Washington explained that while the blacks in the South had a near-monopoly of the trades, that monopoly could soon end. Those who knew trades had learned them in slavery, but now there were few places where young blacks could learn a trade and too few who wanted to work at the trades. At Tuskegee one could learn, and had to learn, all sorts of basic trades:

> The Tuskegee Normal School, with a farm of five hundred acres, carpenter's shop, printing office, blacksmith's shop, and brick yard for boys, and a sewing department laundry, flower gardening, and practical housekeeping for girls, is trying to do its part towards furnishing industrial training. We ask help for nothing that we can do for ourselves; nothing is bought that the students can produce. The boys raise the vegetables, have done the painting, made the brick, the chairs, the tables, the desks; have built a stable, a carpenter's shop, and a blacksmith's shop. The girls do the entire housekeeping, including the mending, ironing, and washing of the boys' clothes; besides they make many garments to sell.[17]

Washington explained that he had entered Hampton Institute with fifty cents in his pocket and had been given a chance to help himself. He wanted to give others a similar chance.

Washington's emphasis on industrial education was designed to provide students with what he considered to be dignity and utility. He concluded, for several reasons, that blacks would not profit from a traditional liberal education. Their chances to secure or use such an education were too limited. He feared that traditional education would only bring the blacks ridicule and disdain from the white society. Washington wanted to demonstrate that black people could learn to work, support themselves, and contribute to society. To earn their rightful place in society, blacks needed to secure an education that would provide more than a thin veneer of uselessness. It was, he believed, imperative that they "learned to appre-

---

16. Booker T. Washington, "The Education Outlook in the South" (July 16, 1884), in *The Booker T. Washington Papers*, ed. Louis Harlan (Urbana: University of Illinois Press, 1972), p. 260.

17. Ibid., p. 261.

ciate the fact that they had been worked, and that one of the great lessons for freemen to learn is to work."[18]

Washington frequently reported with pride that neither Latin nor Greek was taught at Tuskegee, for he questioned their utility. In *Up from Slavery*, he reported that during the period of Reconstruction there was among blacks a "craze for Greek and Latin learning," based on the belief "that a knowledge, however little, of the Greek and Latin languages would make one a very superior human being, something bordering almost on the supernatural."[19] In an address delivered in 1896, he told how, when he decided to add instruction in tailoring to the curriculum at Tuskegee, he could not find any black man who was qualified to teach it, but a surfeit of those who could teach "astronomy, theology, Greek, or Latin." To show how lacking in utility such study was, he described his encounters with those who had a literary education but no practical knowledge for everyday living. He told of meeting women "who could converse intelligently on Grecian history, who had studied geometry, could analyze the most complex sentences," but who "could not analyze the poorly cooked and still more poorly served bread and fat meat that they and their families were eating three times a day." There were too many girls who could "locate Pekin and the Desert of Sahara on an artificial globe" but who could not find the proper place on the table for the dinner ware.[20]

Throughout his career, Washington remained convinced that industrial education was the best possible foundation for black education and black citizenship. As late as 1907 he was still defending the wisdom of his emphasis on industrial education. He believed he was creating a system and building skills that would not allow blacks and whites to maintain a complete separation from each other in their daily lives. "If a black man became a lawyer, a doctor, a minister, or an ordinary teacher," he said, "his professional duties would not ordinarily bring him in touch with the life of the white portion of the community, but rather confine him almost exclusively to his own race."[21] Industrial education was a way to maintain contact between the two races and even to foster cooperation between them:

> The minute it was seen that through industrial education the Negro youth was not only studying chemistry, but also how to apply the knowledge of chemistry to the enrichment of the soil, or to cooking, or to dairying, and the student was being taught not only geometry and physics, but their application to black-smithing, brickmaking, farming, and what not, then there began to appear for the first time a common bond between the two races and co-operation between North and South.[22]

18. Booker T. Washington, *The Negro in Business* (1907), in Brotz, *Negro Social and Political Thought*, p. 409.

19. Booker T. Washington, *Up From Slavery* (1901), in Harlan, *Booker T. Washington Papers*, vol. 1, p. 256.

20. Booker T. Washington, "Democracy and Education," Speech to Institute of Arts & Sciences, Brooklyn (September 30, 1896), in Brotz, *Negro Social and Political Thought*, p. 3.

21. Booker T. Washington, *The Negro in Business* (1907), in Brotz, *Negro Social and Political Thought*, p. 409.

22. Ibid, pp. 409–410.

Washington may have been overly sanguine about the bond that industrial education would forge between blacks and whites. He believed that the black man who learned the fundamentals of agriculture and became a prosperous farmer was "laying the foundation for his children and grandchildren" to secure a literary education and join the professional classes. He did not foresee that blacks would not fully secure their civil and political rights until nearly a century after the Emancipation Proclamation and that capricious social and economic discrimination would last even longer. However, his advocacy of industrial education was shared by many other educators in the late nineteenth and early twentieth centuries.

While Washington was promoting the Tuskegee program, the idea of industrial education for both black and white students was taking hold in other parts of the country. In 1847 Jonathan Baldwin Turner resigned his professorship of classics at Illinois College and began his campaign for a university where students could study the theory and practice of practical pursuits. Mechanics and farmers, he argued, had as much right to a useful higher education as did the clergy, lawyers, and doctors. In 1862, President Lincoln signed the Land Grant College Act (Morill Act), and the states could secure federal lands to support the establishment of schools that would devote as much attention to agriculture and engineering as other schools devoted to languages. In the 1870s Calvin Woodward of the O'Fallon Technical Institute in St. Louis began to criticize traditional education. Schools were preparing their students for lives of "ease and enjoyment" and rendering them "unfit" for honest and productive labor.

Woodward and others who believed that practical education should replace a liberal arts education found more inspiration at Philadelphia Centennial Exposition of 1876. Visitors had the opportunity to see the plans and samples of the work that had been produced in Russian technical schools. What they saw was the work Victor Della Vos created after the Moscow Imperial Technical School had been founded in 1868. Della Vos reasoned that any skill consisted of many separate skills. To teach the component skills in any orderly way, he organized the "instruction shop." From there students advanced to the "construction shop" where they actually made goods.

Among those who saw the Russian exhibit and were impressed by it was John D. Runkle, President of the Massachusetts Institute of Technology. He persuaded the MIT trustees to allow the establishment of instruction shops and to open a new department, the School of Mechanic Arts, for those students who desired to engage in the various mechanic arts rather than pursue a career as an engineer. Before visiting the Philadelphia Exposition, Woodward had taken to teaching his students how to work with tools, finding that many of them could not even build models to illustrate problems in mechanical engineering. In June 1879, Woodward opened Washington University's Manuel Training School, where he undertook to teach students to use their hands, not as preparation for any specific trade but as a way of applying abstract principles to practical and tangible problems.

Soon Woodward and others found themselves in the center of a debate. The topic gained an increasing amount of educators' attention, and manuel training schools began to open. By 1890 at least thirty-six cities had introduced some form of manuel training into their schools. The pressure on the schools to set aside traditional education for practical education continued. In 1892 Edmund Jane James of the Wharton School of Finance told a meeting of the American Bankers Association that they should encourage the establishment of "commercial high schools." A Department of Business Education was set up within the National Education Association in 1896.

Washington agreed that industrial education should assist the community in its profit-making pursuits. He told a story of how George Washington Carver had discovered minerals on a white landowner's property and pointed out their commercial applications and value. For those who needed further reason to believe that industrial education was valuable, Washington cited the example of Germany, long admired by the United States "in the way of education." In Saxony, he pointed out, there was one industrial school for "every 14,641 people," while in the American South there was only one "worthwhile industrial school for every 4,000,000 colored people."[23]

The "Atlanta Compromise"

In 1896, Washington addressed the Cotton States and International Exposition in Atlanta, giving a speech that has since come to be known as the "Atlanta Compromise." Although the pressure for Jim Crow laws was growing almost daily, Washington did not resist the pressure, but pointed out that blacks and whites could coexist peacefully and productively in the same society. Blacks needed to avail themselves of the opportunities all about them in the South. That entailed learning to work and recognizing that there was "as much dignity in tilling a field as in writing a poem."[24] Whites should hire the black workers who had been laboring "without strikes and labor wars" rather than rely on "those of foreign birth and strange tongue and habits for the prosperity of the South." Washington further assured the whites with one of his most famous lines: "In all things that are purely social we can be as separate as the fingers, yet one as the hand in all things essential to mutual progress." He added that for blacks to agitate for "social equality" would be "the extremest folly."[25]

Washington was now hailed as the spokesmen for blacks, as the successor to Frederick Douglass who had died earlier that year. But he continued to maintain the posture of a schoolteacher and deliberately resisted pressure to discuss political questions. When he wrote to the Louisiana State Constitutional Conven-

---

23. Booker T. Washington, *The Negro in Business* (1907), in Brotz, *Negro Social and Political Thought*, p. 416.

24. Booker T. Washington, *Up From Slavery* (1901), in Harlan, *Booker T. Washington Papers*, p. 331.

25. Ibid. pp. 332–333.

tion in 1898 to urge the delegates to adopt fair election laws and to provide educational opportunity for all people, he emphasized early in his letter that he was "no politician." He also reminded the convention that he had "always advised my race to give attention to acquiring property, intelligence and character, as the necessary basis of good citizenship rather than to mere political agitation."[26] He had concluded that "Negroes needed something more than to be reminded of their sufferings and of their political rights." Washington made a career of attending to that "something more."[27]

Toward the end of the nineteenth century, Jim Crow laws were passed, the United States extended its sphere of influence, and a doctrine of Anglo-Saxon superiority was being put forth to justify imperialism. C. Vann Woodward has pointed out that those who advocated a doctrine of white superiority within the United States "thoroughly grasped and expounded the implication of the new imperialism for their domestic policies."[28] In both the North and the South, Americans had little difficulty finding racial differences and justifying racial discrimination.

Though Washington was proclaimed by many to be the spokesman of his race, his position and his views did not go unchallenged. As the conditions the blacks had to endure worsened, and as opportunities for improvement failed to materialize, the efficacy of his apolitical posture and the soundness of his educational views both were questioned. Among those who clearly articulated a different way for blacks was the scholar and historian W. E. B. DuBois.

W. E. B. DuBois

William Edward Burghardt DuBois was born in Great Barrington, Mass., in 1868, after the Emancipation Proclamation and the Civil War's end. Though he grew up in a society dominated by whites, it was not the South. Blacks were not a majority dominated by a minority, but a small minority—about one percent of the population in Great Barrington. Though the ever-present color line existed, it was not as harshly drawn as in many other nineteenth-century communities.

DuBois attended the local schools, took the classical course to prepare himself for college, and then went to Nashville, Tenn., to study at Fisk University. There he learned about the situations of other blacks, especially the poor blacks from the rural South whom he taught during the summer. At Fisk, DuBois continued his study of Latin and Greek and added French, German, science, literature, ethics,

---

26. Booker T. Washington to the Louisiana State Constitutional Convention, (February 19, 1898), in Brotz, *Negro Political and Social Thought*, p. 373.

27. Booker T. Washington, *My Larger Education*, pp. 105–106.

28. C. Vann Woodward, *The Strange Career of Jim Crow* (New York: Oxford University Press, 1957), p. 55.

philosophy, and political economy. He then entered the junior class at Harvard. Except for the customary trip for study in Germany, DuBois remained at Harvard until 1894. Harvard at that time had some of the most notable scholars in the history of American higher education, including William James, George Santayana, and Albert Bushnell Hart. As a graduate student, DuBois attended Hart's seminar in Constitutional and political history and began his dissertation work. It was published in 1896 as the first volume in Harvard's Historical Studies series: *The Suppression of the African Slave-Trade to the United States of America, 1638–1870.* He was given his Ph.D. from Harvard in 1895.

In 1894 DuBois, given a choice of three teaching positions, took one at Wilberforce University in Xenia, Ohio, teaching Greek and Latin. But he found it difficult to accept Wilberforce's religious character and activities. DuBois had been educated at one of the nation's best schools, had studied in Germany and traveled about Europe, had studied with the best of Harvard's faculty and been accepted as a scholar without any significant evidence of prejudice. He had concluded that the scholarly community was free of prejudice and would be the best setting for his work. Wilberforce was not that setting. He left it to conduct a study of the black community in Philadelphia for the University of Pennsylvania, then went to Atlanta University.

DuBois's Challenge

DuBois believed that higher education at its best would bring advancement for blacks, destroy the ignorance that supported prejudice, and lead to a society free from racial injustices and discrimination. In *The Souls of Black Folk* (1903), he challenged the position Booker T. Washington was advocating for blacks in the United States. He questioned the originality of Washington's work, the soundness of his values, and the ultimate price blacks would have to pay for heeding his counsel. Armed with his scholarly skills and a knowledge of history, DuBois challenged an acknowledged leader.

DuBois's criticism of Washington was not gentle. He wrote that Washington "was the most distinguished Southerner since Jefferson Davis, and the one with the largest personal following."[29] He referred to "Washington's cult" and "unquestioning followers." There was, claimed DuBois, some criticism of Washington, but most of it was suppressed. According to DuBois, "educated and thoughtful colored men in all parts of the land" experienced "a feeling of deep regret, sorrow, and apprehension at the wide currency and ascendancy which some of Mr. Washington's theories have gained."[30] DuBois argued that "honest and earnest criticism from those whose interests are most nearly touched,—criticism of writers by readers, of government, of leaders by those led,—this is the soul of democracy and the safeguard of modern society."

---

29. W. E. B. DuBois, *The Souls of Black Folk* (1903), in Brotz, *Negro Social and Political Thought,* pp. 509–510.

30. Ibid., p. 511.

Because American blacks had been *given* a leader, as they were given Washington, they suffered a loss as well as a gain. The "irreparable" loss, he said, was the "loss of that peculiarly valuable education which a group receives when by search and criticism it finds and commissions its own leaders."[31]

DuBois objected to Washington's acceptance of the commercialism of the age and to his disregard for the traditional subject matter of higher education. He explained that Washington had learned "the speech and thought of triumphant commercialism, and the ideals of material prosperity" so well that "the picture of a lone black boy poring over a French grammar amid the weeds and dirt of a neglected home soon seemed to him the acme of absurdities." To challenge that impression which Washington had so effectively communicated, DuBois rhetorically wondered how Socrates or St. Francis of Assisi would assess such a boy.[32] Washington preached "a gospel of Work and Money" and overlooked "the higher aims of life."[33] While trying to build a system of common schools for blacks and providing industrial education, Washington failed to see that the lower levels of education had to rest on the foundation "of the well-equipped college and university."[34]

DuBois emphasized the importance of higher education because he believed the welfare and the dignity of a people depended on educated leaders, not on a mass of skilled workers. Accordingly, he argued for the need to provide education for those whom he called "the talented tenth":

> The Negro race, like all races, is going to be saved by its exceptional men. The problem of education, then, among Negroes must first of all deal with the Talented Tenth; it is the problem of developing the Best of this race that they may guide the Mass away from the contamination and death of the Worst, in their own and other races. Now the training of men is a difficult and intricate task. Its technique is a matter for educational experts, but its object is for the vision of seers. If we make money the object of man-training, we shall develop money-makers but not necessarily men; if we make technical skill the object of education, we may possess artisans but not, in nature, men. Men we shall have only as we make manhood the object of the work of the schools— intelligence, broad sympathy, knowledge of the world that was and is, and of the relation of men to it—this is the curriculum of that Higher Education which must underlie true life. On this foundation we may build bread winning, skill of hand and quickness of brain, with never a fear lest the child and man mistake the means of living for the object of life.[35]

DuBois described how the abolitionist movement had been dominated by intelligent and educated people. The talented tenth who worked in the abolition movement served as examples for other blacks and demonstrated to whites "the possibilities of the Negro race." For those who claimed that the college-educated

31. Ibid.
32. Ibid., p. 510.
33. Ibid., p. 513.
34. Ibid., p. 515.
35. W. E. B. DuBois, "The Talented Tenth," in Brotz, *Negro Social and Political Thought*, p. 518.

black could not find proper employment, DuBois provided statistics to show that was not the case. College education was imperative if a sufficient supply of teachers and professionals were to be available to educate others. They were needed not only to staff the schools for blacks but to serve as leaders and models in the black communities. Unless the talented tenth were identified and educated, blacks would have to rely on "half-trained demagogues" and "vociferous busy-bodies" for leadership.[36] DuBois pointed out that even Washington hired college graduates. He reported that "some thirty of (Washington's) chief teachers are college graduates, and instead of studying French grammars in the midst of weeds, or buying pianos for dirty cabins, they are at Mr. Washington's right hand helping him in a noble work." He pointed out that a number of Washington's able assistants had studied the classics and that Washington's wife had "read Virgil and Homer in the same classroom with me [DuBois]."[37]

DuBois objected to Washington's "Atlanta Compromise" and the support it seemed to give to those who claimed that the blacks were an inferior race. As a historian, he concluded that people were most assertive when the prejudice against them was intense. However, Washington had somehow changed the workings of history. According to DuBois:

> In other periods of intensified prejudice all the Negro's tendency to self-assertion has been called forth; at this period a policy of submission is advocated. In the history of nearly all other races and peoples the doctrine preached at such crises has been that manly self-respect is worth more than lands and houses, and that a people who voluntarily surrender such respect, or cease striving for it, are not worth civilizing.[38]

Washington had, he claimed, convinced many to be submissive in exchange for economic advantage. To DuBois that was not a bargain. He believed the final price for submission would be further degradation and setbacks. Washington had asked blacks not to press for political power, not to insist upon their civil rights, and to forgo higher education for black youth. In exchange, said DuBois, blacks were disenfranchised, saw the enactment of legislation that granted them second-class citizenship, and saw aid for their colleges diminish rapidly. Washington's program seriously discouraged, if it did not disallow, proper education of exceptional blacks. DuBois also pointed out that the exchange would not work in the long run. It would be extremely difficult "for working men and property-owners to defend their rights and exist without the right of suffrage."[39] Although the effects of years of prejudice could not be made to "disappear at the blast of trumpet," DuBois insisted that the only way blacks would secure all their rights was to insist on having them.

---

36. Ibid., p. 529.
37. Ibid., p. 532.
38. W. E. B. DuBois, *The Souls of Black Folk,* in Brotz, *Negro Social and Political Thought,* p. 513.
39. Ibid., p. 514.

Although Washington and DuBois disagreed about the kind of education blacks needed, both agreed that education was essential to black progress and freedom. Much of the focus of the earlier and later stages of the black civil rights movement has been on securing equal educational opportunities for black students. From the Supreme Court's 1954 decision declaring separate school systems unconstitutional to the still-unconcluded debates over busing, open admissions, special programs, and other issues, education has been seen as vital.

The gap between blacks' and whites' opportunities for education has closed steadily. In 1940 the median number of years of schooling for all Americans aged 25–29 was 10.3 years; for blacks it was 7 years completed schooling. By 1972, this gap had almost closed: all Americans 12.7 years, blacks 12.3 years. On the other hand, according to James Geschwender, the increased educational level has not been matched by better jobs. Blacks still hold fewer top jobs than whites with the same amount of education. At each occupational level, blacks are required to have more education than their white counterparts.[40]

---

40. James A. Geschwender, *Racial Stratification in America* (Dubuque, Ia.: Wm. C. Brown Co., 1978), pp. 209–210.

The New Education

Learning a New Lesson

Americans have a persistent need to fiddle with their schools. When classrooms are filled with active students, a plan appears to introduce discipline, quiet, and order. When classrooms are filled with rows of quiet, attentive, children, a plan appears to introduce more activity. In the 1830s and 1840s Americans were persuaded to support efforts to expand and improve their public schools and create a more uniform system. But almost as soon as variability had given way to order and uniformity, there were attempts to reform the schools and break the standard routines. What had been built had to be dismantled and put back together again.

Edward A. Sheldon and the Oswego System

One of the earliest to build and dismantle an educational machine was Edward A. Sheldon. Sheldon wrote that while he was in charge of the schools at Oswego, New York, in the 1850s, he "carried a straight-jacket system of close classification to its highest point of perfection" and "perfected the most complete educational machine that was ever constructed." It was so perfect that he only needed to look at his clock to know "exactly what every teacher in the city was doing." He confessed that it took him "a long time to learn that there was a better way."[1] He discovered the "better way" by chance. In 1859 while on a holiday in Toronto, Canada, Sheldon visited a museum where he saw a display of an English version of Pestalozzian materials. Impressed, Sheldon brought his discovery back to Oswego and embarked upon the building of a new educational machine.

---

1. Edward A. Sheldon, *Autobiography* (1911), *The Educating of Americans: A Documentary History,* ed. Daniel Calhoun (Boston: Houghton Mifflin, 1969), p. 311.

Sheldon had been named secretary of the Oswego Board of Education (comparable to superintendent) in 1853. It was a position for which he had no training and little experience.

In the fall of 1848 he had successfully organized the Orphan and Free School Association of Oswego. Locally known as the "Ragged School," its purpose was to provide education for the community's poor. Fearing the community's interest in the school would not endure, he had left it to begin his own private co-educational school in collaboration with J. D. Higgins. He also spent some time in Syracuse, N.Y., as superintendent of schools. There he established school libraries, opened evening schools, and tended to the establishment of graded schools. In 1851 he had tried to convince Oswego to establish a system of free public schools. In his first years as secretary there, he paid particular attention to the course of study, introduced graded schools, and tried to recruit good teachers.

Building the New System

In the spring of 1860, the *Annual Report* of the Oswego Board of Education admitted that there had been "too much teaching by formulas," but attempts were being made to remedy the situation. Although Sheldon had instructed teachers to use Pestalozzian object lessons, they had no manuals or guides to follow, and consequently had no clear sense of purpose for the new system.[2] To remedy the situation, the *Report* indicated, materials were being secured from the Home and Colonial Infant and Juvenile School Society of London. Sheldon soon acquired both the materials and services of two experienced assistants, Margaret Jones and Herman Krusi, Jr. Krusi's father had been one of Pestalozzi's assistants, and Krusi himself had become a specialist in training teachers how to use object lessons in the classroom. Margaret Jones had been trained in and worked in the Home and Colonial Training School in London.

Success came quickly. The 1861 *Annual Report* recorded that the yearly examining committee had paid special attention to those schools where the new methods had been tried. In those schools where the teachers had "caught the spirit of the plan" and applied it properly, the students displayed an interest and enthusiasm for school that had not been previously known in Oswego. The *Report* stated that:

> It was never our pleasure before to witness so much interest in any class exercise. There was no dull routine of questions and monosyllabic answers, no mere recitation of dry and stereotyped formulas, no apparent unloading of the memory, but we seemed as in the presence of so many youthful adventurers fresh from their voyages of discovery, each eager to recount the story of their successes.[3]

---

2. *Seventh Annual Report of the Board of Education, of the City of Oswego* (1860), in Calhoun, *Educating of Americans* pp. 311–312.

3. *Eighth Annual Report of the Board of Education, of the City of Oswego* (1861), in *Education in the United States: A Documentary History*, ed. Sol Cohen, vol. 3 (New York: Random House, 1974), p. 1781.

In the spring of 1861, the president of the Oswego board reported that the new system had been found to be "very satisfactory," on a limited trial in the primary schools and would be more widely used in the coming year. He explained that the new system looked to nature, to the natural development of human faculties, for its order. It was based on the premise that all human knowledge comes through the senses. Accordingly, it was the obligation of every teacher to base instruction on "the observation of real objects and occurrences." The aim of the new system was not to fill little heads with technical knowledge but to provide "a harmonious cultivation to the faculties of the mind."[4]

With the enthusiasm for the new method came the realization that the child's ability to recite rules, lists, or whatever did not signify knowledge. It was necessary that instruction begin with and build on what children already knew. Teachers were to begin with the concrete and proceed to the abstract. They could no longer teach just the numerals *1, 2, 3,* but now had to provide children with the opportunity to experience the *numbers* 1, 2, 3. Children learned to identify three claps of the hand, three marbles, two pencils, four sticks. After dealing with the objects the teacher could then proceed to teach the symbols (numerals) and the abstractions commonly called rules.

In an account of object teaching that appeared in Barnard's *American Journal of Education,* Sheldon indicated that the new approach to pedagogy began not with subject matter but with the nature of the child. The moral, physical, and intellectual development of children was more important than mastery of subject matter. Children were not viewed as miniature adults but as having "certain marked and distinctive characteristics," the most important of which were "activity, love of sympathy, and a desire for constant variety." Now teachers were to take advantage of these characteristics. In place of logically ordered lessons and drills, the teachers were to provide lessons that would "quicken the perceptions, and give them accuracy, awaken thought, and cultivate language." Children were to be allowed to observe objects so that they could learn to observe, describe, and define what they had seen. However, Sheldon warned that the descriptions and definitions should be limited to those characteristics the students could discern for themselves.[5]

According to Sheldon, there was "a natural order of subjects" just as there was a natural order in the development of children. First in the natural order was mathematics, followed by physics and language. Mathematics included the form and size of objects as well as number. Physics included all the objects of nature and their qualities that could be apprehended by the senses. Speaking, writing, reading, and spelling comprised the province of language. Sheldon related that, according to Pestalozzi, language was second only to observation. There was, said Sheldon, "a natural connection between thought and speech, observation and

---

4. *Eighth Annual Report of the Board of Education. of the City of Oswego* (1861), in Calhoun, *Educating of Americans,* pp. 312–313.

5. Edward Sheldon, "Object Teaching" (1864) in Cohen, *Education in the United States,* pp. 1782–1783.

expression."[6] For Sheldon there was no way to overestimate the value of language:

> Again, of what practical advantage would be the careful cultivation of observation, without a corresponding power of expression? Ideas unuttered are valueless to all but their possessor, but well expressed, they are a power to move the world.[7]

Though language was third in the "natural order of subjects" it quickly became the most important feature of the new education.

Language and Vocabulary

For Sheldon it was imperative that the vocabulary of children be enlarged as they moved from the nursery to the classroom. Although he cautioned that the new terms introduced to the children must be appropriate for their mental states, it was nonetheless essential that teachers encourage the precise use of an expanded vocabulary. It was the duty of the school to foster what he called a "refining" and "civilizing" influence by proper work in language. Sheldon believed that the correct method would enable children to "acquire the power of easy and elegant diction, and readiness in composition.[8]

Critics of the Oswego System

For many who adopted the new pedagogy, proper use of language became the sole aim of instruction. Some teachers were more intent on having children recite the characteristics of an object in a prescribed form than they were in having the children express what they actually observed. One critic of the "Oswego system" charged that the insistence on form inhibited children. In 1865, H. B. Wilbur claimed that many students who could answer quickly in arithmetic were confused and consequently failed because they did not know how "to cloak" their own fully understood answers "in the long syllogistic formula required"[9] by the Oswego system. To make his point he offered a simple question and then gave the kind of answer the students were required to present:

> If 2 bunches of matches cost 4 cents, what will 4 bunches cost? The pupil repeats the question and gives the solution.
> If 2 bunches of matches cost 4 cents, what will 4 bunches cost? 1 bunch of matches will cost one-half as much as 2 bunches of matches. If 2 bunches of matches cost 4 cents, 1 bunch of matches will cost one-half of 4 cents, which are 2 cents. 4 bunches of matches will cost 4 times as much as 1 bunch of matches. If 1 bunch costs 2 cents, 4 bunches will cost 4 times 2 cents, which are eight cents. Therefore, if 2 bunches of matches cost 4 cents, 4 bunches of matches will cost 8 cents.[10]

---

6. Ibid., p. 1784.

7. Ibid., pp. 1784–1785.

8. Ibid., p. 1786.

9. H. B. Wilbur, "Object System of Instruction as Pursued in the Schools of Oswego," *American Journal of Education* 38 (March 1865), p. 197.

10. Ibid., p. 198.

Wilbur also objected to the vocabulary students were taught upon their arrival in the classroom. Within two weeks, he claimed, "one hears from infant mouths such terms as 'graminivorous and chalybeate, iridescent and amorphous, serrated and foliaceous, imbricated and indigenous'."[11] In Wilbur's judgment such vocabulary was not a substitute for science.

Wilbur noted also that one of the cardinal principles of the object method dictated that the teacher develop the idea, then supply the term for that idea, and then proceed to cultivate its proper usage among the children. The method, he observed, seemed to emphasize mastery of the terms. At the end of each lesson, teachers wrote the term on the board and then led the children in "simultaneous repetition." Clearly the terms the children learned were not the "resultant of the workings of the class mind." They were, he suggested, "the set phrase and the stereotyped formula that the teacher furnishes as the summary of the particular class exercise."[12]

A later and more successful attack on Sheldon's new system occurred in 1872. It began when this resolution was presented to the Oswego Board of Education: "*Resolved:* That we discontinue Object teaching in our junior schools and substitute instead Cornell's *Primary Geography* and Appleton's *Elementary Arithmetic.*"[13] Complaints about the new ways of the school began to be heard: Students could no longer move from one grade to the next as easily as they once did. Parents had to spend too much money for books for their children. Some believed that the parents and teachers would rather use textbooks than the oral lessons dictated by the object method of teaching.

During the year a number of people wrote to the newspapers to air their complaints about the new system, particularly its cost. One citizen urged a return to the old ways and complained of the system's cost:

> I believe nine out of ten heads of families here look upon the Oswego system of schools as mischievous, expensive and cruel humbug. If your correspondent, Mr. Editor, had the management of public education in this city, he would make many changes. In the first place, he would discontinue the High School. There is no justice or propriety in levying a tax upon the whole people to teach a few children botany or geometry or Latin. He would drop from the [public school] course of study everything but reading, writing, arithmetic, geography and grammar. In the next place, he would return to the kind and form of school-books that were in use twenty-five years ago. Object teaching and gymnastics should be sent out of doors again. . . . The more teachers we have, the higher price, of course, we must pay for each. A diminished demand would be more economically supplied.[14]

Another citizen promised that "at the election in May the people will have some-

---

11. Ibid., p. 200.

12. Ibid., p. 196.

13. Mary Sheldon Barnes, "Edward Austin Sheldon," in *History of the First Half Century of the Oswego State Normal and Training School* (Oswego, N.Y.: The Radcliffe Press, 1913), p. 45.

14. Ibid., p. 46.

thing to say about a system by which they have been humbugged out of large sums of money and an incalculable amount of time."

According to Mary Sheldon Barnes, with the help of "a few strong friends" her father tried to answer the objections, showed where mistakes had been made, and tried to show that the system was good. He was not, however, completely successful, and after the May election the Oswego schools took action to confine the object lessons in color, form, size, animals, and plants to the first grade. Cornell's *Geography* and Appleton's *Arithmetic* were re-introduced to the schools. Sheldon was instructed not to hire teachers who were not natives of Oswego, and the high school was closed for a time.

Like most other pedagogical systems, the "Oswego system" was frequently only as good as the teachers and just as frequently as bad as the teachers. The system depended greatly on how well teachers were trained to employ it. Boston school superintendent John D. Philbrick noted that several good articles on Pestalozzi's system had appeared in 1839 in Russell's *Journal of Education* and that Josiah Holbrook's apparatus, natural history specimens, and cabinets were placed in several of Boston's primary schools. The method soon died out, however, "because the *teachers were not trained in the system.*" Philbrick also noted that "where the teacher is not interested in it, the results are far from satisfactory."[15]

Teacher Training in Oswego

Sheldon knew from the very beginning that the success of the new pedagogy depended on the ability of teachers to use it properly. He immediately coordinated the introduction of the new methods with a program of teacher training. During the first year of the new system, only the first grade used object lessons. Each Saturday morning Sheldon met with the first-grade teachers to discuss the system's principles and to plan the next week's work. During the week, he visited teachers in their classrooms to supervise their progress. As he trained the teachers, many of them left Oswego to teach where they could earn higher salaries. As Sheldon needed a larger supply of trained teachers, he asked the board of education to allow him to establish a training program. He proposed to enroll high school graduates in a program that would emphasize two major areas: the study of educational principles and their applications to classroom work; and the practice of teaching under the supervision of an accomplished teacher.

Sheldon's new school for training teachers began in May 1861 with the arrival of Margaret Jones from England. The school opened with nine pupils and was conducted in one of the city's primary schools. Sheldon shortened the school day of that school by one hour so that teachers who wanted to learn the new system could join the other students receiving instruction from Jones. With her help,

---

15. *Ninth Annual Report of the Board of Education, of the City of Oswego* (1862), in Calhoun, *Educating of Americans*, p. 315.

Sheldon established a program to train teachers to teach. They established a model school where students could observe teachers using the new methods, a school where the students could practice their teaching, and one school that was staffed only by members of the training class.

After the first year Jones returned to England and was replaced by Herman Krusi. During the second year of the training program, four other people, all trained by Margaret Jones, worked with Sheldon and Krusi. Sheldon served as principal and taught natural history, school organization, and school discipline. Krusi served as the instructor for method in form, number, drawing, and mental philosophy. E. D. Weller taught the proper methods for reading and language instruction. Amanda P. Funnelle taught the methods to use in animal lessons and moral instruction, and also served as the principal of the practice schools. Mary Howe Smith Pratt taught methods for color and geography, and Ellen Seaver instructed students how to use the methods in the advanced lessons on plants and objects.

In 1863 the state of New York appropriated $3,000 for Sheldon's Oswego Primary Teachers' Training School. With the money came the stipulation that Oswego provide suitable grounds, buildings, and furnishings, and the requirement "that there shall be instructed in said school for a period of at least forty weeks in each year, not less than fifty teachers, designing to teach in the common schools of this State."[16] In 1866 the school became the Oswego State Normal and Training School. In the next two years, six more state normal and training schools were opened along the lines Sheldon had established at Oswego.

Oswego became the model for training teachers not only in New York but also in many other cities and states. Visitors came to learn about the Oswego version of Pestalozzian methods and the methods that had been established for practice teaching. In 1887 Krusi reported that Oswego had prepared teachers for the state normal and training schools at Brockport, Potsdam, Genesco, Fredonia, Buffalo, Cortland, and New Paltz (all New York). Students came from all parts of the country. Graduates found positions in several states as well as in Canada, Japan, the Sandwich Islands (Hawaii), Mexico, and South America. After the end of the Civil War, Oswego sent its graduates to several southern schools that had been opened for the freedmen: Fisk University, Atlanta University, Avery Normal Institute in Charleston, and Tougaloo, Mississippi.[17]

Graduates of Oswego were in demand because they had learned not only *about* teaching, but also *how* to teach. Most teaching students could observe teachers in model schools, but those at Oswego also had the opportunity actually to teach in various classes in the practice school.

---

16. "Act Establishing the Training Class at Oswego," in Ned Harland Dearborn, *The Oswego Movement in American Education* (New York: Teachers College, 1925), Appendix VI.

17. Herman Krusi, "History of the Normal School" (1887), in *History of the First Half Century of the Oswego State Normal and Training School*, p. 27.

Reform at Quincy

While Cornell's *Geography* and Appleton's *Arithmetic* were being re-introduced in the Oswego schools, those who had assumed responsibility for the common schools in Quincy, Mass., were trying to find ways to get the schools out of the rut into which they had fallen. The school committee's annual report in 1873 said that a review of the work of the schools over the previous ten years showed no significant improvement. There was no noticeable difference between earlier students and recent graduates in the ability to read, write, spell, or do arithmetic. According to the committee, most who completed the course set out for them in school could "neither speak nor spell their own language very perfectly, nor read and write it with that elegance which is desirable."[18]

Charles Francis Adams, Jr., grandson of John Quincy Adams and a public-spirited citizen, claimed that the curriculum of the schools had degenerated into "all smatter, veneering and cram." Over the years many new studies had been introduced, but no effort had been made to integrate the various subjects into anything approaching a coherent program. Teachers had been allowed to become preoccupied with examinations; they turned their "scholars into parrots, and made a meaningless farce of education."[19] To the school committee it was clear that the town's money was not being spent effectively, and it was determined that "the two points of excellence and economy were to be kept clearly in view, and neither was to be subordinated to the other."[20]

The citizens of Quincy were quite aware of the cost of their schools. In a ten-year period the cost of educating each child had increased 250 percent: what had cost $6 in 1863 cost $15 in 1873. The school committee had considered hiring better teachers, described by Charles Francis Adams as "men and women of ideas, of individuality." But to do so would have driven the expenditure per child up to $30. Taxpayers, they concluded, were already overburdened and there was not much point in having "model schools if no one but the tax-gatherer can afford to live in the town that supports them."[21] Some committee members made suggestions and even tried to introduce reforms. However, they quickly realized that they had neither the time nor the necessary skills to improve the schools. Soon Quincy decided that it could afford to hire one person who had the necessary ability and spirit and then rely upon that person "to infuse his spirit into the others." In 1875 Colonel Francis Wayland Parker was hired to serve as the superintendent of the Quincy schools.

---

18. Charles Francis Adams, Jr., *The New Departure in the Common Schools and Other Papers on Educational Topics*, sixth ed. (Boston: Estes and Lauriat, 1879), p. 31.

19. Ibid., p. 33.

20. Ibid., p. 31.

21. Ibid., p. 35.

Francis Wayland Parker

Francis Wayland Parker was born in Bedford, New Hampshire, in 1837. When he was six years old, his father died and his uncle bound him to a farmer. There Parker was given a home and the opportunity to attend the district winter school for eight weeks each year. At age thirteen he managed to get to Mount Vernon, New Hampshire and attend a regular school. He remained in school and supported himself by working at a variety of odd jobs until he was sixteen. Then he quit school to become a teacher. In 1859 he took a teaching job in Illinois, but when the Civil War began, returned to New Hampshire to enlist in the New Hampshire Volunteers. By the end of the Civil War he was a lieutenant colonel. Although this was the end of Parker's military career, for the rest of his life, he would be known as "Colonel Parker."

After the war he taught in New Hampshire and in Dayton, Ohio, where he was put in charge of the normal school and studied Sheldon's *Object Lessons* to develop new teaching methods. In 1872 he traveled to Germany where he studied the *Kindergartens* and some of the new teaching methods developed by followers of the Herbartan pedagogy. Returning to the United States in 1875, he took the position in Quincy where he worked at introducing the new education into the Quincy schools. He soon gained a national reputation for the reforms he instituted at Quincy in 1875–80 and at Boston as a supervisor in 1880–83.

According to Adams's account, Quincy presented an ideal situation for reform. The school committee did not fear losing its power to the new superintendent, while Parker showed sympathy for their ideas and suggestions. Parker quickly introduced a new system "marked throughout by intense individuality." He demonstrated that he did not subscribe to the belief "that vast numbers of children should be taught as trains on railroads are run, on a time-table principle,—that they are here now, that they will be at such another point tomorrow, and at their terminus at such a date." "The essence of the new system," wrote Adams, "was that there was no system about it."[22]

In place of drills in the A B C's, Parker substituted a variety of activities. Teachers were instructed to allow children to learn to read and write the same way they had learned to speak—by doing it. Instead of learning rules, formulas, names, and sounds, they practiced reading and writing. Classrooms were filled with toys as well as books, and children were allowed to move about. Without knowing that they were learning to read, children learned to read. Soon children, according to Adams, "were happier and more amused and better contented at school than at home." Even the teachers profited from the new system. Though their work was "more exhausting, it was also far more inspiriting."[23]

When Parker reported on the new methods to the Quincy school committee, he emphasized both the impropriety and the inefficiency of the old methods. He explained that the town spent a minimum of $25,000 to prepare one class for the

---

22. Ibid., p. 37.
23. Ibid., p. 38.

high school and that the preparation of that class was not all that good. Within a typical class there could not be found one student with skill in handwriting suitable for business. The students' ability to punctuate, capitalize, and use the English language properly was very poor and "much of the spelling," he related, "is worthy the invention of Josh Billings."[24]

The schools' failure, according to Parker, was not the fault of the teachers, but of the old methods. All good educators (he explained) from the time of Pestalozzi on knew that drill in the A B C's, geography, grammar, arithmetic, or any other subject was ineffective and impractical. The "new" methods were only new to Quincy for they had been intuitively known by all good teachers. They could not even properly be termed "experimental," for they had been "tested for thirty years in Germany."[25]

Parker explained that the essence of his methods was "the *teaching of things,* and not words alone." His defense for his methods came from his observations of children and from the German philosopher Hegel, who had earlier noted that children learn more during their first six years than during the remainder of their lives. Young children spend their time exploring, manipulating objects in their environments, and playing. When children entered school, Parker said, their "imagination, curiosity, love for mental and physical activity are in a state of vigorous development."[26] Too frequently, schools suppressed that natural and vigorous activity and curiosity and insisted that children be quiet and learn the alphabet by rote. They were given books filled with letters that made as much sense to them as a book of Chinese would make to most American adults. The proper school, he insisted, had the same attributes as a cheerful and pleasant home. Children were to be encouraged to be active in the classroom—to play, sing, and draw as well as read, write, and count.

In 1883, Parker left Massachusetts to become the principal of the Cook County Normal School in Chicago. By the 1890s he was interested in more than introducing new methods into schools. He had become convinced that the common school was the institution best suited to preserve democracy. He insisted that:

> No child, no citizen of a republic, can be educated into citizenship outside of the common school; *the common school is not a charity; it is the inalienable right of every child, and common education is the imperative duty of every community.*[27]

The common school, according to Parker, could do what no other institution could do. Society was marked by differences in class, religion, and national origin, all of which kept people apart. The school was the one place where all children

---

24. *Report of the School Committee of the Town of Quincy* (1875–1876), in Calhoun, *Educating of Americans,* p. 320.

25. Ibid.

26. Ibid.

27. Francis W. Parker, *Talks on Pedagogics* (New York: E. L. Kellogg & Co., 1894), p. 438.

could learn to "live together, work together, [and] *know* each other."[28] Parker urged also that boys and girls attend the same schools from the kindergarten to the university. Separation of the boys and girls in schools could only produce "mistrust, misunderstanding, false—nay even impure—fancies."[29] Coeducation in the common school would allow all people who would have to live and work together to know and to understand each other. The school, he felt, could remedy all social ills. Teachers could even cure the problems of the slums; good teachers could reduce the enrollments in the nation's prisons, reform schools, poorhouses, and "lunatic asylums."

The Kindergarten

The kindergarten, like many other educational developments in the United States, was of European origin. Its founder was Friedrich Froebel, a German from Thuringia. In 1805, after many unsuccessful attempts to find a satisfactory occupation, Froebel happened into teaching in Frankfurt at a school run along Pestalozzian principles. The success he enjoyed and the personal satisfaction he found in teaching little children prompted him to journey to Switzerland to study with Pestalozzi. After two years, he returned to study Hebrew and Arabic at Göttingen; from there he went to Berlin to study mineralogy. Throughout his studies Froebel was looking for what he called "unity." He was trying to reconcile his inner self with the outer world as well as find "the equally necessary harmony between aim, career, and method." He found that unity in the study of mineralogy; the study of rocks and crystals somehow made it clear that all parts of the cosmos were related to each other in an orderly manner.

After the end of the Napoleonic Wars, Froebel returned to schoolkeeping. By 1837 he had returned to his native Thuringia where he opened what was to become the *Kindergarten* (although it was originally called "school for little children" or *Kleinkinderbeschäftigungsanstalt*). He envisioned his school as a place where children would be free to develop their personalities under the careful guidance of sympathetic teachers. He supplemented Pestalozzi's methods with play and music. To express his views about how children should be allowed to develop, Froebel adopted the metaphor of nature and objected to those who viewed the child "as a piece of wax, a lump of clay." Plants and animals, he explained, were given the space, time, rest, and freedom from "arbitrary interference" to develop according to natural law. Children, he argued, should have the same opportunity for natural development.[30]

The kindergarten was brought to the United States by German immigrants

---

28. Ibid., p. 421.

29. Ibid.

30. Friedrich Froebel, *The Education of Man*, in *Three Thousand Years of Educational Wisdom*, ed. Robert Ulich (Cambridge: Harvard University Press, 1963), p. 55.

after the 1848 revolution. The first kindergarten in the United States was probably the one established in 1855 in Watertown, Wisconsin, by Margaretta Schurz, who had been one of Froebel's pupils. Schurz's kindergarten and others founded by German immigrants were private schools conducted in German. In large measure, their purpose was to ensure that children would learn the German language and the culture of their forefathers.

Henry Barnard visited Madame Ronge's kindergarten in London in 1854 and became an advocate. As U.S. Commissioner of Education, he urged both the Senate (in 1869) and the House (in 1870) to establish kindergartens in the District of Columbia, but Congress did not act on his recommendations. The first kindergarten to be conducted in English was founded in 1860 in Boston by Elizabeth Peabody with the help of her sister Mary Peabody Mann (Horace Mann's widow).

Most early kindergartens were privately operated for children from prosperous families. As the idea gained popularity, several charitable organizations established kindergartens for the children of the poor. Under the direction of Susan Blow and Wiliam Torrey Harris, St. Louis became the first city to open a publicly supported kindergarten as part of a public school system. In 1868, one year after he became superintendent of the St. Louis schools, Harris took a census of how many children there were in various parts of the city and how long children from the various neighborhoods typically remained in school. The reports revealed that children who lived near the levee and near factories usually attended school for three years or less. Harris concluded that such children were doubly handicapped: They received little schooling and they lived in neighborhoods where negative influences "abounded" in the streets and alleys.[31]

In 1870 Harris sought from the St. Louis Board of Education a suspension of the rule that required children to be at least six years old to enter school. His request was denied and, in fact, the age requirement was raised to seven to solve the city's problem of too few schools for too many students. Harris, however, persisted in trying to help slum children by bringing them into the schools earlier. In 1872 he recommended that the kindergarten be instituted for children who were three years old or older, for he had observed that many slum children went from their third year to their seventh year without proper supervision by their families. As Harris developed his notions about the kindergarten, his explanations of its benefit took on Hegelian overtones. In 1879 he wrote of the kindergarten:

> As regards the claimed transcendence of the system over all others in the way of moral development, I am inclined to grant some degree of superiority to it, but not for intrinsic reasons. It is because the child is then at an age when he is liable to great demoralization at home, and is submitted to a gentle but firm discipline in the kindergarten, that the new education proves of more than ordinary value as a moral discipline. The children of the poor, at the susceptible age of five years, get many lessons on the street that tend to corrupt them.

---

31. Selwyn K. Troen, *The Public and the Schools: Shaping the St. Louis System, 1838–1920* (Columbia, Mo.: University of Missouri Press, 1975), pp. 100–102.

The children of the rich, meeting no wholesome restraint, become self-willed and self-indulgent.[32]

For Harris, the major proponent of the Hegelian philosophy in the United States, to have children left without supervision—particularly in these important years—was to have an intolerable condition.

Susan Blow

As the daughter of Henry Taylor Blow, U.S. Minister to Brazil and a prominent figure in the economic and political life of Missouri, Susan Blow had had every opportunity to travel and to attend good schools. Her education and the Christian character of her upbringing gave her a sense of duty. On her return from Brazil, she became a substitute teacher in St. Louis, tried some Froebelian ideas, and discovered that her duty was to become a kindergartner (a term then used for the teachers also). With Harris's support she went to New York in 1872 to study with Maria Kraus-Boelte, who had recently opened a school to teach mothers and aspiring kindergartners how to tend to the needs of children. In 1873 Blow returned to St. Louis, the first kindergartner to be trained in America by Kraus-Boelte, and opened the first public kindergarten in the United States. The next year she began a class to train more teachers.

With three volunteer assistants, Blow tended to 68 children in the first kindergarten. Soon the idea gained considerable public support in St. Louis. When in 1875 the public learned that her kindergarten might be closed because of its expense, citizens sent letters of objection to the local newspapers and circulated petitions urging its continuation. For a while a fee was charged to those who could afford to pay it, but by 1878 the school board decided to accept the kindergarten as a permanent feature of the school system. By 1880 nearly 8,000 children were enrolled in the kindergartens and were being taught by 166 teachers and 60 volunteer assistants.[33]

The St. Louis kindergarten used Froebelian techniques, but Blow and Harris were more interested in teaching children how to conform to a vision of the good citizen in the good society than in promoting their unfettered unfolding. Self-activity was not a prominent feature, for, as Harris later explained, "the cultivation of self-activity may be excessive, and lead to pertness and conceit."[34] They used games as an important pedagogical method, as did Froebel, but they used them to teach children their duties to themselves and to society. Their use of objects, or what Froebel called "gifts," was designed to prepare children for arithmetic, geometry, and drawing, and to enhance their manual dexterity so they would later be good industrial workers.

---

32. William Torrey Harris, "The Kindergarten in the Public School System," in Cohen, *Education in the United States,* p. 1907.

33. Troen, *Shaping the St. Louis System,* p. 107.

34. Harris, "The Kindergarten in the Public School Systems," in Cohen, *Education in the United States,* p. 1907.

Later Changes in the Kindergarten

After 1878 the St. Louis kindergarten was attacked by those who believed it was not an American institution but a German institution. After some legal battles, Harris had to stop admitting three- and-four-year olds and also had to charge a nominal fee. Nonetheless, the kindergarten survived in St. Louis and spread to other cities, where the St. Louis kindergarten served as the model. Kindergarten teachers trained in St. Louis later helped to establish and run kindergartens in Boston, Baltimore, Chicago, Cincinnati, and other cities.

As the plight of the poor worsened in many industrial cities, settlement houses were founded by philanthropic organizations to assist both Americans and immigrants living in the slums. The settlement houses used the kindergarten to assist children and to teach parents how to rear children. The promise of the kindergarten seemed so great that even the Women's Christian Temperance Union established a kindergarten department, opened over twenty kindergartens of its own, and prepared Froebelian literature for use by its local affiliates. Between 1880 and 1900 hundreds of kindergarten associations were formed, usually by women doing charity work. Many of these associations also conducted training schools for teachers. In time, many of the kindergartens became part of the local public school system; and sometimes the training departments became affiliated with local universities.

Before the nineteenth century closed, the kindergarten was sufficiently established to allow debates about how to conduct it. Some held to the Froebelian philosophy and methods. Some argued that the new methods of child study and the new science of psychology dictated changes in the kindergarten. Some kindergartners were convinced that the ways of the kindergarten had to be consistent with the developmental stages of childhood—social and biological—identified by G. Stanley Hall.

In 1894 John Dewey joined the faculty at the newly founded University of Chicago, and in 1896 he opened a laboratory school to study the best ways of educating children. He was also in the process of developing a new psychology—*functionalism*—and a new philosophy, known as *pragmatism*. The central concern in both the new psychology and the new philosophy was utility: Dewey was to argue that the meaning and value of any object or idea were to be found in how well it served humanity's purposes. He was especially concerned with social purposes. Dewey was so insistent that psychological continuity was more important than logical continuity in the activity of children that he refused to use the term kindergarten to designate the class for four- and-five-year olds in the laboratory school. In its place he used the term, "sub-primary."[35]

As the new psychologies were developed and new methods were built on them, Harris and Blow held to their position. Harris admitted that some knowledge could be gathered from physiological psychology, but insisted that introspection

---

35. Evelyn Weber, *The Kindergarten: Its Encounter with Educational Thought in America* (New York: Teachers College Press, 1969), p. 51.

would tell more about mind and its development than the direct observation of human behavior. Susan Blow remained convinced that one truly capable person could discern more about the development of children than any number of data gatherers.[36]

As the nineteenth century came to a close, debate about the kindergarten continued. Many educators claimed that it should be based not on speculative or philosophical notions about the development of children but on the findings of the social and behavioral sciences, especially psychology. As educators attempted to base educational practices and organization on a scientific basis, the new education became progressive education. However, those who had to convince school committees, school boards, and taxpayers that the kindergarten should be made an integral part of public school systems could not always use philosophical and scientific arguments. They had to argue their case in terms of practicality and utility. Consequently, kindergartens throughout the country were shaped by the elementary schools. They became "prep schools" where children could be prepared to begin "academic" work of the first grade rather than schools to foster moral, emotional, physical, and social development.

---

36. Ibid., p. 50.

PART III

New Institutions in a New Era

By 1850, California had become a state, and the United States spanned an entire continent. The nation's population had increased from 3.9 million in 1790 to 23.1 million in 1850, and its diversity also increased. In half a century, the traditional ways of doing business, manufacturing goods, transporting people and goods, communicating, and farming had changed.

In the midst of these changes, many Americans tried to achieve some sense of order and to preserve traditional ways and values. As changes were introduced, so were alternatives. For the most part Americans avoided revolutionary choices. As the factory system grew, Americans were offered the choice of turning to communal societies, but they did not receive widespread support, and few such societies prospered for long. Education was offered repeatedly as the solution to the social and economic problems confronting Americans, but there were many alternatives. One was to continue the system that allowed the prosperous to support schools for themselves and offer some support for the very poor. Such charity schools were rejected. The major educational innovation of the early nineteenth century—the Lancasterian system—was also rejected. By the middle of the century, however, there was considerable agreement that common schools were necessary. They were seen as an institution that would stabilize society, protect its cherished way and values, and serve as a deterrent to revolutionary change. A resolution offered by Alonzo Potter at a common school convention in Utica, N.Y., in 1842 expresses what many expected of the common school:

> *Resolved,* That the best police for our cities, the lowest insurance of our houses, the firmest security for our banks, the most effective means of preventing pauperism, vice and crime, and the only sure defense of our country, are our common schools; and woe to us, if their means of education be not commensurate with the wants and the powers of the people![1]

To build the common school, Americans had to surrender some of their earlier prejudices against European institutions. In the years immediately following the Revolution, American statesmen counselled against sending youth to Europe for their schooling or imitating European ways. But in the 1830s and after, Americans went to Europe specifically to see how schools might be organized and conducted. Many admired the Prussian school system, which was well organized, orderly and efficient; enrolled all children; and provided for the training and supervision of its teachers. The Americans adopted the Prussian model and attempted to fill it with American content.

---

1. Jonathan Messerili, *Horace Mann* (New York: Knopf, 1972), p. 442.

However, many wanted the American school to do for American society just what they thought the Prussian school was doing for Prussian society. Victor Cousin's *Report* had said that two German words characterized Prussian society—*Schulpflichtigkeit* and *Dienstpflichtigkeit* (roughly, "obligation to school" and "civic obligation"). Many Americans also wanted a citizenry that was willing to accept unquestioningly its duty to support the school and its duty to serve the nation without hesitation. Even on the eve of World War I, Americans were still using German ways of schooling to measure their own educational and national progress. While Germany did not continue as *the* model to follow, Americans did continue to see a relationship between their schools and the strength of their nation.

The schools quickly mirrored much of the confusion and many of the contradictions of American society. Mann, for example, argued that education would create wealth and thereby render unnecessary any revolutionary redistribution of wealth. The texts prepared for use in the schools taught children to love their country, respect authority, work hard, obey all the rules, and observe the Sabbath. McGuffey's *Readers* presented many stories in which children who disobeyed met severe, immediate, and even fatal punishment. On the other hand, children who obeyed were frequently the recipients of instant wealth or promising opportunities that would lead to wealth. The rewards, however, typically came from a benefactor whose appearance could be attributed only to chance or divine providence, not from the children's own knowledge or capability.

Recently, historians of American education have questioned the effectiveness of the common school movement. Michael B. Katz, for example, has argued that it created school systems that were "universal, tax-supported, free, compulsory, bureaucratic, racist, and class-biased."[2] He has further argued that these characteristics, acquired between 1800 and 1880, have not changed materially since. Robert L. Church and Michael W. Sedlak have concluded that "whatever the statistics on attendance and length of school year and magnitude of educational effort show, they do not appear to demonstrate any revolutionary changes in the amount of schooling in the United States that can be associated with the common school movement." They claim that the common school movement was coincidental with an already existing educational movement and that the "essence" of the movement was "its rhetorical commitment to the deliberate use of education as a tool for social manipulation and social progress."[3]

Claims that many leaders in the common school movement were greatly concerned with protecting law and order, promoting social tranquility, and maintaining the social and economic status quo are largely correct. Merle

---

2. Michael B. Katz, *Class, Bureaucracy, and Schools* (New York: Praeger, 1971), p. xx.

3. Robert L. Church and Michael W. Sedlak, *Education in the United States* (New York: The Free Press, 1976), p. 58.

Curti effectively argued that point a generation ago (1935). But Curti has also pointed out that the poor were much worse off in the early 1800s than they had been in colonial times. The rise of the factory system made many social relationships formal and impersonal and destroyed the apprentice system, in which many had not only learned a trade, but also gained some "book" education. In the early 1800s many children, especially poor children in densely populated areas, were out of school and in the factories. When Horace Mann began his educational work in Massachusetts in 1837, he quickly learned that a third of the local school districts did not even have a schoolhouse. In many other states the situation was not significantly different.[4]

In its early years the common school may not have done much more than compete sucessfully with private schools, serving children who were already in schools. Why those who, could afford to send their children to private schools chose to send them to the common school and forgo the alternatives that the private schools offered is a question worth consideration. The common school was accepted, if not used, by many Americans. After mid-century, states began to adopt compulsory school attendance laws (Massachusetts in 1852 and New York in 1853 were the first, and the size of the school population increased. Whether the success of the common schools in attracting students and the compulsory attendance laws constituted a form of opportunity or a form of social imposition is a matter of historical interpretation. Different interpretations start from different assumptions about the nature and obligations of a democracy and about the rights and duties of humanity. Katz has argued that the promises of opportunity offered by the common school have not been kept:

> There is a great gap between the pronouncement that education serves the people and the reality of what schools do to and for the children of the poor. Despite the existence of free, universal, and compulsory schooling, most poor children become poor adults. Schools are not great democratic engines for identifying talent and matching it with opportunity. The children of the affluent by and large take best marks and the best jobs.[5]

Despite its shortcomings, its limitations, and its contradictions, Americans held onto their new institution, the common school. The continued economic expansion in the United States in the 1850s and the concomitant improvement in the standard of living undoubtedly convinced many that the schools *did* produce wealth. By the 1870s many acted as though the school were a long-established institution and set out to reform it once again. All social and economic problems were to be solved by a reformed common school.

---

4. Merle Curti, *The Social Ideas of American Educators*, rev. ed. (Totowa, New Jersey: Littlefield, Adams and Co., 1968), pp. 25-27.

5. Katz, *Class, Bureaucracy, and Schools*, p. xviii.

Most historians agree that the 1890s constituted a great dividing line in the history of the United States. By 1890 it was fairly clear that the United States was to become a great industrial nation with large urban centers. After the 1890s the pace and the nature of that change itself altered dramatically. As Americans entered the new era, they carried old values and old institutions with them. Some survived, some disappeared, and others were modified. One institution they carried with them was the public school.

Many continued to view public schools as the answer to all social ills. And the schools not only survived, but grew. New schools were opened, high school attendance increased, and Americans continued to argue about what should be taught to whom and how it should be taught. Americans tried to reform their schools, and frequently assumed those attempts would also reform society. New methods and new emphases were substituted for old ones, but, in many cases, the changes did not help the people they were supposed to help. Industrial education brought blacks and American Indians neither prosperity nor political and civil rights; it became clear that it was education for those who had not enjoyed opportunity and who were not likely to enjoy it in the future. In 1906 the U.S. Commissioner of Education reported that "industrial training is offered in most of the Negro schools, reform schools, and schools for defectives.[6] In 1909 the *Chicago Daily* reported to its readers that President William Howard Taft supported industrial education for blacks because black graduates of liberal arts colleges became professionals and then agitated for political rights.[7] As late as 1940, Horace Mann Bond described American blacks as "a semicaste in American life" and referred to "the immense inertia of the social structure which stands in the way" of their achievement.[8]

The inertia of a generation ago still persists in many areas. Equality of educational opportunity for all children is a goal that has not been attained. Many minority groups find themselves with economic problems, which often translate into educational inequalities. Yet there is clear recognition that opportunity should be effectively extended to all and there is evidence that many do receive more schooling than they did a generation ago. Women still suffer from discriminatory attitudes that were common a century ago, but many of these discriminatory practices have been challenged and some have been terminated.

In the 1890s a new basis for reforming the schools was discovered — psychology. As Americans learned about the new science of the mind, psychology, they used it to revise the reforms that had been instituted in the

---

6. Quoted in Paul C. Violas, *The Training of the Urban Working Class: A History of Twentieth Century American Education* (Chicago: Rand McNally, 1978), p. 137.

7. Ibid. p. 138.

8. Horace Mann Bond, "Negro Education," in *Encyclopedia of Educational Research,* ed. Walter S. Monroe (New York: The Macmillan Co., 1949), pp. 748–749.

late 1800s and used it to develop something called "progressive education." The new psychology was to be scientific and "objective" yet it would be used to support old claims of racial superiority and inferiority.

PART IV
Modern Times

To emphasize the far-reaching implications of the nation's transformation into an industrialized society, Samuel P. Hays has used the image of "the American of 1914," who, "looking backward scarcely more than forty or fifty years . . . fully recognized that his country had changed rapidly and fundamentally."[1] In 1914 Henry Ford began the "progressive line production" of automobiles, an innovation that was to change the lives of subsequent generations of Americans. But the changes in American society were not confined to how goods were produced and distributed. They went to the very core of American society and transformed many human relationships. Writing in 1924, Walter Lippman said: "We are unsettled to the very roots of our being." According to Lippman, all human relationships were being transformed:

> There isn't a human relation, whether of parent and child, husband and wife, worker and employer, that doesn't move in a strange situation. We are not used to a complicated civilization, we don't know how to behave when personal contact and eternal authority have disappeared. There are no precedents to guide us, no wisdom that wasn't made for a simpler age. We have changed our environment more quickly than we know how to change ourselves.[2]

Americans had to adjust their ways of thought, play, worship, and work to a new economic and intellectual order.

Responses to the new order were varied. Utopian novelists believed that

---

1. Samuel P. Hays, *The Response to Industrialism, 1885–1914* (Chicago: University of Chicago Press, 1963), p. 1.
2. Walter Lippman, *Drift and Mastery* (Englewood Cliffs, N.J.: Spectrum Books, 1961), p. 92.

modern technology was the key to a society free from want and from social conflict. Henry James and Henry Adams found an alternative to the new economic order in looking back to history and European values. Another response was in the form of social disorder—the Pullman strike and other violent labor disputes, Coxey's march on Washington—disturbances demonstrating that the social disorders created by the new economic order could not be resolved by force.

These social and economic developments called for adjustments in systems of education. Old systems were simply inappropriate. Walter Lippman aptly described the situation:

> In former times you could make some effort to teach people what they needed to know. It was done badly, but at least it could be attempted. Men knew the kind of problems their children would have to face. But today education means a radically different thing. We have to prepare children to meet the unexpected, for their problems will not be the same as their fathers. To prepare them for the unexpected means to train them in method instead of filling them with facts and rules. They will have to find their facts and make their own facts and make their own rules, and if schools can't give them that power then schools no longer educate for the modern world.[3]

The scale and the character of the school, especially the secondary school, were changed significantly. As the city increased its numbers, housed an increasingly diverse population, and required more tax dollars, a steadily increasing percentage of the school-age youth began to attend school, the school term was lengthened, attendance grew more regular, and the school consumed more tax dollars than ever before.

In the early 1890s there was considerable debate about the purpose and the curriculum of the high school. Some wanted to revise the curriculum for the needs of city youth or the challenges of the modern world. Others wanted to hold on to older, more established ways. To clarify the situation the National Education Association appointed a Committee of Ten to examine the secondary school program. The report issued in 1893 prompted a debate that was to endure through the first quarter of the twentieth century.

Critics and defenders of the NEA recommendations turned to the new "science of the mind," psychology, to buttress their positions. Some held to old psychological notions and some employed the findings of the new psychology and of other social and behavioral sciences. The new generation of educators was attempting to make a science, or at least an applied science, of public schooling. From the 1890s on, many school practices were to be defended, touted, or instituted because they were seen to be consistent with the latest psychological findings. In psychology Americans found new

---

3. Ibid., p. 93.

directions for running their schools, new conceptions of childhood, and new aims of education.

In Chapter Thirteen we shall examine the new psychology and how it influenced education. In doing so, we shall focus on some psychologists who applied the new science to educational questions: William James, Edward Thorndike, G. Stanley Hall, Arnold Gesell, and Daniel Starch. This group, though far from complete, is representative of those who made important contributions to changing the ways educators looked at problems. In the last part of this chapter we shall note how psychological theory and findings were used to support many old and unfounded prejudices, for it is always important to note that how humanity uses its knowledge is always at least as important as the knowledge itself. Perhaps this chapter will also help us see that questions of right, justice, and morality need to be answered in a way that allows us to use all that we know rather than what we know from one limited area of inquiry.

In Chapter Fourteen we shall review how Americans responded to the increased size of their educational enterprise by looking at the metaphors they used to describe their schools and the educative process. At times metaphors help people understand problems, by describing new and strange elements in terms of what is already known and comfortable. At times, however, they may disguise new and significant changes.

An institution and an experience that has come to be universal for nearly all Americans, the high school, will be examined in Chapter Fifteen. It is an institution that was shaped during the intellectual, social, and economic ferment of the 1890s and has endured. As our industrialized and postindustrial society has required greater technical skills of its members, the high school has become increasingly important.

The New Science of the Mind 13

Education and the New Psychology

Modern psychology began in the second half of the nineteenth century. In England, Charles Darwin, Sir Francis Galton, and Herbert Spencer were developing the study of human behavior from a scientific point of view. In Germany, Theodore Fechner, Herman von Helmholtz, and Whilhelm Wundt were removing psychology from its philosophical base and developing scientific methods for the study of the human mind. In 1870, Wundt opened his psychological laboratory in Leipzig, and many Americans traveled there to earn their psychological credentials just as the previous generation had gone to Germany to learn the ways of schoolkeeping.

William James
The foundations of an American school of psychology were laid by William James. Given an eclectic liberal education, he turned toward science and medicine, receiving his medical degree from Harvard in 1869. In 1872 he began to teach physiology at Harvard, setting up a two-room experimental laboratory for graduate students enrolled in his course, "The Relations between Physiology and Psychology." In 1877, James secured additional space for a laboratory in Harvard's Museum of Comparative Zoology to carry out his own experimental work. America had its own psychologist.

In 1878 James promised the publisher Henry Holt that he would write a psychology text for Holt's American Science Series. He signed a contract and agreed to finish the text in two years. James missed his deadline, but he gave Holt much more than a text. In 1890, he completed the now famous two-volume *Principles of Psychology*. James's text offered a grand synthesis of psychology, a synthesis with an American flavor. James liberated American psychologists from the European origins of psychology and allowed the development of an American psychology that was to emphasize the functional and adaptive behavior of humanity. In the *Principles* he incorporated and presented the work of most of his contemporaries in Europe. But while he used their work, he neither accepted nor advocated their ideologies or world views. James had successfully taken two traditions—the work from the German laboratories and the English theories of evolution and associationism—and incorporated them into his own evolutionary point of view. The view he presented was acceptable because he left the future course of evolution uncharted. He insisted that the human mind acted on the environment while the environment was acting on it. To be able to accept evolution and still have a choice in how humanity would be affected by it was an inviting position.

For many years James's psychology texts apparently were used by nearly every student of psychology. But even before he finished his texts, James began to influence the course of American psychology and American education through his lectures and his teaching.

G. Stanley Hall, The First Student

In June 1878, G. Stanley Hall was examined by William James and four other Harvard professors. He answered their questions satisfactorily and was awarded a doctorate in psychology. It was an historic occasion, for Hall's was the first Ph.D. degree in psychology to be awarded by any university in the United States. In the next twenty-five years Hall became one of the most prominent American psychologists. He helped form the American Psychological Association, founded the *American Journal of Psychology* and the *Pedagogical Seminary,* made Clark University into an outstanding center for the study of psychology and pedagogy, helped forge the link between psychology and pedagogy, and started and promoted the child-study movement.

Hall, born in 1846, was from rural Massachusetts. He began to study for the ministry, but after a year went to Germany to prepare himself for a professorship. There he studied a variety of subjects: philosophy, physics, and anthropology. He returned in 1871, and in 1876 he was asked to teach English at Harvard. That gave him the opportunity to study psychology with James and complete a dissertation on "The Muscular Perception of Space."

Although Hall had his doctorate in psychology, he was unable to find a suitable position. He postponed the problem of finding a job by returning to Germany to study with Wundt at Leipzig. He also spent some time acquainting himself with the latest developments in pedagogical theory and practice in Europe. Upon his return, Charles W. Eliot, president of Harvard, invited him to offer two series of lectures: one on the history of philosophy and one on pedagogy.

Both lecture series were very successful, and according to a recent biographer of Hall, there were numerous reasons for that success: First, Hall presented his lectures on pedagogy not in Cambridge but in Boston and on Saturday mornings, a convenient time and place for teachers. Second, many people in the Boston area were already interested in pedagogy, for in nearby Quincy, Col. Francis W.

Parker had already generated an amount of interest in educational reform. Third, teachers desired whatever help they could find in managing their classrooms more efficiently and professionally. Most teachers were women, poorly trained and poorly paid; and their task was becoming increasingly troublesome because of the growing diversity of the students. Fourth, Hall's lectures seemed "scientific," and in the last quarter of the nineteenth century there was widespread belief that science would solve all human problems and help restore some semblance of order to society. Finally, Hall's lectures contained elements that appealed to both reformers and more conservative thinkers. For example, while he demonstrated that the new science of psychology supported the new ideas on teaching put forth by Pestalozzi and Froebel, he also maintained that physical punishment was often necessary to help children conform to the rules of school and society.[1]

Encouraged by the success of his lectures on pedagogy, Hall submitted two articles in 1882 to the *Princeton Review:* "The Moral and Religious Training of Children" and "The Education of the Will." These also mixed new theories and old values. His advice against forcing religious training at too early an age was consistent with the position of a number of the New England clergy. He was not opposed to religious training, but believed that children would naturally acquire the proper religious outlook. In these early articles he was already expressing the notion earlier articulated by the German evolutionist Ernest Haeckel that "ontogeny recapitulates phylogeny." As children developed, they repeated the development of the race. Education shortened and expedited such natural development. When Hall applied this belief to religious instruction, he concluded that children should not receive any instruction in the doctrines of a religion until they had attained adolescence. Hall also openly discussed adolescents' preoccupation with the problems that puberty presented. He advised that adolescents needed some independence from their parents while sex and religion were their chief concerns. Those who believed that the "new education" (Pestalozzi and Froebel) was too permissive could find in Hall assurance that it was still proper to insist that children learn to obey adults. He cautioned against the dangers of allowing people to follow their impulses and feelings. As children had a natural inclination to abide by the direction given to them by those in authority, that inclination should be used to train the young to obey. In essence, Hall used his version of psychology and evolutionary theory to support traditional values.

In 1883, Hall published a third article in the *Princeton Review,* "The Contents of Children's Minds." He used his knowledge of studies conducted earlier in Germany to explore just what children did and did not know as they entered school. He investigated how many boys, how many girls, how many American children, how many Irish children, and how many children who had been to kindergarten knew what he thought children of their age should know. With the help of assistants from a nearby kindergarten, he assembled lists of concepts and ob-

---

1. Dorothy Ross, *G. Stanley Hall: The Psychologist as Prophet* (Chicago: University of Chicago Press, 1972), pp. 113–117.

jects. They included: beehive, frog, butterfly, ribs, ankles, the origin of butter, the source of milk, growing of dandelions, growing of apples, the number five, right from left, sunset, rivers, and many other items.

Hall described some of the children's ignorance and misconceptions in this way:

> Skeins and spools of thread were said to grow on the sheep's back or on bushes, stockings on trees, butter to come from buttercups, flour to be made of beans, oats to grow on oaks, bread to be swelled yeast, trees to be stuck in the ground by God and rootless, meat to be dug from the ground, and potatoes to be picked from trees. Cheese is squeezed butter, the cow says "bow-wow," the pig purrs or burrows, worms are not distinguished from snakes, moss from the "toad's umbrella," bricks from stones, nor beans from trees. An oak may be known only as an acorn-tree or a button-tree, a pine only as a needle tree, a bird's nest only as its bed, etc.[2]

Hall found that while no one child was completely ignorant of the questions asked, no children knew all that was asked. Knowing that every child had some misconceptions or areas of ignorance about common objects was especially important for teachers. Every idea, then, had to be presented in a way that would ensure its connection with an idea the child already had incorporated into his or her "apperceptive mass." A mistaken assumption about what the child knew could "make utter nonsense or mere verbal cram of the most careful instruction."[3] For instance, many children could explain what a cow was, how it provided people with milk and leather, and yet believe "that it was no bigger than a small mouse." What children learned from their picture books was not always what adults thought they learned.

Hall's study indicated that "country children" knew more and were better prepared for school work than "city children." He explained the difference by noting that the content of the primers was based on life in the country rather than the city. Curiously, Hall did not recommend that the texts be changed to relate to what children knew, but rather, warned that the difference demonstrated that "the danger of unwarranted presupposition is considerable." He observed:

> As our methods of teaching grow natural we realize that city life is unnatural, and that those who grow up without knowing the country are defrauded of that without which childhood can never be completed or normal. On the whole the material of the city is no doubt inferior in pedagogic value to country experience.[4]

To remedy the difference between "country children" and "city children," Hall urged that the "city children" be taken to the country for a few days so their intelligence could be improved.

When Hall spoke to the Young Men's Christian Association in 1901, he told

---

2. G. Stanley Hall, "The Contents of Children's Minds" (*Princeton Review*, 1883), in *Readings in the History of Psychology*, ed. Wayne Dennis (New York: Appleton-Century-Crofts, 1948), p. 260.

3. Ibid.

4. Ibid., p. 261.

his audience that only in the country could humanity be natural and offered a catalogue of ills brought on by life in the city. City life, for instance, restricted "the eye, which normally roves freely far and near, to the monotonous zigzag of the printed page." Other ills that could be attributed to the city were "the pallid, muddy or choloritic complexions, stoop, decaying teeth, premature grayness and baldness" as well as "the great increase of nervous disorders."[5]

City life was especially dangerous for adolescents. The increased mechanization in the city deprived many adolescents of the opportunity to engage in "the strenuous life"—the life that would develop their muscles and prevent their surrender to licentious distractions. Proper use and development of the body during adolescence would not only lead to strength and health but lessen "the power of sin over body and soul."[6]

Hall's obvious preference for country life over city life was not new or unique. Throughout American history there has been dislike, distrust, even fear of the city. According to Morton and Lucia White, there is a "powerful tradition of anti-urbanism in the history of American thought.[7] What the Whites term the "ambivalence and animosity toward the city" has been reflected in the nation's schools. Many reforms in American schooling have been attempts to institute programs that would provide children with the knowledge and values people of an earlier rural age found useful.

A notable example is the program John Dewey implemented in his laboratory school at the University of Chicago in the 1890s. There he engaged children in the occupations of an earlier age so they could develop in the school the sense of community that seemed impossible in an industrialized urban setting. Many other educators sought to recreate the consistencies of an earlier age in the school. Whether that approach helped to develop psychologically healthy individuals or widened the gap between school and society is still an open question.

The Child-Study Movement

In the 1860s and 1870s some school supervisors in Germany had used questionnaires to find out what school children knew. In 1880, Charles Frances Adams, Jr., in Quincy, recommended to the NEA that school programs and practices be based on what was known about the development of children.[8] Yet, those early efforts did not have the impact of Hall's article, "The Contents of Children's Minds." (1883). With that one study and a number of addresses, Hall began a movement.

5. G. Stanley Hall, "Christianity and Physical Culture" (*The Pedagogical Seminary*, vol. 9, September 1902), in *Health, Growth, and Heredity: G. Stanley Hall on Natural Education*, ed. Charles E. Strickland and Charles Burgess (New York: Teachers College Press, 1965), p. 157.

6. Ibid., pp. 158–159.

7. Morton and Lucia White, *The Intellectual Versus the City* (New York: Mentor Books, 1964), p. 15.

8. Ross, *G. Stanley Hall*, pp. 125–126.

While he was preparing the article, he was developing the argument that pedagogy should be based on the scientific study of children and that if it were, it would produce a new state of development for humanity. The responses and inquiries he received from teachers after publication led him to prepare a pamphlet for teachers so they could assist him in his work.

The "Contents" article was reprinted in several publications and issued as a pamphlet. In 1893 Hall and his supporters persuaded the National Education Association to organize a Department of Child-Study. By 1900 he could report that many women's clubs, summer schools, and Sunday-school teachers' organizations were devoting their attention to child-study. He had "received some two thousand letters—either unacknowledged or inadequately answered-from all parts of the world, asking how to organize local work, requesting suggestions for reading, or very often seeking advice concerning children."[9]

Critics of Child Study
Some people believed that the process of studying children would destroy their natural "naiveté." Hall, however, explained, that data could be gathered without children even knowing that they were being observed. The tasks required of the children—to tap their fingers, press down on a dynamometer, count objects, insert a needle into a small hole, read, or name their favorite story—did not seem to bother or strain them. At other times children were subjected to simple examinations of their sight, hearing, speech, or height and weight. It was beneficial to ask children about their fears, for "the very calling of attention to these psychoses, which have often secretly haunted adolescence for years, has, in itself, helped toward their dissipation and control."[10]

Hall's introduction of the questionnaire method into child-study was the beginning of a movement. As the questionnaires flowed out of Clark University, so did the criticism. Among those who raised questions about the work was William James who, in his *Talks to Teachers,* argued that teachers need not be active participants in the new movement:

> Least of all need you, merely *as teachers,* deem it part of your duty to become contributors to psychological science or to make psychological observations in a methodical or responsible manner. I fear that some of the enthusiasts for child-study have thrown a certain burden on you in this way. By all means let child-study go on,—it is refreshing all our sense of the child's life. There are teachers who take a spontaneous delight in filling syllabuses, inscribing observations, compiling statistics, and computing the per cent. Child-study will certainly enrich their lives. And, if its results, as treated statistically, would seem on the whole to have but trifling values, yet the anecdotes and observations of which it in part consists do certainly acquaint us more intimately with our pupils. . . . But, for Heaven's sake, let the rank and file of

---

9. G. Stanley Hall, "Child-Study and Its Relation to Education" (*The Forum,* vol. 29, August 1900), in Strickland and Burgess, *Health, Growth and Heredity,* p. 75.

10. Ibid., p. 79.

teachers be passive readers if they so prefer, and feel free not to contribute to the accumulation.[11]

James believed that the teachers were "overworked already." He also told teachers that he agreed with his colleague Professor Munsterberg who maintained that "the teacher's attitude toward the child, being concrete and ethical, is positively opposed to the psychological observer's, which is abstract and analytic."[12] In the years after James and Hall, many educators would argue about whether students should be treated as children or as instances of psychological laws.

Arnold Gesell and Stages of Development

Through the work of one of Hall's outstanding students, Arnold Gesell, child-study became an enduring feature of American culture and education. Gesell was born in 1880 in Alama, Wisconsin, became football coach and teacher at the high school in Stevens Point, Wisconsin, and attended Stevens Point Normal School. By 1903 he had been awarded a Bachelor of Philosophy degree from the University of Wisconsin. He studied with Hall at Clark University, was granted his Ph.D, and went to Los Angeles to become principal and assistant professor of psychology at the Los Angeles State Normal School. Soon he was invited to Yale University as a part-time assistant professor of psychology. He accepted because he would also be able to earn his medical degree, a necessity for the kind of work he wanted to undertake. In 1915, with his M.D. degree, Gesell began to map the entire course of child development. He had begun the work earlier in the New Haven dispensary; later it was conducted through the Yale Clinic of Child Development.

In 1918, Gesell and his staff undertook a complete mental survey of the children in New Haven's elementary schools. The results of that survey led to the recommendations Gesell prescribed in *Exceptional Children and Public School Policy* (1921). Gesell insisted that the school had to be constantly aware of the principles of mental hygiene, deal with each child as an individual, and have as its primary objective each child's healthy psychological and physical development.

Gesell found a way to gather data about children that was more reliable than Hall's use of teachers' observations. Gesell developed what he called "cinemanalysis," using a movie camera. For the study of infants he developed a dome encased by a one-way-vision screen. On the quadrants of the dome, silent cameras moved back and forth to record the behavior of the subjects. Before Gesell's career ended, he had accumulated nearly fifty-seven miles of film (showing the behavior of 12,000 children. Many of his books were illustrated with photographs of the specific behaviors he discussed. For example, there were 3,200 photographs in his *An Atlas of Infant Behavior: A Systematic Delineation of the Forms and Early Growth of Human Behavior Patterns* (1934). The data he collected enabled him to chart the entirety of child development.

---

11. William James, *Talks to Teachers on Psychology* (New York: Henry Holt and Co., 1901), pp. 12–13.

12. Ibid., p. 13.

Hall, Gesell, and others effectively changed the language of the school. In place of talk about students' accomplishments in traditional school subjects—reading, writing, arithmetic, history, language, geography—there developed a language that emphasized the need for healthy self-concepts and the well-adjusted child. For example, in *The First Five Years of Life,* Gesell suggested that "early reading difficulties would vanish if the natural processes of maturation were given a chance to assert themselves."[13] The problem of reading could be corrected by paying closer attention to the child's development. When cultural pressures and psychological processes conflicted, the best course, he suggested, was to follow the psychological route:

> When culture and child come into conflict it is time to be mindful of growth factors. Reading is a major cultural goal set up by society in an age which is strongly eye-minded. Important as the goal may be, it cannot be realized through sheer drill and direct pressure. Concessions must be made to the nascent needs and to the pattern of individual development.[14]

For some, the norms Gesell developed were used to allow children to do what they seemed to want to do and to support the belief that all children would learn what they needed to know when they were *ready* to learn it. For others, Gesell's norms became a source of concern when the children in their charge did not seem to measure up to what he had laid out.

Edward L. Thorndike

Edward L. Thorndike, the son of a New England clergyman, and a native of Williamsburg, Mass., was born in 1874, one year before James opened his demonstration laboratory at Harvard. Twenty years later, in a required course in psychology at Wesleyan University, Thorndike had to read certain chapters of William James's *Principles* to compete in a "prize examination." Forty years later, Thorndike wrote that the chapters he read "were stimulating, more so than any book that I had read before, and possibly more so than any read since."[15] As soon as he could, he set out to study at Harvard with James.

Thorndike planned to study literature, philosophy, and psychology, but psychology soon consumed all his interests and efforts. He began a series of experiments in which children were to guess what he was thinking about; for guessing correctly they were rewarded with a piece of candy. The Harvard authorities disapproved of his experiments and he had to discontinue them. Unable to work with children, Thorndike turned to chickens. The classic story is that as there was no room for his chickens at Harvard, and his landlady frowned on his keeping them

---

13. Arnold Gesell et. al., *The First Five Years of Life* (New York: Harper and Brothers, 1940), p. 313.

14. Ibid., pp. 313–314.

15. Edward L. Thorndike, "Autobiography," in Geraldine M. Joncich, *Psychology and the Science of Edcuation: Selected Writings of Edward L. Thorndike* (New York: Teachers College Press, 1962), p. 28.

in his room, William James (to the delight of his children) came to the rescue and offered his cellar to Thorndike's chickens.

In 1898 Thorndike received an offer from James McKeen Cattell to complete his work in psychology at Columbia University in New York City. When he set out for New York, he carried with him a basket holding his "two most educated chickens." He had planned to breed them so that he could "test the influences of acquired mental traits upon inherited capacity."[16] The breeding rate of the chickens, he later reported, made that "a foolish plan." He abandoned his fowl, turned to cats, and completed his doctoral dissertation, *Animal Intelligence.* An appointment at the College for Women of Western Reserve University in Cleveland required him to teach education, a subject he had not previously studied. In 1899 he was invited to teach psychology and child study at Teachers College, Columbia University. There he spent the rest of his career, becoming one of the outstanding figures in education and educational psychology.

Transfer of Training

One of the early topics Thorndike investigated was transfer of training. In collaboration with Robert S. Woodworth, he published the first of three articles on this subject in the May 1901 issue of *Psychological Review.* These articles were significant from the vantage point of psychology, educational psychology, and theories of education. The Thorndike-Woodworth experiments and Thorndike's subsequent work on the transfer problem are still often discussed in educational psychology.

The transfer experiments related directly to one of the major educational issues of the time—the public high school. By 1890 there was little doubt that there would be high schools open to all the children of all the people. The major issue was Herbert Spencer's question: "What knowledge is of most worth?" Spencer and his adherents argued that the standard classical curriculum of the nineteenth century was outdated and impractical.

Educators had to decide whether to persist in traditional ways or reform the curriculum. What was to be taught? Latin? Science? They argued about whether the high school should prepare its students for college or for life. They asked whether training should be specific or whether general education should be continued. Then, as now, the possibility or impossibility of transfer of training determined many people's answers.

The debate about the high school curriculum and the psychological defense that it would be provided was crystallized by the 1893 *Report* of the NEA's Committee of Ten. Before, during, and after the time of the committee, its chairman and principal author of the *Report,* Charles W. Eliot, president of Harvard, argued that all school subjects should be training subjects. In so arguing he was arguing for mental discipline and placing himself in a tradition that was at least as old as

---

16. Ibid., pp. 29–30.

the famed Yale Report of 1828 that defended the classics, which maintained that the "discipline" of the mind was far more important than its "furniture."

The Committee of Ten maintained that those school subjects that best prepared students for entry into college also best prepared them for the tasks and problems they would encounter outside college. Students were to have choices, but they were limited to a restricted list of subjects. For those who held to Spencerian views, the committee's recommendations were unacceptable. They did not leave sufficient room for science and other practical studies.

Thorndike and Woodworth's experiments, attempting to determine precisely the extent to which improvement in one activity would transfer to other activities, changed the character of future educational debates. The debates about faculty psychology, mental discipline, and formal discipline would continue, but after Thorndike and Woodworth the concepts would fall under a new heading—transfer of training or transfer of learning. Participants would be required to have either experimental or quantifiable data to support their claims.

The immediate effect of the Thorndike-Woodworth studies and those that followed was to support the claims of those who were trying to replace the classical curriculum with one that would be more "practical" and "relevant" to students in the first years of the twentieth century. Now there was not only theoretical doubt about transfer and discipline and faculty psychology, but also scientific proof.

The Influence of Transfer Studies   Even those who wanted to hold on to old theories and old ways had to deal with the new transfer studies. William C. Bagley, for example, who would later be known for his questions about progressive education, admitted in 1904 that "the doctrine of 'formal discipline' seems doomed."[17] He did not, however, surrender completely. He told the faculty of the University of Chicago College of Education, "Personally, I believe that those who still cling to the dogma in its original form cannot justify their position; I also believe that those who have entirely cast aside the idea of formal training have done so too hastily."[18] He had constructed and would continue to construct his own alternative to the old doctrine. He called it the "ideal." It was similar to a notion that Charles H. Judd was to call the "theory of conscious generalization."

Bagley discussed his "ideal" in *The Educative Process* (1905) and *Educational Values* (1911), texts that were widely used in teacher education classes. In the latter work he reviewed nearly twenty studies on formal discipline from England, America, and Germany, some of which supported his own notion that transfer occurred when students were taught that the "ideal" embedded in the subject matter should be followed in all situations.

---

17. William C. Bagley, "Ideals Versus Generalized Habits," *School and Home Education* 24:3 (November 1904), p. 102.

18. William C. Bagley, "The School's Responsibility for Developing the Controls of Conduct," *The Elementary School Teacher* 8:7 (March 1908), p. 356.

In the 1930s Bagley and others were still trying to combat the legacy of the Thorndike-Woodworth experiments. Bagley then reported that Pedro Orata, a student at Ohio State University, had demonstrated "beyond a peradventure of a doubt" that "the 'transfer' evidence had not only been overworked but actually abused."[19] He referred to Orata's "searching analysis" of 99 transfer experiments conducted between 1890 and 1928, which showed that "the total evidence of these experiments, far from demolishing the theory of mental discipline, actually supports it, although obviously not its earlier naive form."[20] Orata's bibliography on "transfer of training" shows that nearly a generation after the Thorndike-Woodworth studies, psychologists and educators were publishing three or four studies a year on the transfer question. The stream of discussion and investigation into the transfer question continued into the 1960s.

Thorndike's own interest in transfer did not cease with the first set of studies. In the 1920s he and his associates conducted two studies of high school students, which included the performances of nearly 14,000 students. At the beginning and the end of the year, the students were given the *I. E. R. Tests of Selective and Relational Thinking* to determine whether they had made any gains. It was believed that comparison of students with equal abilities who had studied different subjects would show the transfer effect of any given subject. The transfer effects were small, however, and Thorndike concluded that the intelligence of the student was more important than the subjects they studied.[21] For those who argued that some subjects were especially fitted to promote cognitive prowess in students, that was still one more setback. Neither the transfer question nor its relationship to the school curriculum has been satisfactorily resolved. As late as 1953, C. E. Osgood concluded that it was not certain that the old doctrine of formal discipline was invalid.[22]

In the early 1930s, according to Henry C. Ellis, "a shift in emphasis was seen in which laboratory rather than classroom studies became increasingly important, a trend not only true in transfer but of learning in general." With that shift to more laboratory studies there came "much greater emphasis on research designs which permitted detailed analysis of the variables contributing to transfer" and a "lessened interest in broad general conceptions of behavior, such as formal discipline, and greater interest in more limited conceptions of transfer."[23] As those

---

19. William C. Bagley, *Education, Crime and Social Progress* (New York: The Macmillan Co., 1931), p. 126.

20. William C. Bagley, *Education and Emergent Man* (New York: Thomas Nelson and Sons, 1934), p. 37.

21. Edward L. Thorndike, "Mental Discipline in High School Studies," *Journal of Educational Psychology* 15 (1924), pp. 1–22 and 83–98; and C. R. Broyler, E. L. Thorndike, and Ella Woodward, "A Second Study of Mental Discipline in High School Studies," *Journal of Educational Psychology* 18 (1927), pp. 377–401.

22. C. E. Osgood, *Method and Theory in Experimental Psychology* (New York: Oxford University Press, 1953).

23. Henry C. Ellis, "Transfer: Nature, Measurement, and Fundamental Processes," in *Learning: Processes*, ed. Melvin H. Marx (New York: The Macmillan Co., 1969), p. 382.

emphases changed, many educators allowed their attention to drift away from the problems of what should be taught into debates about psychology.

Transfer studies were frequently used to tell educators what they wanted to be told. In the 1927 NSSE Yearbook, *The Foundations and Technique of Curriculum-Construction,* Harold Rugg reported that no major curriculum committee set out to answer whether any school subject as presently taught contributed to increasing the student's ability to think. The way to answer such a question—by careful measurement of the ability of large groups of students before and after instruction in a specified subject—awaited Thorndike's 1924 study. According to Rugg, Thorndike "showed by measuring carefully the ability of 9,000 tenth-grade pupils before and after taking a year of Latin that one year's study of Latin as now organized does increase one's ability to reason—by a small amount—but that the gain is no larger than that due to the study of other school subjects as now organized." Rugg observed that "it is of great importance to find, for example, that bookkeeping, cooking, and sewing increases one's ability to generalize even more in some instances than does the study of the Classics!"[24] To Rugg's chagrin the Advisory Committee of the Classical League devoted only two sentences to Thorndike's investigation. Its *Report* noted that "the study shows that the amount of growth produced by certain school subjects in the ability measured by the test varies so slightly that no definite conclusions can be drawn therefrom."[25] Rather than accept the findings of an extensive study, the committee solicited the judgments of seventy psychologists, psychologists who favored the classics.

Curriculum reforms of the late 1950s and early 1960s showed a similar relationship between what was prescribed for teaching and the psychological justifications given for those prescriptions. Whenever evidence is debatable, public opinion and tradition turn out to be the dominant forces shaping the school's curriculum.

Thorndike's Laws

Thorndike's three articles on transfer of learning, though far-reaching in significance, were only a small portion of his work. He also produced more than 500 articles, reports, and monographs and more than thirty books. He contributed to the testing and measurement movement in education, the development of scientific school administration, the development of school surveys, the nature-nurture controversy; and he influenced what was taught in the schools and how it was taught.

Like his teacher William James, Thorndike was influenced by evolutionary theory. In the *Origin of Species* (1858) Charles Darwin offered a theory that

---

24. Harold O. Rugg, "Three Decades of Mental Discipline: Curriculum Making *via* National Committees," *The 26th Yearbook of the National Society for the Study of Education: The Foundations and Technique of Curriculum-Construction,* ed. Guy Montrose Whipple (Bloomington, Ill.: Public School Publishing Co., 1926), p. 61.

25. Quoted in Rugg, "Three Decades of Mental Discipline," p. 62.

explained variations and development of species in terms of their successful responses to threatening situations in their environments. Thorndike similarly subscribed to an "emergency" theory: organisms adapted and learned when confronted with a critical situation. Through trial and error, people learned what responses were satisfying and successful. The psychology Thorndike developed was thus basically a stimulus-response psychology. It examined not only people but how people responded to their environment. Thorndike also examined how people's responses changed them. The psychology he developed came to be known as *connectionism*. For Thorndike, learning consisted of the formation of bonds, or connections, between the stimuli in a situation and people's responses to them.

By 1914 Thorndike had completed a one volume version of his *Educational Psychology* (1903), *The Principles of Teaching* (1906), and his three-volume *Educational Psychology* (1913, 1914). In these works he discussed his principles of learning in terms of school situations. He articulated four chief principles, which were taught to thousands of teachers for at least half a century: the law of effect; the theory of identical elements; the law of readiness; and the law of exercise.

Thorndike's *law of effect* maintained that bonds were strengthened when the subject derived pleasure from making the appropriate response and that bonds were weakened when the required response was annoying. To use this principle to good advantage in the classroom, teachers needed to structure the work of the students in a way that would allow them to derive pleasure from their studies. In Thorndike's approach, it was not necessary for the teacher to dispense rewards directly. Rewards were found in the work itself. In *The Psychology of Arithmetic,* for example, Thorndike explained that:

> . . . computation is not dull if the pupil can compute. He does not himself object to its barrenness of vital meaning, so long as the barrenness of failure is prevented. We must not forget that pupils like to learn.[26]

The law of effect also required teachers to build their lessons in accordance with the interests of students. That prescription was consistent with both the doctrines of the new education and the teachings of G. Stanley Hall.

The *theory of identical elements* was derived from the work on transfer. It maintained that what students learned in one learning task would not transfer to another unless both tasks contained identical, or very similar, elements. Thorndike offered an application of this principle by producing a series of arithmetic texts (1917) and publishing *The Psychology of Arithmetic,* (1920), in which he showed how the content of arithmetic could be organized to take maximum advantage of the theory of identical elements. In those works he revolutionized the teaching of arithmetic by showing that teaching could be more effective if the subject matter was organized not according to the logic of a discipline but according to how students actually learn.

---

26. Edward L. Thorndike, *The Psychology of Arithmetic* (1922), in Joncich, *Psychology and the Science of Education,* p. 89.

The *law of readiness* maintained that when the student was in a state conducive to the formation of a bond, forming that bond would be satisfying. But if the situation were not satisfying, attempts to form the bond would annoy the student. This law was also consistent with the teachings of the new education. It recognized that there were developmental stages in the life of the learner. It also reinforced earlier notions that held that learning should be associated with pleasure rather than pain.

The *law of exercise* held that connections were strengthened by use and weakened by disuse. This law was directly applicable to the time-honored practice of classroom drills. As Thorndike investigated its practical application, he discovered that distributed practice, or drill, was more effective in many instances than concentrated practice. As a result, countless students were required to practice their spelling words, penmanship, arithmetic, and other skills a few minutes a day rather than until they achieved mastery at one sitting.

Throughout his career, Thorndike seems never to have lost sight of the teacher and the classroom. While he described individual differences and argued that special attention had to be paid to students with special problems or special abilities, he seems always to have remembered that teachers have to contend with many students at one time, not just one. He did not urge teachers to become psychologists, but he did provide them with laws and applications to make their work more orderly and efficient.

Daniel Starch: The Move to Measurement

Like Gesell, his contemporary, Daniel Starch was a native of Wisconsin, born in LaCrosse in 1883. All his early training in psychology was in the Midwest. After graduating from Morningside College in Iowa in 1903, he secured a fellowship from the State University of Iowa (Iowa City) where Carl Emil Seashore had been recently appointed professor of psychology. Starch studied psychology and education with Seashore, was awarded an M.A. degree in 1904, and decided to remain at Iowa to continue work in psychology. After being awarded his Ph.D. in 1906, he remained at Iowa for one year as an instructor in experimental psychology, then moved to Massachusetts to teach experimental psychology at Wellesley College and study it at Harvard. In 1908 he began a twelve-year tenure at the University of Wisconsin, where he began several books in which he tried to apply the findings of the new science to education and to advertising.

Starch's applications of psychology to practical affairs, education and advertising, were very successful. His growing reputation in the psychology of advertising led to his appointment as a lecturer at the Harvard Graduate School of Business in 1919. From that time on, most of his professional work was in advertising.

Starch did most of his work in education between 1906 and 1919, mainly at Wisconsin. He concentrated on the measurement of pupil achievement, the reliability of grading practices, and the determination of the worth of the various school subjects. He also published a text, *Educational Psychology* (1919). For nearly ten years it was the most widely used text in the field, was reprinted thirteen times, and for a time was more widely used than Thorndike's text.

In 1912–13, Starch collaborated with E. C. Elliott in publishing three articles in the *School Review* on the reliability of grading in high school English, history, and mathematics. The Starch-Elliott studies were among the first of their kind. They set out to determine how widely grading practices varied, and their findings consistently showed that marks assigned to a given paper by different readers varied widely. The wide ranges of variations prompted Starch to write the text *Educational Measurements* (1916).

While Starch admitted that most educational measurements were still in the experimental stage, he also claimed that "the need of definite, objective measures of educational products" was great enough to proceed with the work.[27] A year earlier, he had concluded that "the current movement for measuring school products is one of the three or four most important fields of investigation in the scientific study of educational 'programs'."[28] For Starch there was no doubt about the propriety of educational measurement. The old pedagogy was to be replaced with "quantitative studies, objective measurements, and carefully observed facts." In a statement very much like one made by Thorndike a few years earlier, Starch told his readers that "any quality of ability of human nature that is detectable is also measurable."[29] All that educators needed to do was to find better ways to make such measurements and further refine their tests and scales.

There was no need to defend educational measurement; it was an integral part of the daily work of the school, used or misused each time a grade or mark was given. Moreover, decisions about "promotion, retardation, elimination, honors, eligibility for contests and societies, graduation, admission to higher institutions, recommendation for future positions" all depended on the grades a student had been assigned. Educators, Starch believed, should refine their judgments so that they could "express them in terms of known units of a definable character." He wanted educators to be able to report "that a pupil can read three words per second of a certain passage and to repeat so and so much of it, that he knows the English meaning of 2,000 Latin words and can translate without error sentences of specified difficulty." If there were educational "products or by-products" that could not be judged to exist in some quantity, then, Starch advised, "we may be suspicious of their actual existence."[30]

Although most teachers were generally so confident of their marking systems that they often used fractions of a percentage point, Starch claimed there was no

27. Daniel Starch, *Educational Measurements* (New York: The Macmillan Co., 1917), p. 1.

28. Daniel Starch, "The Measurement of Efficiency in Reading," *Journal of Educational Psychology* 6:1 (January 1915), p. 1.

29. Starch, *Educational Measurements*, p. 2.

30. Ibid., pp. 2–3.

good reason to believe that the grades assigned were reliable. Studies had demonstrated that there were wide ranges of differences in grading practices from school to school and even from teacher to teacher within a department. The percentage of "excellent" grades and of "failures" in the same subject in the same department varied too widely too frequently. Even the folk wisdom about grades was mistaken. "Contrary to current belief," Starch was able to report, "grades in mathematics are as unreliable as grades in language or in history."[31] Investigations had demonstrated that "the mathematics instructors did not agree any more closely with their own marks than the language or science instructors."[32] For instance, he found that the grades assigned to a set of papers in plane geometry by 116 teachers ranged from 28 to 92.

To remedy the wide diversity of grading practices, Starch urged the adoption of appropriate marking scales and standards for the distribution of grades. Scales that used 100, 99, 98, 97.... 0 percent were inappropriate, for they had no "objective validity." The divisions on a marking scale had to be large enough to allow 75 percent of all measurements of a student's paper to fall within that division in order to ensure validity. Starch's calculations led him to recommend a scale with five marks. He described that scale in this way:

A or Excellent, which should be assigned to approximately 7% of the pupils.
B or Superior, which should be assigned to approximately 24% of the pupils.
C or Average, which should be assigned to approximately 38% of the pupils.
D or Inferior, which should be assigned to approximately 24% of the pupils.
E or Unsatisfactory, which should be assigned to approximately 7% of the pupils.[33]

He further advised that letters and symbols were preferable to words such as Good or Fair or Poor.

Applying the Normal Curve

Starch recommended that "marks on the whole and for large groups of pupils of usual ability should be distributed with a reasonably close conformity to the normal, bell-shaped, probability curve." He reasoned that since measured human physical traits and psychological traits conformed to the probability curve, there was no reason why marks should not also be normally distributed. While he acknowledged that there were factors that tended to skew the curve in one direction or the other, he claimed they ultimately counterbalanced each other. For example, the elimination of poor students from schools, especially in the upper grades, and the improved performance of students because of good teaching would be offset by the lower performance of students who did not always employ maximum effort. He also argued that the elimination of the poor student was "not a cutting off at a definite point of the curve, but rather a smooth shaving off along

---

31. Ibid., p. 8.
32. Ibid., p. 9.
33. Ibid., p. 15.

the entire range." Grades would "be assigned much more justly if they are assigned with reasonably close conformity to the probability distribution."[34] Harold O. Rugg presented data showing "that the normal distribution did not hold in some cases and that many factors affecting marks were not susceptible to an assumption of normality,"[35] but Starch and others at the time continued to urge that all educational data be made to conform to the normal curve.

In his text *Educational Psychology*, Starch employed the normal curve to explain the nature of human variation. He did not consider the idea that the normal curve may represent only how widely distributed variations are, not what they mean to an individual or a society. To know that human abilities varied in accordance with the normal curve was, for Starch, to know the nature of human variation. To illustrate the nature of human variation, he presented in graphic form a number of different distributions. They included such data as the memory ability of 173 university students; the ability of 164 university students to cancel A's in one minute; the ability of 164 persons to cancel a specified geometrical figure in a page of figures in one minute; the chest measurements of English soldiers; the height of 1,052 women; and the number of "heads" in tossing ten pennies 1,000 times. Starch sought to teach future teachers that all distributions of human traits and all human performance approximated the normal distribution.

Eliminating Waste

For Starch, as for many of his contemporaries, waste in education was a major problem. He and other researchers began to measure time usage. At times the measurement bordered on the absurd:

> ... We do not know with any definite assurance what is the most economical amount of time to devote to any one of the school subjects. From such investigations as have been made, we may infer that there is an enormous waste in our educational practices. ... If by some means it were possible to save one minute a day for every school day during the eight years of a child's school life, we would be able to save one entire week of school time. If we could save four minutes a day for the same length of time, we would be able to save one month; if we were able to save 18 minutes a day, we would be able to save one-half a school year; and if by more economical methods of learning and distribution of time we were able to save 36 minutes a day for eight years, we would be able to save an entire school year.[36]

Although enough was not known about how students learned to enable educators to shorten the school day and the school year for all students, it was possible, Starch maintained, to effect some reductions for some students. He was confident that waste could be eliminated and that economies could be introduced into schools. All facets of students' performances could be reduced to differences in

---

34. Ibid., p.12.

35. Ann Z. Smith and John E. Dobbin, "Marks and Marking Systems," in *Encyclopedia of Educational Research*, 3rd ed., ed. Chester W. Harris (New York: The Macmillan Co., 1960), p. 484.

36. Daniel Starch, *Educational Psychology* (New York: The Macmillam Co., 1919), pp. 3–4.

either time or amount. For example, Starch explained, "we find that on the average the best pupil is able to do the same task from two to twenty-five times as well as the poorest pupils."[37]

Starch also believed that school time could be saved by considering students' varied abilities. He reported that "the differences in abilities in school subjects are fully as wide as in special psychological capacities."[38] Since the differences were "probably due primarily to native ability rather than to differences in opportunity, training or environment," a wide range of ability could be expected in every class and in every school. Even after students' abilities in the various school subjects were averaged, the superior second and third grade students were nearly equal to the poorest eighth grade students. Starch felt that *this enormous range of ability, and the resulting overlapping of successive grades, is probably the most important single fact discovered with reference to education in the last decade.*[39]

Starch suggested that the proper promotion and classification of students would permit 33 percent of them to complete eight grades of schooling in less than eight years; 33 percent could finish in eight years; and the remainder would need more than eight years to finish eight grades satisfactorily. Not to separate students according to their abilities was wasteful, for students at both ends of the distribution would suffer if the necessary attention were given to the other end. That was clearly unfair to the superior students.

The Needs of the Superior Students

Starch saw two ways to meet the needs of the superior, industrious students. One was to "attempt to keep the pupils of a given class together but vary the manner of instruction for the pupils of different capacities;" the other was to "keep the manner of instruction uniform but promote or retard pupils according to their achievements."[40] He warned that plans that relied on individualization of instruction were unreliable and likely to neglect the necessary "social stimulus" that all students need. He favored programs that allowed for rapid acceleration.

One practical program of acceleration was the St. Louis promotion plan as described by W. J. Stevens in 1914. In the St. Louis schools, each grade was divided into four ten-week quarters. At the end of each quarter, average students were promoted according to schedule, and the superior students were allowed to move on to the "next higher class." Stevens's study of 1,439 students in four elementary schools showed that "about 1% of the pupils required approximately four years, 6.3% five years, 22.8% six years, 34.6% seven years, 24.9% eight years, 7.6% nine years, 1.7% ten years and 1.3% eleven to thirteen years to complete the eight grades."[41] Stevens's data agreed with Starch's own calculations.

---

37. Ibid., p. 29.
38. Ibid., p.33.
39. Ibid., p. 39. Starch's emphasis.
40. Ibid., p. 42.
41. Ibid., p. 44–46.

At least 5 percent of the children who enrolled in the public schools were, said Starch, "so inferior physically, mentally, educationally, and socially that they may properly be identified as 'special class children'."[42] These students had to have special instruction, which emphasized concrete operations and avoided abstractions; they also needed to be trained for useful jobs that would make them economically independent. But while Starch agreed that children with special problems needed special attention, he did not agree that they should be given more attention than the superior children. "Society would be compensated far more for paying at least equal attention to the gifted pupils since they primarily will determine the future progress of mankind."[43]

Starch argued that just as adults of superior drive and ability were allowed to compete and earn rewards in society, children should be given the same opportunity in school. As a corollary, he argued that children who performed in a superior fashion in school were also of superior character. He related that:

> Considerable information concerning the character traits of a child may be inferred from his mental and educational test data. If in educational attainment a child is one quartile position above that customary for children in his intelligence quotient, excellent character traits are likely to be present; if his educational attainment accords with the customary for children of his intelligence quotient; average character traits may be inferred; if, however, his educational attainment is one quartile position below that customary for children of his intelligence quotient, poor character traits are probable.[44]

Successful people in society were deserving of their success because of their superior character; those who met with misfortune could be considered to have earned their just reward. Such views were consistent with the era. For example, in 1908 the general agent for the New York Association for Improving the Condition of the Poor proclaimed that "the modern Diogenes does not go about with a lantern seeking goodness; he looks for efficiency and expects goodness to be thrown in."[45] For those who believed that people varied only in the quantities of traits they possessed, that may not have seemed unreasonable.

An Alternative to "Instincts"

Starch's *Educational Psychology* (1919) offered educators an alternative to Thorndike's view. A review of his text in the *Journal of Educational Psychology* noted that Starch "points out that instincts as such have very little significance for education, and that the chief educational doctrines based upon instincts (dynamic theory of instincts, transitoriness, recapitulation) have very little justification in verified fact." The review emphasized that Starch's was a "sane view" and ex-

---

42. Daniel Starch, *Educational Psychology*, rev. ed. (New York: The Macmillan Co., 1927), pp. 45–46.

43. Starch, *Educational Psychology* (1919), p. 47.

44. Ibid., pp. 45–46.

45. William H. Allen, *Efficient Democracy* (New York: Dodd, Mead and Co., 1908), p. 6.

pressed hope "that it will tend to neutralize the overemphasis of instincts that has been prevalent in educational discussion since James."[46]

Although Starch reproduced Thorndike's list of forty-two instincts, he had very little use for it. He questioned the true number of instincts as well as how much learning they involved. He was even more skeptical about the relationship between instincts and the learning of a given school subject. He was confident that "two-thirds or three-fourths" of the instincts were "only indirectly concerned in school exercises, and most of the remaining ones, such as rivalry, cooperation, collecting, and hoarding, are serviceable chiefly as general motives."[47]

Starch's position was a rejection not only of James and Thorndike, but also of much of G. Stanley Hall. As such it was a departure from the prevailing point of view. According to Bird Baldwin, writing in 1911, James had successfully changed how the basis and the aims of education were defined and discussed. James's emphasis on native tendencies or instincts had "directed attention to the native resources of the child and the place these native tendencies to reaction must necessarily have in any scheme of education in which children are concerned."[48] The emphasis on the child's own native tendencies had provided educators with an alternative to the Herbartian pedagogy and psychology, which stressed the organization of subject matter. Starch stressed the importance of testing, measurement, and reliable grading of student performances in the various school subjects, and so moved the emphasis back to subject matter. But rather than allowing the content of school subjects to be determined by aims of education, Starch allowed the requirements of a good test to shape the content and organization of schooling. Standardized tests now had the potential to minimize the teacher's role in the classroom. What a teacher could personally offer students would have to fit the test. The specification of the product so that it could be tested in specified ways, would determine what materials were used and how they were used. At least, that was the grand logic of Starch's position.

The Science of Education

Starch and other educators who were part of the "cult of efficiency"[49] emphasized economy of time and searched for ways to measure educational progress; in so doing they sometimes gave undue emphasis to a nebulous notion of an educational product. This approach was one of many taken by those who were trying to build a science of education. Many educators believed there were laws

---

46. "Starch's Educational Psychology," *Journal of Educational Psychology* 11:9 (December 1920), p. 535.

47. Starch, *Educational Psychology* (1919), p. 12.

48. Bird T. Baldwin, "William James' Contributions to Educational Psychology," *Journal of Educational Psychology* 2 (1911), p. 376.

49. Raymond E. Callahan, *Education and the Cult of Efficiency* (Chicago: University of Chicago Press, 1962).

that governed the educative process, that those laws could be discovered, and that education could be improved by following them. For example, in 1905, William C. Bagley announced (in *The Educative Process*) that there were "basal principles of the educative process" that could be subverted by even an experienced teacher who had mastered the techniques of teaching. It was necessary that "an adequate conception of principles based on the best data that science can offer . . . be added to a mastery of technique." He explained that "clear and definite notions of the functions of education and of the laws which govern the educative process will do much toward eliminating the waste of time and energy that is involved in the work of the school."[50]

Bagley offered the view, one shared by many of his era, that the study of education, or of any other complicated process, initially reveals "a vast noisy machine, the various parts of which appear to work with little references to the needs and nature of the whole." Science, however, had revealed "the harmonious cooperation of all these factors toward a definite end."[51] Just as scientific investigation had been able to identify the organic world's components, education also needed to be reduced to its lowest possible terms so that educators could gain control of it and give it proper direction.

In the first years of his career, Bagley believed that psychology would contribute to the development of a science of education. Later he began to argue that a proper science of education would have to stand on its own. By 1912 he was arguing that education would have to develop its own science independent of other sciences. He wrote in the *Kansas School Magazine:*

> It is out of the question to solve satisfactorily the problems of education by deductive inferences from the principles that have been worked out in what we call the "pure" sciences. We cannot for example, take the principles of psychology and deduce from these conclusions regarding educational problems that will unerringly "work." We can get useful hypotheses, but these must be relentlessly subjected to the crucible of actual test under educational conditions. . . . Agriculture has made its great progress not by neglecting what chemistry and biology had to teach, but by the experimental investigation of its own problems in the light of these teachings. Education cannot hope to progress rapidly until it has reached a similar point in its development. We must, in a sense, declare our independence, take the scientific method which is our most precious heritage from the basic sciences, and with its aid work out our own salvation.[52]

Bagley continued to argue that the problems of education could not profitably be reduced to problems of psychology. To attempt to do so was to impose on education extra-educational abstractions that promised more than was ever delivered. Many others, however, held to the belief that psychology was the proper foundation for education. According to David C. Berliner and N. L. Gage, at the turn

---

50. William C. Bagley, *The Educative Process* (New York: The Macmillan Co., 1905), pp. v–vi.

51. Ibid., p. 2.

52. William C. Bagley, "A Plea for the Scientific Study of Educational Problems," *Kansas School Magazine* 1:2 (February 1912), p. 54.

of the century "empirical research, primarily psychological, seemed to be only a few short years away from solving the problems of education by providing the scientific underpinning for instructional practice." However, the marriage of education and psychology turned out to be a "disappointing marriage."[53] Some might call it barren.

Mental Tests and Measurement
Measurement is perhaps the most successful technology borrowed from psychology by educators. The measurement movement in psychology originated in the work of Sir Francis Galton, who in the 1870s was promoting the new study of "anthropometry" and urging that anthropometric records be made and stored. Galton believed that through the study of human performance, outstanding people could be identified and recruited into civil service, ensuring the efficient progress of society.

Galton's tests of people caught on quickly. He opened a laboratory in 1882 at the South Kensington Museum in London. For a small fee, patrons could have their physical measurements taken and their reaction times tested. In 1893 Joseph Jastrow of the University of Wisconsin found many visitors to the World's Columbian Exposition in Chicago who were willing to have psychological tests administered.

James McKeen Cattell, Thorndike's mentor at Columbia, was probably the first to use the term "mental tests" when he administered a battery of tests on 100 University of Pennsylvania freshmen. At Clark University, Franz Boas was teaching courses in anthropometry and anthropological statistics in 1889; in 1891, with encouragement from G. Stanley Hall, he began measuring various characteristics of 1500 Worcester school children. Hall had already analyzed the contents of several children's minds and encouraged others to take countless measures of the characteristics of countless children. In 1896–97, Frederick W. Smedley provided a catalogue of the measurements being taken of children at the University of Chicago's primary school:

> Measurements were taken in sight, ascertaining the visual acuity, testing also for astigmatism, color discrimination, sensitiveness to light, power of coordinating the eyes, and judgment of division of length by sight.
> In hearing, the auditory range and discrimination of pitch were tested.
> In feeling, tests were made determining the minimum of discernible pressure, the span of double touch, discrimination of weights, using active lifting and passive pressure, and the ability to discriminate different temperatures.
> Smell and taste were tested by determining the pupils' ability to detect different solutions.
> Besides these sensory tests motor measurements were made of the strength of the grip, and also tests in reaction time.
> In addition to the above tests, anthropometrical measurements were taken in connection with the gymnasium.[54]

---

53. David C. Berliner and N. L. Gage, "The Psychology of Teaching Methods," in *The Psychology of Teaching Methods: The 75th Yearbook of the National Society for the Study of Education, Part I*, ed. N. L. Gage (Chicago: University of Chicago Press, 1976), p. 1.

Smedley reported that so many measurements of the children were taken that "one gentleman was led to remark that the children were in danger of becoming shop-worn through much handling."[55] Educators and psychologists did not persist in administering such a large battery of tests to children, but they did persist in testing. They concentrated on those tests that could be given with only a paper and pencil and sought tests that could be administered to large groups of children at one sitting by one untrained test-giver. Curiously, World War I gave them the opportunity to develop and to popularize their technology.

Army Alpha and Army Beta

Soon after the United States entered World War I, Robert M. Yerkes, a Harvard psychologist and president of the American Psychological Association, organized several committees of psychologists. One was the Committee on Psychological Examining of Recruits, later called the Psychology Committee of the National Research Council. Besides Yerkes, the members of the committee were W. V. Bingham, head of the Division of Applied Psychology at the Carnegie Institute of Technology; H. H. Goddard, who had earlier introduced the Binet scale to the United States; T. H. Haines, a psychiatrist and psychologist; L. M. Terman, who had recently finished the Stanford Revision of the Binet test; F. L. Wells, a clinical psychologist who had co-authored the Woodworth-Wells Association tests; and G. M. Whipple, who had assembled a comprehensive survey of published psychological tests. Though Yerkes had done most of his work in the area of animal psychology, he had worked on the Yerkes-Bridges Point Scale of Intelligence, a test that some thought was better than the Binet.

The Yerkes committee wanted to construct an instrument that would facilitate classification of recruits according to their abilities and talents. They wanted to be able to identify both those recruits who would be able to complete successfully the course for officers, and those whose lack of ability would interfere with the operation of an organized military machine.

When Yerkes assembled his group (May 1917), individual intelligence testing of children was only a decade old, and little was known about measuring the intelligence of normal adults. Individual testing of the recruits was impractical, and so the committee agreed that a group intelligence test was needed. There would have to be two forms: one for those who were literate and another for those who were either illiterate or who could not read and write English. The committee also specified twelve criteria for the test:

1. Adaptability for group use.
2. Correlation with measures of intelligence known to be valid.

---

54. Frederick W. Smedley, "A Report on the Measurements of the Sensory and Motor Abilities of the Puplils of the Chicago University Primary School and the Pedagogical Value of Such Measurements," *Transactions of the Illinois Society for Child Study* 2:2 (1896–97), pp. 85–86.

55. Ibid., p. 86.

3. Measurement of a wide range of abilities.
4. Objectivity of scoring preferably by stencils.
5. Rapidity of scoring.
6. Possibility of many alternate forms so as to discourage cheating.
7. Unfavorableness to malingering.
8. Unfavorableness to cheating.
9. Independence of school training.
10. Minimum of writing in making responses.
11. Economy of time.[56]

Intelligence was to be defined not by what the recruits could do, but by what the examiners could easily measure.

In seven working days, the committee agreed on ten major areas for the test and selected enough items for ten forms of the test. The first form was printed and administered to almost 500 subjects, including recruits in the officers' training course; aviation recruits; and inmates from a psychopathic hospital, a school for retarded children, and a reform shcool. The psychologists then correlated the subtest scores with the total score, and the total score with the Binet. Later a group of statisticians under the direction of Thorndike analyzed the scores of the tests administered to 3,129 soldiers and 372 mental patients. Thorndike was satisfied that it was one of the best group intelligence tests ever constructed. After further testing, a final form with eight subtests was constructed—Army Alpha. The subtests included: Oral Directions, Arithmetical Reasoning, Practical Series, Completion of Analogies, and Information.

Army Beta was designed for illiterates and recruits who did not speak or write English. Up to that time there had been no successful nonverbal group intelligence tests. Army Beta in its final form consisted of pictures and diagrams. Administration of the test proved difficult and confusing. Even recruits who understood English were frequently confused by the pantomime instructions of the examiners. The Beta form proved to be not as reliable as Alpha, and many recruits apparently were wrongly classified by their scores.

The Army accepted the tests, and Yerkes and his associates received commissions as officers. Yerkes recruited other psychologists to join the effort, and a school to train examiners was set up at Fort Oglethorpe. Eventually nearly two million tests were administered to recruits at thirty-five different camps by 120 officers and 350 enlisted men. (Among the enlisted men who administered the tests was David Wechsler, who published his own intelligence tests some twenty years later.) Even though the tests were used for recommending the discharge of 8,000 Army recruits and the specific placement of 19,000 recruits in low-level jobs, they did not accomplish as much as had been expected in terms of increased efficiency or the savings of millions of dollars through appropriate placement of recruits.

---

56. Phillip H. DuBois, *A History of Psychological Testing* (Boston: Allyn and Bacon, 1970), pp. 62–63.

The Test Results and Biases The impact of the Army Alpha and Beta tests on American psychology and American society was considerable, however. In a recent assessment of these World War I tests, Franz Samelson reported that "all through the war activities, there runs a slender thread indicating some conflict about whether the focus of the work should be practical-applied or basic scientific research."[57] Before the war, both Terman and Yerkes had been working on intelligence tests and had sought grants from the General Education Fund to gather "large-scale normative data." The war gave them more data than either had originally tried to assemble. After the war, the General Education Fund granted $25,000 of Rockefeller funds to the National Research Council so it could construct a group intelligence test for schoolchildren. In 1918 Otis published his group test and in 1919 Thorndike published a test for high school graduates. After the war the Army disposed of its unused copies of the tests, and they soon found their way into the hands of educators who used them in the schools. Group intelligence testing became standard school practice.

One indication that the psychologists also used the testing program for their own research was the nature of the data they collected. Recruits were asked to give information about their home town or birthplace. After the war those data were correlated with the test results. Some used the test results to demonstrate that blacks were intellectually inferior to whites. The tests also showed a high correlation between what the psychologists took to be intelligence and the amount of schooling a recruit had completed. That correlation was interpreted to mean that "native intelligence is one of the most important conditioning factors in continuance in school."[58] However, the Jim Crow laws had just been firmly established in the South, and frequently there were no educational opportunities available to blacks, no matter how intelligent. Another factor the testers overlooked was that those who failed the Beta test were suppposed to be given an individual intelligence test but often were not. Samelson reports that some blacks "capable of understanding English even if not capable of reading it, were so mystified by the nonverbal pantomime instructions for the Beta test, that they dozed off en masse."[59]

Blacks were not the only Americans to suffer from the "results" of the Alpha and Beta tests. According to the interpretations, those who held more lucrative jobs and occupied higher positions on the social status scale were more intelligent than those with less prestigious jobs and in lower social positions. The tests were also used as evidence that those born in northern Europe were more intelligent then those from southern Europe. Such interpretations helped to support those who wanted to restrict immigration from southeastern Europe as well as those who were promoting the eugenics movement. When in 1921 the Congress began to

57. Franz Samelson, "World War I Intelligence Testing and the Development of Psychology," *Journal of the History of Behavioral Sciences* 13:3 (July 1977), p. 277.

58. Robert M. Yerkes, ed., *Psychological Examining in the United States Army* (1921). Quoted in Samelson, "World War I Intelligence Testing and the Development of Psychology," p. 279.

59. Samelson, "World War I Intelligence Testing and the Development of Psychology," p. 280.

debate restrictions on immigration, Yerkes himself wrote to Congress to draw their attention to what the Army tests had revealed about the abilities of foreign-born soldiers. During the 1920s and 1930s, those who claimed that the Nordic "race" was superior to the Alpine and Mediterranean peoples had the support of what many believed to be scientific facts.

The judgments about various races that the psychologists supported with their test data were not invented by the psychologists. The psychologists simply found data to support what many Americans believed long before the beginnings of modern psychology. For example, Crevecoeur in his *Letters from an American Farmer* (1793) described the "great metamorphosis" experienced by immigrants after their arrival on the American continent. He also noted that not all immigrants were equally successful, and offered his own observations on these differing rates of success:

> From whence the difference arises, I know not; but out of twelve families of emigrants of each country generally seven Scotch will succeed, nine German, and four Irish. The Scotch are frugal and laborious; but their wives cannot work so hard as the German women, who on the contrary, vie with their husbands, and often share with them the most severe toils of the field, which they understand better. They have therefore nothing to struggle against, but the common casualties of nature. The Irish do not prosper so well; they love to drink and to quarrel; they are litigious, and soon take to the gun, which is the ruin of everything; they seem, beside, to labour under a greater degree of ignorance in husbandry than the others; perhaps it is that their industry had less scope, and was less exercised at home.[60]

Crevecoeur explained the differences among the various peoples in terms of the environments from which they came, but the differences he expressed became stereotypes that endured. In an 1851 article on immigration in the *Massachusetts Teacher,* teachers were told that the problems attended to immigration deserved the attention of the nation's best and wisest minds. Immigration could either pollute the country with ignorance, vice, crime, and disease just as the Missouri River muddied the clear water of the Mississippi River, or the country could take action to protect itself from "the threatened demoralization" and take action to "improve and purify and make valuable this new element."[61]

The author of the article in the *Massachusetts Teacher* also found that there were differences between German immigrants and Irish immigrants. The differences between the two peoples were described as follows:

> Our chief difficulty is with the Irish. The Germans, who are the next in numbers, will give us no trouble. They are more abstinate, more strongly webbed to their own notions and customs than the Irish; but they have, inherently, the redeeming qualities of industry, frugality, and pride, which will

---

60. Michel-Guillaume Jean de Crevecoeur, *Letters from an American Farmer,* 1793, Letter III, in Willard Thorp, Merle Curti, and Carlos Baker, *American Issues Volume I: The Social Record,* rev. ed. (New York: J. B. Lippincott, 1955), p. 110.

61. "Immigration," *The Massachusetts Teacher* Vol. 4 (October 1851) in Michael B. Katz (ed.), *School Reform: Past and Present* (Boston: Little, Brown and Co., 1971), p. 169.

save them from vice and pauperism, and they may be safely left to take care of themselves. But the poor Irish, the down-trodden, priest-ridden of centuries, come to us in another shape. So cheaply have they been held at home—so closely have they been pressed down in the social scale—that for the most part the simple virtues of industry, temperance, and frugality are unknown to them; and that wholesome pride which will induce a German, or a native American, to work hard from sun to sun for the smallest wages, rather than seek or accept charitable aid, has been literally crushed out of them.[62]

To solve the "Irish problem" the author recommended that society take three measures. The first was that a proper police force be established so that the Irish children could "be gathered up and forced into school." Any parent or priest who resisted such a measure, it was recommended, was "to be held accountable and punished." Compulsory schooling was the only alternative. Without it the Irish children would be left to the care of their parents who were too often "unfit guardians" and who allowed their children to develop "idle, dissolute, vagrant habits." Other necessary measures to solve the problem included employment of enough policemen to carry in all the drunkards and set them before the magistrates and elimination of "street begging."[63]

In 1909 Ellwood P. Cubberley drew attention to the large number of immigrants who came to America, and emphasized the changing character of those who had arrived in the most recent years. In his highly successful and widely used text, *Public Education in the United States* (1919), Cubberley repeated and expanded upon his earlier observations. In describing the character of immigration to the United States before 1882, Cubberley related that nearly all who came to America "were from race stock not very different from our own." The immigrants who came before 1882 "possessed courage, initiative, intelligence, adaptability, and self-reliance to a great degree." The Irish were characterized as co-operative, good-natured and as having "executive abilities." The Germans were noted for their "intellectual thoroughness" and the English for their "respect for the law and order." The Scandinavians, according to Cubberley, contributed their "thrift, sobriety, and industry" to American life.[64]

After 1882, immigration from northern and western European declined while immigration from eastern and southern Europe increased. In addition to Italians who were coming at the rate of 20,000 a year, people from places that were unknown to many Americans began to arrive in great numbers. The arrival of these new and different peoples was a cause for concern. As Cubberley put it, "these Southern and Eastern Europeans were of a very different type from the Northern and Western Europeans who preceded them." The new immigrants were "largely illiterate, docile, lacking in initiative, and almost wholly without the Anglo-Saxon conceptions or righteousness, liberty, law, order, public decency, and govern-

62. Ibid., pp. 169–170.

63. Ibid., pp. 170–171.

64. Ellwood P. Cubberley, *Public Education in the United States* (Boston: Houghton Mifflin Co., 1919), pp. 336–337.

ment." The immigrants of the last quarter century had, claimed Cubberley, given the nation "a serious case of racial indigestion." Only the southern states were free from the problem of the foreign-born, but in its place those states had "the problem of the negro and his education." While earlier statesmen had worried about the Irish and German immigrants, the present generation had cause to "be alarmed at the deluge of diverse people which has poured into this Nation."[65]

In his description of the cosmopolitan nature of American society, Cubberley provided an entire catalogue of stereotypes. Examination of the catalogue reveals that the white collar jobs in American society were held by those whose names indicated that they came from northern or western Europe. Peddlers, keepers of small shops, and those who engaged in manual labor or service occupations came from southern and eastern Europe. Cubberley's characterization of the newer immigrants was not a unique characterization; it was shared by many educators. As late as 1953, Stuart G. Noble, in a history of education text written for prospective teachers, offered the judgment that "before the passage of the Quota Law (1924) the later immigrants came, to a considerable degree, from the lowest order of European society." He described the later immigrants as "backward people" who were incapable of adjusting themselves readily to democratic society." They helped to increase crime and lower traditional standards of decency and "were useful only as factory workers or day laborers."[66]

Notions about racial superiority were not confined to politicians and social and behavioral scientists. By the 1920s such talk was a common part of the popular culture. For example, early in *The Great Gatsby,* the host of a small dinner party, Tom Buchanan, Daisy's husband, expresses his concern for the survival of the white race. Tom asks his guests whether they have read Goddard's *Rise of the Colored Empires* and goes on to explain that "it's a fine book, and everybody ought to read it. The idea is if we don't look out the white race will be—will be utterly submerged." He then tried to assure his guests that "It's all scientific stuff; it's been proved." Daisy observes that Tom has been turning "very profound" and the conversation continues.[67]

As educators continued to reflect the prejudices and fears of American society, they placed themselves in a paradoxical position. While they argued that schools were necessary to Americanize the immigrants and thereby create a unified social order, they also claimed that not all people were truly capable of being educated and becoming thoroughly American. For many prospective teachers that double message must have been confusing. For immigrants and members of minority groups it was patently unfair.

---

65. Ibid., pp. 338–340.

66. Stuart G. Noble, *A History of American Education,* rev. ed. (New York: Rinehart and Co., 1954), p. 372.

67. F. Scott Fitzgerald, *The Great Gatsby* (Charles Scribner's Sons, 1953), pp. 11–12.

From Schoolhouse to Factory 14

New Metaphors

The language of a people tells us about their values and aspirations as well as how they met the challenges of their times. Every age develops its own heroes, images, and metaphors. As Americans moved from the nineteenth century into the twentieth, it became apparent that the structure and character of American society were changing. Those who were charged with the responsibility of operating the public schools were soon confronted with the problems of its growth. Those who studied the processes of public schooling and tried to find ways to make them more effective and orderly also could not ignore this growth and the problems it brought. To conceptualize those problems, many Americans frequently turned to ideas borrowed from other large organizations—specifically, the military and industrial business enterprises. In the process, some began to think of the schools and their problems as "management problems," not as human and educational problems. The guardians of the schools frequently saw them as large organizations whose personnel—students and teachers—were to be treated like soldiers, enemies, or factory workers. As Americans became concerned with the efficiency of their industrial enterprises, they also became concerned with efficiency in other areas of their lives. That concern led some to develop a program of "social efficiency" for the schools. As some adopted the language of the military, they came to assume that the schools sometimes had power comparable to that of an army.

The Little Red Schoolhouse

In an address to the City Club of Chicago in 1907, George Herbert Mead of the University of Chicago's philosophy department told his audience that the days of the little red schoolhouse were over. To understand the problems of the public school, they would have to consider its magnitude:

It is a commonplace of the student of education in America, that our system, even in the large city, has had as its unit the little red schoolhouse of glorious memory. But the mere multiplication of rooms and teachers and even principals and superintendents does not adapt the schoolroom any better to the task which the great city presents to its school system. We are finding out in very various ways that when children are multiplied and the rooms piled up into huge structures we have entirely different problems from those which gave rise to the public school system in the United States.[1]

Americans' commitment to the public school and their desire to have the schools assume a greater responsibility for the care and development of children presented Americans with "a qualitatively different problem" from those faced by earlier generations. The increased scale of public schooling "magnified the importance of conditions which, in the little schoolhouse, were quite imperceptible."[2] As little red schoolhouses gave way to large school buildings, educators had to attend to physical details: how many square feet each child needed, how to provide ventilated lockers for the students' wraps, how large the assembly halls and gymnasiums had to be, how to provide for medical examinations, school lunches, and textbooks. They had to be certain that fire escapes were adequate in number and properly placed, that laboratories and shops were properly and safely equipped. Educators now had to ask: "Is the physical life of the child in the schoolroom what his physique and his surroundings call for?"[3]

According to Mead, what took place in the schoolroom itself also was changing; and while those changes were not always so obvious as those in the school buildings, frequently they were even more complicated. There was the contest between the "old education" and the "new education," between what Mead termed "the three R's and the so-called fads and frills." As Mead expressed it:

> We are told from one side that the children leave the schools by the time they reach the fifth grade, because the work is so unmeaning to them, has so little relation to their life, that the school has no power to hold them, and that we must introduce more of the constructive outgoing activities into their school life. We are told on the other side that they leave by the time they reach the fifth grade, and therefore they should be drilled, drilled, drilled so that they may acquire this control over language and number, which is to become a necessity for them in after years. Here is the same contest of old and new ideals in education. . . .[4]

There was a new ideal. At times it was expressed by what children did in the classroom—manual training, shop work, drawing, music, working with clay, training in the domestic sciences, training for trades. At times educators could abandon these newer educational activities, but they could not long abandon the new criterion by which schooling was evaluated: not just how well the student had mastered the three R's but also "the mental, moral and physical health of the

---

1. George Herbert Mead, "The Educational Situation in the Chicago Public Schools," *The City Club Bulletin* 1:11 (May 8, 1907), p. 131.
2. Ibid.
3. Ibid., pp. 131–132.
4. Ibid., p. 132.

immediate life that the child is leading in the schoolroom and on its playground."[5]

Large school systems also brought changes to the teachers. Mead's assessment of the teacher in the new "huge structures" was that "there is no social functionary who is more unfortunately isolated than the teacher in the schoolroom of our city schools."[6] Teachers received their orders from the school administrators. They were told what curriculum to teach, how to teach, and what materials to use. In turn, they were expected to administer the curriculum in the prescribed manner to the students. This sytem thus also isolated the teachers from the students. Mead's 1907 speech predicted one consequence:

> People who feel themselves isolated naturally organize themselves on the basis of that isolation. Until there is a natural method by which the teacher may be felt in the school administration, by which her judgment on books and methods and the ordering of school life may be heard, until she is recognized as a part of a social organization and not a machine, there will always exist the situation out of which irresponsible bodies like the Teachers' Federation will arise. If the teacher, as a teacher, is not consulted by those who lay tasks upon her shoulders, she is bound to make demands as a member of an externally organized association.[7]

As the schools grew and as the educational problems grew in number and in complexity, many seemingly forgot that schools were social institutions, organizations of people. They began to talk and to write about the schools as though they were either large businesses, industrial enterprises, or massive military organizations. At times some educators confused the reality of public schooling with the language they had used to try to make sense of its problems.

One who strongly objected to the new language of schooling and the treatment it suggested was Charles Francis Adams, Jr., the reformer who was partly responsible for the reforms in Quincy, Mass. In a speech before the NEA in the 1880s Adams complained that too many professional educators had the wrong view of their job:

> Most of you, indeed, cannot but have been part and parcel of one of those huge, mechanical, educational machines, or mills, as they might more properly be called. They are, I believe, peculiar to our own time and country, and are so organized as to combine as nearly as possible the principal characteristics of the cotton-mill and the railroad with those of the model state prison. The school committee is the board of directors, while the superintendent—the chief executive officer—sits in his central office with the time-table, which he calls a programme, before him, by which one hour twice a week is alloted to this study, and half an hour three times a week to that, and twenty hours a term to a third; and at such a time one class will be at this point and the other class at that, the whole moving with military precision to a given destination at a specified date. . . . From one point of view children, are regarded as

---

5. Ibid.
6. Ibid., p. 135.
7. Ibid.

automatons; from another, as India-rubber bags; from a third, as so much raw material.[8]

Not all educators and commentators on public schools were as perceptive as Mead and Adams. Many succumbed to the language of the era. Schoolrooms became shops or battlefields, teachers became workers or soldiers, and students became not participants in the educative process but objects to it.

The "Great Army of Teachers"

Even John Dewey, who made a career of trying to emphasize that education was the process by which the human organism achieved its essential human characteristics, was not immune to the language of his day. In 1896 he wrote an article outlining why pedagogy should be a university discipline: "There must be some schools whose main task is to train the rank and file of teachers—schools whose function is to supply the great army of teachers with the weapons of their calling and direct them as to their use."[9] There should also be, he urged, schools that directed their energies "to the leaders of our educational systems." By arguing for the separation of the two kinds of schools and the personnel each kind would train, Dewey was endorsing the system that isolated teachers from the school superintendents, supervisors, and principals, and from the professors of pedagogy.

When William James lectured to teachers in the early 1890s, he reminded them that "the science of psychology, and whatever science of general pedagogics may be based on it, are facts much like the science of war." He carried the comparison further and advised the teachers that:

In war, all you have to do is to work your enemy into a position from which the natural obstacles prevent him from escaping if he tries to; then to fall on him in numbers superior to his own, at a moment when you have led him to think you are far away; and so, with a minimum of exposure of your own troops, to hack his force to pieces, and take the remainder prisoners. Just so, in teaching, you must simply work your pupil into such a state of interest in what you are going to teach him that every other object of attention is banished from his mind; then reveal it to him so impressively that he will remember the occasion to his dying day; and finally fill him with devouring curiosity to know what the next steps in connection with the subject are.[10]

James indicated that victory would be easy if it were not for one "incalculable quantity." That was the human mind. He explained to the teachers that the mind of their "enemy, the pupil" worked against them just "as keenly and eagerly" as did the mind of one's opponent in war. Both the warmaker and the teacher needed to know how the mind of the enemy was working.

8. Quoted in Michael B. Katz, "The 'New Departure' in Quincy, 1873–1881: The Nature of Nineteenth-Century Educational Reform," *The New England Quarterly* (March 1967), pp. 27–28.

9. John Dewey, "Pedagogy as a University Discipline," *University [of Chicago] Record* 1:25 (September 18, 1896), p. 353.

10. William James, *Talks to Teachers* (New York: Henry Holt and Co., 1901), pp. 9–10.

The military metaphor sometimes brought educators into political stances. At the 1891 meeting of the National Educational Association, J. R. Preston, the Mississippi State Superintendent of Public Instruction, spoke to the delegates about the problems of patriotism and national unity.

After listing problems that were dividing the country—from protective tariffs to the concentration of wealth—Preston specified that a nation was held together by "common sympathies, identity of race and descent, the same language, the same religion, [and] identity of political antecedents." Unfortunately, none of those elements could be found to run throughout the national life. Instead, he found that those aspects of American society that had a national basis all fostered the interests of special groups. Representatives in Congress served local rather than national interests. Railroads connected all parts of the country, but still were not used to promote an identity of interests, only people's desire to move their goods to make a profit. The press typically addressed itself to the sectional interests of its readers. The public school was the sole agency capable of promoting national unity. Preston recommended that the public schools'

> ... army of half a million teachers, sustained by popular devotion to the cause, must in times of peace and through peaceful measures fight this continuous battle for the perpetuity of national life. This army stands today holding the hands and hearts of tomorrow's nation.[11]

According to Preston, the schools could ensure national unity by teaching students what their rights and duties as citizens were, and at the same time kindling the fires of patriotism.

Similarly, in his 1899 presidential address to the National Educational Association, Eliphalet Oram Lyte of the Principal State Normal School (Millersville, Pa.), celebrated the successful conclusion of the Spanish-American War and told the delegates that the teachers of the United States constituted one of the world's greatest armies:

> Our history has demonstrated that we have no need of a great standing army. It has demonstrated that in every school district may be found a company, in every township a regiment, in every county a brigade or division, in every state a corps, if not an entire army, ready at a moment's notice to defend our flag against every foe. And this army is not marshaled by military chieftains, but by educational chieftains. A strong nation is made, not by barracks for troops, but by schoolhouses for children; not by recruiting officers, but by schoolmasters; not by rifled cannon and Mauser bullets and war vessels, but by books and newspapers and churches.[12]

In the United States people obeyed the law not because there was a standing army to enforce the law but because they learned to obey the law in school. Lyte had no difficulty accepting the fact that an Army was needed "to subjugate the Filipi-

---

11. Quoted in David B. Tyack, ed., *Turning Points in American Educational History* (Lexington, Mass.: Xerox College Publishing Co., 1967), pp. 257–258.

12. Eliphalet Oram Lyte, "President's Address," *Addresses and Proceedings of the National Education Association* (1899), p. 67.

nos." However, use of a standing army to enforce the law in the United States would, he explained, be a distinct loss of "moral tone."

Lyte was not content with the recent victories of the Spanish-American war. It was now time, he instructed the delegates, to carry the victory forward. Teachers had a new responsibility: "Whether we will or not, the problem of carrying the benefits of our public institutions to the islands beyond the sea must be solved, in part at least, by the men and women of this association." Lyte acknowledged that there would be those who might disagree with him but for himself he could not but help to "rejoice to watch the onward progress of our ever-conquering republic, and the triumphant march of the Anglo-Saxon race." The sea was no longer a barrier but "a great highway on which we can convey the material and spiritual benefits of a Christian civilization to the benighted children of our enforced adoption." For Lyte there was but one question: "Are the schoolmasters ready?"[13]

The School Hierarchy

In 1904 the National Educational Association held its annual meeting in St. Louis in connection with the Louisiana Purchase Exposition. At that meeting Aaron Gove, Superintendent of Schools in Denver, Colorado, spoke to the teachers and school administrators about the "Limitations of the Superintendents' Authority and of the Teacher's Independence." He presented a stern account of what rights and responsibilities superintendents had and what rights teachers did not have. He warned his audience that "a dangerous tendency exists toward usurpation by teachers, thru organization, of powers which should be retained by the superintendent." To Gove's dismay there seemed to exist the notion "that the public-school system should be a democratic institution, and that the body of teachers constitute the democratic government." Such a notion, he emphasized, was "a false conception of true democracy."[14] For Gove, the school board constituted the representative body that had the authority to legislate educational policy.

Teachers were "instruments" to be used by the superintendent to secure the results the board of education desired. Their role was "comparable to the turning out of work by an industrial establishment, the performance of a task assigned by the chief of police of a city, or communicated to a soldier while on duty." As Gove explained it,

> The teacher has independence and can have independence like that of the man in the shoe factory who is told tomorrow morning to make a pair of No. 6 boots. The independence of that workman consists in the fact that he can sew four stitches in a minute or forty, can work rapidly or slowly, as he chooses or as he is able; but his dependence is that the boots must be made and made exactly, according to the order both in size and quality and execution.[15]

---

13. Ibid., p. 68.

14. Aaron Gove, "Limitations of the Superintendents' Authority and of the Teacher's Independence," *Addresses and Proceedings of the National Educational Association* (1904), p. 153.

15. Ibid., p. 155.

As schools grew in number, Gove continued, it became increasingly difficult for the superintendents to maintain adequate inspection schedules. He suggested that the best method of ensuring proper inspection was for schools to use the War Department as a model. He told his audience:

> Those who are fairly familiar with that department of our government understand how emphatic and essential is regarded the inspection of garrisons, posts, divisions, battalions, and regiments. The commanding officer at headquarters keeps in touch with all stations in his department by occasional personal inspection, but frequent and detailed inspection is necessary, and is performed by officers of the inspector-general's department.[16]

Nearly all the authority and all the rewards were to be in the hands of the superintendent. According to Gove, "the most valuable power, that which deserves and must receive more compensation than any other, is the directive power—the superintendent—whether it be of a transportation company, or of a great industrial enterprise, or of schools."[17] He stopped short of suggesting that classrooms could be viewed as trolleys and teachers as conductors.

In his second text, *Classroom Management* (1907), William C. Bagley attempted to provide beginning teachers with a compendium of precepts that would help them master the techniques of teaching. Through the years many seem to have found it useful. Over 100,000 copies of it were sold and it did not go out of print until 1946. Bagley also undertook to explain the proper relationship of the teacher to the principal, the supervisor, and the superintendent. He informed the students of teaching that teachers were directly responsible to the chief officer of the school system, the superintendent. However, in most cases the "principal of the building" served as an additional link in the chain of command. Bagley likened the school principal to the captain of a ship. In this structure, the captain read the orders (the course of study) to the teachers who, in turn, were to apply them to the students. Students were to acquire whatever habits and ideals had been specified in the orders as well as master the assigned skills and knowledge. For this system to work efficiently, it was imperative that teachers give their complete loyalty to the principal. That meant, wrote Bagley, *"unquestioned obedience."*[18] Teachers who were not able to comply had but one alternative—resignation.

Bagley claimed that "in practice, this condition is not so arbitrary and autocratic as it may appear in cold print." In most instances, principals and superintendents simply required that all teachers work toward the same objectives. How to realize those objectives was an area in which teachers could exercise some choice and initiative.

16. Ibid.
17. Ibid., p. 156.
18. William C. Bagley, *Classroom Management* (New York: The Macmillan Co., 1907), p. 262. Bagley's emphasis.

Teacher Cadets

In 1911 Lotus D. Coffman published what was probably the first sociological study of American teachers, *The Social Composition of the Teaching Population*. Coffman demonstrated that the American system of education was not training enough teachers to meet the demand of the growing schools. Schools throughout the country were staffed by teachers who were either poorly trained or not trained at all. The schools needed 125,000 new teachers each year to replace those who were leaving, but teacher training institutions were graduating only 19,000 teachers a year. Even if most teachers remained in the schools longer than the average tenure of four years, the number of new teachers was not enough to fill the positions created by the increase in specialization and in the total school population.

Reviewing Coffman's study, Bagley reported that one suggested solution to the problem was to upgrade certification requirements and provide better salaries for teachers. He pointed out, however, that this would cause the sociological base of the teaching profession to shift to those families who could afford to send their children to schools for appropriate training and away from those from poorer families who were becoming teachers. Bagley asked: "Should we not leave the profession of teaching open to any youth of the land irrespective of his parents' economic status, provided only that he himself shows capacity for the work?"[19]

Bagley's idea was that, if the public would admit "that public school service is at least as important and fundamental to social welfare as military and naval service," the solution was to establish a system whereby normal schools would pay their students just as the naval and military academies at Annapolis and West Point paid their cadets. Such a system would give all who were able to teach the opportunity to do so, as well as ensure that all teachers would be properly trained. The "teacher cadets" were to be paid a living wage and required to "pledge that they will enter the service and remain for at least five years after graduation."[20]

During World War I, President Woodrow Wilson recommended that married women be allowed to teach in the schools of the District of Columbia and Ella Flagg Young urged that the rule of the Chicago schools that disallowed the employment of any married women within two years of childbirth be amended to allow women to be hired one year after childbirth. Bagley endorsed those recommendations as "gratifying indications that the prejudice against the employment of married women as public school teachers is breaking down." And, once again he made his point with a military image. "With the great bulk of elementary teaching in the hands of women," he wrote, "the only way to insure a relatively permanent and experienced teaching corps is to permit married teachers to continue in the service of the schools."[21]

---

19. William C. Bagley, "The Remedy: Normal School Training at Public Expense," *School and Home Education* 31:3 (November 1911), p. 93.

20. William C. Bagley, "A Further Advantage of Paying Salaries to Normal-School Cadets," *School and Home Education* 31:3 (November 1911), p. 94.

The Ultimate Aim of Education: Social Efficiency

For Bagley, the school's purpose was the control of children's experiences during their most plastic period of growth. The standard by which and toward which the process of control was to be guided was called "social efficiency." Social efficiency was not a doctrine peculiar to either Bagley or to American education. It was one of the many verses of the "gospel of efficiency" that was being preached through the land during the Progressive Era.

The high point of the efficiency craze was reached just after the hearings on the Eastern Rate Case of 1910–11. At those hearings before the Interstate Commerce Commission, Louis Brandeis, armed with the testimony of an assortment of ten engineers and industrial managers and Harrington Emerson, argued that the railroads could save up to a million dollars a day by applying the new science of management to their daily operations. At the center of the testimony was Frederick W. Taylor, whom the witnesses frequently credited as the originator of "scientific management." The news of efficiency and its manifold benefits spilled over into the Sunday supplements, the weekly magazines, and the muckraking journals.

The fascination with efficiency spilled over into nearly every quarter of the nation's life. As Samuel Haber put it, there was "an efficiency craze—a secular Great Awakening, an outpouring of ideas and emotions in which a gospel of efficiency was preached without embarrassment to businessmen, workers, doctors, housewives, and teachers, and yes, preached even to preachers."[22] While efficiency meant many different things to many people, it is possible (according to Samuel Haber) to delineate four categories: (1) mechanical efficiency; (2) commercial efficiency; (3) personal efficiency; and (4) social efficiency. While mechanical efficiency is expressed as an output-input ratio of matter or energy, commercial efficiency is usually expressed as the ratio of income and expenditures. As American business and industry became interested in commercial efficiency, they adopted cost accounting and double-entry bookkeeping. In *Education and the Cult of Efficiency,* Raymond Callahan recorded how school administrators adopted these techniques and the language of efficiency to the problems of operating schools.

Personal efficiency was used by many to describe personal character traits. "An efficient person," Haber has reported, "was an effective person, and that characterization brought with it a long shadow of latent associations and predispositions; a turning toward hard work and away from feeling, toward discipline and away from sympathy, toward masculinity and away from femininity."[23] In 1902 George E. Vincent of the University of Chicago offered a definition of personal

21. William C. Bagley, "Married Women as Public-School Teachers," *School and Home Education,* Vol. XXXIV, No. 8 (April, 1915), p. 281.

22. Samuel Haber, *Efficiency and Uplift* (Chicago: University of Chicago Press, 1964), p. ix.

efficiency that shows how its meaning covered a wide range of personal characteristics and attitudes:

> At first thought the word efficiency brings with it the idea of bustling activity, or perhaps of strong, firm-handed mastery. One sees a pragmatic person, sure, swift, accomplishing. Visions of great factories, railways, banks, with captains of industry and Napoleons of finance, come sweeping through the mind. Pictures of great leaders, generals, admirals, statesmen, paint themselves in fancy. There is a certain strut about the word, efficiency. It seems to describe only strong men doing great things. Yet it carries a general idea, the ability to meet situations, to solve problems whatever they may be. Efficiency is problem-solving, adequacy. . . . It describes the faithful service of the humble follower as well as the brilliant achievements of the conspicuous leader.[24]

A variation of personal efficiency is the application of the concept of mechanical efficiency to human performance. The best-known example is probably the time-and-motion study—a study in which engineers attempt to establish standards of job performance. Studies of teachers' behavior, language, and teaching styles are also examples of attempts to apply the concept of mechanical efficiency to people.

Proponents of social efficiency usually emphasized the need for the leadership of the competent and the need for social harmony. As reformers during the Progressive Era demanded that the school have a clear social mission, educators adopted a version of social efficiency that contained two major elements: social control and social service. At times these elements were not at all compatible.

Social Service vs. Social Control

On the side of "social control" were the first users of the term, Albion W. Small and George E. Vincent; its popularizer at Stanford University, Edward A. Ross; Ross's student, David Snedden, who developed a position that maintained that every school activity had to be related to a clearly productive and useful function needed in society; and Charles A. Ellwood, who desired to sentence every child to meet a minimum requirement of competence in school. On the side of social service were Samuel T. Dutton and John Dewey, who tried to discern and specify the relations between school and society; and the advocates of the social center movement who had their origins in the Grange, the Lyceum and the Chautauqua movements.

When Bagley adopted "the development of the socially efficient individual as the ultimate aim of education," he claimed that he was accepting an aim that was "implicit in all recent educational writings."[25] He indicated that recent works by

---

23. Ibid.

24. Quoted in Laurence R. Veysey, *Emergence of the American University* (Chicago: University of Chicago Press, 1965), p. 117.

Michael Vincent O'Shea, Samuel Dutton, and John Dewey all expressed similar views. In *Education as Adjustment* (1903), O'Shea maintained that the responsibility of the school was to teach students to conduct themselves "in harmony with the rules essential to the well-being of the social whole."[26] In social terms or psychological terms, education was the process whereby individuals were to learn to adjust to whatever situations had been provided for them. In *Social Phases of Education* (1899), Dutton urged that the schools prepare students to live in an ideal society, the kind of society Bellamy described in *Looking Backward.*[27] Dutton thought the school could create a harmonious and orderly society by teaching students how to be free, co-operative, and altruisitic.

In *The School and Society* (1899), Dewey emphasized both the individual and the society that defined the individual. Like many others of his era, he wanted to promote order and social harmony. Early in his text he promised that "when the school introduces and trains each child of society into membership within . . . an embryonic community life, saturating him with the spirit of service, and providing him with the instruments of self-direction, we all have the deepest and best guaranty of a larger society which is worthy, lovely, and harmonious."[28] Organization was the way to achieve economy and efficiency.

The waste Dewey sought to eliminate, however, was the waste of human life. In *Democracy and Education* (1916), he addressed himself directly to social efficiency as the aim of education. He suggested that it was an appropriate aim if it promoted the active employment of individuals' abilities in socially significant activities and avoided what he termed "negative constraint" of individuals. As a specific aim, social efficiency had advantages and disadvantages. It was, according to Dewey, entirely proper for schools in a democratic society to teach youth to maintain and support themselves. He warned, however, that if social efficiency were defined in too narrow a fashion, "existing economic conditions and standards will be accepted as final."[29] Dewey was too committed to progress and growth to accept any condition as final.

One who objected to social efficiency as the aim of education was William Carl Ruediger, professor of educational psychology in the Teachers College, George Washington University. In his *Principles of Education* (1910), he protested that those who advocated social efficiency had reversed the proper order of the individual and the society. They failed to understand that "society exists for the individuals, and not the individual for the society, for it is the individual that really lives and experiences, and not the group." He agreed that efficiency was desir-

25. William C. Bagley, *The Educative Process* (New York: The Macmillan Co., 1905), pp. 58 and 66.

26. Michael Vincent O'Shea, *Education as Adjustment* (New York: Longmans, Green, 1903), p. 95.

27. Samuel T. Dutton, *Social Phases of Education in the School and Home* (New York: The Macmillan Co., 1899), p. 17.

28. John Dewey, *The School and Society* (Chicago: University of Chicago Press, 1956), p. 29.

29. John Dewey, *Democracy and Education* (New York: The Macmillan Co., 1959), p. 139.

able, that the social form of life did promote efficiency, and that well-ordered societies became more important as civilization grew increasingly complex. But the social organization was not to be the end toward which people were to work, only "a means for the full realization of individual lives."[30]

Ruediger pointed out that strict adherence to social efficiency disallowed the schools from offering instruction in art, music, and other subjects that did not have any obvious practical applications. "Man indulges his taste in music, art, literature, philosophy, and even science," maintained Ruediger, "largely for his own immediate enjoyment, without any thought of social benefit, and it is conceivable that such benefit might not ensue." That such encounters and indulgences did not have clear and immediate socially useful consequences did not disturb Ruediger. He found that the "social aim" was "but a partial statement of the aim of education."[31]

The Teachers Are Sent to War

Three months after the United States entered World War I, the National Educational Association held its annual meeting in New York City. Patriotism was the order of the day. The first general session was held on the afternoon of July 3, 1916, and in the address of welcome, New York's Governor Whitman spoke of the importance of fostering American citizenship. He asked the members not to underestimate the importance of teaching the nation's youth and to be mindful of the influence the schools had on the development of American citizenship in the nation's 20,000,000 school children. He was confident that the nation's "army of over one-half million teachers" could do the job. When he contemplated "the proper marshalling of these mighty forces" and he observed "the earnest and patriotic devotion of the American teacher," he knew "that the ideals of our republican institutions are established on enduring foundations."[32]

In October 1916, A. Caswell Ellis told his colleagues in the department of education at the University of Texas about "the Pedagogue and Preparedness." In Ellis's judgment, the nation was not sufficiently prepared for the dangers that faced it. The schools, he said, had the capability to assist the nation in achieving the necessary state of preparedness in three areas: economic, social and civic, and spiritual. Whether the nation would be able to provide the physical necessities for war and for peace depended, he claimed, "upon the efficiency of its schools." The schools needed to provide the appropriate armies. Americans, he explained had been wasting their resources. They were abusing their virgin soil, stripping their forests, and failing to make proper use of water for power and irrigation. The nation needed the schools to train experts capable of properly managing the country's timber and minerals. Moreover, "another army of educated leaders and

30. William Carl Ruediger, *The Principles of Education* (Boston: Houghton Mifflin, 1910), p. 61.

31. Ibid., pp. 60–61.

32. Quoted in *School and Society* 4:80 (July 1916), p. 75.

skilled workmen must be prepared to take over the rich stores of raw materials and turn them into the manufactured articles of commerce." The nation could only hope "to defend its integrity against the embattled armies of earth from without," if the schools produced people who could make the nation "independent of the world for the material necessities of life."[33]

To preserve the country from internal dangers, Ellis said, schools had to teach citizenship, which would eliminate "the ugly viper of class hatred" and give students "an understanding of the services of every class of our citizenship," "an appreciation of the mutual dependence of man," and "a sense of service."[34] Once the schools had trained an efficient economy army and promoted good citizenship, they were to turn to the spiritual battle for the souls of the nation's youth. As Ellis stated the matter,

> The field of the nation's never-ending battle for existence is the souls of the new generation. The generals and captains and soldiers that alone can save the nation are the teachers, principals and other leaders in our great common schools and colleges who calm the savage instincts, develop the efficiency, and inspire the ideals of our nation.[35]

The use of the military metaphor to depict the importance and especially the magnitude of education in the United States has continued to the present. In trying to explain why the nation's schools had seemingly not responded quickly to the "war on poverty" in the late 1960s, Harry S. Broudy again likened American education to a great army. Like others before him, Broudy depicted the teachers as soldiers and the school administrators as officers. He suggested that it is a very difficult army to command and may in fact be leaderless. After pointing out that there is no supreme five-star general in charge of the great army of teachers, Broudy suggested that it may be "more realistic" to picture the 46 million teachers and 2 million "officers" as "thousands of herds of varying sizes, all moving more or less in the same general direction at differing speeds over a vast terrain."[36]

A New Version?

In 1975, John I. Goodlad offered his colleagues and the public an analysis of some attempts at educational reform in the 1950s and 1960s. In *The Dynamics of Educational Change,* he argued convincingly that teachers cannot be isolated from the teaching situation, and that the individual school with its principal, teachers, pupils, parents, and community relationships is the critical unit of study and the obvious target for the school reformer. Attempts at school reform that

33. A. Caswell Ellis, "The Pedagogue and Preparedness," *School and Society* 4:104 (December 1916), p. 950.

34. Ibid., pp. 950–951.

35. Ibid., p. 952.

36. Harry S. Broudy, *The Real World of the Public Schools* (New York: Harcourt Brace Jovanovich, 1972), p. 23.

impose changes on teachers are less likely to succeed than those that include the teachers in the determination of the ends and means of school reform. As Goodlad tried to assign new roles, behaviors, and responsibilities, he described teachers and school administrators in a new version of the old metaphor.

In Goodlad's system, the superintendent of a public school system was compared to the general manager of a shipping company, the principal to a ship's captain, and the administrative and supervisory staff of the school to the support personnel who tends "to the care of the ships carrying the freight—educating the children in their care." The principal, Goodlad suggests, should be well schooled in modern management skills and "participating in a continuous program of personal updating." Teachers then become crew members "participating actively in all aspects of running the ship."[37] Like the metaphors of the earlier part of the century, Goodlad's still placed the teacher at the bottom of the pile. Teachers are not officers. They are simply the crew. Students, it may be presumed, are even lower than that. In the last chapter of his work, Goodlad appropriated the ecological metaphor to show that the school and the society in which it exists are interdependent, that students are subject to a variety of influences outside the school, and the schools are polluted with an overload of functions they should not have to perform.

As Americans turn to images and metaphors to describe their schools and how they work or do not work, they risk not asking the proper questions about their schools. Unless such metaphors are set aside, it is not likely that Americans will be able to ask whether schools still need the large cadre of supervisors who became part of the school systems at the turn of the century. Questions about whether teachers are to be at the bottom of the pile and questions about how schools view children may be more useful than either new or old metaphors.

---

37. John I. Goodlad, *The Dynamics of Educational Change* (New York: McGraw-Hill, 1975), pp. 185–186.

The High School 15

The People's College

The American high school grew rapidly in size and popularity after 1890, when it was a relatively small, new institution. In the 1889–90 school year only 202,963 people were attending high school, less than one percent of the nation's population. Yet many educators in this period argued long and hard about the high school. Many insisted that it was to be a "people's college," not a preparatory school for the nation's colleges. Like the common school of the previous generation, it was to be the school where the daughters and sons of all the people would learn to live and work together. As early as 1879, an Illinois high school principal likened the high school to a family table. It was the place where "the children of the rich and the poor, the lords and the peasants, exercising a healthful influence upon one another, are fed from the same table."[1] Though the statistics on school attendance did not support that principal's claim, it was a vision that became for many an ideal to be pursued. Many believe that high school has become *the* universal American experience. Ralph Keyes, for instance, has remarked that "once you grow alert to the impact of high school on this society it registers like blips on a radar screen." He suggests that school has become "our most universal experience as Americans.[2]

The origins of the American high school are complex. It is one of many forms of higher education that Americans used to meet their educational needs and aspirations. Indeed, Americans, as did their European ancestors, invented and adapted educational institutions to suit their purposes and aspirations. The acade-

---

1. Quoted in Edward A. Krug, *The Shaping of the American High School* (New York: Harper and Row, 1964), p. 13.
2. Ralph Keyes, *Is There Life After High School?* (Boston: Little, Brown & Co., 1976), p. 8.

my is one form of schooling that stood parallel to the high school for a time and then began to decline. It was originally invented to meet new conditions and aspirations in both seventeenth-century England and eighteenth-century America.

The Academy

European nobility began to establish academies in the middle of the sixteenth century to provide their children with training in practical subjects—subjects they needed for their social station and their future life at court. In the academies, young men received instruction in mathematics, a bit of science, gymnastics, and basic training in the use of arms as well as the traditional tutelage in languages. In *c.* 1570, Sir Humphrey Gilbert proposed that an academy be built in London for the education of children of nobility who were the legal wards of the crown. He proposed that masters be employed to teach the traditional subjects: Grammar, both Greek and Latin, Hebrew, Logic, Rhetoric, and other languages. He also proposed that training be provided in a number of other subjects that would fit youth for services to the Crown:

> Also there shall be placed two mathematicians, and the one of them shall one day read Arithmetic, and the other day Geometry, which shall be only employed to Embattlings, fortifications, and matters of war, with the practice of Artillery, and use of all manner of Instruments belonging to the same. And shall once every month practice Cannonry. . . .[3]

Sir Humphrey concluded his recommendation by arguing that the establishment of the Academy would ensure that every gentleman would be "good for some what," while "now the most part of them are good for nothing."

The crown did not act on Sir Humphrey's recommendations, and his plan remained but a plan. However, there were other plans, and eventually academies were established as alternatives to existing schools. John Milton offered his ideas for an academy in 1644.[4] Although Milton suggested extensive and intensive study of the traditional subjects, he also, like Gilbert, urged that the students be given instruction in practical subjects and outlined how they might proceed in mathematics from trigonometry through fortification, architecture, engineering, and navigation.

The course of study Milton laid out for students was probably too rigorous except for very extraordinary students, but his plan became a model for Puritans after the Act of Uniformity was enacted by Parliament in 1662. That Act drove the Puritans from the universities. Those who had already completed their university course but subscribed to non-Anglican beliefs found it impossible to secure from the church authorities a license to teach in an endowed school or a university. The Puritan alternative was the academy. Although the academies founded by the

---

3. Sir Humphrey Gilbert, "Queene Elizabethes Academy," in *The Educating of Americans: A Documentary History,* ed. Daniel Calhoun (Boston: Houghton Mifflin, 1969), p. 6.

4. John Milton, "Of Education," in *Milton on Education,* ed. Oliver Morley Ainsworth (New Haven: Yale University Press, 1928), pp. 57–58.

Puritans were manifestations of their religious convictions, they were also, according to Theodore R. Sizer, "a reaction against the narrow curriculum so entrenched in the schools and universities of the time."[5] Along with the subjects of the grammar schools, the curricula of the academies also included practical subjects that would enable one to work and compete in the emerging mercantile society.

The American Academy

The first secondary schools established by the immigrants to the American continent were Latin grammar schools. Like the grammar schools in England, which were college preparatory schools, the American grammar schools taught young men Latin and Greek. As Americans found a need for a school that would teach something other than a college preparatory course, they asked the grammar schools to expand their offerings. Some grammar schools, reluctantly, taught arithmetic, writing, and even English. Some parents sent their children to private venture schools where instruction in modern subjects suited to the daily commercial world was available.

An early instance of a plan for an American academy was Benjamin Franklin's 1749 Proposal (discussed in Chapter 3). Like others who had proposed academies, Franklin wanted a course of study that would include practical studies. Franklin did not urge training in the use of arms, but he did emphasize that it would be essential to maintain the students "in Health, and to strengthen and render active their Bodies" and urged that the students "be frequently exercis'd in Running, Leaping, Wrestling, and Swimming, etc."[6] Franklin also recommended the study of agriculture and engineering, subjects that would be interesting as well as useful. Franklin's Academy never took the form he envisioned. In increasing numbers, however, Americans turned to some form of an academy for secondary education as the eighteenth century came to its end. By 1850, Henry Barnard reported, there were 6,000 academies in the United States, and Sizer has suggested that Barnard "was probably conservative in his estimate."[7]

According to Sizer, the distinguishing characteristics of the American academy were its form of control and its curriculum. The academies usually were not controlled by locally elected boards and supported by public funds, but were essentially private enterprises. Their curricula were broader than those of the grammar schools. Besides Latin, and sometimes Greek, there were modern subjects and practical studies. In the academy it was possible to learn navigation, agriculture, and bookkeeping; sometimes there was a pedagogical course. The practical subjects were not vocational courses in the modern sense of the term; like other subjects, they were taught from books.

---

5. Theodore R. Sizer, ed., *The Age of the Academies* (New York: Teachers College Press, Columbia University, 1964), p. 7.

6. Benjamin Franklin, "Proposals Relating to the Education of Youth in Pennsylvania," in *Benjamin Franklin on Education*, ed. John Hardin Best (New York: Teachers College Press, Columbia University, 1962), pp. 148–149.

7. Sizer, *Age of the Academies*, p. 1.

For eight decades the academy was the dominant form of secondary school in the United States. Its form and its quality varied greatly. Some academies offered little more than basic instruction; others successfully prepared their students for college. Still others equipped their students for the activities of the commercial world. The academy was not a school for all the people. Many were boarding schools, and not all parents wanted, or could afford, to send their children away. Unlike the earlier grammar schools, the academies were usually more receptive to female students.

By the end of the nineteenth century, the academy gradually gave way to the high school. But as late as 1884–85, there were still more than 1,600 academies. For a period there were two forms of secondary education in the United States. The high school took hold in the urban areas while the academies persisted in the less densely populated areas.

The Development of the High School

The term "high school" had been used long before the high school became a standard feature of American education. During the Renaissance, for instance, "high school" (*Hochschule* or *Hohe Schule*) was the German name for those schools that were controlled by local authorities rather than the Church and that had recently adopted the humanistic curriculum.

The first high school in the United States was probably the English High School in Boston. It was founded in 1821 as the English Classical School but changed its name in 1824. In 1826 Boston opened a high school for girls, but it was closed after two years because so many girls applied that the authorities could not meet the demand. In its place, the Boston authorities offered an expansion of the common schools. John Griscom opened a high school for boys in New York in 1825. In 1827, James G. Carter persuaded the Massachusetts legislature to enact a law that required a town of 500 families or more to provide instruction in algebra, American history, bookkeeping, geometry, and surveying in addition to the common branches of the common school. Towns with a population of 4,000 or more were required to provide additional instruction in Latin, Greek, general history, rhetoric and logic. The law was generally ignored and two years later was revised simply to allow towns to provide such instruction. The Massachusetts law did, however, serve as a pattern for other parts of the country.

On the eve of the Civil War there were some 300 high schools in the United States. By 1880 there were 800, and by 1910 there were more than 10,000. Many of those schools were but modest extensions of the elementary schools. The now familiar pattern of large numbers of students and different teachers for each subject was not the rule. The *Cyclopedia of Education* (1911) reported that "in a little less than one third of these schools there are not more than three teachers; in about two thirds, not more than ten teachers."[8] In many places, the high school

---

8. "High Schools in the United States," in *Cyclopedia of Education*, ed. Paul Monroe (New York: The Macmillan Co., 1911), p. 263.

was housed in the elementary school. Frequently, the local common school added Latin, algebra, and perhaps a few other subjects to its offerings and announced the addition of a high school department.

The Debate over Curriculum

By the late 1800s, American colleges and universities had been established and were concerned with how well their applicants would be prepared for a course of collegiate level. Many institutions of higher learning were dissatisfied with the preparation of their applicants. Some universities maintained their own academies where students could acquire the necessary preparation. Many faculty members, however, objected to the presence of any work on the campus that was not truly college level work. Some universities had high school visitors who traveled about the state to determine which high schools properly prepared their students for the university. The work of the high school visitors frequently created political problems for the university. Citizens who took pride in their local high school did not look favorably on the university that would not accept its graduates.

For the colleges and universities, some uniformity in the work of the high schools and a guarantee of at least minimal preparation for college work were essential. Before the end of the nineteenth century, they achieved much of what they wanted. The National Education Association addressed itself to the high school question, and its Committee of Ten issued a report that all but standardized all future debate about the high school.

The Committee of Ten

In the summer of 1892, Nicholas Murray Butler of Columbia University introduced to the NEA's Council of Education a resolution calling for the appointment of an executive committee whose charge would be to organize a series of educational conferences. Each conference was to include secondary school teachers and college teachers of a given school subject. Colleges could communicate to the high schools what students needed for entry into college; the secondary schools could better determine what the colleges required and what kind of certifications were needed. Ten members were named to the executive committee, and Charles W. Eliot, president of Harvard, was appointed chair. (The Council appropriated the then generous sum of $2,500 to enable the committee to complete its work.)

The Committee of Ten was not specifically instructed to come to terms with the issue of uniformity in the secondary schools' programs, but the issue of uniformity was the paramount issue.[9] Eliot, who had introduced the elective system at Harvard, explained to a general session of the NEA that he did not understand why all students who applied to the nation's colleges had to have the same

---

9. Edward A. Krug, ed., *Charles W. Eliot and Popular Education* (New York: Teachers College Press, Columbia University, 1961), p. 8.

preparation. He advocated uniformity with variations. Secondary school students should have some choices in the program of studies, but educators, he argued, should standardize the various subjects. For each subject there should be, he suggested, agreement about how much time students would spend at study, what topics would be included as part of the subject, and how the subject would be taught. The committee's report was to bear the mark of Eliot's ideas.

In December 1892, conferences on each school subject were conducted simultaneously. According to Krug, the most important question for the conferences was: "Should the subject be treated differently for pupils who are going to college, for those who are going to scientific school, and for those who, presumably, are going to neither?"[10] To Eliot's satisfaction, all conference reports answered that there should be no difference. Not all educators agreed, however. Some wanted to segregate the college-bound students from the others.

In their final report, the Committee of Ten presented four sample programs of study. They were identified as Classical, Latin-Scientific, Modern Languages, and English. The titles of the programs and their contents reveal that the committee had constructed an artful compromise. The obvious emphasis on language shows that the committee was not able to break from tradition completely. On the other hand, the committee's recommendation that any student who completed any of the sample programs should be admitted to its corresponding course in either a college or a scientific school was a setback for those who wanted strict uniformity in all the high schools. Yet the options allowed in high school were essentially determined by the options that were becoming available in the colleges.

Further examination of the sample programs reveals that those who advocated that Latin and Greek were the best preparation for college had suffered a serious setback. Greek was confined to the Classical program, and then it was recommended that it be studied in only the third and fourth years. Latin was required in only two of the programs, the Classical and the Latin-Scientific.

After several years of discussion and debate, most American high schools offered programs that were very much like those recommended by the Committee of Ten. Most high schools offered some form of a classical and a scientific track. Commercial and vocational tracks were added later. Contrary to the recommendations of the Committee of Ten, however, many high schools developed a two-track system, one for the college-bound and one for those who were presumably "preparing for life" (that is, a job). As they did so, they allowed class distinctions and courses of study to become closely correlated. Subsequently, high schools were charged with being agents for vested interests in the society, sorting students along social class lines.

The debate about the Committee of Ten's final report took an unfortunate form. The participants tended to argue for "preparation for college" or "preparation for life" as though the two were mutually exclusive. Many too easily over-

---

10. Ibid., p. 10.

looked the possibility of conceiving of the high school as a truly educational institution. It became the fashion to argue about what school subjects were best and what school subjects would develop the most intellectual power rather than to see the high school as an institution where students might be introduced to the cultural life of the nation and even of Western civilization. To those on both sides of the issue, the high school was seen as a time and a place for utilitarian preparation for narrowly defined future pursuits—job or college. Educators thus placed themselves in an awkward and untenable position. They would always have to be judged by how many students went to college, how well those students did in college, how many got jobs upon being graduated, and how well satisfied their employers were with their performances. Rarely were schools judged simply on how well they taught what they did.

The High School of the Future

In 1891, just one year before the NEA formed its Committee of Ten, W. R. Garrett spoke to the group about "The Future High School." Garrett's vision turned out to be different from that presented by the Committee of Ten, for it was shaped more by a desire to create an institution that would be responsive to the desires of the people than by a desire to improve the articulation between the colleges and the high schools.

Garrett saw an unrest among the people, that called for a reform of the high school. The laboring classes were beginning to understand that their children could gain a chance at true equality in the political, social, and business spheres only if they were properly educated. The high school was the institution with the power to "level the distinction between the rich and the poor." He described his vision:

> The high school is the people's college. It draws its pupils from all classes of society. Here come the sons and daughters of the farmer, the mechanic, the laborer, the miner, the merchant, the professional man, the capitalist. The education secured must be of such a character as to be serviceable where sound the hammer, anvil, and loom; where struggle men for mastery in the avenues of trade; where is exerted the power of logic, rhetoric, and eloquence; where are seen and felt the grace, culture, and conduct of educated men and women. If our high school is to do for all classes, and furnish finished products exhibiting such varied qualifications, then it must present a variety of subjects and branches. Its sphere must be enlarged so as to put it into closer touch with the activities of daily life.[11]

Although Garrett wanted the high school to be all things to all people and admitted that "the varying interests of communities demand different courses in different places," he set down three general principles of liberal education. With each principle he indicated the kinds of courses that would enable one to realize it. Garrett's ideas show that he could see the aims of education and its subject matter as related:

---

11. W. R. Garrett, "The Future High School" (*NEA Proceedings*, 1891), in *Turning Points in American Educational History*, ed. David B. Tyack (Waltham, Mass.: Ginn and Co., 1967), p. 388.

1. A knowledge of nature, or those branches which acquaint the student with man's abode—geography, geology, botany, zoology, physics, chemistry, and astronomy.
2. A knowledge of man, or those branches which set forth the achievements of the race—language, literature, history, civics, arts, and psychology.
3. A knowledge of fixed relations, or mathematics—arithmetic, algebra, and geometry—studies which enable man to determine the relations of number and space. . . .[12]

Besides a Classical course and an English course to equip students for college, Garrett wanted a business course that would allow students to choose electives from the college preparatory courses, and a manual-training course and a domestic-economy course that would prepare students for the industrial sphere of human activity. He also suggested that the typewriter would eventually be a universal feature of the high school, for it would "fulfill an important educational mission." Music and physical culture were also necessary features of a good high school, as were properly illustrated textbooks.

Growth and Popular Control

As high school attendance increased, some educators recognized that public interest in the work of the high school would also increase. One who saw very clearly that relationship was George B. Aiton, the inspector of state high schools for Minnesota. In 1898, he noted that the development of regional accrediting associations, national committees, and conference after conference had placed college entrance requirements "on the rapid road toward national uniformity.[13] The high school was becoming a national institution. As schools adjusted their offerings to the colleges' entrance requirements, they quickly came to resemble each other. Soon a student could move from one end of the state to the other or from one end of the nation to the other and find a high school that would not be significantly different from the one he or she had left.

Aiton predicted that more than eighty percent of the students probably would not attend college, and so educators would somehow have to protect all students' rights. He saw the problem like this:

We shall soon have a round million of young people in secondary schools. We desire to retain the best traditions of the past; we desire our best influence and our best effort to go with the overwhelming majority immediately into the life of the community. We *must* have the respect of the educated; we *must* retain the confidence of the public. These apparently conflicting purposes may be reconciled in one way, and only one. I give you this as our first principle. *Whatever is truly best for the people is best for the school, and ultimately best for higher education.* The converse is also true. Whatever is best for higher education is best for the school, and ultimately best for the people, but the second proposition is more difficult to maintain. The real interests of the

---

12. Ibid., p. 390.

13. George B. Aiton, "Principles Underlying the Making of Courses of Study for the Secondary Schools," *School Review*, 6:6 (June 1898), p. 369.

common school, the high school, and the university, the academy and the college, are identical.[14]

While Aiton maintained that the interests of the people and of their various schools were essentially common, he also observed, "What these interests are cannot be determined by pure reason." Rather, he said, "the principles of education, like all principles of sociology, are matters of opinion."

Aiton urged that "the persistent preferences of any considerable portion of the community should be recognized" in the school program. Colleges should recognize all courses provided they agreed with other courses in what he termed "intensity" and the length of time students studied them. If a course was good enough to build a citizen, then it was good enough to prepare one for college. Conversely, if a course was good enough to prepare one for college, then it was good enough to prepare one for citizenship. Aiton believed that it was, at least in principle, possible to "brush away all conflict of interest between the people and institutions of higher learning." However, like most educators of his era, he had to discuss the high school in terms of preparation for college.

The Quest for Uniformity

The period of the report of the Committee of Ten was also a time in which, according to L. A. Cremin, "political, economic, and social changes of the first magnitude were beginning to occasion new demands on the school—demands destined profoundly to alter the outlook of 1893."[15] The committee's recommendations resolved few questions about the high school. Not only were more people beginning to attend high school, but the people who were attending were different from those who had attended a decade or two earlier. They were different because the society was different. The problem confronting educators—a problem they had difficulty seeing because they were in the midst of it—was not how to resolve the difference between the college bound and the non-college bound. It was the need to conceive of a high school that would be responsive to the needs and aspirations of the twentieth century. Yet for nearly three decades, educators continued to see the high school problem as one defined by the requirements of colleges and universities.

In an attempt to bring uniformity to college entrance requirements, the College Entrance Examination Board was founded in 1900. In June 1901 nearly 1,000 students at 67 centers took the first examinations prepared by the Board. Though many colleges and universities preferred to admit their students on the basis of a diploma or certificate from an accredited school, the Examination Board endured. In 1906, another step toward uniformity resulted from Andrew Carnegie's

---

14. Ibid., pp. 370–371.
15. Lawrence A. Cremin, "The Revolution in American Secondary Education, 1893–1918," *Teachers College Record*, 56:6 (March 1955), p. 297.

gift of $10,000,000 for a pension fund for college professors. Because the fund was not large enough to provide funds for all retiring professors, the Carnegie Foundation for the Advancement of Teaching limited applications to those whose colleges required incoming freshmen to have completed fourteen units in a four-year high school course. Colleges moved to adjust their requirements to ensure compliance with the requirements of this pension fund, and the high schools followed. Within a few years those who wanted high schools standardized had won. The measure of standardization was the Carnegie unit, determined by time spent in a class.

The drive for uniformity grew ever more complicated. In 1913, the NEA appointed another committee—the Commission on the Reorganization of Secondary Education. It was given the responsibility of reviewing and coordinating the work of a dozen subject-area committees appointed earlier. After five years of work this commission published its report, *The Cardinal Principles of Secondary Education.*

The Cardinal Principles
In the quarter century that elapsed between the reports of the Committee of Ten (1893) and the Commission on the Reorganization of Secondary Education (1918) there was, according to Cremin, a revolution in American secondary education: "a shift in the conception of the school, of what could and should be its primary goals and responsibilities."[16] The contrast between the two reports is nearly as great as that between the times they appeared. The Committee of Ten conceived of a school for the few; the CRSE conceived of a school for all. The CRSE recommended as well that colleges accept all graduates of accredited high schools. Unlike earlier committees, it urged that the high school become universal. All children, it suggested, should remain in high school until they were eighteen years old. The CRSE saw the high school not as the preparing ground for the colleges, but as a "pivotal point in the public school system, one which carried forward objectives yet unfinished by the elementary school and opened new vistas leading on to the college." From an institution concerned primarily with the development of individual intellectual power, the high school became a vehicle for "progressive amelioration of every individual and social need."[17]

The CRSE did not try to set down a program for secondary education but rather tried to set down principles that should govern the construction of such programs. According to the CRSE, "secondary education should be determined by the needs of the society to be served, the character of the individuals to be educated, and the knowledge of educational theory and practice available."[18] It emphasized that all the factors that demanded consideration were dynamic. As

---

16. Ibid., p. 296.

17. Ibid., p. 307.

18. Commission on the Reorganization of Secondary Education, *Cardinal Principles of Secondary Education,* U.S. Bureau of Education, Bulletin No. 35 (Washington: Government Printing Office, 1918), p. 7.

the society changed its ways of production from manual labor to extensive use of machinery, the family structure and the needs and aspirations of people also changed. The school had to respond to those changes.

The CRSE also noted that educational psychology had recently made many contributions to educational theory that effectively challenged traditional conceptions of education. It had shown that "capacities and aptitudes" of secondary school students varied widely. Schools had recognized that variability, but they needed to pay even more attention to it. The CRSE tried not to take sides on the question of "general discipline" but noted that "while the final verdict of modern psychology has not as yet been rendered, it is clear that former conceptions of 'general values' must be thoroughly revised."[19] It was no longer sufficient to determine whether school subjects were logically organized. It was now necessary to show how knowledge could be applied to the activities of living and to determine whether teaching methods were consistent with the laws of learning. Psychology had also shown, according to the CRSE, that the development of children was a continuous process. The "sudden or abrupt" break that was often found between the work of the elementary school and the secondary school was contrary to the continuous process of child development.

The Committee of Ten had offered sample programs with lists of courses. The CRSE offered seven educational objectives: (1) health; (2) command of fundamental processes (reading, writing, arithmetic, and oral and written expression); (3) worthy home-membership; (4) vocation; (5) citizenship; (6) worthy use of leisure; and (7) ethical character. The CRSE's report and objectives were widely accepted with practically no objection. Soon the objectives were taken to be the "cardinal principles" of the report's title, and thousands after thousands of students in teacher training institutions were required to memorize them. Many students were taught that comprehensive high schools operated along the lines set down by the CRSE would help to bring social solidarity to a nation whose people seemed to be growing ever more diverse.

While it is difficult to determine how much influence the "cardinal principles" had on the principals, superintendents, and school board members who actually ran the nation's secondary schools, for decades educators persisted in discussing the secondary schools in their terms. In 1973 when the National Commission on the Reform of Secondary Education, established by the Charles F. Kettering Foundation, issued its report, it compared its recommendations with the "cardinal principles." The 1973 commission concluded that its last six goals—knowledge of self, critical thinking, clarification of values, economic understanding, the achievements of man, and nature and environment—were unrelated to the CRSE's "worthy home membership," "worthy use of leisure," and "ethical character." Thus, two generations after the CRSE set down its vision of the secondary school,

---

19. Ibid., p. 8.

educational reformers still found it necessary to explain their views in the terms it set down.

The Vocational High School

During the last quarter of the nineteenth century, while educators were debating the goals of the high school, some educators successfully introduced manual training into the schools. The demonstration of the work of the Moscow Imperial Technical Institute, which was presented to Americans in 1876 at the Philadelphia Centennial Exposition, helped American educators construct a defense for manual training. The Russian system separated the instruction of manual training from the actual productive processes. Such separation helped American educators argue that manual training was not practical vocational training but cultural training. So considered, manual training became a liberal study.

In the 1880s and 1890s educators debated the merits of manual training while it was finding its way into the schools. By 1900 the arguments had changed. Many educators, especially in the cities where school enrollments were increasing dramatically, began to recognize that industrialism was to be a permanent feature of American life. Vocational education became the way both to prepare youth for the new social-economic order and to solve the problems it brought. Vocational education somehow would put an end to strikes and labor riots, increase the efficiency and productivity of the American factory, and allow American business to compete successfully with Germany and Japan in the world marketplace.

After the turn of the century, the movement for vocational—(then called "industrial") education received support from many directions. Manufacturers wanted skilled workers. Social workers and social reformers saw in vocational education a means of remedying the plight of the poor and many social ills. Educators saw it as a way to attract and to hold students. Labor, sometimes afraid that business and management interests would dominate the movement, also supported it, though sometimes reluctantly.

In 1905 the Massachusetts legislature appointed a Commission on Industrial Education to determine whether it was advisable for the state to begin a system of industrial schools. The commission held hearings and even hired professionally trained personnel to help find the facts. When it issued its report in 1906, it was able to proclaim that there was widespread support for industrial education as a panacea that would solve social problems, help the poor, give the public schools a new vitality, and assist the state's economic system. In 1906, Massachusetts created a permanent commission empowered to establish vocational schools.

While proponents of vocational education took heart from events in Massachusetts, another society for the promotion of industrial education was being organized in New York. In November 1906, about 250 people met at the Cooper Union to organize the National Society for the Promotion of Industrial Education (NSPIE). They included industrialists, labor leaders, educators, and social workers. The group quickly adopted a constitution, elected Henry S. Pritchett of the Massachusetts Institute of Technology as president, and elected a Board of Managers. Arthur G. Wirth has described this board as "about as diverse a collection of Progressive Era spokesmen as one could imagine."[20] Its membership included the president of AT&T, Frederick Fish; a Worcester manufacturer, Milton Higgins; Anthony Ittner from the National Association of Manufacturers; the early pioneer in scientific management, Frederick W. Taylor; Jane Addams and Robert Woods who were active in the settlement houses; Samuel Donnelly of the New York Building Trades Union; and F. J. McNulty of the International Brotherhood of Electrical Workers.

Although the NSPIE represented divergent interests and viewpoints, all seemed to agree that vocational education was necessary. It began to lobby actively and effectively for establishment of vocational education at both state and national levels. At its 1908 national convention, the NSPIE voted to send the President and the Congress a message pointing out how important vocational education was to the nation's welfare. In 1912 the Society hired Charles Prosser as its executive secretary so that it could coordinate and concentrate efforts to secure federal support for vocational education. Prosser proved to be an effective lobbyist. In 1914 when the Congress appointed a Commission on National Aid to Vocation, Prosser secured an appointment for himself. As a member of the commission, he supplied it with the arguments and views of the NSPIE. Since many of the other members had expressed support for vocational education prior to their appointments, it was not surprising that the federal commission discovered an urgent need for education that would "prepare workers for the more common occupations in which the great mass of our people find useful employment." The commission stated:

> There is a great and crying need of providing vocational education of this character for every part of the United States—to conserve and develop our resources; to promote a more productive and prosperous agriculture; to prevent the waste of human labor; to supplement apprenticeship; to increase wage-earning power of our productive workers; to meet the increasing demand for trained workmen; to offset the increased cost of living.[21]

In the view of the commission, there was no doubt that support for vocational education would be a "wise business investment for this Nation." The Commission also found "an overwhelming public sentiment" for vocational education, coming from "every class of citizenship."[22]

To those who might claim that education was a local, not a federal, responsi-

---

20. Arthur G. Wirth, *Education in the Technological Society* (Scranton, Pa.: Intext Educational Publishers, 1972), p. 80.

21. "Report of the Commission on National Aid to Vocational Education," in *American Education and Vocationalism,* ed. Marvin Lazerson and W. Norton Grubb (New York: Teachers College Press, 1974), pp. 116–117.

22. Ibid., pp. 117–118.

bility, the commission answered that the mobility of people was increasing and that many communities simply could not afford to train people who would employ their skills in other parts of the country. In 1914, Congress enacted the Smith-Lever Act, which provided federal support for agricultural extension programs. Charles Prosser of the NSPIE had helped Senator Page of Vermont draft the bill. In fact, the advocates of vocational education lobbied for the agriculture bill in exchange for promised help in securing favorable Congressional action on their own bill. Attempts to pass the Smith-Hughes bill failed in 1914 and 1915. In February 1917, however, two months before the United States entered World War I, the Congress sent President Woodrow Wilson the bill and he signed it on February 23. Federal funds were now available to support vocational education in the United States.

The Smith-Hughes Act

By the terms of the new act, funds granted to the states would be administered by a Federal Board for Vocational Education. During the first year the board was to distribute 1.5 million dollars; by 1926 the Board's funds were to be increased by 7 million dollars. States that were willing to match the federal funds could secure support for training teachers; and for the salaries of the people who taught, supervised, or directed programs in agricultural education, home economics education, and vocational training for specific jobs. The advocates of vocational education envisioned the creation of vocational high schools where students would be taught by teachers proficient in a trade or skill. The curriculum would be entirely and directly related to the skill or trade. Mathematics, English, and science, for example, would be taught by the vocational teachers at the time when the students needed them to progress in their vocational programs.

The composition of the Federal Board for Vocational Education reflected the desire of the NSPIE to have a system of vocational high schools in the United States that would be effectively separated from the non-vocational high schools. The Smith-Hughes Act specified that the board's membership would include the secretaries of the Departments of Agriculture, Commerce, and Labor; three other members to be appointed by the President and confirmed by the Senate; and the U.S. Commissioner of Education. (The appointment of the Commissioner of Education was a concession to the National Education Association and other interests that did not want to see vocational education completely separated from the already existing educational systems.) Individual states were allowed to decide whether to administer vocational education programs through separate boards under the auspices of their existing boards of education.

The Consequences of the Vocational Movement

The significance of the vocational movement's success was not so much the number of programs and students that were devoted to vocational education as it was the influence it had on how Americans thought about their schools. For example, in 1912–13, when the idea of vocational education had been accepted but there was no federal aid, 6.9 percent of the nation's high school students were enrolled in vocational courses.[23] Most students who took advantage of vocational programs conducted with the support of federal funds enrolled in part-time programs. Though people did not press their school boards to convert their schools into vocational schools, they did come to believe that schooling and employment opportunities were closely linked. The Americans' view about their schools assumed a vocational component. According to Lazerson and Grubb:

> The triumph of vocationalism lay less in the numbers enrolled in trade training courses than in the belief that the primary goal of schooling was to prepare youth for the job market, in the redefinition of equality of educational opportunity that accompanied the differentiated curriculum, and in growth of vocational guidance, educational testing, and the junior high school to select students more effectively for educational programs on the basis of their predicted future economic roles. Vocationalism's importance thus extended far beyond the confines of the vocational classroom, for its assumptions and practices pervaded the education system.[24]

"Somebody Else's Children"

One common assumption was that vocational education was for the slow student or for students who did not belong to the dominant racial or social group in the community. Equally important was the belief that Americans began to hold that the high school was to prepare their children for jobs, jobs that would enable them to move up on the socio-economic ladder. As long as the economy provided profitable jobs for most of the population, that belief served the schools well. When the economy faltered, however, schools were blamed for events they did not control.

The vocational guidance movement begun in the first decades of the twentieth century by Frank Parsons also led to some false expectations. After World War I, many believed the newly developed psychological tests and inventories would allow students to be properly evaluated, screened, and assigned to courses of study where they would be successful. The instruments, however, were less than perfect. Job success depended on so many outside factors that the schools could not guarantee it. In too many places it was assumed that vocational education was for the slow student or for students who did not belong to the dominant racial or social group in the community.

In the 1960s critics of vocational education concluded that the vocational programs were too narrowly defined and failed to respond adequately to changes in the economic system. They also charged that by limiting itself to the secondary school, vocational education failed to reach those students who dropped out of school after a brief stay in the junior high school.

Even as late as 1969, proponents of vocational education were not satisfied with its status and effectiveness. The National Advisory Council on Vocational Education in its 1969 report described the major problem:

---

23. Ibid., p. 32.
24. Ibid.

At the very heart of our problem is a national attitude that says vocational education is designed for somebody else's children. This attitude is shared by businessmen, labor leaders, administrators, teachers, parents, and students. We are all guilty. We have promoted the idea that the only good education is an education capped by four years of college.[25]

In 1971, the United States Commissioner of Education, Sidney P. Marlan, announced a new concept—career education—that was designed to make education relate more effectively to students' lives and aspirations. Career education is a collection of ideas expressed and tried earlier. Under this plan, students would be introduced to various occupations in the early grades and be given the opportunity to prepare for them in the later grades. Basic subjects, what the CRSE would have called the fundamental processes, would be related directly to various careers. Whether career education will be for all students or "for somebody else's children" remains to be seen.

---

25. Quoted in the National Commission on the Reform of Secondary Education, *The Reform of Secondary Education* (New York: McGraw-Hill, 1973), p. 51.

PART IV

Modern Times

By the early twentieth century, the United States had become larger, more powerful, and wealthier; it was on its way to becoming a mass, urban, industrialized society. People had had to make adaptations in their daily lives and in their institutions. The new ways, the concentration of people in urban areas, and the nation's increased wealth all helped to make schools more feasible, more accessible for many (but still not for all), and more important than they had been earlier.

As educators tried to design schools that would satisfy the needs and aspirations of Americans in the new age, they were promised a new source of knowledge—psychology. Psychology did become an important part of American education. Teachers were required to study it, and educators claimed it as the basis for new teaching methods and improved curricula. Frequently, however, psychology was used to support the interests of the established order and to change the educational process into something that looked like the new industrial processes.[1] Time, measurement, discrete steps, and finished products became the categories of thought used by educators to fit the schools to a new age. People in turn were made to fit the requirements of the new tools.

At the turn of the century, educators predicted that the high school would become a permanent part of the American educational system. In 1890, less than 7 percent of the nation's high-school-aged youth were actually attending high school. By 1920, one generation later, that proportion had increased to one-third. In 1950 three-fourths of the high-school-aged youth were in school, and by 1970 high school had become nearly universal (90 percent). As more young people have entered the schools, educators have tried to reform and revise the high school to meet the demands and aspirations of their times. As will be discussed in the next section, Americans in the 1950s decided that the high school was closely related to nation's requirements for national defense and turned back to the 1890s version.

The American high school continued to be an institution whose characteristics were determined by the colleges and universities. This notion was not even challenged by the Progressive Education Association when, in 1930, it decided to address once again the issues taken up by the NEA in the 1890s. At its 1930 meeting, the PEA decided to make a study of college entrance requirements and the relationship between high schools and institutions of higher learning. The result was the now frequently cited Eight-Year Study (1933–41). The PEA persuaded a number of colleges to

---

1. Clarence J. Karrier, *Shaping the American Educational State* (New York: Free Press, 1975), pp. 161–165.

accept "experimental" students who did not meet the conventional entrance requirements—they did not have the required number of "units" in the typically required subjects and did not complete achievement tests. The PEA did agree that the students would have to make satisfactory scores on the College Board Examination. The Study showed that students from high schools where curricular experimentation was allowed did as well as students from schools that followed college-oriented courses. These results prompted many educators to think about curriculum as something other than a series of courses, but the measure of success remained the same—performance in college.

The Eight-Year Study also allowed teachers to pay attention to how school affected the students' attitudes, how well they reasoned, how well they used and interpreted data, and how sensitive they were to social issues and problems. Under the direction of Ralph Tyler, the Study's evaluation staff helped to devise paper-and-pencil tests to measure such outcomes. As they tried to look at nontraditional outcomes and tried to measure them, they came to insist that all objectives be expressed in behavioral terms. As Edward A. Krug noted, that insistence was "prophetic of what would remain for at least forty years a major preoccupation in curricular planning and theory."[2] There was apparently no question whether such objectives could be met or could be measured. The aims and how they would be taught depended on the process of measurement. In an industrial society Americans thought about their schools like all other institutions. Production goals and schedules were specified, and teachers and students were expected to meet them.

In the 1970s the high school was singled out as an institution that cannot survive unless its many problems are solved. In 1973, the National Commission on the Reform of Secondary Education charged that:

> Education is warped by the tension between a rapidly changing society and a slowly changing school. In an effort to discover the best way to accelerate educational change, millions of dollars have been invested in educational research. Unfortunately, this substantial effort has produced few significant findings and even fewer practical recommendations.[3]

Like other committees and commissions before it, the NCRSE tried to convince the public that the problems of the schools are also the society's problem, for the school simply reflects the condition of the society. However, unlike earlier groups, the NCRSE did not predict continued growth for the nation's high schools. Rather it predicted that in the 1980s the total high school population will decrease, school personnel will be older, and fewer

---

2. Edward A. Krug, *The Shaping of the American High School, 1920–1941* (Madison: University of Wisconsin Press, 1972), p. 264.

3. National Commission on the Reform of Secondary Education, *The Reform of Secondary Education* (New York: McGraw-Hill, 1973), pp. 3–4.

new people will be brought into the system. Those charged with operating and maintaining the schools will have to learn how to be responsive to the needs and aspirations of students and society during a period of decline.

New economic conditions and changes in the nation's demography also may bring about changes in the schools. In addition, the many "rights" movements of the 1960s and '70s made their mark on how educators think about the schools. Now educators must consider not only the psychological needs of the students and the needs of the society, but also the students' political rights and aspirations. As high schools learn to deal with decline and with the necessity to conduct programs that are fair to students of different races, ethnic groups, and sexes, they may find a way to fashion a high school that is something other than a preparatory school for college. Or they may surrender the notion of compulsory attendance and simply allow young people to explore whatever alternatives exist for them.

PART V

A New World and a New Generation

The 1920s and the 1930s are decades that offer a study in contrasts. One gave Americans the taste for prosperity and affluence. The other not only showed the misery a crippled economic system could bring, but also prompted many Americans to question seriously whether democracy and capitalism were viable principles for social organization in the modern world. Germany's invasion of Poland and the Japanese attack on Pearl Harbor, however, turned people's attention away from these questions. World War II gave Americans, men and women, work to do. During the Depression, Americans hoped things would get better. During the war, they expected things to get better once the war was over. Returning veterans and all other Americans were in a hurry to pick up where they left off and make things better. Their earlier hopes had become expectations, and these in turn became demands. The race for educational credentials, jobs, and the good life was on. The differences between the prewar years and the postwar years, whether judged in terms of the lives of the Americans, the values and make-up of society, or the refinement and proliferation of technologies, make the differences between the 1920s and the 1930s appear insignificant. Henry Malcolm has observed that most American adults "do not realize that while the twenties and thirties heralded the end of the nineteenth century, the sixties and seventies proclaim the end of the twentieth century as we have known it."[1] During and after the war, Americans developed a mass culture, a culture

---

1. Henry Malcolm, *Generation of Narcissus* (Boston: Little, Brown and Co., 1971), pp. 9–10.

that Malcolm describes as unlike anything previous generations have known.''[2]

It is easier to state that there are differences than it is to specify and assess their importance and significance. Any attempt to provide an historical account of the last generation is difficult, for it is barely in the past; it may be too soon to give it a history. Yet the recent past deserves attention. It has shaped and continues to press upon the present.

In Chapter Sixteen we will examine the significance of the transition from atomic physics to nuclear physics and nuclear weapons, and the demands that those developments placed on the schools. In the twentieth century many came to see the schools as a vital part of the nation's defense and security. In Chapter Seventeen we will look at another unique aspect of the present—the proliferation of print media and electronic media, which are working a true transformation of education in American society. The availability of information *seems* unprecedented. The forms in which information and ideas are transmitted, and how those forms shape the message and its audiences, are issues that our generation and the next will have to address.

2. Ibid., p. 5.

Education for Defense 16

The Italian Navigator

On December 2, 1942, under the west stands of Stagg Field at the University of Chicago, a refugee Italian physicist, Enrico Fermi, and his associates successfully tested an atomic pile. The amount of energy the pile produced—one-half watt—was not great, but the achievement was. Now there was no question that the scientists could release the power contained in the nucleus of the atom. Equally important was the ability of the scientists to sustain and control that power.

That afternoon, Arthur Holly Compton telephoned James Bryant Conant to tell him of Fermi's success. To maintain security Compton used code. His message was: "Jim, you'll be interested to know that the Italian navigator has just landed in the new world."[1] Compton's message was a concise statement of what had and was happening to Americans. They were indeed entering a new world.

The industrial system would soon turn out consumer goods in unprecedented quantities, new technologies would be introduced and rapidly spread across the nation, and a new mass culture would be fashioned. A new kind of war, the so-called "cold war," was to follow. Preparation for war would become a continuous process. What scientists investigated, how they worked, for whom they worked, and how their investigations were organized and supported were all radically transformed by World War II and by the advent of the nuclear age. American education, from the first grade to graduate school, was to become part of the defense establishment. In earlier eras, friends of public education had proclaimed that the strength of the nation depended upon the strength of its schools, but most everyone understood such claims to be platitudes. Now, such platitudes were admonitions.

---

1. Arthur Holly Compton, *Atomic Quest* (New York: Oxford University Press, 1956), p. 144.

The Scientists and the Soldiers

In June 1916, the National Academy of Sciences established the National Research Council (NRC) to foster scientific research that would enhance the welfare and the security of the country. The NRC sought to organize the nation's scientists, engineers, and industrialists to promote, in cooperation with govermental agencies, the research and development necessary for defense. When war began, the NRC organized scientists to work on the development of systems for the detection of enemy submarines, the increased production of optical glass, chemical warfare, and other areas. At the end of World War I, many military leaders and politicians agreed that science had made significant contributions to the war effort. It was in the national interest to support and to train even more scientists. In April 1919, the Rockefeller Foundation granted $500,000 to the NRC to support post-doctoral study in chemistry and physics for a five-year period. In the same year the Carnegie Corporation provided $5 million to the National Academy to build quarters and to support the NRC's work. The National Defense Act of 1920 gave the United States Army permission to send up to two percent of its officers to colleges and universities for advanced technical training.[2]

The relationship that had been established during World War I between the scientific community and the government did not endure. Many in the military were not willing to surrender control of scientific endeavors to civilian scientists, whom they found too inclined to pursue interesting but impractical questions. Moreover, in the 1920s many people questioned whether it was proper for the government to provide financial support for scientific research. For some, such support was contrary to the ideal of pure science. During World War II, however, the relationship between the government and the scientific community had been reestablished, and the new union proved to be one that could not be easily broken. Only the government, it seemed, had sufficient resources to maintain essential scientific activity.

Many scientists returned to their campuses after World War I with new expectations. They wanted new and bigger laboratories and equipment they had not had previously. During the 1920s they were able to secure much of what they desired. The practical value of a college education had been demonstrated to the public during the war. In the decade of the 1920s undergraduate enrollments increased by nearly 100 percent; graduate enrollments increased by more than 300 percent.[3] Scientists learned how to use the media to their advantage and also learned to enjoy the acclaim and support of the public. In the 1930s this acclaim and support diminished somewhat, but the scientists did not lose all they had gained. By 1940, for instance, Ernest O. Lawrence convinced the Rockefeller Foundation to grant him $1,150,000 to build a gigantic cyclotron. Daniel J. Keveles has observed:

---

2. Daniel J. Keveles, *The Physicists: The History of a Scientific Community in Modern America* (New York: Alfred A. Knopf, 1978), pp. 149–150.

    3. Ibid., p. 157.

The venture signaled the coming of a new kind of physics in the United States. It was a physics of many practitioners and considerable reliance on theorists as well as experimentalists, a physics whose salient intellectual challenges led inexorably to expensive machines and massive organizations. . . . in the phrase of a later day, it was "big physics."[4]

Though the scientific community did not receive any significant government support in the 1930s, and the military had meager funds for research, the American scientific community continued to grow. In June 1940, President Franklin D. Roosevelt established the National Defense Research Committee and subsequently the Office of Scientific Research and Development (OSRD). Under the leadership of Vannevar Bush, OSRD decided to inventory existing research facilities in the United States and to assemble lists of scientists so that the appropriate contracts for research and development could be granted. The nation's university laboratories were to become centers of research and development for military weapons and technology. At the Massachusetts Institute of Technology, a group of scientists were assembled to perfect radar. At Johns Hopkins, the scientists worked on developing the proximity fuse. At the California Institute of Technology, they worked on solid fuel rockets. The Metallurgical Laboratory was organized at the University of Chicago where Fermi was to build his successful atomic pile. At the University of California at Berkeley, E. O. Lawrence began conversion of his cyclotron to a large mass spectrograph for the magnetic separation of U-235 from U-238. Special research facilities were built at Oak Ridge and Los Alamos.

The work of the scientists in World War II had a lasting effect on American science and on all of American education. During the war years, the average annual federal expenditure on scientific research and development increased from $48 million to $500 million. Many scientists had grown used to requesting and receiving whatever equipment they needed. University administrators quickly realized that scientists would not be willing to return to the conditions of the 1930s.

At the same time, many people realized that the war had in a way diminished the country's scientific capability. According to James B. Conant, the war had denied American science 150,000 first degree scientists and nearly 17,000 scientists with graduate degrees. In 1945 Vannevar Bush predicted that by 1953 the nation would have 2,000 fewer Ph.D. physicists than were needed.[5] There was also the realizaton that if there were another war, there would be no time to assemble and train scientists. Postwar defense requirements required the continuous contribution of the scientific community.

As the political climate of the nation changed during the postwar era, there was less willingness to rely on the private sector to support scientific research. Some feared that the private sector would support only those endeavors that would bring a quick profit, rather than those that were what the nation needed for defense or were even socially useful. The federal government was to become

---

4. Ibid., p. 286.
5. Ibid., p. 341.

increasingly involved in the support of scientific research in all fields. By the end of the 1950s, the public was linking defense needs to the quality of its public schools.

Postwar Critics of the Schools

In the 1920s and 1930s the American high school grew larger and lost some of its selective character. Although there was little change in total school enrollments, because of declining birth rates, the high school enrollment increased rapidly. In the 1930s many young people who would ordinarily have left school to find jobs remained in school because there were few, if any, jobs. Some were even paid by the WPA to remain in school and not compete for scarce jobs. As the character of the school population changed, educators developed new conceptions of schooling and defined new purposes. The superintendent of schools in St. Louis, for instance, reported in 1936:

> This growing enrollment in all of the secondary schools has an important social significance. Actually, whether we accept it as a part of our idealism or not, the high schools can no longer function as selective agencies for higher institutions of learning. Children who are mentally and physically capable of remaining in school are in most cases continuing their attendance beyond the elementary school age. In other words, the concept of a common school education has grown to include twelve grades instead of eight.[6]

In the 1940s and early 1950s educators emphasized that the schools were to meet the needs of all students no matter how great or how limited their abilities. The schools were to prepare students to earn a living and to be good citizens. The revised concept of the school demanded revised curricula. Traditional academic fare was no longer adequate. In St. Louis, it was observed that "many of the students now entering high school are not inherently academic minded." Some were slow learners, some were a "year or more retarded in mental maturity." Either the content of the curriculum had to be reduced, or a different course of study had to be designed to satisfy the needs and abilities of the students now enrolled. In St. Louis, for instance, nine options were now provided: classical, scientific, general, commercial, drawing, music, home economics, industrial arts, and something termed "modified general." Later, similar attempts to meet the needs of all students for work and life in a democratic society were to be called "life adjustment education." Other attempts to revise school activities were called "progressive education." "Progressive" was a term of both approbation and opprobrium. For reasons that may never be completely clear, John Dewey and William Heard Kilpatrick were usually credited with the responsibility for progressive education.

The postwar economy brought a prosperity that was curiously manifested in

---

6. Board of Educaton of St. Louis, *Eighty-Second Annual Report,* (1936), p. 18.

conformity, alarming some social observers. As always, dissatisfaction or concern with what is happening in American society prompted some to direct their attention to the nation's schools. If a growing and conforming mediocrity is spreading through the land, then, it was reasoned, the schools must be awry. In 1953, Albert Lynd, who cogently titled his book *Quackery in the Public Schools,* charged that the nation's youth were not adequately prepared for life and work. "Mere literacy," he wrote, "is the quality most difficult to find in the young men and girls coming into offices from the schools today."[7] Lynd acknowledged that in a system of universal education it may not be possible to teach all children how to read and write. He claimed, however, that even capable students had little chance to learn because those who controlled the schools had so little regard for such fundamental skills.

Lynd charged that control of the nation's schools no longer rested with the citizens, but with an "Education bureaucracy" that made "all basic decisions about the aims and methods of schooling."[8] These "educationists" were promoting "the new Education," and Lynd was not willing to let the old education go. The old education, he explained, consisted of three major elements: "the students, the teacher, and the body of knowledge which the teacher endeavored to communicate to the student." In the old education, it was likely that some of the knowledge would "stick to the more intelligent children" even if the teacher did not communicate very well. However, as Lynd expressed it, "the New Education stakes everything on the wisdom or the limitations of the teacher, while encouraging him to throw out most of the accumulated wisdom of the race."[9] For Lynd, there was more of worth to be found in subject matter than in the teachers.

Another critic, Mortimer Smith, warned in his book *And Madly Teach* (1949) that the schools were suppressing individuality and teaching students to obey the herd instinct. The schools' failure to cultivate the students' intellect and to maintain intellectual values was sure to lead to a society of robots programmed for political and economic exploitation. In *Crisis in Education* (1949) The Reverend Barnard I. Bell argued that the nation's culture was bound to disintegrate unless the schools were improved. Bell suggested that schools should be freed from political meddling and be better supported so that class size could be reduced, and the students' efforts be directed only to worthwhile studies. Improved schools and proper cultivation of the intellect would save the nation's culture and give it direction. So that the schools could embark upon a program of cultural salvation, Bell suggested that the schools cease assuming those responsibilities which belonged to the parents. Curiously, Bell did not object to having the schools assist churches in accomplishing their mission; in fact, he indicated that if education was to have a basic purpose worthy of pursuit the schools would have to teach those values enforced and taught by most American churches.

---

7. Albert Lynd, *Quackery in the Public Schools* (New York: Grosset and Dunlap, 1953), p. 23.
8. Ibid., p. 37.
9. Ibid., p. 69.

At the 1952 meeting of the American Historical Society, Arthur Bestor, professor of history at the University of Illinois, proposed that the community of scholars assume responsibility for watching over the nation's public schools, especially the high schools. He offered his proposal in a series of resolutions that received the support of nearly 700 scholars from colleges and universities throughout the country. Bestor's proposals attracted the attention of the press, and a number of newspapers wrote editorials about them. In 1953, the proposals were published in full in *School and Society*. Bestor had attacked the educational establishment and it responded, bringing his position to the attention of the public.

In 1955 Bestor presented his book *Educational Wastelands,* which received wide attention and stirred much controversy. Like other critics of the era, he complained that the schools had fallen into the hands of educationists who had no appreciation for the cultivation of the intellect. He charged that the educators were constructing an "iron curtain" across the land, behind which were "slave-labor campuses" where classroom teachers were imprisoned by the educationists. Only the public could save the teachers and the schools by insisting that schools be supervised not by educationists who advocated narrow vocational education and life adjustment education, but by the kind of educator who could command the respect of scientists, scholars, and other professionals.

The attention Bestor's first attack created prompted a second work, *The Restoration of Learning* (1955). Once again he emphasized that the school should be "a place of thorough and disciplined intellectual training" and advocated "rigorous intellectual discipline." Although he maintained that there were fundamental disciplines and called for a "restoration of learning", Bestor did not deny that the school's curriculum had to relate to the modern world. His reason for the return to a traditional curriculum—science, mathematics, history, English, foreign languages—was that such disciplines are the foundation for "contemporary intellectual life." If students were to be able to understand their world, they needed something other than "the simple-minded conception of mathematics as primarily a matter of making change and figuring out how many cups of punch can be dipped from a gallon bowl." They needed algebra, trigonometry, and calculus. To understand the television that had recently entered their homes, they needed to know advanced physics. The use of vitamins and antibiotics required the students' knowledge of biochemistry. The use of plastics and detergents dictated that students learn chemistry.[10]

The Role of Government

As the media drew the public's attention to the importance of science and education, legislators also began to consider those topics. In 1945, a bill to create a

---

10. Arthur Bestor, *The Restoration of Learning* (New York: Alfred A. Knopf, 1956), pp. 40–41.

National Science Foundation was drafted by Vannevar Bush and introduced in the Senate by Sen. Warren G. Magnuson. That bill was rejected, but in 1947 Congress agreed on a bill to create such a foundation and sent it to President Truman. He vetoed it, however, because he was unwilling to create a governmental agency over which the President would have no direct control. In 1950 Congress and the President finally agreed on a new bill, and the National Science Foundation (NSF) was created. NSF was to promote and fund pure (not military) research as well as support the training of scientists. Its director was to be a presidential appointee. The nation's scientists had some assurance that their pure research would be supported by the government, and the government had acknowledged its obligation to support such research.

Sputnik Goes Up

Americans' traditional opposition to federal school aid was abandoned quickly in 1957 after the launching of *Sputnik I.* Across the nation, the morning papers of October 5, 1957, announced that the Soviet Union had successfully launched the first man-made Earth satellite. About once every hour and a half, a twenty-two-inch sphere circled the earth and sent back signals. The satellite's orbit and size indicated to American experts that the Soviets had made significant advances in rocketry. On November 3, 1957, the Russians dealt American prestige a second and harsher blow. Their second satellite circled in a higher orbit, and it weighed six times more than *Sputnik I.* More significantly, it contained an air-conditioned apartment carrying a live dog. The Defense Department hastily announced that the United States would launch its own satellite from Cape Canaveral, Fla., on December 4, 1957. December 4, came and the rocket needed repair. On December 6, the first launch was attempted. Within seconds it was a clear failure. On January 31, 1958 *Explorer I* was successfully launched, but it did not put the American fears to rest. *Explorer I* was not much larger than *Sputnik I* and much smaller than *Sputnik II.*

The Russian space successes gave the critics of American education a nearly instantaneous credibility. In *The Restoration of Learning,* Bestor had produced statistics that showed that enrollments in high school mathematics, science, and foreign languages had declined significantly. Since the beginning of the twentieth century, the percentage of students studying science had dropped from 83.9 percent to 53.8 percent; in mathematics the drop was 85.6 percent to 54.7 percent; and in foreign languages, 72.7 percent to 21.8 percent.[11]

Shortly afterwards, John Gunther's *Inside Russia Today* let Americans see how their schools compared with Soviet schools: Russian children attended school six days a week. They were required to complete a stiff curriculum: ten years of mathematics, four years of chemistry, five years of physics, and six years of biology. American students seemed to study comparatively little science. Only half

---

11. Ibid., pp. 42–43.

the American students studied physics, and then for only a year. Nearly two out of three studied chemistry, but that also was for only a year. Gunther's account convinced many that the Russian high school graduate knew more science than most American college graduates.

In the spring of 1958 *Life* magazine turned its attention to the mediocrity of the nation's schools. Readers were told that the entire public school system needed to be overhauled. Bright students were neglected in favor of dull ones. Schools were overcrowded. More attention was given to social adjustment and to teaching students how to be consumers than to solid academic fare. There were too many electives. As for teachers, *Life* thought they deserved better salaries, but that many did not deserve what they were already being paid. Educators had to respond to the criticisms and to the questions and demands of parents. Some defended their ways, but for the most part, the educationists and the public set out to seek "excellence." Students were suddenly expected to do more faster. Those who complained about the schools a few years earlier earned new popularity, and sometimes new profits. For example, in 1955 Rudolf Felsch published *Why Johnny Can't Read—and What you Can Do About It*. It received little notice, but after *Sputnik* it became a best seller.

The National Defense Education Act

While it had taken Congress and the President five years to agree on a bill to create the National Science Foundation, *Sputnik* prompted quick agreement on legislation. In January 1958, President Eisenhower asked the Congress to increase NSF's appropriations by 500 percent and to support a series of other measures designed to strengthen the schools' ability to contribute to the nation's defense requirements. NSF was granted money to support its earlier work in the development of a new physics curriculum. The National Defense Education Act (NDEA) was passed, allowing the Department of Health, Education, and Welfare to implement new programs in the nation's schools through its Office of Education. NDEA authorized the Office of Education to provide funds to improve instruction in science and mathematics, to strengthen programs in foreign languages, to encourage the nation's youth to choose teaching as a career at all levels, and to implement sound guidance programs.

Curriculum Reform

The "New Physics". The NDEA funds for science and mathematics programs completed work that NSF had begun in 1956 when it agreed to sponsor the Physical Science Study Committee. The PSSC was initially organized by a physicist from the Massachusetts Institute of Technology, Jerrold Zacharias. Zacharias and other physicists believed that an improved physics curriculum would attract more students to physics as a career. The course would emphasize basic ideas rather than practical applications of physical laws. Classical Newtonian physics would be replaced by nuclear physics. To effect such a radical reconstruction of the physics curriculum, Zacharias proposed to produce 90 twenty-minute films that could be used in classrooms. Teachers would show the films, then use the study questions, problems, and equipment that were to be produced to accompany them.

After 1956 the PSSC received millions of dollars annually from NSF and private foundations to produce what came to be known as the "new physics." The PSSC organized summer workshops to produce the new materials and a textbook and to train teachers. By 1960, the materials had been tested in 500 schools. With funds recently made available to them through NDEA, public schools were able to purchase the equipment the new physics courses required.

The "New Math." Like the new physics, the "new mathematics" originated before *Sputnik.* Early in the twentieth century, a minority of mathematicians, mathematics teachers, and scientists were arguing that traditional methods of mathematics instruction, which emphasized "memorization, drill, speed in calculating, and the use of prescribed formulas rather than thinking, reasoning and understanding computational operations,"[12] were not providing students with an adequate foundation for further progress in mathematics or for success in their chosen careers. As early as 1919, a radical change in mathematics curriculum and instruction was recommended by the National Committee on Mathematical Requirements appointed by the Mathematical Association of America. The Committee recommended that "formal demonstration (proof) should be preceded by 'a reasonable amount of informal work of an intuitive, experimental, and constructive character, and that drill on the manipulation of symbols should be kept in perspective as a means of improving speed and accuracy after understanding has been developed.' "[13]

The University of Illinois Committee on School Mathematics (UICSM) was organized in 1952 by Max Beberman of the College of Education and Herbert E. Vaughan of the mathematics department. Working in the university's Laboratory School, Beberman, Vaughan, and their associates began to build and teach a mathematics curriculum that emphasized the understanding of mathematical relationships rather than computational skills. Students were taught set theory so they could learn how to relate mathematical concepts rather than being taught how to apply rules that produced the correct sums but little or no understanding of mathematics. The College Entrance Examination Board appointed a Commission on Mathematics that reported in 1959 that conventional ways of teaching mathematics failed to foster either an understanding of or a liking for mathematics. In 1957 the University of Maryland established its Mathematics Project to investigate the best way to teach mathematics in the junior high school. Like the other groups, the

---

12. Helene Sherman, *Commcn Elements of New Mathematics Programs* (New York: Teachers College Press, 1972), p. 12.

13. Nathaniel Gage, ed., *Handbook of Research on Teaching* (Chicago: Rand McNally, 1963), pp. 1009–1010.

Maryland project endeavored to build a curriculum that promoted the student's ability to deal with mathematical abstractions and abandoned the traditional approach of drilling students in rules they did not understand.

In 1958 Edward G. Begle from the mathematics department of Yale University received an NSF grant to plan a program to improve the school mathematics curriculum. That was the beginning of the School Mathematics Study Group (SMSG). During the summer of 1958, the SMSG decided that the most effective way to transform the teaching of mathematics was to produce new textbooks. Accordingly, they began making preparations for a series of texts for grades seven through twelve. Less than a year after its founding, SMSG was able to provide schools with experimental materials. When schools opened in the fall of 1959, a new series of SMSG texts was ready for use by over 25,000 students in grades seven through twelve. In the spring of 1960, SMSG began work to revise the elementary mathematics curriculum.

Other Reforms. Groups also were formed to revise the curriculum in other school subjects, but they did not receive as generous support from NSF. The American Institute of Biological Sciences Curriculum Study (BSCS) was organized in 1959 to produce new biology materials. In 1960 the Chemical Education Material Study (CHEM Study) began work on a new chemistry curriculum using films, a new text, laboratory manuals, and a teachers' guide. Attempts were even made to provide new humanities and new social studies courses. In 1962 the American Council of Learned Societies and Educational Services, Incorporated tried to do for the social sciences and humanities what had been done for mathematics and the sciences. Their funds were meager, however, and they could not identify a comprehensive and unified structure that would allow them to create an analogue to the other new courses. Funds were made available through NDEA to promote the study of foreign languages, especially the languages of the Third World, and to encourage social scientists to turn their attention to those areas.

The money made available through NDEA for guidance programs was used in a similar way. Many people believed that the most efficient way to produce the needed scientists, mathematicians, engineers, and other experts was through early identification of able students in the early grades. To ensure that there would be enough properly trained guidance counselors, NDEA sponsored summer training programs as well as fellowships for those who wished to participate in the selection and sorting of the nation's youth.

Professional educators objected to the specific features of NDEA. Many advocated unrestricted aid to local school districts on a per capita basis. But after *Sputnik,* neither Congress nor the public was willing to accept the advice of professional educators. They were convinced that the schools needed to abandon the anti-intellectualism that the professional educators had introduced and return to a rigorous program. All the public needed was a comprehensible description of what a good school was. Shortly after *Sputnik,* James Bryant Conant provided such a description.

James Bryant Conant

James Bryant Conant, born in Dorchester, Mass. in 1893, was educated in private schools, and took his doctorate in chemistry (1916) at Harvard. After World War I, he returned to Harvard, became a full professor, and in 1929 was appointed the Sheldon Emery professor of organic chemistry. In 1931 he won the Chandler Medal for his work on hemoglobin, and in 1932 the Nichols Medal of the American Chemical Society for his work on chlorophyll. In 1933 he was named the twenty-third president of Harvard University. When World War II started, Conant quickly became an important figure because of his scientific accomplishments and his administrative ability. In 1940 he joined the National Defense Research Committee; he was sent to England that same year to work out ways to exchange scientific information. When the NDRC was reorganized in 1941, as the Office of Scientific Research and Development, Conant was named to succeed Vannevar Bush as its chairman.

When the Manhattan District was organized in June 1942 to administer the building of the atomic bomb, Conant became the scientific advisor to its director. He was a member of the committee that advised President Truman on the use of the bomb. In 1947 Conant returned to Harvard, but in 1953 President Eisenhower named him High Commissioner to the new West German government in Bonn. When West Germany was granted autonomy in 1955, Conant became U.S. Ambassador. In February 1957, he returned to the United States to begin a study of the nation's schools funded by a grant from the Carnegie Foundation and administered through the Educational Testing Service.

Conant had limited experience with the nation's public schools. He had written several college chemistry texts and, as a professor of chemistry at Harvard, worked with physicists and demonstrated interests in history, literature, and philosophy. He was one of the founders of the Harvard Shop Club where faculty members from a variety of disciplines assembled to talk to each other about their work. In 1925, he devoted eight months to a study of how German universities conducted their research and instructional programs. In 1948 he had published *Education in a Divided World,* in which he tried to show that the strength of a democracy depended on its public schools.

As Conant and his associates set out to study the American high school, they demonstrated the traditional American bias and ignored the major cities. The schools they visited "were located for the most part outside metropolitan areas in cities with populations between 10,000 and 100,000."[14] They visited schools in twenty-six states, avoiding the South except for Kentucky, Maryland, and Virginia. Conant's team visited four school systems and 103 schools; he himself visited three systems and 55 schools.

Their findings were published in 1959 as *The American High School Today:*

---

14. James B. Conant, *The American High School Today* (New York: McGraw-Hill, 1959), p. 14.

A First Report to Interested Citizens. From the very beginning of his report, Conant avoided comparing the American educational system with European systems. He explained that the American school was rooted in a different social, economic, and political tradition, and offered a vision of a high school that could be nearly all things to nearly all people.

Conant explained that the comprehensive high school was an invention of the twentieth century, that no other country in the world had a comparable institution, and that it was to be found in nearly all communities. There was only one major question to ask:

> Can a school at one and the same time provide a good general education for *all* the pupils as future citizens of a democracy, provide elective programs for the majority to develop useful skills, and educate adequately those with a talent for handling advanced academic subjects—particularly foreign languages and advanced mathematics?[15]

An affirmative answer to that question was necessary to ensure not only the future of American education but also the future of the nation. If that question could be answered affirmatively, then "no radical change in the basic pattern of American education would seem to be required."[16] Moreover, Conant believed it was possible for most, if not all, communities to have a comprehensive high school. If it were large enough to have a graduating class of one hundred students, the school could offer all the courses all the students needed in an efficient manner and at a reasonable cost.

So that "interested citizens" could determine how good their schools were, Conant provided the checklist he developed during his own survey. It contained fifteen items divided into four major sections. The first section was devoted to "general education for all"; it focused attention on the school's program in composition and literature (both American and English), social studies, and American history, and asked whether students were grouped according to their abilities in the required courses. The second section raised questions about the "non-academic elective program." An appropriate program would provide "vocational programs for boys and commercial programs for girls," offer "opportunities for supervised work experience," and make "special provisions for very slow readers." The third section of the checklist was directed at the program for the "academically talented students." For such students the good school was to have programs that challenged the gifted, such as "special instruction in developing reading skills," summer sessions for enrichment, and "individualized programs" that were characterized by an "absence of tracks or rigid programs." The last section of the checklist asked about the guidance program, student morale, the organization of homerooms, and "effective social interaction." Schools, according

---

15. Ibid., p. 15.
16. Ibid.

to Conant, were to foster "understanding between students with widely different academic abilities and vocational goals."[17]

Conant indicated that he tried to give each school he visited a simple yes or no for each question. Presumably, interested citizens could visit their schools and do the same. He paid special attention to the teaching of mathematics, science, and foreign languages in all the schools he visited, and found that school officials could not report with certainty what portion of the academically talented seniors enrolled in physics, senior mathematics, and a foreign language course. He asked twenty-two principals to prepare an "academic inventory" for him, showing what courses the top 25 percent of the senior class had taken during their stay in high school. Those inventories showed Conant that there were only eight schools "satisfactorily fulfilling the three main objectives of a comprehensive high school." It was clear to Conant that "the majority of the bright boys and girls were not working hard enough."[18] It was also clear that the schools were not offering a sufficiently wide range of academic courses.

Conant urged school boards to adopt policies that would require academically talented high school students to complete an eighteen-course program, consisting of four years of mathematics, four years of one foreign language, three years of science, four years of English, and three years of social studies. Students in such a program were also expected to do three hours of homework nightly. Provision should also be made, he suggested, for the academically talented to take extra courses in foreign language and social studies. Conant explained that such policies could be defended from two points of view:

> From the point of view of the individual, failure to develop talent in school may be the equivalent of locking many doors. For example, without mathematics and science in high school, it would be difficult later to enter an engineering school, to take a premedical course in college, and impossible to begin a scientific career in a university.[19]

The neglect of "the 15 percent of the youth who are academically talented" meant either a diminution of the pool from which "professional men and women" could be drawn or a group of professionals who were not as well prepared for the social roles as they might be.[20]

Conant believed strongly that "academically talented youth ought to elect a full program of stiff courses in high school and ought to go to college," but deliberately avoided describing his recommended program as a "college-preparatory program."[21] The variation in admission requirements and courses of study in the colleges and universities made it impossible to give any one program that label.

---

17. Ibid., pp. 19–20.
18. Ibid., pp. 22–23.
19. Ibid., p. 59.
20. Ibid., pp. 59–60.
21. Ibid., p. 60.

To many parents and educators, however, his recommendations appeared to be a restatement of what for years had been the traditional college-preparatory program. Richard Hofstadter observed that there was a "close similarity" between Conant's program and that recommended by Charles W. Eliot and the Committee of Ten in 1893.[22]

In 1961 Conant published a second report, *Slums and Suburbs.* For this book, Conant and his staff visited those metropolitan areas that were left out of the earlier study. Conant's own description was that this was "a book of contrasts." The differences he found between slum schools and suburban schools—schools frequently no more than a twenty-minute drive from each other—were enormous. In the school districts he visited for the first report, he found a "sense of social and economic cohesion"[23] that simply did not exist in the nation's ten largest metropolitan areas. The differences between the slum schools and the suburban schools were "appalling."[24]

Although Conant tried to assure readers in his first report that radical change was not necessary, he now tried to convince readers that immediate changes were needed in American schools and society. He warned that Americans were allowing "social dynamite" to build up to a point of explosion in their cities:

> I have sought to create a set of anxious thoughts in the minds of the conscientious citizens who may read these pages and who, while living in the suburbs, may work in the city. To improve the work of the slum schools requires an improvement in the lives of the families who inhibit the slums, but without a drastic change in the employment prospects for urban Negro youth relatively little can be accomplished.[25]

In the slums, approximately two-thirds of the young black people who dropped out of school were unemployed. Telling them to stay in school to increase their chances for a job made little sense, for about half of those who completed high school were also unemployed. Conant feared that "the fate of freedom in the world hangs very much in balance." He further warned that "Communism feeds upon discontented, frustrated, unemployed people." To the unemployed youth of the slums the words "freedom," "liberty," and "equality of opportunity" could have no meaning. Those youth could not be expected "to understand the relentless pressures of communism."[26] In the 1950s Americans were told that they needed to improve their schools to protect themselves from external threats. In the 1960s they were told that they needed to improve their schools to protect themselves from internal threats.

To defuse the "social dynamite" of the cities, Conant proposed "an educational heresy." He urged *"that in heavily urbanized and industrialized free society*

---

22. Richard Hofstadter, *Anti-Intellectualism in American Life* (New York: Alfred A. Knopf, 1963), p. 330.

23. James B. Conant, *Slums and Suburbs* (New York: McGraw-Hill, 1961), p. 5.

24. Ibid., p. 2.

25. Ibid., p. 147.

26. Ibid., p. 34.

the educational experiences of youth should fit their subsequent employment."[27]
He called for "a smooth transition" from school to job even if a student left as early
as the tenth grade. Schools had to provide vocational programs *and* vocational
guidance; he proposed that they also assume responsibility for job placement.
Schools needed more guidance counselors, and they *"ought to be given the
responsibility for following the post-high school careers of youth from the time they
leave school until they are twenty-one."*[28]

Conant recognized that more job preparation would be fruitless if the jobs did
not exist. At the time, a bill to create a Youth Employment Opportunity Act was
in Congress. One proposed program was similar to the Civilian Conservation
Corps of the Depression era, but Conant questioned its relevance for urban youth.
Other programs called for job training programs conducted by local employers,
trade unions, and schools, and for public service jobs. He endorsed them, but
emphasized that they would help "only if a non-discriminatory provision is included
and enforced."[29] He suggested that the Congress appropriate funds for 300,000
jobs for youths between the ages of sixteen and twenty-one. That was a
quantitative solution to a qualitative problem; for jobs were becoming more
dependent on schooling than ever before. While jobs were needed, new
conceptions of schooling were also needed to answer the demands of the
post-World War II society.

New Demands and New Conceptions

In the post-World War II years, the schools were assigned several new, and
sometimes contrary, tasks—tasks different from and in addition to the sorting and
training of a new technical elite. Simply stated, the task was to serve a school
population it never previously had had to serve. The United States had reached
the point in its industrial development where it could no longer rely upon the
marketplace to finish the job of socialization and elementary job training for those
who found the schools uncomfortable or not suited to their needs, purposes, and
backgrounds. The marketplace now demanded the equivalent of successful completion of high school as a minimal entry requirement.[30] For a short while, this new
demand was set aside while schools reacted to the *Sputnik* signals. They were
allowed, even forced, to devote their limited resources and expertise to the
preparation of a new technical elite.

But while this elite was being identified and trained, a new school population
was growing. Eventually those students whom the St. Louis superintendent de-

27 Ibid., p. 40. Conant's emphasis.

28. Ibid., p. 41. Conant's emphasis.

29. Ibid., p. 39.

30. Morris Janowitz, *Institution Building in Urban Education* (New York: Russell Sage Foundation,
1969), p. 9.

scribed as not "academic minded" were given new names: the poor, the deprived, the disadvantaged, the culturally different. Soon the new population, which had been so long ignored, began to be heard. The politics and priorities of American society had to be rearranged. President John F. Kennedy proclaimed a "new frontier" and asked Americans to work on behalf of their country. President Lyndon B. Johnson turned that request around and proclaimed the "great society"—an attempt to finish the New Deal, which had been an attempt to complete the work of the early twentieth-century progressives who, in turn, had tried to extend the work of the populists. The accumulated social vision held that the children of all the people would go to good schools together.

In the 1960s, there was almost a surfeit of ideas, enthusiasm, hope, money, innovations, and new programs that promised to usher in the "great society." Just as the schools figured out how to meet the demands for excellence, they were told to wage a war on poverty. Though the two assignments were not incompatible, most Americans—in and out of the school business—saw them as different. American schools quickly fashioned new objectives and new programs, which clearly were needed to deal fairly, justly, adequately, and competently with a population it had previously ignored. But both society and the schools assumed that the objectives of schooling somehow also had to be different. American society and American schools needed to be looking at what kinds of schooling all American youth needed, not simply doing more to defend themselves against external and internal threats.

Media and Messages 17

Gutenberg, Before and After

There were schools (and school crises) long before there were books. In the bookless schools, the teachers lectured to their students. The teachers, or lecturers, read ("lecture" comes from the medieval Latin *lectura,* "a reading") their manuscripts (literally, *handwritten* books) to the students. A student with a good ear and a fast hand could reproduce with few or with many errors the teacher's lecture. After Gutenberg and the development of the printing press, eventually it became possible for every student to have a book, or at least have access to books in libraries. Eventually, the printing press was improved, and books became cheaper to make and cheaper to buy. Later still, other means of reproducing print quickly, easily, and cheaply became available.

Yet, though printed material is accessible everywhere in the modern western world, schools remain much as they were hundreds and even thousands of years ago. Teachers continue to lecture (read) to students. Some minor variations on that practice have been introduced. Sometimes students are required to read to the teacher. Commonly, all the students read from identical books at the same time in the same place. Teachers have continued to expect all the students with the same books in the same place to get the same meaning from what they have read. At times students are required to return written words to the teachers in the form of term papers and reports. Technological innovations, in fact, permit students and teachers to exchange nearly any amount of print in an expeditious manner. The curiosity is that the school is so frequently designated as the place where the exchange is to occur.

At one time the school may have been a convenient place to transmit the spoken word. For centuries, teachers could lecture only to a limited number of students, those who could hear them. The invention of the telephone, the radio, public address systems, and other devices allowed teachers to read to virtually an unlimited number of students at one time. Later, the phonograph, the wire recorder, and the tape recorder relieved the speakers of even having to be present. The transistor and miniaturization of electronic circuits made sound equipment easily portable. For those who need visual images as well as sound, there are instant photographs, slides, filmstrips, instant movies, and television. Now we are even promised telecommunication, a process that will enable two viewer-speakers to view and to speak to each other across space at any time.

Each time an innovation in technology promised to make spoken words more accessible or more portable, there were predictions that the ways of schooling would be revolutionized, immeasurably improved, or at least made more economical. In 1919 the radio station of the University of Wisconsin's broadcast special programs to the state's public schools. In the 1920s and 1930s educators were predicting that school exercises would be conducted by the country's best teachers via the radio and were enthusiastically announcing that radio instruction would be cheaper than instruction provided by teachers. However, the enthusiasm for radio rose rapidly and then died. Robert Potter noted that the *Education Index* listed twelve columns of articles about radio for the period January 1929–June 1932. Thirty years later, there was not even one full column of articles on the radio and education.[1] In 1922, Thomas A. Edison predicted that motion pictures would revolutionize education. He claimed that while schoolbooks were about two percent efficient, movies were one hundred percent efficient. Television, too, was seen as a medium that would bring a new day to the classroom.

In the early 1950s the Federal Communications Commission specified that some television channels would be reserved for educational purposes. Later the federal government made funds available for educational use of television through the Educational Television Facilities Act, the National Defense Education Act, the Economic Opportunities Act, and the Elementary and Secondary Education Act.

Despite technology, schools have not changed significantly. In many essential features, they are little different from the pre-Gutenberg days. Teachers still hand out previously manufactured words, and students are typically expected to return those words or other previously manufactured words at a later date. It may be safe to speculate, therefore, that if the basic social structure and social relationships of the classroom were going to be revolutionized by the media, they would have changed by now.

Those charged with the responsibility for the schools (along with most other members of society) have consistently failed to perceive what new developments in the media could mean for both society and the schools. Frequently, our ways of thinking preclude our seeing the full import of an invention or a new technique. We tend to create metaphors that reduce the new to a variation of the old. For

---

1. Robert E. Potter, *The Stream of American Education* (New York: American Book Co., 1967), p. 521.

example, we may say that television is like radio with pictures, that a light bulb is a glass candle. We prefer the familiar to the new and unsettling elements in our environment. We assume that new inventions will allow tomorrow to be pretty much like today but even better. When the new invention or technique is not easily incorporated into old patterns, or does not produce the results we expected, we become unsettled and look for someone to blame.

Charles Weingartner has suggested that the schools have failed to acknowledge that American young people in the 1960s did not acquire their value system from the formal program of the school, family, or church but from the electric and electronic media.[2] While schools were emphasizing the print medium, students were listening to and adopting the values of television and the long-playing record. According to Weingartner the messages received via the long-playing record "shaped both the appearance and behavior of millions of youth around the world in a relatively brief period of time, producing what was probably the first international (or transnational) sub-culture in human history."

The media have played an enormous role in the education of all Americans. Statistics accumulate on how many hours how many Americans watch television, how many listen to their radios, how many crimes how many children see on the tube, and on and on. Educators and public-minded lay persons report these statistics with grave concern and frequently implore the public to use the electronic media to turn youth toward the medium of print. For example, during prime time on three evenings in August 1978, the Columbia Broadcasting System presented a three-part documentary on public education, "Is Anyone Out There Learning?" The third segment focused on the role of television and its possible uses in the schools, demonstrating that many still believe that television can be used in the classroom to turn students toward books. While such an approach probably made sense to many, it was an attempt to add peaches and peanuts and count the results in marbles. Books and television are not similar; each makes different demands on the individual, and each requires the individual to participate in different ways. As long as our primary attention is paid to how the various media can be used to promote the schools' version of the print medium, we will not be in a position to understand how Americans have been educated and miseducated outside the school by the comic book, the radio, the motion picture, or television.

Instructional Comic Books

Attempts to use comic books for instructional purposes began in 1941—just three years after *Action Comics* introduced Superman—when the publishers of *Parents'*

2. Charles Weingartner, "No More Pencils, No More Books, No More Teachers' Dirty Looks." Paper delivered at Educational Future Conference, University of Houston (October 21, 1978), typescript. Used with permission.

Magazine presented George Heckt's *True Comics,* which offered young readers true adventure stories about historical figures. Although *True Comics* were praised as a well-conceived instructional effort, children did not buy many, and they were discontinued after a few years. During World War II, comic books were used by the government to disseminate propaganda. Comics devoted to war themes were quickly produced and sent overseas to armed services personnel. In 1945 a new company, Educational Comics, began to publish comic-strip versions of the Bible, American history, world history, science, Shakespeare, and mythology. All the series were not equally successful, but by 1971, more than five million copies of *Picture Stories from the Bible* had been sold. Some instructional comics were for adults. *Desert Dawn* was produced for the American Museum of Natural History, and *The Bible and the Working Man* for the C.I.O. Another instructional form of the comic book was the Gilberton series *The World Around Us.* Its *Classics Illustrated* series tried to interest readers in the world's great literature. At the end of each *Classics Illustrated* comic was a statement telling the readers that the original work could be found in either the school or the public library.

More recently, the Marvel Comics Group has developed a series based on the works of well-known authors, including Mary Shelley's *Frankenstein,* Bram Stoker's *Dracula,* H. G. Wells's *War of the Worlds,* and Edgar Rice Burrough's *Tarzan.* Marvel also has published "Spidey," a comic book that uses characters from public television's "The Electric Company" and a vocabulary designed to encourage rather than frustrate the reader. With help from the Department of Curriculum and Teaching of Teachers College, Columbia University, King Features has published the King Comic Reading Library. Instructional features in this series include a glossary on the inside back cover, definitions of words in the picture frame where they occur, and puzzle pages of exercises that claim to develop reading skills.

It may be difficult to assess precisely the contribution comic books have made to the education of Americans, but both the government and educational institutions have used the format to get their messages to the public. That critics of comic books attempted to regulate their content in the mid-1950s is further evidence that many believed the comics did make a difference to the nation's youth.

Radio

In the early 1920s many saw radio only as a variation of what already existed—a telephone without wires. Some saw it as a way to do better what was already being done. Newspapers reported that schools and colleges were planning to use the radio to transmit courses to countless numbers of people across the land. In 1930, Joy Elmer Morgan, the editor of the NEA's *Journal,* enthusiastically reported that the radio was "lifting the level of informed intelligence among the masses." Morgan was sure that radio would provide "to all that common background of information, ideals, and attitudes which binds us together into a vast community of thinking people."[3] Schools were outfitted for radio reception, educational experiments showed what subjects students could best learn via their ears, and teachers learned how to speak over the radio and use the microphone.

According to Morgan, radio would contribute to the physical, mental, and emotional well being of nearly all Americans, even those living in out-of-the-way places. Radio would help to keep people in their homes and thereby maintain the integrity of home life. In fact, Morgan looked forward to the day when radio would offer courses on home planning and design that would enable Americans to create homes that could come closer to the reasonable standards that had been set down by the experts.

Radio, predicted Morgan, would bring to millions of people the "thinking processes of the best minds," and those minds would stimulate people to learn. Radio would create a "world language" and rapidly raise "the quality of thinking among the masses." Through the broadcasting of political speeches and debates, radio would promote an interest in government that would create both a "new interest in citizenship on the part of the masses and a new integrity on the part of officers responsible for the management of our public affairs." Radio even had the capability to contribute to the development of sound ethical character by widening both the family circle and the school circle "to include the ablest teachers, the most earnest preachers, and the noblest statesmen." Once youth were so exposed, it seemed all but inevitable to Morgan that the nation's youth would come to value the proper "qualities of character."[4] Morgan tried to assure teachers that neither the radio nor any other invention could take the place of teachers. However, in the nation's sparsely settled areas where teachers were very young and not very well trained for their jobs, radio programs promised to improve the work of the school.

Morgan's assessment of the role of radio in education was not shared by all educators. J. J. Tigert, a former U.S. Commissioner of Education, reported in 1929 that "the field of education in its formal sense has scarcely been touched by the radio."[5] A survey of state superintendents of public instruction revealed that in New Jersey nearly 50 percent of the schools had radios, and in Nebraska 25 percent, but in most other states few radio sets were being used for instructional purposes.

Tigert found that all educators did not agree that radio would or even should be used widely in the public schools. Many felt "that while radio may be of use in the high school or even in the junior high school, it can be of little value in the first six grades."[6] Others believed there was no place for radio in formal education, but most agreed that it had unlimited value as a medium for entertainment and culture. It would help promote a general diffusion of culture and could contribute to education in those areas where the objectives were easily specified—music and

---

3. Joy Elmer Morgan, "Radio and its Future," in *Radio and Its Future*, ed. Martin Codel (New York: Harper and Bros., 1930), p. 68.

4. Ibid., pp. 70–74.

5. J. J. Tigert, "Radio in the American School System," in *Radio*, ed. Irwin Stewart (The American Academy of Political and Social Sciences, 1929), p. 71.

6. Ibid.

agriculture, for instance. Many believed that the more educational a program was, the more restricted was its potential audience. It was also thought that educational material had to be transmitted in the form of a formal lecture. The only alternative, claimed Tigert, was "the so-called informal lecture, sugar-coated with a variety of scientific facts unusual enough to catch the interest and intrigue the imagination of the casual listener."

Certainly, the effective use of the radio required a form of delivery different from that typically used in the classroom. Moreover, using the radio would have required a reconstruction of the classroom, or it would have dramatically changed the nature of what typically happens in a classroom. Teaching and public speaking were very similar in that each was a "live" public event. Radio, it turned out, was very much like the telephone, a form of person-to-person communication that allowed the development of new forms of privacy, intimacy, and informality. Radio personalities did not address their audiences; they conversed with them. Unlike those who spoke to people from a platform or in the classroom, radio speakers did not know precisely who was listening. Radio audiences had the potential to be much larger than a live audience and so created a new privacy for the listener. As Daniel Boorstin has observed, "now for each listener the public message could be a one-to-one experience, no matter how many others were listening."[7]

The relationship between radio and people was, and is, different from that between people and their schools. In the 1920s and 1930s students could not easily walk out or tune out as the radio audience could. Schools did not have to change their programs, or at least the need to change their programs was not so clear. To maintain its audience the radio had to offer a variety of programs to appeal to a variety of needs and interests.

Films

In 1888 Thomas Edison informed the U.S. Patent Office that he was developing a kinetoscope, a device that would reproduce pictures in much the same way as the phonograph reproduced sound. The first Kinetoscope was a box through which the viewer watched a piece of illuminated film move from one spool to another. Initially, Edison believed that his device would be used by one person at a time, but he was wrong. People were soon able to visit neighborhood movie theatres.

As a medium, the motion picture industry has successfully and successively adapted its fare to the moods of the country. When one studio struck a responsive chord, others followed, so that there have been cycles of gangster movies, war movies, anti-racist movies, bad Westerns, "serious" Westerns, anti-Communist movies, Bible movies, and social problem movies. As the attitudes of the Americans have changed, the themes and content of the movies have changed, too.

---

7. Daniel J. Boorstin, *The Americans: The Democratic Experience* (New York: Vintage Books, 1974), p. 470.

Movies depend upon young people for a large share of their audience, and in turn, young people have learned from the movies how they might direct their lives and their relationships with the world and others about them. It is, however, not easy to discern exactly what the movies have taught several generations of American youth, or what American youth has learned from the movies. There is no clear, simple relationship between the two. Robert W. Wagner observed:

> The content of the films affects the motion-picture audience. This does not mean that the effects are simple, linear, or immediate. Certainly it is clear that immediate effects may be slight and that there is no reason to believe that movies are the prime cause of juvenile delinquency or divorce or any social ill. Their role may be to maintain present attitudes or outlooks or, indeed, to reinforce them. But motion pictures, like other mass media, are not innocuous. They maintain, reinforce, or shift learning.[8]

The meaning and the effect of a film may be very different from what its makers foresaw or intended. Audience interpretation of a film varies even from one geographic region to another, illustrating that the culture and history of people does give meaning to their experiences.

Themes treated by movies and how well or how poorly they have been handled have varied widely. In 1935 W. W. Charters analyzed five hundred feature films and found that three themes accounted for seventy-two per cent of the films he classified: love, crime, and sex. Other observers of the film have concluded that in the mid 1940s, Americans were presented with an appealing but perhaps over-simplified picture of life and its struggles. Heroes were usually men who found themselves in strange places populated by untrustworthy people, and usually had to face adversity and resolve conflict. Typically, the conflict and the dangers resided not within the individual but within the environment. The hero could and usually did overcome them. There is no doubt that many such films were specifically designed to convince the viewer that one way was better than another, especially during the World War II era.

Movies as Propaganda

After the U.S. entered World War II, Pres. Roosevelt, who believed that the movies could be used effectively to inform and influence the American people, instructed Lowell Mellett to establish the necessary channel of communication between the government and the motion picture industry. By June 1942, a set of guidelines was issued—the "Manual for the Motion Picture Industry." Later in the year, a Media Division was established in the Bureau of Intelligence of the Office of War Information. The division prepared weekly summaries and analyses of Hollywood's major films.

The "Manual for the Motion Picture Industry," according to recent historical accounts, was representative of the social and intellectual ferment of the 1930s.

---

8. Robert W. Wagner, "Motion Pictures in Relation to Social Controls," in *Mass Media and Education: The Fifty-third Yearbook of the National Society for the Study of Education*, Part II, ed. Nelson B. Henry (Chicago: University of Chicago Press, 1954), pp. 63–64.

Many believed that the nation's ills, tensions, and dislocations would be improved by a "commitment to some large ideal or movement." For many, "the war seemed to offer that unifying commitment and reduced intellectual content to an *uncritical adulation* of America and [its] Allies."⁹

Movies were expected to depict the war in clear and simple terms: the common person fighting against fascism in all its forms. The movie version of Hemingway's *For Whom the Bell Tolls* was criticized for instance because it depicted the Spanish Loyalists as violent. Musicals and comedies were not encouraged because they did not emphasize the gravity of the war. Neither were movies that portrayed "the melodramatic exploits of swash-buckling American heroes who conquered the enemy single-handed," for that kind of activity was contrary to the concept of teamwork being promulgated. Movies about sabotage and espionage were discouraged because "the overemphasis on an unseen enemy at work within this country was poor diet for a nation striving to become fully united in order to fight the most important war in its history."¹⁰ There was also fear that such movies would adversely affect many innocent aliens. Movie producers sometimes disagreed with the government attitudes. Walter Wanger, newly elected president of the Academy of Motion Picture Arts and Sciences, complained in 1943 that the government had an inadequate understanding of both the motion picture industry and the American public. From the filmmakers' viewpoint, "the film with a purpose must pass the same test that the escapist film more easily passes—theater-goers must want to see the picture."¹¹ Americans simply would not tolerate obvious propaganda and boring movies.

As the war took its course, the needs and the mood of the American public changed and Hollywood responded. In the early years of the war, there was a need to offer movies that informed as well as inspired the public. After 1943, newsreels and other media satisfied the need for information about the war. From Hollywood Americans wanted entertainment.

Film critics agree that Hollywood did offer a number of sensitive, informative, and realistic films about the war. Yet not all officials in the OWI were satisfied with Hollywood war productions. After Dorothy Jones analyzed more than 1,300 films made in the first three years of the war, she concluded that the filmmakers had had no "experience in making films dealing with actual social problems" and that when they were asked to produce films that would educate the public they "did not know where to begin."¹² In her judgment, no more than forty-five or fifty of those films contributed significantly to Americans' and their allies' understanding of the war and its issues. Jones also objected to how Hollywood depicted the war's effect on American youth. During the 1940s juvenile delinquency was increasing.

---

9. Clayton R. Koppes and Gregory D. Black, "What to Show the World: The Office of War Information and Hollywood, 1942–45," *Journal of American History* 64:1 (June 1977), p. 92.

10. Dorothy Jones, quoted in Garth Jowett, *Film: The Democratic Art* (Boston: Little, Brown and Co., 1976), p. 317.

11. Ibid., p. 308.

12. Ibid., p. 319.

Although Hollywood turned its attention to the problem, government reviewers complained that it portrayed the situation sensationally and failed to provide solutions.

Educational Films

To provide an effective alternative to the typical orientation lectures given to teach recruits about the issues of the war, director Frank Capra was asked to make the series, "Why We Fight." All seven Capra films were shown to new recruits and distributed for showing to the Allies. The first in the series, *Prelude to War,* was, at President Roosevelt's suggestion, also shown to American moviegoers. The "Why We Fight" films eventually became the basis of research studies that "encouraged some of the most sophisticated theoretical discussions of the factors involved in film communication effectiveness then known." According to Garth Jowett:

> Several of the films were used extensively in a series of studies by the Experimental Section of the Research Branch in the War Department's Information and Education Division, as part of a large-scale attempt to utilize modern sociopsychological research techniques in the evaluation of educational and "indoctrinational" films. Significantly, these wartime experiments heralded a new age of research into the uses of instructional media, and involved several prominent experimental and educational psychologists.[13]

The researchers also laid the foundation for further investigations into the uses and effect of media by looking into the long- and short-term results of propaganda films, the advantages and disadvantages of presenting one or both sides of controversial issues, and the merits of allowing the audience to participate in teaching-learning situations.

During the war, the government produced more than 5,000 movies. Some were propaganda films; many were training films. After the war, there were thousands of movies available for use in classroom's at every level of schooling. Most of the films made for school use were in social studies, even though some critics believe that educational films (movie or television) would be "more effective in science and engineering courses than in social sciences and humanities courses."[14] Many educators lament that films are not used properly. Often they are seen as supplements to, or substitutes for, what the teacher does. Rarely are they integrated into what the teacher has planned. How the movie has influenced school audience is often overlooked. Ruth C. Peterson and L. L. Thurstone, however, concluded "that movies have a definite, lasting effect on the attitudes of children regarding nationality, race, crime, war, capital punishment, and prohibition."[15] Educators also have overlooked the fact that students have to learn

13. Jowett, *Film: The Democratic Art,* p. 321.

14. Wilbert J. McKeachie, "The Impact of the New Media on Other Aspects of American Education; Higher Education," in *The New Media and Education,* ed. Peter H. Rossi and Bruce J. Biddle (Garden City, N.Y.: Anchor Books, 1967), pp. 293–294.

15. Ruth A. Inglis, *Freedom of the Movies* (Chicago: University of Chicago Press, 1947), p. 21.

how to learn from films just as they have to learn how to learn from books. Further, getting concepts and information via the film may be detrimental to student performance if that performance is to be measured by paper and pencil tests.

Television

In 1948—the year that "Hopalong Cassidy" came to television—there were thirty-six TV stations and just over a million home receivers in the United States. By 1970 there were nearly 650 commercial stations and 80 million sets. By 1975, television was as widespread as indoor plumbing; at least 97 percent of the homes in the United States had one or more sets. It is now estimated that more than 20 percent of the homes in the United States have two or more sets, which are turned on between five and seven hours a day. By the time most children reach kindergarten age, they have already spent more time learning about their world from television than they will spend in college classrooms to receive a college degree. An 18-year-old will have spent about 11,000 hours in school, but between 15,000 and 22,000 hours watching television. Nearly a third of Americans rely on television as their sole source of news, and almost two-thirds say it is their prime source of news.

The Impact of Television

The effect of television on its audience is less easy to state. Max Lerner noted in 1957 that "the psychic and cultural deposit left on young and old alike by the broadcasting arts is not likely to be resolved easily."[16] He quoted a TV columnist, Harriet Van Horne, who predicted dire effects some twenty years ago:

> Our people are becoming less literate by the minute. . . . As old habits decline, such as reading books and thinking thoughts, TV will absorb their time. By the twenty-first century our people doubtless will be squint-eyed, hunch-backed, and fond of the dark. Conversation will be a lost art. People will simply tell each other jokes. . . . The chances are that the grandchild of the Television Age won't know how to read this.[17]

An imaginative assessment of the fantastic potential power of television is the basis of Jerzy Kosinski's novel, *Being There*. Its anti-hero, Chance, has spent his childhood, his youth, his adolescence, and a number of his adult years confined to a back room of a house set in a garden surrounded by high walls. Chance has a television set. It and the garden comprise his entire world. Through turning the dial, he has been able to control most of his world. When chance turns Chance out into the world, he adjusts and responds by behaving as he saw others behave on television. Though he does not understand the questions put to him, his replies are consistently interpreted as brilliant and incisive. At the novel's end, Chance is

---

16. Max Lerner, *America as a Civilization* (New York: Simon and Schuster, 1961), p. 843.
17. Ibid., pp. 843–844.

being selected as a vice-presidential candidate, and he has no idea of what is happening to him.[18]

While Kosinski's portrayal of Chance and his non-experiences may border on the fantastic, some realistic assessments of the impact of television are nearly as forceful. For instance, Henry Malcolm has noted that adults and children view the television set differently:

> Every adult over the age of thirty-five has seen the entrance of the television set into the house, not as another piece of furniture but as an ultimate source of information about the world beyond the home.
>
> The vast majority of children, on the other hand, see the television set as a part of the home environment—like beds, chairs, and record players.[19]

The difference between the experiences of adults and youth with television is significant. From the point of view of the adult, the television has revolutionized the world. For youth, it is a device that allows them to bring what adults perceive as the world "out there" to themselves on command simply by turning a dial. With the help of television, youth believe that they can make reality conform to what they want. If Malcolm's contention that youth consider traditional pressures to conform to be unwarranted and illegitimate invasions of their world is correct, then we *are* witnessing a new world and a new generation.

As Marshall McLuhan has pointed out, most innovations in the media have been seen as extensions of what already existed. The movie was to be an illustrated and moving book. Similarly, television was to be defined by radio: "a radio with pictures." However, television turned out to be much more. It brought many experiences to the Americans in ways they had never before had them. Public events of all sorts—political conventions, rallies, riots, sports events, artistic performances—could all be seen and experienced "live." There were sometimes advantages to observing the event rather than being there. For many adults, television provides an easier, better, or more economical way to view many events. For children, however,—the "post-television generation"—television is not just a medium that brings an event to them. While such programs as *Sesame Street* attempt to involve young children in learning, objections have been raised to the short segments that make up program formats, for these seem to encourage children's short attention spans. Classroom teachers find it difficult to compete with the constantly changing, highly visual aspects of educational television programming, and its lasting benefits have been called into question by educational researchers.

Educators can continue to express their difficulty in even defining what the media are (as is done in the most recent *Handbook on Research in Teaching*) but the media will continue to influence their students. Jacques Ellul contends that propaganda has the power to create people who are not comfortable unless they are "integrated in the mass," people who reject "critical judgments, choices, and

---

18. Jerzy Kosinski, *Being There* (New York: Bantam Books, 1972).
19. Henry Malcolm, *Generation of Narcissus* (Boston: Little, Brown and Co., 1971), p. 4.

differentiations" because they prefer to hold on to the "clear certainties" the media provided.[20] As long as the media provide students with "clear certainties," schools will encounter many difficulties, especially if they persist in seeing the media as simply an improved way to deliver information.

The Educational Message

A survey of the many educational messages that the various media present to their readers, listeners, and viewers reveals that Americans have a surfeit of educational problems and programs. For a generation, all areas of schooling—aims of education, curriculum, teaching methods, the ways in which schools are organized and administered, and how schools are financed—have been revised, criticized, and sometimes revised again. Yet, not too many schools appear to be significantly different from what they were a generation ago.

A quarter century ago, when the Supreme Court declared that segregation of students on the basis of race was unconstitutional, some were criticizing the schools for their lack of academic standards. A few years later, the Soviet Union successfully launched Sputnik and, as was related in Chapter Sixteen, Americans expected their schools to prepare an elite to enable the nation to compete successfully in both the arms and the space races. Then, busing of students was frequently proposed as the way to desegregate, if not integrate, the schools. Since then, Americans have had to try to balance two contradictory tendencies in their educational system: egalitarianism and elitism. As Christopher Lasch has recently stated the case, "the struggle over desegregation brought to the surface the inherent contradiction between the American commitment to universal education on the one hand, and the realities of a class society on the other."[21]

The Americans had fashioned an educational system designed to prepare youth for its economic system. Some were expected to participate as workers, while others were selected to be leaders and managers. As Americans were forced by circumstances to confront their ideal of equality of opportunity, many saw that non-white minorities and the poor were consistently denied the opportunity to achieve either educational or economic success.

For decades many were content to believe that supposed racial inferiority adequately explained why some failed to achieve educational or economic equality. However, as notions of racial inferiority lost their credibility in light of the theories and investigations of social scientists, new explanations for the failure to educate blacks and other minorities had to be found. The explanation most commonly accepted was "cultural deprivation." In some instances, this explanation provided a ready rationalization for the failures of many students: the students who failed came from culturally deprived backgrounds, and the schools had no effec-

20. Ibid., p. 146.
21. Christopher Lasch, *The Culture of Narcissism* (New York: W. W. Norton & Co., 1978), p. 142.

tive control over the cultural backgrounds of its students. However, cultural deprivation proved to be an explanation that differed significantly from that of racial inferiority. While there is not much that a society can do about racial inferiority there is much that a society can do about the conditions in which many of its people live. It can change those conditions, or it can attempt to fashion programs to enable people to overcome the disadvantages with which their cultural setting has handicapped them. Thus, during the 60s and 70s, Americans witnessed the inauguration of many programs designed to help individuals overcome their cultural disadvantages. It was presumed that these programs would equalize educational opportunity, defeat poverty, and bring about the Great Society.

Equality of Opportunity

The decision that the Supreme Court rendered in the Brown v. Board of Education case only declared that segregation of the races in schools was unconstitutional. It did not directly address other areas of segregation and racial discrimination in American society. It did, however, mark the growing Civil Rights movement. After a decade, the participants in the movement witnessed some measure of success. In 1964 Congress passed the Civil Rights Act, which declared that segregation on the basis of race in any enterprise covered by the Constitution's interstate commerce clause was illegal.

The Civil Rights Act of 1964 specified that the United States Commissioner of Education was to "conduct a survey and make a report to the President and the Congress, within two years of the enactment of this title, concerning the lack of availability of equal educational opportunities for individuals by reason of race, color, religion, or national origin in public educational institutions at all levels in the United States, its territories and possessions, and the District of Columbia."[22] In July, 1966, Commissioner Harold Howe II presented the report, *Equality of Educational Opportunity*. It quickly came to be known as the "Coleman Report," a name that identified the director of the study, James Coleman of Johns Hopkins University.

The Coleman Report paid particular attention to the educational opportunity available to six racial and ethnic groups: "Negroes, American Indians, Oriental Americans, Puerto Ricans living in the continental United States, Mexican Americans, and whites other than Mexican Americans and Puerto Ricans often called 'majority' or simply 'white'."[23] The investigation that Coleman and his associates conducted sought to gather information in four major areas. (1) It attempted to determine to what extent the various racial and ethnic groups were segregated from one another in the nation's public schools. (2) It tried to determine whether all schools did in fact offer equal educational opportunities to all students. To do this, several characteristics were examined: laboratories, textbooks, and libraries;

---

22. James S. Coleman, *et. al.*, *Equality of Educational Opportunity* (Washington, D.C.: U.S. Government Printing Office, 1966), p. iii.
    23. Ibid.

the curricula (academic, commercial, and vocational); teacher characteristics such as training and education, experience, salaries, attitudes, and verbal ability; and several student characteristics including socio-economic backgrounds, parents' education, academic goals, and other attitudinal measures. (3) The study attempted to determine how much students learned by examining the students' performances on standardized tests. (4) Coleman tried to ascertain what the relationship was between student achievement and the kinds of schools students attended.

Coleman found that a full decade after the Brown v. Board of Education decision a great measure of segregation and inequality persisted in the nation's schools. It was reported that

> In its desegregation decision of 1954, the Supreme Court held that separate schools for Negro and white children are inherently unequal. This survey finds that, when measured by that yardstick, American public education remains largely unequal in most regions of the country, including all those where Negroes form any significant proportion of the population.[24]

A majority of the nation's children were attending schools that had not been desegregated. Among all groups, white children were the most segregated. Among the minority groups, black children were the most segregated.

While the conclusions of the Coleman Report were many and frequently qualified, the conclusion that was accepted by many readers of the report was that suggesting that racial integration of the schools would not harm white pupils but would help minority students. It was maintained in the Report that

> . . . It appears that a pupil's achievement is strongly related to the educational backgrounds and aspirations of the other students in the school. Only crude measures of these variables were used (principally the proportion of pupils with encyclopedias in the home and the proportion planning to go to college). Analysis indicates, however, that children from a given family background, when put in schools of different social composition, will achieve at quite different levels. This effect is again less for white pupils than for any minority group other than Orientals. Thus, if a white pupil from a home that is strongly and effectively supportive of education is put in a school where most pupils do not come from such homes, his achievement will be little different than if he were in a school composed of others like himself. But if a minority pupil from a home without much educational strength is put with schoolmates with strong educational backgrounds, his achievement is likely to increase.[25]

Although only three of the 737 pages of the Coleman Report were devoted to the possible benefits students would enjoy from attendance at racially mixed schools, the Report was frequently used to support claims that black children would benefit by being bused into predominantly white schools. As Seymour W. Itzkoff has observed, the Coleman Report "was the statistical source of much of

---

24. Ibid., p. 3.
25. Ibid., p. 22.

the pressure for busing."[26] In 1971 the Supreme Court decided that busing for the sake of ending a dual system of education was constitutional (Swann v. Charlotte-Mecklenburg Board of Education).

Attempts to desegregate schools by busing have met with considerable resistance in many communities, and the resistance often receives attention from the mass media. However, the attention given to busing in the media may have given Americans a distorted impression of the issue. Manouchehr Pedram has recently reported that "statistically, 40 percent of the school-aged population or twenty million youngsters are bused daily; only about 3 percent of this number are bused for desegregation purposes."[27] The *Eleventh Annual Gallup Poll of the Public's Attitudes Toward the Public Schools* (1979) suggests that busing may not be a major issue for the majority of Americans. In that poll, only 9 percent of the respondents declared that "integration/busing (combined)" was one of "the biggest problems with which the public schools in [their] community must deal." Ahead of busing were five other school-related problems: lack of discipline (24 percent); use of drugs (13 percent); lack of proper financial support (12 percent); poor curriculum and poor standards (11 percent); and difficulty in getting good teachers (10 percent).[28]

Compensatory Education. In 1965 the Congress enacted the Elementary and Secondary Education Act—"an Act to strengthen and improve educational quality and educational opportunities." Since then Congress has provided between $1 and $2 billion a year for compensatory education programs under Title I of the Act. Congress hoped to achieve three major goals: (1) to provide supplementary funds for those school districts that enrolled large numbers of students from low-income families; (2) to make funds available for special services and programs in schools with students whose achievement was below average; and (3) to fund programs that would enhance the cognitive, social, and emotional development of the students.

Title I programs were aimed at all levels of schooling, from preschool to college. Through these programs a variety of educational services were introduced into many schools. Besides providing resources for revising curricula and providing guidance counseling services, there were attempts to tend to the medical, nutritional, social, and psychological needs of disadvantaged students. To increase educational opportunity at the college level, open admissions programs were instituted whereby traditional entrance requirements were suspended. At the beginning of the educational ladder, Project Head Start, probably the most popular of the many programs, was designed to ready disadvantaged youth for the ele-

---

26. Seymour W. Itzkoff, *A New Public Education* (New York: David McKay, 1976), p. 153.

27. Joseph F. Callahan and Leonard H. Clark (eds), *Innovations and Issues in Education* (New York: Macmillan, 1977), p. 139.

28. George H. Gallup, "The Eleventh Annual Gallup Poll of the Public's Attitudes Toward the Public Schools," *Phi Delta Kappan,* Vol. 1, No. 1 (September, 1979), p. 34.

mentary school by providing them with cultural and educational experiences that they were typically denied.

Although the federal government provided up to $2 billion a year in Title I funds for compensatory education programs, that amount was relatively small compared to total expenditures for education. Title I funds have represented one third of the total funds made available for elementary and secondary education by the federal government. In some school districts Title I funds accounted for nearly a third of the district's expenditures. However, Title I funds comprise only 3 percent of all the money spent for elementary and secondary education in the nation.

The Moynihan Report. As Americans seemed to commit themselves to equality of opportunity, some attention was turned to non-school factors. For example, in 1965 Daniel P. Moynihan, then Assistant Secretary of Labor in the Johnson administration, published *The Negro Family: A Case for National Action.* While Moynihan's study drew much unfavorable public attention because many believed the study reenforced racial prejudices and misconceptions, it did not offer much more than an update and rewrite of what Gunnar Myrdal had described a generation earlier.[29] The Moynihan Report described the variety of difficulties suffered by many black families because of past and present discriminatory practices, and how those families, especially in urban areas, were in a situation that was "getting worse, not better. . . .the gap between the Negro and most other groups in American society [was] widening."

Following a model provided by Myrdal, the Moynihan Report presented the claim that the lower-class black families were caught in a vicious cycle. As black males were denied economic opportunities, their abilities to maintain and support strong and stable families decreased dramatically. As the families disintegrated, the opportunities available to its members diminished further. The Report concluded by urging that the United States adopt a policy "to bring the Negro American to full and equal sharing in the responsibilities and rewards of citizenship." It further urged that programs "be designed to have the effect, directly or indirectly, of enhancing the stability and resources of the Negro American family."[30]

A Reassessment. By the early 70s it was clear that it was easier to declare that equality of educational opportunity should be achieved than it was to achieve the desired results. In *Inequality: A Reassessment of the Effect of Family and Schooling in America* (1972) Christopher Jencks and his associates at the Center for Educational Policy Research at Harvard University offered their examination and analysis of the relationship between education and economic status. They discov-

---

29. Gunnar Myrdal, *An American Dilemma: The Negro Problem and Modern Democracy* (New York: Harper and Brothers, 1944).

30. *The Negro Family: The Case for National Action* (Washington, D.C.: U.S. Government Printing Office, 1965), p. 48.

ered a widespread belief that poverty could be eliminated through educational reforms. Folk wisdom maintained that middle-class children rarely wound up poor and that poor children could be led out of poverty if they were provided with compensatory educational programs. Thus, it seemed that compensatory education and true integration of all classes and racial and ethnic groups in the schools would enable all children to learn the skills they needed to escape poverty. The Jencks report concluded that the commonly-held beliefs about the relationship between poverty and education were not entirely true, and that the vast economic and social differences among the people in the United States could not be eliminated solely through educational reforms. According to this report,

> We have seen that educational opportunities, cognitive skills, educational credentials, occupational status, income, and job satisfaction are unequally distributed. We have not, however, been very successful in explaining most of these inequalities. The association between one variable of inequality and another is usually quite weak, which means that equalizing one thing is unlikely to have much effect on the degree of inequality in other areas.[31]

The evaluations of compensatory education programs that Jencks and his associates reviewed showed that students in those programs "do worse than comparison groups as often as they do better."[32] Those evaluations may underscore the fact that in many instances compensatory education programs did not employ new methods and materials but frequently assumed "that what disadvantaged children need is pretty much what they have been getting, only more: more teachers, more specialists, more books, more audio-visual devices, more trips to museums, and so forth."[33]

Paying the School Bill

Integration and compensatory education may be the most popular strategies (but certainly not the only strategies) that have been employed for equalizing educational opportunity. A strategy that did not receive widespread attention until the late 70s is the financing of public education. While some were questioning traditional financing methods, others seemed to be trying to limit public school funds. The media brought this to the attention of the public during 1977–78 as they reported on the campaign of Howard A. Jarvis, Director of the United Organization of Taxpayers, to lower local property taxes in California. In the fall of 1977 Jarvis and his organization had succeeded in collecting more than 1.2 million signatures on a petition to place a proposition before the California voters that would limit property taxes. On June 6, 1978, the voters approved by a 2 to 1 margin what the entire nation then knew as Proposition 13. The three chief features of Proposition

---

31. Christopher Jencks, *et. al.*, *Inequality: A Reassessment of the Effect of Family and Schooling in America* (New York: Basic Books, 1972), p. 253.

32. Ibid., p. 94.

33. Ibid., p. 107.

13 were: (1) the stipulation that the tax on property could not be greater than 1 percent of its fair market value; (2) specification that increases in the assessment of property could not be greater than 2 percent a year; and (3) the stipulation that the legislature could increase other taxes to compensate for any loss of revenue at the local level only if there were a two-thirds vote in favor of such an increase.

James W. Guthrie has explained that Proposition 13 effectively placed the responsibility and control of the public schools at the state level. Before Proposition 13 (1977–78) the state provided between 40 percent and 45 percent of the revenue for schools and over 50 percent of the schools' funds came from locally-levied property taxes. After Proposition 13 was passed it was estimated that 65 percent to 70 percent of the school funds would come from the state and the local portion was expected to fall to 28 percent or 21 percent. What was not funded by either the state or local government was funded by the federal government. Proposition 13 took away "effective discretion over the raising of revenues" from the local school districts. As Guthrie states, "for practical purposes, California has a mandatory statewide property tax, and school boards will not be able to raise or lower it."[34]

The longstanding practice of supporting schools in each of the states (except Hawaii) with locally-levied property taxes has served to maintain the belief that schools were locally controlled. It also provided the schools with some protection from the fluctuations of the nation's economy. In California the proceeds from the property tax increased faster than the rate of inflation. For over four decades there was no decline in property tax yields, even during recessions. However, as the portion of the schools' budget supported by the state increases, it will be more subject to changes in the economy.

The case of California is not entirely unique. Efforts have been made in several states to have the state assume more or even total responsibility for the financing of public education as a way of eliminating the inequalities between poor and rich districts. Observers such as Charles S. Benson drew attention to the disparities among districts in the 1960s.[35] In 1971 the California Supreme Court (Serrano v. Priest) ruled that it was unconstitutional for the quality of education to vary from one district to another because of variations in wealth. In June 1972 the United States Supreme Court agreed to hear a similar case (Rodriguez v. San Antonio), and in March, 1973 reversed the decision of Texas District Court. That decision was a defeat for both those who believed that funds other than local property taxes were needed for the schools and for those who believed that only total state support of the schools would remedy inequalities among poor and rich districts.

Adequate support of the public schools remains a problem in the 80s. Many cities have seen their problems increase while their tax bases have decreased.

---

34. James W. Guthrie, "Proposition 13 and the Future of California's Schools," *Phi Delta Kappan*, Vol. 60, No. 1 (September, 1978), p. 13.

35. Charles H. Benson, *The Cheerful Prospect* (Boston: Houghton Mifflin, 1965).

People in the suburbs sometimes believe they have no responsibility to pay for education in the cities, complain that their taxes are already too high, and resist any fundamental changes in the tax structure. Yet the 1979 Gallup Poll on Public Schools reveals that only two problems are considered to be more important than adequate financial support for the schools. While only 12 percent of the people indicated that "lack of proper financial support" was a major problem confronting the schools, it seems significant that those surveyed indicated (by a 4 to 3 margin) that they were opposed to placing a ceiling on school budgets. Those in favor of a ceiling pointed to waste in the schools. Those opposed indicated that the quality of education was an important consideration.[36]

The last quarter century has been a period in which there have been many significant changes in our society. Whether we look at social or economic issues, all that seems clear is the uncertainty we face. Old as well as new issues will have to be faced. While it can be argued that much has been accomplished, there is little doubt that equality of opportunity will demand further attention. In the fall of 1979, Linda Brown Smith, who was eleven years old when the Supreme Court decided that she had a right to attend an all-white school, was among a group of parents in Topeka asking a U.S. District Court to hear their complaint that the Topeka schools have not yet been desegregated. The Court ruled in the parents' favor.

The Challenge of the Eighties

While Americans may not have found a way of extending equality of opportunity to all who attend the public schools, there is an awareness that did not exist a few decades ago of the needs and aspirations of its many peoples. During the 60s and 70s, it was seen that there were many ethnic groups that had special educational needs and interests, and there is now recognition that English is not the primary language of all Americans. The creation of the United States Department of Education (1979) also specified that there would be an Office of Bilingual Education and Minority Languages Affairs.

To some degree, the work and view of the schools have been expanded so that the needs of those who were previously neglected have begun to receive some attention. Public Law 94-142, passed in 1975 and sometimes mistakenly called the "mainstreaming law," recognized that only about 50 percent of the 8 million handicapped children in the United States were receiving the educational services they needed. The law attempted to ensure that all children who need special educational services—the mentally retarded, the hard of hearing, deaf, the physically impaired, health impaired, speech impaired, visually handicapped, emotionally disturbed, and the specific learning disabled—would receive such services. The law requires that the handicapped child have access to an educational

---

36. George H. Gallup, "The Eleventh Annual Gallup Poll of the Public's Attitudes Toward the Public Schools," p. 38.

setting that is best suited to his or her needs and is as close to a regular classroom as is possible in "the least restricted environment."

How Americans will address the contradictory tendencies in their educational system in the next decade remains to be seen. Certainly, the recent past indicates that educational reforms and emphases are frequently short-lived. In the 60s there were many discussions about decentralization and community control of the schools.[37] Soon, those discussions were overshadowed by the attempts to have the states (and even the federal government) assume more responsibility for the schools. While recognition has been given to the claims and needs of various groups, there has developed a "back to basics" movement, a movement that suggests that there are only a few simple and readily-identifiable subjects and skills that schools must teach and that are appropriate for all students. In the 60s and early 70s a "free-school" or alternative-school movement developed. Unlike traditional schools, alternative schools frequently gave students the responsibility for deciding what they wanted to study, and maintained that effective and meaningful learning could take place in several nontraditional settings. Some of the alternatives have been incorporated into the public schools and some have quietly disappeared.[38]

Whether public schools can and should continue as they have for at least five generations is a question that Americans will have to address as they face the social changes that their economy promises to bring in the 80s. Certainly, there have been a number of revisions and reforms in public schooling. Whether more reforms and revisions will be sufficient or whether a totally new institution will come to take the place of public schooling is the order of question we should begin to ask.

---

37. One of the most well known proposals for community control was the Bundy Plan that was presented in 1967. See: Mayor's Advisory Panel on Decentralization of the New York City's Schools, Reconnection for Learning: A Community School System for New York City (1967). For discussions of the topic in general see: Marilyn Gittell and Alan G. Hevesi (eds.), The Politics of Urban Education (New York: Frederick A. Praeger, 1969).

38. Margaret Shapiro, "Area's 'Free Schools' on Way Out," Washington Post (November 9, 1979), p. B 1.

PART V

A New World and a New Generation

In the last generation, Americans have witnessed many changes in their society. They have also encountered many paradoxes and contradictions as they looked at their schools. In the years immediately after World War II, they were told—and they believed—that schooling was more important than ever before. The defense requirements of the nation as well as the requirements of a post-industrial economy seemed to demand increased investments in the range of schooling available to Americans and in the quality of the schools. Later they were told by Ivan Illich and others that they should "de-school" their society. Others have proclaimed that the ills of school and society would be quickly remedied if only the schools could be pushed back to the basics.

But while the schools are being told to return to the basics of the previous era, the society has entered a new age. Whether schools will be important in the next generation and whether schools will even survive remain to be seen. At present, schools are neither the most pleasant nor the safest places to be. Too frequently they are the sites of robberies, gang fights, and even homicides, and the school officials are trying to figure out why attendance is declining. The National Institute of Education has found it necessary to study violence in the nation's schools. According to the NIE report, the annual cost of school crime is $200 million a year. More than 25 percent of the nation's schools are likely to be vandalized in any given month.

Whether schools can be reformed to meet the requirements of the next generation is a moot question. At the 1978 Educational Future Conference, Charles Weingartner observed:

> The history of school reform is a depressing chronicle in itself. For all of the efforts made by one person or another, or one institution or another, in one place or another at one time or another, there is virtually nothing to show for it. The relentlessness of the inertia in the conventional school bureaucracy is truly impressive. It has been almost totally unaffected by dramatic changes in society resulting from technological developments, by knowledge of how human learning proceeds, and by the efforts of informed, and even subsidized school reformers. Even church conventions and prison conventions are characterized by more innovation than are school conventions. By and large, schools, both public and private, at all "grade levels," have been impervious to change from within and without.[1]

The Ford Foundation's report on its success in implementing school reform

---

1. Charles Weingartner, "No More Pencils, No More Books, No More Teachers' Dirty Looks." Paper delivered at Educational Future Conference, University of Houston (October 21, 1978), typescript. Used with permission.

between 1960 and 1970 supports Weingartner's conclusion. After spending $30 million, the Ford Foundation could point to few significant changes in public schooling.

Reform, if it comes, according to Weingartner, will not result from a new and better educational philosophy or a new social vision but from the collapse of the public school system. In the future the public schools will have to face the consequences of what he terms the "big X"—one ascending line that represents the increasing cost of schooling, and a descending line that represents the declining size of the school population, a decline due not only to the birth rate but to the loss of faith in the public schools by its traditional supporters, the middle class. The collapse that has been predicted need not be a catastrophe. It can, claims Weingartner, be an opportunity to use what we know about technology, computers, and computer-based instruction to teach just about anyone anything they might want to know.

Doubtless there will be (and are) those who will claim that a computer in every home will not mean the end of public schooling, even though each home in the country could be equipped with a mini-computer for less than half of what it now costs to maintain a student in school for nine months. But then Socrates judged writing to be a debasement of human speech and a threat to memory, and the medieval schoolmen viewed the book as an inferior sort of manuscript.

A Guide to Educational Research

This guide has been prepared for those who may want to investigate topics presented in the text or other educational topics of interest in further depth. It includes references to works that will be useful to those who are interested in the history of education, current educational problems, and other areas. References are to standard works that are commonly available in college and university libraries and in most public libraries.

For those who are interested in comparing the development of public education in their states to the development of public education in the nation or to the other states, a good beginning is Jim B. Pearson and Edgar Fuller (eds.), *Education in the United States: Historical Development and Outlook,* Volume I, (Washington, D.C.: National Education Association, 1969). Its companion, Volume II, *Education in the States: Nationwide Development Since 1900* is a good beginning for more recent developments. Together these volumes provide good summaries of the organization and development of public education in the states. They also provide references to the standard and the detailed histories of education for each of the fifty states.

Good accounts of the issues and problems attendant to teaching in general and to the teaching of the various school subjects, as well as a review of the research related to those issues and problems, can be found in Robert M. W. Travers (ed.), *Second Handbook of Research on Teaching* (Chicago: Rand McNally, 1973). Still very useful is the earlier edition: Nathaniel L. Gage (ed.), *Handbook of Research on Teaching* (Chicago: Rand McNally, 1963).

Information and bibliography on teaching as well as other educational topics such as school surveys, school libraries, reading, school transportation (busing), and testing can be found in one of the four editions of the *Encyclopedia of Educational Research,* completed under the auspices of the American Educational Research Association. The complete citations for these four volumes are: Walter S. Monroe (ed.), *Encyclopedia of Educational Research* (New York: Macmillan, 1941); Walter S. Monroe (ed.), *Encyclopedia of Educational Research,* rev. ed., (New York: Macmillan, 1950); Chester W. Harris (ed.), *Encyclopedia of Educational Research,* 3rd. ed., (New York: Macmillan, 1960); and Robert L. Ebel (ed.), *Encyclopedia of Educational Research,* 4th. ed., (New York: Macmillan, 1970). A fifth edition should soon appear. Comparison of articles on the same topic in the several editions can provide one with an overview of its historical development. At the end of each article in the *Encyclopedia* there is typically an extensive bibliography of the best work in the area. The American Educational Research Association has also established an annual *Review of Research in Education.* The first issue in this series appeared in 1973. In these annual reviews readers can find information and bibliography on a variety of educational topics, including learning and instructional sequence, the impact of school resources on students, the process of organizational change in schools, test theory, and the impact of policy decisions on schools.

Less compact than the works already cited are the *Yearbooks* of the National Society for the Study of Education, which have been published since 1902 and, as a series, cover just about every educational topic imaginable; the *Yearbook of Education,* which began in 1932 and became the *World Yearbook of Education* in 1965, and the Teachers College, Columbia University Contributions to Education, a set that now contains nearly one thousand volumes.

Other useful works are: Edward W. Smith, *et al.* (eds.), *The Educator's Encyclopedia* (Englewood Cliffs, New Jersey: Prentice-Hall, 1961); Lee C. Deighton (ed.), *The Encyclopedia of Education,* 10 volumes (New York: Crowell-Collier, 1971); and Paul Monroe (ed.), *A Cyclopedia of Education,* 5 volumes, (New York: Macmillan, 1911). While Monroe's *Cyclopedia* is over half a century old, it is still useful and interesting. From it one can see how education, as a field, was conceptualized and organized at the turn of the century, and how that basic conceptualization and organization has endured. Contributors to the *Cyclopedia* were those who gave modern public education much of its shape and character.

Biographical sources for leaders in American education, past and present, are plentiful. Two that are readily available are *Who's Who in American Education* and John F. Ohles (ed.), *Biographical Dictionary of American Educators,* 3 volumes (Westport, Connecticut: Greenwood Press, 1978). For material on those in the field of education as well as those in related areas, one or more of the following should be consulted: Maxine Block (ed.), *Current Biography: Who's News and Why* (New York: H. W. Wilson, 1942) and/or one of the supplementary Yearbooks; *Who Was Who in America,* which covers historical figures from 1607 to the present; *Who's Who in America; Who's Who,* which has been in existence for over one hundred and thirty years; *Who Was Who,* a companion to *Who's Who;* and the original *Dictionary of American Biography* and its more recent supplements.

In recent years many directories to works by and about blacks and other minority groups have appeared. The compilations of materials of women and women's studies are increasing rapidly. Some recent and useful works are Edward T. James, *et al.* (eds.), *Notable American Women, 1607–1950: A Biographical Dictionary,* 3 volumes (Cambridge, Massachusetts: Belknap Press, 1971), and Patricia O'Connor (ed.), *Women: A Selected Bibliography* (Springfield, Ohio: Wittenberg University, 1973), which lists books and articles under several categories: Anthropology and Biology; Psychology; Economics; Social Condition and Theory; Law and Political Science; History; Biographies and Autobiographies; and Education. Also useful are Audrey B. Davis (ed.), *Bibliography on Women: With Special Emphasis on Their Roles in Science and Society* (New York: Science History Publications, 1974), and Helen Rippier Wheeler, *Womanhood Media: Current Resources About Women* (Metuchen, New Jersey: Scarecrow Press, 1972).

A good beginning for literature on minority groups is Jack F. Kinton, *American Ethnic Groups and the Revival of Cultural Pluralism,* 4th. ed., (Aurora, Illinois: Social Science and Sociological Resources, 1974). It includes direction to books and articles on the various ethnic groups in the United States and references to works on race relations and ethnic group theory. For literature on various aspects of the experiences of American Indians and black Americans, appropriate sections of the *Harvard Guide to American History* should be consulted (a full citation appears below). The reader may also want to consult *The Negro in America : A Bibliography,* compiled by Elizabeth W. Miller and Mary L. Fisher (Cambridge: Harvard University Press, 1970).

Several excellent bibliographies pertaining to American Indians are available. A superb bibliography that contains a listing of the library of a former Commissioner of Indian Affairs is Carolyn E. Wolf and Karen R. Folk (eds.), *Indians of North and South America: A Bibliography based on the collection of the Willard E. Yager Library-Museum, Hartwick College, Oneonta, N.Y.* (Metuchen, N.J.: The Scarecrow Press, 1977). William Nelson Fenton's *American Indian and White Relations to 1830: Needs and Opportunities for Study: an Essay* (Chapel Hill: University of North Carolina Press, 1957) provides a selected bibliography that brings together, in one list, studies of Indian-white relations in both the Humanities and the Social Sciences. The U.S. Department of the Interior has published the *Biographical and Historical Index of American Indians and Persons Involved in Indian Affairs,* 8 volumes (Boston: G.K. Hall, 1966), which is a subject catalog developed by the Bureau of Indian Affairs. Another extremely helpful volume is *The American Indian in Graduate Studies: A Bibliography of Theses and Dissertations* (New York Museum of the American Indian—Heye Foundation, 1957, 1974). The second of the two volumes contains an index to both.

Many like to examine documents from the period they are studying. For those who do there are many good collections. A recent and very ambitious collection is Sol Cohen (ed.), *Education in the United States: A Documentary History,* 5 volumes (New York: Random House, 1974). Cohen provides not only an extensive collection that covers the last four centuries, but also some very useful introductory essays. Other standard collections are: John Hardin Best and Robert T. Sidwell (eds.), *The American Legacy of Learning: Readings in the History of Education* (Philadelphia: J. B. Lippincott, 1967); Daniel Calhoun (ed.), *The Education of Americans: A Documentary History* (Boston: Houghton Mifflin, 1969); Ellwood P. Cubberley (ed.), *Readings in Public Education in the United States: A*

Collection of Sources and Readings to Illustrate the History of Educational Practice and Progress in the United States (Boston: Houghton Mifflin, 1934); Carl H. Gross and Charles C. Chandler (eds.), *The History of American Education Through Readings* (Boston: D. C. Heath, 1964); Edgar W. Knight and Clifton L. Hall (eds.), *Readings in American Educational History* (New York: Appleton-Century-Crofts, 1951); S. Alexander Rippa (ed.), *Educational Ideas in America: A Documentary History* (New York: David McKay, 1969); David B. Tyack (ed.), *Turning Points in American Educational History* (Waltham, Massachusetts: Blaisdell, 1967); and Rena L. Vassar (ed.), *Social History of American Education,* 2 volumes (Chicago: Rand McNally, 1965).

The standard collection devoted to education in the South is Edgar W. Knight (ed.), *A Documentary History of Education in the South Before 1860,* 5 volumes (Chapel Hill, North Carolina: University of North Carolina Press, 1949-1953).

An outstanding collection on American youth is Robert H. Bremner, *et al.* (eds.), *Children and Youth in America: A Documentary History,* 3 volumes (Cambridge, Massachusetts: Harvard University Press, 1970).

Periodical literature on education is more than abundant. Direction to articles either by topic or by author can be found in the *Education Index* which has been published continuously since 1929. For identification of earlier articles there are: *Poole's Index,* which covers most of the nineteenth century (1802-1881); *Poole's Supplement* (1882-1907); and the *Nineteenth Century Reader's Guide* (1890-1899).

There are hundreds of journals and periodicals that may be of interest and use. The following is a selected list of generally available educational, historical, and other journals with the year of their first issue. *American Historical Review* (1895); *Educational Forum* (1936); *Educational Record* (1920); *Educational Research* (1958); *Educational Review* (1948); *Educational Studies* (1970); *Educational Theory* (1951); *Elementary School Journal* (1900); *Historical Journal* (1958); *Historical Review* (1952); *History* (1912); *History of Childhood Quarterly* (1973), which became the *Journal of Psychohistory* in 1976; *History of Education Quarterly* (1961); *Journal of American History* (1964); *Journal of Education* (1875); *Journal of Educational Psychology* (1910); *Journal of Educational Research* (1920); *Journal of Social History* (1967); *Journal of Contemporary History* (1966) became *Journal of Popular History* in 1967; *Phi Delta Kappan* (1915); *Paedagogical Historica* (1961); *Mississippi Valley Historical Review* (1914), which became *Journal of American History* in 1964; *Review of Education* (1975); *Review of Educational Research* (1931); *Women's Studies Abstracts* (1972); and *Women's Studies Newsletter* (1972).

The standard guide to materials in American history is Frank Freidel (ed.), *Harvard Guide to American History,* rev. ed., 2 volumes (Cambridge, Massachusetts: Belknap Press, 1974). The earlier edition, edited by Oscar Handlin, *et al.* in 1963, is still useful.

The most recent attempt at a guide to works in the history of education is Joe Park (ed.), *The Rise of American Education: An Annotated Bibliography* (Evanston, Illinois: Northwestern University Press, 1965).

Index